# Autobiographies, Biographies and Memoirs in English

PRISTINE WAVES

# Autobiographies, Biographies and Memoirs in English

PRISTINE WAVES

Arvind M. Nawale
Ankita Khanna
T. N. Kolekar

GNOSIS
Nurturing the Aspirations

Worldwide Circulation through Authorspress Global Network
**First Published 2013**
by
**GNOSIS**
(An Imprint of Authorspress)

*Editorial*
Q-2A Hauz Khas Enclave
New Delhi-110 016

*Marketing*
E-35/103, Jawahar Park
Laxmi Nagar, Delhi-110 092

e-mails: authorspress@rediffmail.com; authorspress@hotmail.com
Website: www.authorspressbooks.com



**Autobiographies, Biographies and Memoirs in English: Pristine Waves**
**ISBN 978-93-81030-48-6**

DISCLAIMER

The contents of all the articles included in this volume do not necessarily reflect the views of the editors. The contributors of the articles are responsible for the opinions, criticisms and factual information presented. They are also responsible for ensuring the proper adherence to the scientific rules of writing and copyright regulations. While the editors have tried their best to carefully review, format and make necessary corrections in the manuscripts, if there are still any lapses, the onus lies only with the contributors of the articles.

Printed in India at Krishna Offset, Shahdara.

This literary venture is dedicated to...

***Hon'ble Shree Ashokrao Patil, Ekambekar***
*(President, K.S.P. Mandal, Udgir)*

and

***Hon'ble Shree Adv. C.P. Patil,***
*(Secretary, K.S.P. Mandal, Udgir)*
*All members of K.S.P. Mandal, Udgir*

***Hon'ble Dr. Babasaheb Bandgar***
*(Vice Chancellor, Solapur University, Solapur)*

***Hon'ble Dr. Shivraj Nakade***
*(Former Vice Chancellor, Dr.B.A.M. University, Aurangabad)*

***Hon'ble Dr. J.M. Waghmare***
*(Former Vice Chancellor, S.R.T.M. University, Nanded)*

***Capt. Dr. Nitin Sonaje***
*(Registrar, Solapur University, Solapur)*

We are highly indebted in their constant love, inspiration and support.

—*Editors*

# Preface

Autobiographies, biographies and memoirs occupy an important place in literature for various reasons. Authors used this genre to communicate their worldviews to people. Gandhi's *The Story of My Experiments with Truth* is an excellent example. *My Truth* by Indira Gandhi is yet another example of communicating the message of an individual to a larger world. *Jivansmriti (Reminiscences)* of Rabindranath Tagore narrates his early years of life, while in *Toward Freedom: the Autobiography of Jawaharlal Nehru,* conveys Nehru's own views to his "own countrymen and women." Nirad C. Chaudhuri's *The Autobiography of an Unknown Indian,* published in 1951, stands apart as a great masterpiece, combining personal life experiences with a strong motivated worldview ("the conditions in which an Indian grew to manhood in the early decades of this century").

Talking about non-Indian writers, *A Stolen Life* by Jaycee Dugard is one such autobiography where everyone's heart goes out to this girl who was kidnapped and imprisoned at the tender age of 11. Another autobiography that took away the hearts of readers is *Sliding into Home* by Kendra Wilkinson, a former resident of the Playboy mansion and star of The Girls Next Door. She manages to tell a lot more about her life than most people would be willing to. *War* by Sebastian Junger takes us inside an Afghanistan war zone to learn what it is like to be in combat.

Similarly the renowned Biography *Jonathan Edwards* by George Marsden where the author brings to life the great preacher and theologian Jonathan Edwards is praiseworthy. Another truly portrayed biography that we came across is *Love Queen of Malabar: Memories of Friendship with Kamala Das* by Merrily Weisbord where she wanders into the restricted zones of Kamala Das's life.

Jawaharlal Nehru writes in his autobiography *Toward Freedom*, "... this account is wholly one-sided and, inevitably, egotistical; many important happenings have been completely ignored and many important persons, who shaped events, have hardly been mentioned. In a real survey of past events this would have been inexcusable, but a personal account can claim this indulgence." Gandhi justified writing an autobiography with these words:

> But a God-fearing friend had his doubts, which he shared with me on my day of silence. 'What has set you on this adventure? He asked. 'Writing an autobiography is a practice peculiar to the West. I know of nobody in the East having written one, except amongst those who have come under Western influence. And what will you write? Supposing you reject tomorrow the things you hold as principles today, or supposing you revise in the future your plans of today, is it not likely that the men who shape their conduct on the authority of your word, spoken or written, may be misled. Don't you think it would be better not to write anything like an autobiography, at any rate just yet?

Indira Gandhi's work is a compilation of her writings in a manner that the book has an autobiographical format. Nehru wrote his autobiography in English. Gandhi and Tagore wrote their autobiographies first in their mother tongues (Gujarati and Bengali, respectively) and then they got it translated or recreated their works into English. Nirad Chaudhuri wrote his celebrated work in English.

Autobiographies, biographies and memoirs may raise controversies of various types: political, social, familial, regional, religious, etc. A recent biography-like book on Muhammad Ali Jinnah by Jaswant Singh, *Jinnah: India-Partition-Independence,* raised a hue and cry among his own party members. Earlier in recent times, actor Om Puri's biography *Unusual Hero* by his wife created strong and deep controversies. Such controversies arise out of revelations in public of private personal acts and thoughts that may involve others and thus hurt the feelings, careers and interests of people referred to. It looks like that the autobiographer or biographer never asks the permission of others to narrate the incidents which involve them! But due to such pristine waves of unfold truth, autobiographies, biographies and memoirs became most popular forms of literature.

However, autobiographies and biographies have their own aspects difficult to master. Even the authors of these works are burdened with the responsibility of ensuring that the readers are with them and are comfortable with the journey they choose to undertake with the authors. The goal of this special volume *Autobiographies, Biographies and Memoirs in English: Pristine Waves* is to make a survey of some of the major autobiographies and biographies written in English. It is assumed that the work should try to bring out some pristine waves to unfold truth, hidden fact or incident of the life of the person studied in present book.

The very first paper 'Autobiographies, Biographies and Memoirs in English: An Appraisal', jointly written by the editors of present book, Arvind Nawale & Ankita Khanna, intends to explore the historical and chronological traces of the three selected genres: autobiography, biography and memoir. Next to it, Nawale explores voices from DNTs in Laxman Gaikwad's autobiography *The Branded*. In the third paper again Nawale with Vittal Jaybhaye jointly capture the insights of the inspiring life of A.P.J. Abdul Kalam reflected in his *Wings of Fire*. The second editor Ankita Khanna's paper 'Defying Societal Norms: *My Story* by Kamala Das', depicts Das's voice against patriarchal Indian society. It is an analytical study of Kamala Das's *My Story* where she leaves no stone unturned to voice out the sufferings and pain caused to her by the rigid norms of the society. "*Growing up Bin Laden* –A Peep into the Private Life of Osama Bin Laden" is a paper by another editor T. N. Kolekar, jointly written with Annie John. It reveals to us the hidden aspects of the life of Osama Bin Laden.

"*Wings of Fire*: An Autobiography: A Construction of Kalam's Identity and Nation's Identity" by A. Edwin Jeevaraj is an attempt to define how Kalam's identity constructed is in the Wings of Fire and how this autobiography becomes the representation of his nation's identity. The importance of identity comparing with the other major autobiographical subjects like memory, experience, and embodiment agency are discussed in the paper. Omana Antony in her paper "*My Story*: A Naked Portrait of Womanhood" reveals how this autobiography has a revolutionary effect among the women of not only Kerala but also the entire nation. Malshette Yogesh and Shete Sonali in their paper "Kamala Das's *My Story*: A Confessional Feminist Modern Autobiography" explores a unique courage and frankness in exposing the urges of autobiography in the autobiography of Ms. Das. Abhilash Nayak's paper "Kamala Das's *My Story*: A Compendium of Confessions, Convictions or Contradictions?" attempts to bring out the confessions, convictions and contradictions contained in Das's autobiography *My Story*. Shobhaa De's writing is centred on the psychology of women's sexuality and so is Das's. Mayur Agravat in his paper "A Critical

Study of Autobiographies – Kamala Das's *My Story* and Shobhaa De's *Selective Memory—Stories from My Life*" takes up the challenge to compare De against a classic poet like Kamala Das whereas Anita Mudkanna investigates bold confession of Kamala Das's premarital life in her *My Story.* Dr. Rajnish Mishra in his paper "Truth in Auto/biography: Rousseau's *The Confessions and My Experiments with Truth*" attempts to present *The Confessions* of Rousseau and Mahatma Gandhi's *My Experiments with Truth* as examples of autobiography in its general analysis of truth that is present in biographies and autobiographies. He also attempts to explore the various strands of truth—historical, psychological and philosophical in the texts under analytical gaze, while G.B. Shelkikar explores a note of confession in Gandhi's *The Story of My Experiments with Truth.* J. David Livingston and Sophia Livingston in their paper "Reflections on the Confessions of Jean Jacques Rousseau" explore *The Confessions of Jean-Jacques Rousseau,* one of the first autobiographies in which an individual wrote of his own life mainly in terms of his worldly experiences and personal feelings. "Against All Odds'—A Spiritual Autobiography' The Story of God TV's Visionary Pioneers, Roy and Wendy Alec'" by S. Jeyachandra is an attempt to review this book as a historical autobiography of an institution—God TV, a spiritual autobiography and an inspirational or motivational autobiography.

Bhaskar Roy Barman, in his paper, presents "Perspectives on Nehru's *An Autobiography.* "Taslima Nasrin's" *My Girlhood: An Autobiography of a Known Architect*" contributed by Indrani Singh Rai explores the darkness of a community that often forgets to be flexible and responsive towards its partakers. She also depicts Nasreen questioning the *Quran* and strongly makes people trust that not every word written in any holy book is indeed holy, and not every attempt to bring resurgence to a closed society is ignored by considering as 'cultural imperialism.' Archana Bhattacharjee explores the tradition of Guru-disciple relationship in *Autobiography of a Yogi.* Rajiv Kumar presents a case study of childhood reflected in Lal Behari Day's *Recollections of My School Days* while Brajesh Sawhney offers a feministic study of Doris Lessing's autobiographies *Under My Skin* and *Walking in the Shade.* Chung Chin-Yi in her paper "Revelation as Divine Truth in St Augustine's *Confessions*" explores the autobiographical *Confessions* of St Augustine, a journey made from darkness and a life of sin and debauchery to light and gradual acceptance of divine truth. Varsha Gosavi assesses the journey of Amrita Pritam's artistic mind in *The Revenue Stamp* while J. Ravindranath offers a fresh perspective on Nirad C. Chaudhuri's *Autobiography.* Krati Sharma in her paper "Gender Identity: A Case Study of Durga Khote's *I, Durga Khote*" makes an attempt to see that how Durga Khote, an actor, writes her autobiography and approach to the people at large.

Next, Deepali Patil explores how Sadhana Amte's *Samidha* is a beacon of light for posterity. Shubha Acharya assesses the making of a woman in Urmila Pawar's *The Weave of My Life: A Dalit Woman's Memoirs* while Kunal Ray examines 'Self' in Andre Agassi's autobiography *Open.* Minu Susan Koshy in her paper "Autobiographies as Negotiations, Religion as Subterfuge: A Study of *Amar Jiban, My Story,* and *Amen: The Autobiography of a Nun*" focuses on three autobiographies by women. Rashsundari Debi's *Amar Jiban,* Kamala Das's *My Story* and Sr. Jesme's *Amen: The Autobiography of a Nun.* This paper attempts to look into how *Amar Jiban, My Story* and *Amen* are negotiations of the kind mentioned above, making the authors "acceptable resisting subjects". Jyoti Sharma picks up one of the best poetic-psychological autobiographies of the modern times, *Life Studies* by Robert Lowell, and analyses it as a unique psychoanalytical autobiography in her paper, "A Critical Analysis of Robert Lowell's Life Studies: Confessional Poetry as Psycho-Analytical Autobiography". Grishma Khobragade reflects on the experience of discrimination and dalit identity in Omprakash Valmiki's *Joothan.*

"Partial Confessions in Bill Clinton's *My Life* and Michael Jackson's *Moonwalk*" by V. Rajesh & J. Jaya Parveen talks about the autobiographies written by two eminent personalities of all times, Bill Clinton and Michael Jackson, in which they have made confessions which are not complete but only partial. "Biography and Other Cognate Forms of Narrative Prose" by Dhara K. Chotai aims at analyzing the difference between the form of biography and other forms of narrative prose like novel, story and history. An attempt has made by the contributor to understand different aspects of biography with reference to other forms of writings. Charusheela Patil in her paper "Knowing the Unknown" examines with a difference an overall scenario of autobiographies of Indian women. Payel Dutta Chowdhury studies William Styron's *The Confessions of Nat Turner* as a historical truth while R. K. Bhushan offers a fresh perspective on autobiography, biography and memoirs as popular forms in English literature. Arvind Nawale interviews Dr. Sharankumar Limbale, a writer of renowned Autobiography, *The Outcaste.*

We are hopeful that this critical anthology would prove to be a very valuable companion to different teachers, postgraduate and undergraduate students, and doctoral research scholars who are intent on acquainting themselves with different aspects of autobiographies, biographies and memoirs in English. We are grateful to the publisher of this anthology, Mr. Sudarshan Kcherry, Managing Director, and the whole team of Authors Press, Gnosis and Access Publishing House, New Delhi, for pursuing us to bring the present volume and for helping our project to reach teachers and students internationally. Thanks are also due to our Management, Principals for their support and our family members for allowing us to work together and their love and support.

Arvind M. Nawale, Ankita Khanna & T. N. Kolekar

# Our Contributors

**Abhilash Nayak**, Regional Director, IGNOU Regional Centre, Koraput, Odisha.

**Ajit Kumar**, Assistant Professor, Department of English, Maharani Lakshmi Bai College for Girls, Bhiwani Rohilla (Hisar), Haryana.

**Anita Mudkanna**, Principal, Jawahar Arts Science Commerce College, Andur, Dist: Osmanabad.

**Ankita Khanna**, Lecturer in English & Communication Skills, Sardar Vallabhbhai National Institute of Techonology, Surat.

**Annie John**, Associate Prof. & Head, Department of English, A R Burla Womens' College, Solapur (M.S.).

**Archana Bhattacharjee**, Associate Professor, Department of English, Kakojan College, Jorhat, Assam.

**Arvind M. Nawale**, Head, Department of English, Shivaji Mahavidyalaya, Udgir, Dist: Latur (M.S.).

**Bhaskar Roy Barman**, Agartala, West Tripura, India.

**Bhushan, R. K.**, Professor, Lovely Professional University, Punjab.

**Brajesh Sawhney**, Professor, Department of English, Kurukshetra University, Kurukshetra, Haryana. India.

**Charusheela H. Patil**, Head of Dept. English, Sinhgad College of Arts and Commerce, Narhe, Pune (M.S.).

**Chung Chin-Yi**, National University of Singapore.

**David Livingston, J.**, Assistant Professor in English, Salem Christian College of Arts and Science, Salem, Tamil Nadu.

**Deepali Patil**, Associate Professor, Department of English, S.B. B alias Appasaheb Jedhe College of Arts, Commerce and Science, Shukrawar Peth, Pune (M.S.).

**Dhara K. Chotai**, Faculty in English, Centre for English Studies, School of Language, Literature & Culture Studies, Central University of Gujarat, Gandhinagar.

**Edwin Jeevaraj, A.**, Professor and Head, Department of English, Adhiyamaan College of Engineering, Hosur.

**Grishma Manikrao Khobragade**, Assistant Professor, Department of English, Birla College, Kalyan, Dist. Thane (M.S.).

**Indrani Singh Rai**, Associate Professor and Head, Department of English, MATS University, Raipur (Chhattisgarh).

**Jaya Parveen, J.** Assistant Professor, Department of English, VV College of Engineering, Tisaiyanvilai, Tuticorin District, Tamil Nadu.

**Jeyachandra**, S., Assistant Professor, Department of English, Karunya University, Coimbatore.

**Jyoti Sharma**, Assistant Professor, Manav Rachna International University, Faridabad.

**Kolekar, T. N.**, Assistant Professor, Department of English, D B F Dayanand College of Arts & Science, Solapur (M.S.).

**Krati Sharma**, Assistant Professor, Department of English, Jaipur National University.

**Kunal Ray**, Lecturer in English Literature, Foundation for Liberal and Management Education, Pune (M.S.).

**Malshette Yogesh Trimbakrao**, Assistant Professor, Dept. of Humanities & Basic Sciences, Abhinav Education Society's College of Engineering & Technology, Wadwadi, Pune. (M.S.)

**Mayur R. Agravat**, Faculty, Department of English, Shri Chimanbhai Patel Institute Of Business Administration, Ahmedabad & Rita Dabhi, Faculty, Dept. of English, L. J. Polytechnic, Sanand, Ahmedabad.

**Minu Susan Koshy**, English and Foreign Languages University, Hyderabad.

**Omana Antony**, Head, Dept.of English, Lingaya's University, Faridabad.

**Payel Dutta Chowdhury**, Course Coordinator, Department of Languages, Garden City College, Bangalore.

**Rajesh V.** Assistant Professor, Department of English, VV College of Engineering, Tisaiyanvilai, Tuticorin District, Tamil Nadu.

**Rajiv Kumar**, University Department of English, Sido Kanhu Murmu University Dumka, Jharkhand.

**Rajnish Mishra**, IMS Engineering College, Ghaziabad.

**Ravindranath, J.**, Associate Professor & HoD, Department of English, GVP College of Engineering Madhurawada Visakhapatna, Andhra Pradesh.

**Shelkikar, G. B.**. P.N. College, Pusad, (M.S.).

**Shete Sonali Shivraj**, Assistant Professor, Department of Humanities and Basic Sciences, Abhinav Education Society's College of Engineering and Technology, Wadwadi, Pune. (M.S.)

**Shubha Acharya**, Associate Professor, Shri M D Shah Mahila College of Arts & Commerce, Malad, Mumbai. (M.S.).

**Sophia Livingston**, Assistant Professor in English, St. Bonnie White College of Nursing, Salem, Tamil Nadu.

**Varsha Gosavi**, Associate Professor, Department of English, Vasantrao Naik College Nanded (M.S.).

**Vittal Jaybhaye**, Assistant Professor in English, Late Ramesh Warpudkar College, Sonpeth, Dist.Parbhani (M.S.).

# Contents

# 1

# Voices from DNTs: A Subaltern Study of Laxman Gaikwad's Autobiography *The Branded*

Arvind M. Nawale

It is over and over again argued that all men are born equal but the social reality is that not all men are born alike. The social category generally known as the Denotified and Nomadic Tribes (DNTs) of India, along with other downtrodden casts are considered 'untouchables'. Their being branded as 'criminals' during the long period of British rule, and the lack of rehabilitation following independence, has left a mark of 'outcastes' on them. In the words of Sharan Kumar Limbale, "The DNTs are the most depressed sections of society and all of them are regarded as Dalits" ( 137). K.S. Chalam has also observed that "They are excluded from mainstream social and economic development and as a result they are found to be most vulnerable to hunger and poverty" (Chalam 81). They live as outcastes, outside the villages and are not permitted into schools or even for jobs considering them as criminals. They are being subjugated, oppressed and underprivileged since colonial period. They take up the lowest step of the ladder in the social hierarchy.

They suffered from embarrassment and wanted to defend against but they were not empowered to do so. They could not get easy admission to schooling that could educate them how to stand against heavy odds and complain in opposition to their oppressors. But with the passage of time, things changed and some of them got education and took it as their responsibility to fight against the wrongs done to them

Laxman Gaikwad's *The Branded* (1998) (Translated from the original Marathi autobiography *Uchalya,* 1987 which was awarded by India's Central Literary Academy in 1988), is a throbbing account of dejected life rooted with dishonour and cruelty. This research paper highlights how Laxman Gaikwad, a dalit writer, belonging to DNT, dared to give his voice to the traumatic experiences of those who belong to his community which is named as Uchalya or Bhamta (Branded).

The writer himself is the protagonist of this autobiographical novel but his own experiences, instead of being sole and personal, represents the whole Uchalya community. The novel is set in Dhanegaon, a small village in Latur district (just 75 km from my location) and depicts the life of Laxman Gaikwad an Uchalya (DNT) from childhood to youth. The starting lines tell us the misery of him and his community:

> No native place. No birth-date. No house or farm.
> No caste, either. That is how I was born (01).

In it, we hit upon accounts of horrifying incidents of atrocities done to this Uchalya tribe. The tribe had to produce a pass to move from one place to another as they were under the Habitual Offenders Act:

> We were reduced to the level of animals; for just as permits are needed for cattle to be moved to other places or to be sold in the market; we had to have passes to move about (3).

In one such incidence the police grab Anna for pilfering an oil-tin from the bazaar. They thrust chilli-powder in his eyes. They lash out at him naked and pull out all family members out of their huts and lash out at them also. They barefacedly press and squeeze the breasts of Dhondamai, Anna's innocent mother, who never known stealing. They grab her "mangalsutra" and other ornaments on wrong charge that everything in her house is a stolen property. A policeman tells his mother: "Bring two hundred rupees, then they will be released" (15-16). Here, the police themselves are seen accountable for creating circumstances in which dalits are left with no option but to steal.

Laxman Gaikwad admits that their caste does not permit them to learn. The community is so poorly informed that sending the children to school would annoy the goddess Yellamma:

> We are not merchants and Brahmins to admit our children to school. Has anybody from the thieves' community ever gone to school?'(16).

They make threats to call the panchayat and banish the family of those who send their children to schools. On the other hand Gaikwad also says how dalit students are humiliated in schools:

> I had just started going to school, it was all novel and strange to me. All the urchins started harassing me, as if a poor lamb had entered a pack of wolves. They threw stones at me because an Uchalya child had dared come to school. (10)

Laxman Gaikwad also admits how the paucity of food and hunger forced them to steal grain from the others' fields. When one day Gaikwad and his band had gone to steal something from a farm and when a former saw them plucking "ears of the grain crop", he began to shout: "Thieves ! 'Thieves" and started hurling stones. So, they threw down the plucked ears. But his dada was aware that all the persons at home were waiting for him to bring something to eat. He then ran with the load of plucked grains.

A stone hurled through the sling, hit his head. This shows how they had to move to gratify their starvation.

Poverty and hunger drive them to beg and thefts. Laxman would eat from the offering left for evil spirits and from plates thrown after a feast. Once out of sheer desperation, he and his family plucked leaves of sweet potatoes from the farm where his father worked. His father was suspended from work for eight days "for taking leaves which animals do not eat readily" (40). Fed up with his poverty Laxman once wrote a long letter to Prime Minister Indira Gandhi when he was a young boy, "Please take steps to see that the poor get one square meal a day at least" (79).

Laxman Gaikwad narrates an incident of a guiltless Pardhi woman named Hirabai Kale, who was locked up with her newborn baby by the police. She had nothing to eat after her delivery, as her spouse had been in prison on charges of thievery. So she underwent tubectomy for which she received Rs.200 with which she bought half a gunny bag of high jawar. The police arrested her when they found her bag of jawar in her hut on charges that she had stolen it from a neighbouring village. Even though she pleaded innocent and showed the medical papers regarding her operation she was taken into custody along with her baby. The Uchalya or any other 'Criminal Tribe' cannot wear new clothes or costly ones for fear of being arrested for theft. When the police came to Laxman Gaikwad's hut in search of his family members, they beat his mother even though she never stole. They asked her:

> You harlot, where did you get such a costly sari?
> Do you have the cash memo for this sari? (61).

In this way we see how the life of the Uchalya community is beset sting, suffering, cruelty and disgrace as depicted in this autobiography. The different forces rampant in the social order inflict pain on them. The stigma of Uchalya is so subterranean and evil that it has made their life a practical hell on this earth.

The story of dishonour and prejudice against dalits is not new in our society. It dates back to the time of the *Ramayana*. In this epic we see a low born, Shambuk killed only because he refused, having studied the *Vedas*, to consider Rama and Sita as the perfect models of Indian society. Even after 64 years of independence, we time and again come across news reports about a dalit woman being paraded unclothed or gang raped. There are also news about how dalit students are made to sit separately while mid-day meals in school are served.

Laxman Gaikwad makes us aware of the voice that was silent for ages. He gives expression to the marginalized voice of the downtrodden. This disgrace and cruelty left deep scars on their consciousness. The entire narrative of the text gains a representative quality and imparts the true feeling of the sting the Uchalya communities have suffered. It also provides an insight into the living conditions of an economically marginalized and socially detested community of Maharashtra, the DNTs. India gained freedom from the British sixty-four years ago, but these tribes are yet to be freed from the disgrace of 'Criminal Tribes', attached to them by the British.

## Works Cited

Chalam, K.S. *Caste-based Reservations and Human Development in India.* New Delhi: Sage Publications, 2007. Print.

Gaikwad, Laxman. *Uchalya (The Branded).* New Delhi: Sahitya Akademi, 2005. Print.

Limbale, Sharankumar. *Towards an Aesthetic of Literature.* New Delhi: Orient Longman, 2004. Print.

# 2

# Kalam's *Wings of Fire*: A Powerful Autobiography of Courage and Belief

A.M. Nawale & Vittal Jaybhaye

> Every text participates in one or several genres; there is no genre less text; there is always a genre and genres: yet such participation never amounts to belonging. And not because of an abundant overflowing or a free, anarchic, and unclassifiable productivity, but because of the trait of participation itself.
>
> —*Jacques Derrida*

In comparison to the different genres of Indian English literature, the Indian English autobiography is not as developed as the Indian English poetry or fiction. The Indian English autobiography is as neglected as the Indian English drama. That's because a good number of autobiographies are lacking in literary styles. None the less, the autobiographies of M.K. Gandhi, Pandit Jawaharlal Nehru, Nirad C. Choudhary, Dom Moraes, C.D. Narsimhaih and A.P.J. Abdul Kalam are good works among the Indian English autobiographies.

The first phase of autobiography, such as the autobiographies of M. K. Gandhi, Pandit Jawaharlal Nehru and others, is devoted to the Indian freedom struggle. But the autobiographies after the 1980's are devoted to the self and social analysis of the Indian history and its various aspects. The autobiographies of C.D. Narsimhaiah's *N for Nobody: The Autobiography of an English Teacher* (1991), P. S. Sundaram's *Simple Simon* (1998), Ruskin Bond's *Scenes from a Writer's Life: A Memoir* (1997), R.K. Laxman's *The Tunnel of Time* (1998), P. Lal's *Lessons* (1991), Karan Singh's *Heir Apparent: An Autobiography* (1982), T.N. Kaul's *Ambassdor's need not lie* (1989), K.P.S.Menon's *Thousands Full Moons* (1987), P. N. Haskar's *One More Life* (1990) and A.P.J. Abdul Kalam's *Wings of Fire* (1999) are the important documents of the postmodern Indian English literature. The present paper studies the autobiography of Dr. Kalam – *Wings of Fire*—as a saga of courage and belief.

A.P.J. Abdul Kalam's *Wings of Fire* can be called as an influential autobiography of courage and belief. It is the saga of India's search for scientific and technological potentials. It describes how an innocent boy from a remote corner of Tamil Nadu attained greatness in rocketry and missiles technology, and thereby raised his country's position in applied science and technology to the global standard. It "constitutes an extraordinary reading for the young and old, for a common man and professional including management pundits, and for the uninitiated and the technically trained alike. There is something that everybody can extract from this book" (Mukunda 85). He believed in, "We are born with a divine fire in us. Our efforts should be to give wings to this fire." The fire to achieve and the wings of determination helped him to climb the ladder of success.

Dr. Avul Pakir Jainulabdeen Abdul Kalam is a notable scientist and an engineer of India. He is referred as 'The Missile Man' of India. He played a key role in developing the first and indigenously made ballistic missile of India. He has major contributions to nuclear-strike development, and guides the Missile Development Programme and various ISRO projects of the nation. During his presidential period, he became a popular president due to his active participation in the various cultural and national programmes of India. He is a famous president, who has a special affinsty with children as well as the youths of India. He is the ideal and hard working scientist-president. He is the first Chancellor of the Indian Institute of Space Science and Technology, Thiruvanantapuram (IIST). As President of India, he was awarded the Bharat Ratna, India's highest civilian honour, in 1997. Apart from this, he received numerous awards including the Padma Bhushan (1981) and Padma Vibhushan (1990).

Dr. Kalam is a versatile figure of the 3G India. He is known as an aspiratory writer, poet and autobiographer. Most of his books are about the future and the youth of the nation. He works for 18 hours a day, also write books and articles on various issues of the nation. His books such as *Scientist to President, Ignited Minds: Unleashing the Power Within India, India 2020: A Vision for New Millennium, India—My Dream, Evincing an Empowered Nation: Technology for Societal Transformation, Guiding Souls: Dialogues on the Purpose of Life, Indomitable Spirit, My Journey* are great contributions to Indian English literature and philosophy.

Among his literary contribution, his autobiography, *Wings of Fire: An Autobiography of Dr.A.P.J. Abdul Kalam* (1999), is well known, highly intellectual and a supra aspiratory autobiography. The autobiography was written by him with the help of the writer Mr. Arun Tiwari. The autobiography was first published in English and later on translated and published in 13 languages of India. The autobiography was also translated in Chinese by Ji Ping. Arun Tiwari, the writer of the book, writes in the preface of the book:

> For myself, writing this book has been like a pilgrimage. Through Dr. Kalam, I was blessed with the revelation that the real joy of living can be found in only one way-in one's communion with an eternal source of hidden knowledge within oneself-which each individual is bidden to seek and find for himself or herself. Many of you may never meet Dr. Kalam in person, but I hope you will enjoy his company through this book, and that he will become your spiritual friend (x).

It shows that the life of Dr. Kalam is open for us like a wide open book or like the autobiography of Mahatma Gandhi (*My Experiments with Truth*).

The autobiography *Wings of Fire* unfolds in eight sections including Orientation, Creation, Propitiation and Contemplation which seem more important. The section 'Orientation' opens with the quote from the *Atharva Veda:*

> *This earth is His, to Him belong those vast and bundles skies;*
> *Both seas within Him rest, and yet in that small pool He lies. (1)*

This *shloka* from the *Atharva Veda* implies the omnipotent, omniscient and omnipresent nature of the Almighty (God, Allah, Eshoo, Buddha etc.). The section covers Dr. Kalam's birth, childhood, school and high-school education, from a middle class Tamil Muslim family of Ramnathapuram in Rameshwaram (Tamil Nadu). He writes about his childhood and family:

> I inherited honesty and self-discipline from my father; from my mother, I inherited faith in goodness and deep kindness and so did my three brothers and sister. But it was the time I spent with Jallaluddin and Samsuddin that perhaps contributed most to the uniqueness of my childhood and made all the difference in my later life. The unschooled wisdom of Jallaluddin and Samsuddin was so intuitive and responsive to non-verbal messages, that I can unhesitatingly attribute my subsequently manifested creativity to their company in my childhood. (8)

Dr. Kalam also writes about his undergraduate education in aeronautic engineering from Madras Institute of Technology. This section ends with his moving to United States for a training programme at NASA. He writes about his struggling journey from a small town, rameshwaram, to a Megacity like Bombay (Mumbai) and New York City (USA-NASA). The 'Orientation' contains the aspiratory life and writings of Dr. Kalam, which is the lesson to all lower-middle class students, hard working for the success. This section became the source of energy to the readers of the book.

The section 'Creation' covers seven chapters. It covers the life of Kalam from 1963 until 1980. He writes about the days from NASA and Langley Research Centre (LRC), Goddard Flight Centre (GFC) and WFFW Island in Virginia. In NASA, Kalam was influenced by the rocket scene paintings on the walls of NASA. The paintings caught his attention where he found the army of Tipu Sultan (Indian King) fighting with the British army. He was happy to see an Indian hero on the walls of NASA and glorified with the rocketry by the Indian hero. He writes about the rocketry efforts done by Dr. Vikram Sarabhai and Pandit Jawaharlal Nehru, who rejuvenated the rocket in India, after the eighteenth century Tipu Sultan. The death of Dr. Vikram Sarabhai (31 Dec. 1971) shocked Kalam and it was a huge loss to Indian science. Then he met to Prof. Satish Dhawan, the Head of ISRO. He writes about Dhawan in the book:

> He could hold the listener enthralled because of the logical, intellectual acumen he could bring to bear on his analysis of any subject. I found him full of optimism and compassion. Although he often judged himself harshly, with no allowances or excuses, he was generous to a fault when it came to others.

Another scientist, Dr. Brahm Prakash, played a very crucial role in the career of Dr. Kalam, for he developed leadership skills in Kalam. He writes about Dr. Brahm Prakash's advice could be heard in Emerson's poem on Brahma:

> If the red slayer think he slays,
> Or, if the slain think he is slain,
> They know not well, the subtle ways.
> I keep, and pass, and turn again. (97)

He concludes the section with the launching of SLV-3, the first Satellite Launch Vehicle (SLV) of India.

The 'Propitiation' covers the lifespan of Kalam from 1981 to 1991. The five chapters from this section depict the scientist Kalam's journey towards becoming the 'Missile Man of India.' This section is important among the other sections, because he got the major achievement in his life. In this period, he successfully launched five missiles—Prithvi, Trishul, Akash, Nag and the most awaited one Agni. In this way he proved his dreams to be cherished for his nation. He was jubilant among his colleagues, because India became the fifth country to achieve satellite launch capability. In the next year he received the Padma Bhushan (1981) and was appointed as the Director of DRDL. After launching five missiles, in 1984, the P.M. Indira Gandhi, too, took notice of his contribution to the new missile development of India. In 1990, he was honoured with the Padma Vibhushan.

The fourth section 'Contemplation', describes the devotion of Dr. Kalam to the nation. He writes about the launch of Agni, the Pride of India. It was a great achievement of Dr. Kalam, who successfully launched rockets for the nation. In 1997, he was honoured with the Bharat Ratna, the highest honour of India, for the appreciation and the excellent efforts of the scientist. Dr. Kalam is the name, which enriched the annals of Indian science in the world. The great scientist, the Missile Man of India, concludes the book with following words:

> I will not be presumptuous enough to say that my life can be a role model for anybody; but some poor child living in an obscure place, in an underprivileged social setting may find a little solace in the way my destiny has been shaped. It could perhaps help such children liberate themselves from the bondage of their illusory backwardness and hopelessness. Irrespective of where they are right now, they should be aware that God is with them and when He is with them, who can be against them?
>
> But God has promised<br>Strength for the day,<br>Rest for the labour<br>Light for the way.
>
> ...Let the latent fire in the heart of every Indian acquire wings, and the glory of this great country light up the sky. (167-168)

The autobiography *Wings of Fire* is firing the next generation of India as well as the world. Every word and quotation from the book aspires the reader. The book is full with powerful, energetic quotations about courage, beauty of human life, achievement, struggle and shaping the future of India. At the end, in the 'Epilogue' of the autobiography, Dr. Kalam writes:

> I earnestly hope and pray that the development resulting from these two plans-*Self Reliance Mission* and *Technology Vision-2020*-will eventually make our country strong and prosperous and take our rightful place among the ranks of the "developed" nations. (180)

In this way the autobiography of Dr. Kalam, *Wings of Fire*, is an aspiratory document of the Indian English literature. The book is embedded with the characteristics of the modern Indian literature and its various aspects in comparison to the world literature. *Wings of Fire* is a great chronicle of India's search for scientific and technological prospectives, and is a powerful autobiography of courage and belief.

## Works Cited

*A Little Dream: A Life Documentary on A. P. J. Abdul Kalam* (documentary film). Dir. P. Dhanapal, Minveli Media Works Private Limited, 2008. DVD.

Das, B.K. *Post Modern Indian English Literature.* New Delhi: Atlantic Publisher's, 2006. Print.

Kalam, A.P.J. Abdul, Tiwari, Arun. *Wings of Fire: An Autobiography of APJ Abdul Kalam.* New Delhi: University Press, 1999. Print.

Mukunda, H.S. *Wings of Fire* Rev. *Resonance* September 1999. Print.

# 3

# Defying Societal Norms: *My Story* by Kamala Das

Ankita Khanna

Kamala Das requires absolute no introduction as an Indian, English poet. Although she is better known for the controversial poetry that she wrote yet what she was instantly famous for was her autobiography *Ente Katha* later published as *My Story* in English. The popularity of this autobiography can be judged by the fact that it has been translated into more than fifteen languages since its first publication. She, in her strident voice, challenged the norms of the society in which she lived. In her autobiography she lays before us her life as it was. She did not make any deliberate efforts to hide or conceal anything from the public. She portrays with equal charm the beautiful and the ugly; the acceptable and the rejected; the composed and the piercing.

She talks about her loveless childhood, forced marriage, extra-marital affairs, link-ups, break-ups, pregnancies, and deliveries; all with the same ease and dexterity. She also explores her relationships with almost all the people who are a part of her life. She talks about warmth that she receives from her grandmother and aloofness that her husband gives her. She also talks about how she spent her childhood with her brother though strangely he finds no mention anywhere in the book once she gets married.

Her controversial creation *My Story* also throws light on her stale relations with her father and mother. She is unlike conventional Indian women. She comes in the line of Mamata Kalia and Gauri Deshpande. As Mithilesh K. Pandey says:

> Armed with Indian austerity, Kamala Das has manifested her own realization of life's predicament as a woman in her poems with utmost sincerity....

What makes Kamala Das different from others is that she does not grudge over insignificant matters and also that her discontent is healthy. She has raised herself much above the personal grievance, and voices out the problems faced by many others in general and women in particular. She has discovered the means to release the energy of her hidden anger by creating powerful literature. One may recount the situation of her unhappiness by referring to what Germaine Greer has told about the predicament of women today, be it in India or elsewhere, by using the 'castration' of women as her central metaphor. The claim of Greer is as follows:

> ...women have been deprived of their natural power, pressured towards self-sacrifice but denied any notion of what the self is. (qtd. In Patricia Meyei Spacks in *A Chronicle*. 160)

To put it briefly, suffering and humiliation are undoubtedly the dominating themes in Kamala Das's poetry. She airs her views with boldness unparallel and she hopes that the society might change its attitude to those who suffer and are humiliated. She is essentially a poet of modern Indian women's ambivalence giving expression to it more openly than any other Indian woman poet.

Kamala Das's poetry has her autobiography written into it. She is not any woman or the incarnation of 'essential womanhood' if at all there is one. She is an Indian poet, writing in English when Indian poetry in English is breaking free from the rhetorical and romantic traditions when her male counterparts like Nissim Ezekiel and A.K. Ramanujam are struggling hard to form a dense, pity and ironic idiom in their poems, and Jayant Mahapatra is trying to relate his poetry to his immediate environment with pain and anger.

Theoreticians of feminine condition describe the stereotypes of body, mind and soul imposed upon women, and acquiesced in by them, and go on to recount the inequities of marriage and education. They also emphasize the meaningless destructiveness that develops from such psychic states. Kamala Das asserts their views and describing the brutality of the forced physical relations, she says:

> Forced sex is like an auto crash,... fear, pain, blood, and confrontation accompany both, ...girls forced to have sex begin to look at men with fear in the same way as people are afraid to get into a vehicle after an accident. That is why their eyes seem dilated and their palms grow cold like lotus stems. Gradually they come to know that sex is a war and that lust is a kind of terrorism.

The male domination on the feminine psyche can be diminished and eradicated by the woman when she lets herself participate in the world of nature and in the amelioration of her status independently. Compelled by the circumstances Kamala Das presently deserts her Hindu religion and adopts the religion of Islam, putting on a veil. Her transformation of religion is a vivid picture of woman's identity and liberty. She is not the gentle cow of M.R. Anand's *The Old Woman and the Cow*. She knows how to combat against the age-old customs in society. She, undoubtedly, presents a new paradigm shift in the coming generation in India and abroad.

In contemporary literature, written by women, the feminine voice revolves largely round a claim for perfect freedom in personal matters, chiefly in relation to love and sex. The old customs yield place to the all-pervading spirit of modernism which has crystallized predominantly in the elimination of the status quo in every conceivable walk of life. It appears perfectly natural that Indian women raise their voices against the established order and try to affirm their distinct identity, breaking the traditional taboos on love and sex which is the outcome of a male-dominated society. Das's protest against such a system made her turn a 'rebel'. Her offended feminine self went on emotional wanderings attempting to explore an identity and freedom. Nevertheless, her traditional make-up of a conventional woman was a factor which persistently forbade her from breaking away completely from the role of a traditional wife. A conflict naturally arose between the passivity and rebellion against the male-oriented universe. And the conflict persisted all through her life.

This has been amply demonstrated by Kamala Das who goes beyond her own personal crisis to achieve freedom. The language in which she has written her poems is symptomatic of freedom. In her poetry she challenges the phallocentric idea of society. At a deeper level her poetry seeks to declare through her writings that for a woman writing what she had written is not something totally unexpected. Her writing necessitates a feminist reading. Her ability to depict, not as a male but as a female, the situations, characters and dilemmas straight out of everyday dogmatic life, particularly her own, needs to be recognized.

## Works Cited

Das, Kamala. *My Story* New Delhi: Harper Collins, 2009.

Pandey, K. Mithilesh. "Kamala Das: A Study in Evolving Vision," *Indian English Poetry: New Perspectives* (ed.) K.V. Surendran, New Delhi: Swarup & Sons, 2002, 56.

Greer, Germaine. *The Female Eunuch*, New York: McGraw-Book Company, 1981.

Satchidanandan, K. "Transcending the Body," *Only The Soul knows How to Sing,* Kottayam: DC, 1996.

Weisbord, Merrily. *Love Queen of Malabar: Memories of Friendship with Kamala Das*, Gurgaon: Research Press Private Limited, 2010.

Khanna, Ankita. "Kamala Das's Poetic Work: A Tantalizing Portrayal of Feminine Longings", *Labyrinth* (1-2), Sep. 2010, pp.98-102.

# 4

# *Growing up Bin Laden*: A Peep into the Private Life of Osama Bin Laden

T.N. Kolekar & Annie John

> Now that it is over we look back, and with minute and searching care, seek to find its criminals and its heroes. Where are they? Where are the villains who made the war?
>
> ... We ought to know; we mean to know, smarting under our wounds, enraged by our injuries, amazed by our wonderful exertions and achievements, conscious of our authority, we demand to know the truth, and to fix the responsibilities.
>
> —*Sir Winston Churchill*

A single word "Fascinating" (*The Sunday Times*) speaks volumes about the book. This book by Jean Sasson, co-authored by Najwa bin Laden (Osama bin Laden's first wife) and Omar bin Laden (Osama's fourth son) provide rare glimpses into an unknown world of terrorism and violence. This very first book about Bin Laden written with the support and cooperation of his family members voyages us through their secret world—a gripping read providing authentic details and astonishing secrets of a man whom many people would wish to erase from their memory.

The words of Jean Sasson in her 'A Note to the Reader' is worth pondering. She says, "People are not born terrorists. Nor do they become terrorists in a single stroke. But step by step, like a farmer preparing a field for planting, their lives unfold in a pattern that leaves them prepared to receive the seed of terrorism".

Jean Sasson began writing in 1991 and her literature centres around women in the Middle East. She focuses on the patriarchal society and the injustice meted out against the helpless women.

She found adventure in writing and this led her to travel and work abroad. She worked at the King Faisal Specialist Hospital (Saudi Arabia) as Administrative Coordinator in Medical Affairs. During her stay in the Middle East, she made a number of friends including some from the royal Al-Saud family. Her friendship with Princess Sultana hit off well and her 'The Princess' trilogy is around her (the princess). Her other interesting works include: *The Rape of Kawait, Mayada: Daughter of Iraq, Love in a Torn Land: Joanna of Kurdistan* and *Ester's Child* (a historical fiction). Sasson lives in Southern United States but happily travels all around the globe, visiting the Middle East countries every year.

Omar bin Laden, the son of Osama, being a man of great compassion and a propagator of peace, decided to reach out to the world and share his experience as the son of the most sought—after terrorist. Being a witness to many of the severe crimes committed by his father, he was also greatly terrified by him. Najwa, a shy but determined woman, supported her son strongly and helped him break away from a life that had nothing but violence in store.

Omar approached Jean Sasson with his intention, and after much thought, decided to bring out to the reading public an intimate portrait of the Al Qaeda leader. Everything written comes from the memories of the two people who once greatly revered him.

The chapters in the book alternate between Najwa and Omar; and remain unfiltered by their own opinions and interpretations. The book begins with details by Najwa regarding her early life with her cousin Osama, who later became her husband. Najwa was raised in Syria and Osama in Saudi Arabia. However, they met often as Osama along with his mother Allia and stepfather visited them. (Allia was the sister of Najwa's father). Najwa reminisces, "Osama, of course, was part of the group. My cousin, already a year-old at the time of my birth, was always in my life." (9)

Osama being gentle, serious and conscientious was a kind of mystery to all around him.

Najwa's memory about Osama as her young cousin is truly in contrast to the Osama the world knew. She says, "He was proud, but not arrogant. He was delicate, but not weak. He was grave, but not severe.... I had never been around such a soft spoken, serious boy. Despite his serene demeanour, no one ever thought of Osama as being weak-willed, for his character was strong and firm (10). The happy childhood days passed rapidly and as Osama and Najma grew up to be teenagers "unanticipated emotions began to swirl". They began to share a special relationship and never realized then that their lives would change forever.

They had an early marriage, with Osama going to school in the morning and to work at the Laden construction company in the noon.

Although Najwa knew that marriage to Osama and migrating to Saudi Arabia would change her life, she was not aware that the change would be so drastic. She stayed at home all day as women were not allowed to move about in public unless accompanied by a male relative. She longed for Osama to come home in the evenings and spend time in his sweet company. There were many things that held her in awe about him including the fact that he had the entire *Quran* memorized. As a youth he was highly regarded by his family, was extremely quiet, studious, highly intelligent, a mathematical genius, staunchly religious and well mannered. Marriage brought about a radical change in Najwa. Osama spent a considerable time patiently explaining to her how important it was to live as an obedient Muslim. Fiercely protective he assured her:

> Najwa, for me, you are a prized pearl who must be protected. Just as the hard shell of the sea protects the exquisite pearl, I will be the hard shell protecting you. (20)

Osama's protective nature made her proud and she considered him an expert in all matters including religion. He, being ruthlessly stubborn, harsh with his sons and a believer of violent jihad, came to the fore much later. He believed in simple living including frugal food and amenities, and did not permit his wives to use modern appliances for their convenience and comfort.

Osama behaved in many ways more than his age. His understanding and reaction to things were that of a veteran. His activities included assistance to the beleaguered brethren in Afghanistan. He financially aided the tribal leaders in Afghanistan who were fighting against the invaders.

Osama's increasing political activities kept him away from home for a long time. His mind was always filled with business not pertaining to the domestic front. Although Najwa considered he him a 'kindly partner', she never failed to notice his unconcern towards the family. She says:

> I was always supportive, and I yearned for success on the battlefield for two reasons: one, that the Afghans could live without danger and rebuild their shattered nation; and two, that my husband and the father's of my children might come home so we could resume the life we had once know. (34)

Unlike most Saudi men (as mentioned in *The Princess* trilogy by Sasson), Osama was not indulgent with his sons but disciplined them harshly believing that suffering would discipline and make them stronger. However, he was easy with his daughters and was considerate towards his wives. Again, as mentioned in the same book, it is customary for Saudi men to have four wives and most men do not consult their first wife regarding the same. Interestingly, Osama discussed with Najwa his desire to obtain more wives and even sought her help to seek an alliance. His purpose of getting married was to increase the number of Muslims in the world.

For some months the topic of Osama marrying another woman was constantly discussed between the two. He promised that he would not marry another woman unless she (Najwa) agreed. He even revealed his deepest thoughts, confessing that his sole aim of re-marrying was purely to have many children for Islam. He even reminded her:

> Najwa, if you are contented in your heart for me to take a second wife, you will gain in heaven. It is certain that your life will end in paradise. (61)

Najwa was content that Osama was taking a second wife not out of discontentment but for the greater good of Islam.

Even in the case of divorce, women are usually not allowed the custody of their children. However, Osama permitted one of his wives custody of her children after their divorce. However when Najwa and Omar sought his permission to leave

Afghanistan, he permitted her to take only the youngest child with her.

It's amazing that there was no rivalry between Osama's wives and they lived as one big happy family. Najwa even refers to her husband's wives as 'sister wives'. Even Osama treated all his wives equally and every year began to add a new member to the bin Laden household. However, happy times were not meant to last forever here as Osama began spending a good amount of time away from home.

Osama believed in austerity and simplicity in life. This restricted their home furnishings to being plain, clothing modest and food simple. "The only area where Osama splurged was on his cars, which were always the latest model" (66). Therefore his wives and children never got all those modern goods and personal items loved by many.

Osama was very strict with his sons. Even when they were young children, he would take them out to the desert for long walks. He never permitted them to drink any water when on the hike, not even think about it. He believed that the bin Laden sons should be physically immune to inhospitable conditions. This would make the body and mind strong. In his own way he was preparing "his sons to face desert warfare when the infidel West attacked the Muslim world" (75).

One activity that Osama truly loved was farming. He liked working on the land, growing the best corn and the biggest sunflower. He always discovered new ways of producing the world's largest sunflowers. Displaying these huge sunflowers pleased him endleslly. During the harvest season, he took the entire family to the farms and these outings were truly memorable which Najwa treasured.

When the country was invaded by Soviet Union in 1979, it greatly disturbed Osama; and he began involving himself in the same by supporting the tribal leaders to resist the Russians by providing funds. His involvement in the political activities put him on the wrong side with the Saudi Royals and he was forced to leave the country. His expulsion from the country and his wealth being confiscated by the government embittered him. He was again outraged when the US went into Kuwait. He deeply resented the Western intervention into Islamic affairs and his hatred for the US reached its peak.

Osama along with his family moved to Khartoum, Sudan. The family began adjusting to everything new offered by him. In addition to his mission (still a secret from his family), he engaged himself in other social activities like building schools, roads etc. However, his political activities put him again on a wrong footing and once again he was forced to leave Sudan for the same reasons. This made him very bitter in the light of monetary benefits he had provided the country.

The state of the world not being a very happy place, Osama felt that his wives and daughters must also be trained to become resistant, patient and courageous. He would take the family to some undeveloped place without any overnight supplies. With no beds, blankets or mosquito nets they had to spend the entire night under the starry sky. Asking the older boys to dig hollows, each person had to sleep alone in a dirty hole. When someone complained about the chill, he would simply advice, "cover yourself with dirt and grass. You will become warm under what nature provides" (122).

This was his way of making the family gallant, and prepared them for the future with all its trials and challenges. Although Najwa shudders at the memory of these training sessions, she is thankful that in the process she and his children became strong enough to endure much hardships. She quips, "Wouldn't everyone be surprised when my children and I popped up alive because we knew how to endure the harsh desert climate without water supplies or without the benefit of modern conveniences?" (122)

Osama wanted his sons to be disciplined but was very often cruel to them. He was against giving them pocket money or money for school snacks. He wanted them to know the pangs of hunger and thirst, and the need to minimize their wants. When any of his sons complained (which was something rare), he would say, "No, you need to suffer. Hunger pangs will not hurt you" (142).

Although his sons disagreed with him on various issues, none dared oppose him directly. On certain occasion when there was a protest he would quietly order them to stand to be beaten. His favourite weapon was his wooden cane and as Omar narrates, "there were times he became so excited when hitting his sons that his heavy cane broke into two pieces. When the cane snapped, he rushed to grab one of our sandals by the door, using that to hit us" (143). The statement, "It was not unusual for the sons of Osama bin Laden to be covered with raised red welts on our backs and legs" (143) sends shiver down our spine. However, he had a very different attitude when the women of his family were concerned. He never shouted at any of the women nor did he ever strike them.

From there they moved on to Afghanistan. With all the money gone, they had to live very austere lives and in constant threat of danger to their lives. Najwa recalls how they were running short of food and she feared the little children would fall off the tall mountain cliffs. None of the family members dared to question Osama, but just in case the topic surfaced, he always said that everything happens according to God's plan and should be accepted.

Osama believed that he was sent into this world by the Almighty for a specific reason. He was here with a predestined task which he had to complete. He once told Omar:

> I was put on this earth by God for a specific reason. My only reason for living is to fight the Jihad and to make sure there is justice for Muslims. Muslims are the mistreated of the world. It is my mission to make certain that other nations take Islam seriously (219)

The need of the hour was to be patient. Someday, he believed that both America and Israel would be defeated and the entire world would become one large Islamic country.

However, Omar never agreed with the views of his father and felt that there were other vital things to do in life than just change the world. His heart went out to all those people who believed death to be a great reward. He never had any urge to die, and wanted to stay alive. Though his life was far from being happy, he wanted to live and pursue God's blessing of life on earth. For the first time in his life he realized "that he was of the past, and I was of the future. I felt myself a man" (223).

Negative propaganda about the US had it adverse effect on Omar too. The various talks held against them in meetings and in the mosques had everybody raging. Talks by Osama like "America is the only power in the world with any army capable of patrolling and controlling the world. They have gained a foothold in every region. And for what purpose? To destroy our Islamic society" (242) caused a great alarm and Omar began to visualize the dangers he faced as a Muslim. There were times when he felt a great anger at the West (for propaganda he accepts is a powerful truth). Facing half-truths, he began believing that the US was an evil nation and their only agenda was to kill the Muslims. Now he had only one real goal and that was to figure out how to escape the life ordained by his father.

Osama was obsessed with a kind of lunatic fervour and wanted Islamic jihad to take over the world. The Jihadist fervency was stirred up by him frequently convincing the soldiers that the American military had presence in 150 places all over the world because their sole purpose was to kill all the Muslims and destroy Islam from the face of the globe.

His goal was to take over the entire Middle East by removing all secular governments and replacing them with fervent Islamic regimes. His desire was that "one day Muslims will rule the world" (221).

In Afghanistan, Osama began grooming his son Omar to become his number two man. He began confiding more and more in him and Omar was both mesmerized and shocked by his father's revelation. Osama spoke to his son at length about his childhood, his father, many a venture taken up as a child and the painful memory of the death of his father in an air crash when he was only 10 years of age. Osama had fond memories of his mother (to whom he was very close) and stepfather (whom he considered the most gentle person). These recollections were a treat to young Omar, but slowly he began coming face to face with the other side of his father's personality so far unravelled. Osama's words: "I was put on this earth by god for a specific reason. My only reason for living is to fight the Jihad and to make sure there is justice for Muslims.... Muslims are the mistreated of the world. It is my mission to make certain that other nations take Islam seriously" (219) shocked Omar to the core. The intents of his father now became clear and Omar was in for more shocks as the days passed.

He wanted to exterminate America from the face of the earth. He made his intents very clear to Omar in the following words.

> First we obliterate America. By that I don't mean militarily. We can destroy America from within by making it economically weak, until its markets collapse ..... We have to be patient. Their defeat and collapse may not come in my lifetime. It may not come in your lifetime, but it will come... That is God's plan, Omar, for Muslims to rule. (220, 221)

In addition to this, Omar also began understanding another aspect of his father's character, which he terms as 'hypocrisy'. When asked about the many Muslims killed in attacks initiated by Osama, he would say it was God's chosen time for them to go. There was a lot of hue and cry regarding the Muslims killed by the US troops, but the deaths of the thousands Muslim soldiers used as cannon fodder and as fuel to increase the Islamic furore was viewed differently.

Similarly, after the attacks on American embassies in Kenya and Tanzania, Osama was ready for counter-attacks, as he knew that Bill Clinton was planning to retaliate. He made all the necessary arrangements to move men to another area but did not intend to do the same with the women and children. When asked, he was quick to reply that Clinton would never attack women and children. The irony and hypocrisy here is truly evident.

Osama had other plans for his sons as well. He wanted his sons' names to be added up on the martyr's list. The sons were shocked to hear their father say:

> My Sons, there is a list on the wall of the mosque. This list is for men who volunteer to be suicide bombers. Those who want to give their lives for Islam must add their names to the list (326).

Most of the sons were shocked at their father's proposal; but even shocking was the fact that one of the younger sons, one too young to comprehend the concept of life and death, volunteered to be a suicide bomber and ran towards the mosque. Omar wondered how his father could even ask for this. When he courageously questioned his father, all that Osama said was: *"You hold no more of a place in my heart than any other man or boy in the entire country. This is true for all of my sons"* (326). After this proclamation Omar realized that for his father, love for his sons was only superficial and *"did not sink further than the outer layer of his flesh"* (327). This revelation was painful and Omar realized that his father hated his enemies more than he loved his sons.

This was exactly when Omar decided to leave his father, his work and Afghanistan, and go back to lead a life of peace. He says, "that's when I knew that I was not leaving Afghanistan to look for happiness. I was searching only for peace" (330).

Fighting, killing, bloodshed, violence, brutality, bombardment was the order of the day, and people did not think much about it. Osama desired that Omar would take his place but the sensitive and compassionate Omar had other dreams than being a warrior. A propagator of peace, he wanted to spread the message of goodwill and peace to the world. Although he tried to oppose and argue he was unsuccessful in the beginning. He spoke and convinced his mother, and surprisingly both were permitted to leave just a few days before the WTC attack on September 11, 2004. However, Najwa was only permitted to take the youngest child along. Her heart broke to leave her children behind to an unknown fate.

The book powerfully presents both the personal and paradoxical roles played by Osama. His only vision was that the entire world should be Islam, and for this he was ready to stake just anything and everything. It was his interpretation of religion and his belief in the same that drove his towards the fulfilment of his goal. Passionate about just everything, he believed whatever he did to be right. A fire burning within him and without any passivity, lethargy or hesitation he just went about doing what his heart told him. However, this does not justify his conduct or his deeds.

The bombing of the WTC and Osama's confessing that he masterminded it (in audio-tapes) were the last that Omar and Najwa heard about him.

There is a lot of movement in the book and along with the bin Laden family we literally voyage through the land of Syria, Saudi Arabia, Sudan, Afghanistan, and this journey keeps us hooked.

There are so many questions that keep coming to our mind before and after reading the book.

1. Who are the people behind the acts of terrorism, and what are they like?
2. What drives their passion insane?
3. Why are they willing to sacrifice their life?
4. Why do they toy with the lives of others?

Many questions remain unanswered and certain deeds cannot be justified because violence is not the solution for anything.

In an interview with Parvez Chowdhary, Jean Sasson confesses that "practically everything in the book was a revelation to me."

Osama died believing he had made the right choices. Jean pities that a man with his kind of intellect, charm and money did not use it all to foster Islam in a different way, in a more constructive way. Jean was genuinely satisfied with the book and this sense of accomplishment was possible for her only when she had a passion for the subject or the person concerned. No doubt the writer was passionate about the subject, but more than that she felt a sense of affinity and an emotional attachment towards Omar and Najwa. She wanted the world to know what it meant to be the wife and son of Osama bin Laden. Although the book is a biography on Osama, his son Omar plays a pivotal role, strongly supported by the emotions of his mother. Jean wanted this book *to be a reflection of THEIR lives and THEIR emotions.*

After 15 months of talking to Omar and Najwa, and understanding Osama's personal and political life, Jean was successful in bringing out this book. She was even happy because the book also has multiple stories and interesting facts (never known before) brought to the fore. Najwa refused to talk or comment about the militant and political life of Osama, but as it was impossible to separate the two, Jean (as a writer) interjected some facts about the al-Qaeda.

Truly obliged to Omar and Najwa for their authentic information regarding the man whose life was guarded so secretly, she says:

> A hundred years from now, when someone is studying upon, Osama bin Laden and his family, they will turn to Omar and Najwa's memories for important information.

The final comments of the author and her actual purpose for writing this book is beautifully brought out in her own words. She says, when

> we look back it becomes clear that the acts and accomplishments of human beings are the signatures of history. Human signatures have created an enormous chasm between the joyous light of the age of the Renaissance to the dark shadow of Sept 11, 2001. Those of us living on that fateful day experienced the lower depths of mankind. As an author, avid reader, world traveller and person of enormous curiosity, my life experiences have taught me that discord often erupts from a lack of knowledge and education. To discourage future dark moments, I believe we must nourish the minds of our young with bearing that creates understanding between ethnic and religious groups. Perhaps, understanding will lead to a marvellous day when we see the last of the violence that is so harmful to so many. I sincerely believe that nothing will further the cause of peace more than the education of our young. I would like readers to know that a percentage of the profits from the sale of this book will be devoted to the cause of education. May all roads leads to peace! (360)

(Ever since Najwa and Omar left Afghanistan in 2001, the family has not been together like earlier. Later the other sons, Osman and Mohamad, along with their wives and children caught up with them. They were later re-united with Ladin and Iman, the youngest of the siblings. Fatima was married off very early and with a daughter (named after her mom) stayed back in Iran. After the 9/10 disaster, Osama fled into the mountains and left behind the frightened children to fend for themselves. The children joined the other al-Qaeda families and sought their way into Iran where they were housed by the Iranian government).

## Works Cited

Sasson, Jean, Najwa Bin Laden and Omar Bin Laden. *Growing up Bin Laden.* One-world Publications, England, 2009.

www.jeansasson.com

www.newscommando.com

# 5

# *Wings of Fire*: A Construction of Kalam's Identity and Nation's Identity

A. Edwin Jeevaraj

The statement by Kalam given in his introduction part of *Wings of Fire: An Autobiography*, as "The story is an account, I hope not just of my personal triumphs and tribulations but of the successes and setbacks of the science establishment in modern India struggling to establish itself in the technological forefront" (xv) proves that he intentionally wishes to construct his identity on the basement of his nation. He has a vision which becomes the vision for India. He realized the fact that an individual's weakness is the weakness of the nation. So keeping the nation's progress and development in the centre he started to think and act. *Wings of Fire* is indirectly an outcome of his desire to sow the seeds of constructing individual's identity to build a strong technologically developed and free nation in the future. The co-author of *Wings of Fire: An Autobiography*, Arun K.Tiwari, while talking about the impressions of Abdul Kalam in an interview for rediff news, said:

> I learnt about the power of dreams.

This kindling nature is one of the many natures of Kalam, portrayed by all the readers of *Wings of Fire*. Thus, this paper is attempted to define how Kalam's identity constructed in the *Wings of Fire: An Autobiography* becomes the representation of his nation's identity.

Sidonie Smith and Julia Watson in their 'Reading Autobiography A Guide for Interpreting Life Narratives' claim, 'Identity' as one of the major constructive parts among the five major autobiographical subjects such as 'Memory', a source and authenticator of autobiographical act; 'Experience', that seems to be more personal interpretation of the past in a culturally and historically specific present, meditated through memory and language; 'Identity' by which the subject is said to be so conscious; 'Embodiment', which is believed to be the knowledge of the life narration and autobiographical narrators; and 'Agency' which is told to relate actions in which people exercise free choice over the interpretations of their lives and their true selves.

Jens Brockmeier, in his article, 'Identity', says that identity is a subject or a theme that runs through a life and its various accounts. It is one of the functions and motivations of writing a life of a person as a quest for an answer to the questions 'Who am I?' and 'Who is someone else'. Brockmeier points out three principle aspects for understanding the identity. They are (1) Identity as something that remains unchanging (2) Identity as something that is multiple, and (3) identity as sense of self.

Stuart Hall argues that identity is a production which is never complete, always in process and always constituted within, not outside, representation. He further says, personal identity has been seen by identity of consciousness through duration often with memory as the guarantee of such duration. Identity is also marked in terms of many categories: gender, race, ethnicity, sexuality, nationality, class, generation, family, genealogy, and religious and political ideologies, to cite the most obvious. Identity is said to be filled with the discussions on a wide variety of logical, philosophical, psychological sociological and political exposure.

Formally and logically identity is a relational term. It defines the reader's as well as nations' relationship with the author. Because identities are marked by time and place they become historically specific models of a nation too. At the same time, as the nations are imagined as a community, individuals' identity are also accounted for and become an inseparable part of the nation's identity.

Betty Ann Bergland in her article on 'National Identity and Life Writing', points out that historicity and modernity are the central parts for understanding the nation, national identity and their relationship with life writing. Homi Bhabha in his 'Nation and Narration' points out that seeing nations rather than natural helps us to appreciate the complexities at the intersection of life writing and national identity. Hobsbwan traces the nation and national identity in the link of nation with the emergence of industrialization. Anderson traces the development and identity of the nation from the cultural roots.

The impact of World War I and World War II forces the critics to trace the nation and its identity in the liberty and in the official nationalism. After this period, in the modern era the nation and its identity means a concept associated mostly with liberalization and people's voice for their rights which leads to the concept of equality. It also means in one way a justification on the impact of colonialism.

The positive expression of one's national identity is Patriotism, and the negative is Chauvinism. Multiple and hybrid identity of life writing also become one of the scale points to measure the nation and nation's identity. Moreover, a nation's identity is also found through the collective voice of authors.

Various studies have shown that a person's national identity is a direct result of the presence of elements from the "common points" in people's daily lives.

Identity in colonialism was provided with the impetus for numerous crossover, genetic, intellectual and discursive element. For the postcolonial critics, the idea of hybrid becomes an extremely important one in trying to understand the kind of mobility, cross-over and Diaspora generated by colonialism. It is said to be preserving the difference between the colonizers and the colonized. Moreover, sometimes the narrators are aware of the conflicts and contradictions, sometimes not. Sometimes narrators thematize the conflictual nature of identity in the narrative, often they do not.

Autobiographical acts involve narrators in identifying themselves and in conveying their identifications to the reader. That is, writers make themselves known by the acts of identification and by implication. The stuff of autobiographical story-telling then is drawn from multiple, desperate and discontinuous experiences, and the multiple identities constructed from constituting those experiences. Personal identity has been seen by an identity of consciousness through duration often with memory as the guarantee of such duration. The co–author Arun K. Tiwari would not have faced any problem in filtering and extracting the expected information from Kalam's memory, which is the store-house of the background knowledge for compiling *Wings of Fire* because Kalam's research experience in the scientific field, his writing experience and his focus behind writing the book might have provided the flow of expected information.

According to the theory of Brockmeier the unchanging factor of a person's identity is the nature of a personality. Nature constantly changes. The best examples for this unchanging nature found in Kalam are his simplicity and his optimistic thoughts. His father's belief in his son's potential, his spiritual maturity, and his prophetic vision about his son's future might have provided the base for Kalam's optimistic nature. A thirst for knowledge, wisdom, growth, circumstance, evolution of dreams, hard work, working with a unique mind for completion and perfection are some of the tools that exposed the multiple identity of Kalam to the world, so that he was able to excel in all the tasks he undertook.

Kalam is so sensitive not for himself but for the nation. His thinking without selfishness, love for his nation, his experience in various honourable and sensitive positions of the country, his meeting with the children, leaders and youth of the nation, and his broad view of his nation helped him to sense the status of India in the universe, and motivated him to picture the result of his sense in his writings, particularly in his *Wings of Fire: An Autobiography*.

*Wings of Fire: An Autobiography* is an extraordinary story of a true Indian's identity transformation. It is a transformation of a humble, modest, poor and rural person's life turning from obscurity to be an extraordinary, talented scientist a spiritual guru, the president of India, and the great humanitarian's achievement of the noble goals through personal, physical, psychological and professional struggles. It doesn't glorify the successful events in a man's history. It flashes the passion he maintained with his parents, his mentors, his teachers and with his colleagues. It teaches us how to be a good leader, a good motivator, a good project manager and, above all, someone with a passion and devotion towards work. It's filled with the everlasting energy and spirit especially for young students, managers, scientists and technocrats who can cherish their dreams and inculcate a spirit of integrity, unity, teamwork and honesty. It also presents the saga of an independent India's struggle for technological self-sufficiency and defensive autonomy. It is also one of the most eye-opening, inspiring, thought-provoking and educative pieces of work. In this book, Kalam explains his experience as a child, as a student, as a member and then as a leader through four sections: Orientation, Creation, Propitiation and Contemplation.

Kalam's special nature is curved even from his childhood stage itself through his personal examination of his mental and emotional process. Generally autobiography presents one's life as a journey or as a process of self-finding constituted. According to the researchers this constitution occurs after the 'turning point', particularly in Western autobiographies the constitution occurs after the turning point or conversion. Prof. Sponder's advice to Kalam when he was in a dilemma over his selection of course, was:

> . . . the trouble with Indians was not that they lacked educational opportunities, or industrial infrastructure—the trouble was in their failure to discriminate between disciplines and to rationalize their choices." (18)

Professor Srinivasan's special nature of identifying the place where students have to be stricken in order to get their identity applied on Kalam are some of the turning points which helped Kalam to get his real power and real identity as a hard worker. As in many of the Indian autobiographies of science, politics and art, in *Wings of Fire* also, the protoganist, Kalam, is the constructive agent of his identity. But Kalam used the help of his co-author, Arun K. Tiwari, in constructing his identity.

Another notable quality of Kalam's autobiography that has become the major factor of constituting the protagonist's unique identity is the timely motivation of Kalam's father, his teachers of different periods, his professors, his guides and some spiritual gurus. According to the theory 'Gestalt of coherence', the local or temporary selves may change in the same way that children grow up and become adult or that adult change under different conditions and at different times of their lives. But these selves can also exist simultaneously and independently from each other. It's true that Kalam may also have a chance to have some temporary selves like having interest in literature, business, physics etc. But the motivation of all the characters whom Kalam admired and portrayed in his autobiography, united his constellation of selves under one major identity, humanitarian-cum-scientist. For example, each phase of his academic education, ends up with one quote focusing future. They are:

> "Kalam I want you to develop so that you are on part with highly educated people of the big cities" (10) – Sastry. (I phase)
>
> "Your soul dwells in the house of tomorrow which none of us at Rameshwaram can visit, not even in our dreams". (11) – Kalam's father. (II phase)
>
> "Take my word, this boy is going to bring glory to his school and to his teachers"(13)—Rama Krishna Iyer (III phase)
>
> "you are my best student and hard work will help you bring a great name for your teachers" (21)—Prof. Sponder (IV phase)

It is a fact that whenever Kalam was motivated he was able to search the areas where he could achieve. The earnest search for achievement guided him to identify successful ways to achieve. It also helped him to decide what his autobiography had to be. And to find what story of his life did he find appropriate and fitting. So that he was able to say after the narration how his success has been shown to the world, through continuous motivation as well as personal hard efforts:

> Some poor children living in an obscure place in an underprivileged social settings may find a little solace in the way my destiny has been shaped. It could perhaps help such children themselves from the bondage of their illusory backwardness and hopelessness (167).

This focus not only leads to utilize the personal identification as a motivational tool for the suffering humanity but it also transforms the personal identity into a national identity, as the main motto of this book is to liberate the socially bounded common people.

Kalam's *Wings of Fire* deals with an actual recollection, particularly, of his childhood which prompted the dream about his being an astronaut and his successful attempts for his nation. Significantly, the methodology of teaching a concept practically applied by his teacher, Iyadurai Solomon, an ideal guide for young minds, initiated the first step into his identity as a scientist. Kalam's regular observation on his father's regular prayer at home and in mass, his discussions with other spiritual leaders, and his discussions on hard spiritual philosophies with his father initiated spirituality in the heart of Kalam. Kalam was able to attain the unique nature of religion not only with the help of his father and the traditions followed in the home, but also with the help of the teachers like Iyadurai Solomon, Ramananda Sastry, Lakshmana Sastry etc.

Kalam as a fascist is longing for the rejuvenation of his nation based on his people's commitment to a united national community where its individuals are united together as one and based on people's national identity connected by traditional and modern culture, good-education and big dreams. His recollections are presented not only through combined spiritual thoughts but also through social construction. This way of portraying recollections resembles one of the new elements of nationalism which is called invented tradition, by the historian E.J. Hobsbawm. Kalam's focus in the autobiography is not to raise a call of reaction or of revolution against the nation's policies but it's a call of demanding an inward reaction and revolution of every individual of his nation through big dreams, creative thinking for scientific and technological growth. Both liberal nationalism and integral nationalism are supported by Kalam in his *Wings of Fire.* Liberal nationalism which is also called civic nationalism is compatible with liberal values of freedom, tolerance, equality and individual rights. At the same time there is a small note of anti–colonization found in the *Wings of Fire* when Kalam talks about technological growth. He raises his voice for India as it should be liberated from the technological domination of developed countries.

Generally, the process of identity defines individuals to others and themselves. But the process of Kalam's identity construction is different from his moulders. It defines first others to the world and next it defines him to others and to the world. Kalam in his book defines the observed characters of the personalities like, Prof. Vikram Sarabhai, Dr. Brahm Prakash, Prof. Satis Dhawan. Prof. Srinivasan, Prof. Sponder, Ramananda Sastry and others. Personal praising of Kalam is nowhere found in his *Autobiography.* But the result is a contrast; he was elevated to the peak of praise and was honoured in many ways by the world. These pieces of Kalam's actual identity include a sense of continuity, a sense of uniqueness from others, as well as the identity of his nation's growth and future. His autobiography prognosticates that the identification of his nation and its abundant growth are in the growth of ordinary villages and its people, in Indian youths' broad vision and dreams for their nation, in their active involvement to execute the activities for fulfilling their dreams and visions, and in the nation's scientific technological, research and spiritual development. Moreover, the identification of different facets of Kalam, as a scientist, a great humanitarian, an admirable philosopher, a notable spiritualist, a man of gratitude, an untiring hard worker, a motivator, a creative thinker, a perfect leader and a remarkable writer becomes more visible to the whole world.

Kalam's achievements portrayed in the *Wings of Fire: An Autobiography* are already registered in the scientific history of India. His stress on the technological and scientific development for future India, though not completely yet slightly focuses on the urgency of industrial emergency. Through his narration on how his mother would serve food to him and the kind of relationship between his mother Ashiamma and his father Jainulabudeen, and his teacher Siva Subramania Iyer and his wife, one can understand the traditional practice of various cultures of religion as well as the unity found in the Indian tradition among verities. The traditional Indian guru-shishya relationship, the state and reaction of an innocent Indian's quest, the sufferings and struggles of a poor Indian soul while adopting different atmospheres and failures are pictured realistically in this book. The culture of globalization didn't affect Kalam much in this regard. Though the writing is focused on conveying his gratitude to his moulders, he doesn't fail to raise his voice for freedom from the western colonization on other nations by their technological supremacy. His passion for India and its growth is the main reason for all his attempts and successes. It would be impossible to present detailed discussions of all the identity theories because of the complexities and objections. So this paper is limited to the focus on discussing only the theoretical interpretations that seem necessary for a heuristic understanding of the narrated phenomena of Dr.A.P.J. Abdul Kalam's individual identity in particular, and national identity in general.

## Works Cited

Brockmeier, Jens, "Identity", *Life Writing, Autobiographical and Biographical Forms,* ed., Margaretta Jolly, Rouledge, 1999.

Madhan, Nidhi, *Writing the Self: Subjectivity and Representation in Autobiographical Narratives, Creative Forum,* Vol. 23, pp.15-26, Bahri Publications, New Delhi, 2010.

Kalam, Abdul A.P.J. & Arun K. Tiwari, *Wings of Fire: An Autobiography*, University Press (India) Private Limited, Hyderabad, 1999.

http://en.wikipedia.org/wiki/Nationalism

http://www.rediff.com/news/2002/jun/21inter.htm

http://www.answersingenesis.org/articles/2009/07/13/results-evolution-bloodiest- religion-ever

# 6

# *My Story*: A Naked Portrait of Womanhood

Omana Antony

"Women are not born; they are made." Kamala Das's *My Story* is a concrete representation of this statement. It is a unique, strange and intensely personal autobiography, which projects a woman so naked in both her outer and inner self. The so-called feminism, the issues of woman which no woman dared to confess, finds a true and bold expression in the personal utterances of Das.

Any woman can identify the working of her mind and body with that of the feelings and experiences Das has confessed in her autobiography. *My Story* is the bare depiction of what a female dreamt, felt, desired and experienced in this society that treated her as a woman. It is always the bitter experiences that make a person either to fall into the chaos of calamities or resurrect like a phoenix. In the case of women usually the former situation is seen natural; but Das became different or rather a controversial figure by her courage to throw away her culturally defined self and the traditional Indian morality to winds. Kamala, the 'good' girl, is an ordinary girl turned into a rebel by the circumstances of deprivation and the callousness of the society. Das, in the most honest and daring way, expresses the social, psychological, emotional, physical and even sexual issues of her most personal life in her autobiography. The whole woman kind could identify their hidden feelings and experiences and aspirations with that of Das with a cathartic effect.

Das grew up with a lot of complexes. She believed that even her birth was not a desired one by her parents. When her childhood passed uncared and unsupervised by her busy father and sick and depressed mother, her only brother, her sibling, became her soul companion. Being a victim of negligence at home and of apartheid at school, her attack on William, the white boy, who bullied her brother, was not at all a surprise. It is quite natural to the society to label such a girl as a perverted one. If a girl is once labelled negatively by the society, it is impossible to get rid of it. Nobody will listen to the whimpering of her soul. Here Das is pointing at the worst luck of a woman in the hands of a society that is both deaf and blind. Women always fall victim to this injustice of the society.

It is quite natural for children in their teens to have a fascination for the opposite sex. Das also developed a kind of fascination for one of her schoolmates, Govinda Kurup, an eighth standard boy, just because of his rebellious nature. She even showed the boldness to confide in her grandma that she wanted to marry him. Usually when boys love rebelliousness they will become rebels; girls suppress such feelings just because they are girls. Women usually cherish such desires and feelings in their innermost heart as their purely personal and inner experiences; but Das stands different in her honesty in exposing her inner self.

Das again calls our attention to yet another ill-fate of women through the description of the plight of women in her own family, and even in her own life. It is shocking to see how the elders of a prestigious family could send one of its girls (Das's mother) in marriage to a person neither from any royal family nor a Brahmin. Being afraid of the elders and knowing the conspiracy behind this selfish act, without any protest the girl went with the dark stranger whom she was mortally afraid of. The same was the case with Das. The elders selected the son-in-law suitable to the status of the family instead of the wishes and dreams of the girl. Das very strongly expresses her mental anguish and helplessness at this crime of her elders. Even at the first meeting itself she was victimized by the literary visitor who later became her husband. Unable to confide to her father about the immoral behaviour of the proposed groom, she frantically turned to her girlfriend for consolation; but being helpless she bowed to her fate letting herself be a victim of a young man's carnal hunger, to be a middle-class housewife. Her wedding was a highly expensive and grand one. Her father was very particular to make it a lavish one and was highly extravagant. With scorn she comments that a marriage is an opportunity for the bride's father to show off his wealth; the bride is unimportant and her happiness a minor issue.

In chapter 9 Das introduces her grand-uncle's mother, Madhavi Amma, whom she called 'Valliamma', and admires her capacity for silence. Her silence was so great that she remained dumb when the elders drove her beloved and loving husband out of the house though she had a child by him and within weeks she was married off to her cousin who was not sensitive and gentle like the former. With a heavy heart yearning for her lost beloved one and with the unbearable prick of conscience towards her son for making him a fatherless child, she pulled on her new life within the four walls of the Nalappat house for 30 years till her body and the suppressed desires were devoured by the flames of the funeral pyre. Throughout her life, "Hers was a hard face, a shut safe of iron, that locked in all the bitterness of her unhappy life" (32). If this person had shown a bit of courage to protest against the injustice done to her, she wouldn't have lost her 30 years of life with a conscience of guilt and pain. The root cause of all the predicaments of woman is her muteness towards the injustice and exploitations she is subjected to. This is one of the most serious feminine issues. The muteness or rather the inability of women to protest is exploited by the male selfishness. In general, marriage is taken as the final act for the family to get rid off their responsibilities on the girl. She herself should face as her sole responsibility the adversities or misfortunes or sufferings that she comes across in the rest of her life. Here the society appreciates the woman for her stamina to keep the domestic harmony, but the same society declares her as the weaker sex. What an incongruity! What else can a woman do here other than mock at the hypocrisy of the society?

The incident of the kitchen-maid of Nalapat (Das's maternal family) described in chapter 7 is like a mirror to the conditions of the women of the lower strata in the present society. The way how the small but sweet and beautiful dreams of an innocent young maid of Nalapat family was shattered by the fancy of a rich member of the family tells yet another tale of woman's woe in this male-dominated society. Man, in the guise of high education, family background and financial status appears as a gentleman in public, but blows away all the morality to the winds in privacy. The gentleman who upholds his family tradition and caste superiority in public becomes a mere 'man' when he quenches his sexual thirst stamping down the dreams, tears and weakness of a girl, irrespective of her caste, colour or status.

The revelation of Das's inner self with all its feelings, aspirations and experiences confided in her autobiography is an electric shock to the whole womankind since it is an excavation of the isolated ranches of a female mind where she has hidden her inner self, a replica of what Das has revealed.

The change in the attitude of a girl when she attains 'age' is really surprising and the same was true with Das. Her attempts to make herself look beautiful and impressive, to get the love and affection of the opposite sex etc., are quite common to the feminine world, but she projects herself out from the common women folk while she expresses her longing to be a grown-up woman, a wife, a mistress, a lover etc. Her honesty and boldness reach the climax when she confesses her desire to fall in love with the most wicked, cruel and dark man and to be his mistress. She stands contradictory in her views when she talks about her own dreams about her better-half as she expresses, "I had expected him to take me in his arms and stroke my face, my hair, my hands and whisper loving words....my life" (87). A paradox between the wild mad love and the gentle tender love!

Definitely a girl with the excitement and innocence of the teenage becomes an easy target for sexual exploitation. Unless there is somebody to guide and counsel properly at this age, it becomes the fate of many innocent girls to fall prey to the sexual victimization at this budding stage itself. Her infatuation towards her art teacher made her even travel alone to his lodge room on a rainy day with a desire to fall in love with the art him by making herself look big and beautiful in a sari. The intensity of her infatuation led her to visit her art teacher in his room, fully drenched. Though she was impressed by the tenderness with which he undressed her, dried her body and took her back home, she was disappointed at the way her femininity was ignored by him. It is an unusually exceptional situation in the present world to see a man who treats with remarkable care and concern a teenage girl who visits him alone in his room with a body burning with lust. The world is so corrupted and selfish that no woman can expect such a selfless man even in her dreams. Usually the male world exploits this immaturity of the young girls. She knew where and when to put an end to these sorts of flirting. This common sense enabled her to ignore the older and strange-natured girl in the hostel who caressed and kissed her while on the train and almost succeeded in developing an unwanted relationship with her.

Das's description of her wedding arrangements and the related things unveil the pompousness, extravagance and the meaninglessness of most of the weddings in the present-day society. The elders in the family selected the man who came to her house as a literary visitor as her life partner. This particular attitude of the elders is believed by the present women as the basic cause of their predicament in marital life; that a woman is supposed to live and spend the rest of her life with a stranger selected by the elders without a bit of consideration about the girl's aspirations.

Motherhood exemplifies self-transcendence through self-effacement. The birth of the first child and the consequent experiences was the greatest turning point in Das's personality and life. The birth of her first child whom she called Monoo, who resembled the English poet Lord Byron as she wished (not her husband) was the fulfilment of her motherhood. The sacrificial love of a mother in Das is vivid in the incident where her son fell fatally sick after eating some castor seeds. The lady who wished to be a snob, loved jewels and desired for the luxuries of life vowed to Lord Krishna that she would forsake all her ornaments to restore her son to life. Nowadays the women who categorize them as society ladies or modern women feel it a shame to breast-feed or take care of their babies. Maternal love can be hired now under the title 'ayah'.

Das, a lonely girl, expected a soul-companion in her husband who with his gentle love and tender caresses would make her life a sweet lullaby, but she faced a male-oriented world of sex and lust in her married life. Recollecting the first sexual experience from her married life she writes, "Then without any warning he fell on me, surprising me by the extreme brutality of the attack." This inconsiderate and raw sexual approach of the husband to her who was then a girl of fourteen was definitely a psychological shock. Later she realized that her husband "was obsessed with sex". Heartbroken, she recollects how her womanhood was humiliated while her husband ignored her and eagerly flirted with the maids of Nalapat. The most unbearable thing for a woman, whether she is a wife, a mother or a lover is the neglect from her male partner and his infatuation for another woman.

A very realistic picture of the household predicaments of a married woman in the company of her mother-in-law and husband is projected during Das's stay at Bombay. The first spark of suicidal attempt emerged in Das during this period of her miserable life. She was constantly reminded and forced to be confined to her familial role of a mother and a wife. She was stripped of her personal freedom of having fun and joy in the company of her friends. Seeing this condition her friends glanced at her with pity in their eyes. Her life became more miserable during her second stay in Bombay. She felt a coldness slowly gripping over their marital relationship. She says, "I let him take my body every night, hoping that that would relax his nerves and make him tranquil. At night after all had slept, I sat in our tiny sitting room, sobbing and trying hard to believe in a destiny that might change for the better" (108). This warns us of the developing vagueness of marital relationship. Nowadays Lils and Alberts are increasing in marital life showing how married life is reduced to a sterile and mechanical 'game' when self-possession is absent.

Das then points to the terrible and unimaginable situation that a woman has to face when she returns home as a divorcee. A broken marriage is as distasteful and horrifying as an attack of leprosy. Added to it no man will be there to give a new life to a divorcee, complemented with a two-year-old child; and hence she has to remain as a lifelong burden and disgrace to the family. With regret Das confides that her lack of qualification and her intense love for her husband made her a misfit in getting a job or in opting for a life of prostitution. Just to safeguard the family status and the prestige of elders, with a sacrificial mentality she decided to continue her marital life with her husband...with whom she had lost all emotional contact. This particular context in her life has greater significance in the present world where marriage and marital life has lost all its sanctity and meaning. When a woman discards her feminine qualities the beauty of life is lost. It is essential for a woman of the present world to be aware of the significance of her feminine role for the beautiful and peaceful existence of life in this world.

Whether reality or illusion, Das's confession of the sexual assault on her by the midnight visitor implies a very significant psychological aspect of marital relationship. In the present world the number of women trying to get sexual satisfaction in extramarital relationship is increasing. The disappointment and dissatisfaction in their sex life make them look for it outside, or in some cases they easily fall a victim to sexual exploitations. Sexual satisfaction and mutual understanding are the foundations of marital life. Any defect in this will result in friction between husband and wife. The man will resort to other sources for sexual satisfaction as though it is an approved thing; but the woman who is labelled as the 'good girl' will suppress all her dissatisfaction and aversion towards her husband. Some will succeed in leading this life of tolerance till the end, while others will become vengeful and become victims to sexual exploitations and severe guilty consciousness. The experiences dealt in *My Story* show that Das belongs to the second category. Men generally believe that women will be happy if they are provided with sexual relationship and money. And this is the main cause of all the problems in marital relationship. More than money and sex, a wife needs love and tender care from her husband. Of course money is important, but a loving, tender care will be influencing a wife more than lakhs of rupees. Every man must be made aware of this fact before he takes the hand of a girl in marriage.

Das's relationship with the grey-eyed man stands as an exceptional case in this world (121). Here, though the woman is ready to yield to lust, the man looks at her as though she is a goddess and adores and respects her, disappointing her to the core. This also points to a particular aspect of the man-woman relationship; that is a woman though, married may be submissive to the man who satisfies her with his tender care and affection. When Mr. Das comes to know of Kamala's affair, he blasts her just like any other husband, asking, "Don't I feed you, clothe you and provide warm shelter? Don't I discharge the connubial responsibilities competently whether you ask for love or not..." (124). In the first meeting with Carlo, Das's pen-friend, she could recognize the enormous sex appeal in him, but she didn't feel any physical attraction; whereas her feelings for the grey-eyed friend was like that of Radha's love for Krishna. Das spent her days yearning for her Krishna. This hope made her survive all her unhappiness and disappointments (129). There are wives who share the bed with their husbands whereas their minds are with their beloved lovers.

Whether feminine or feminist, in a world of illusion or reality, Das the woman makes her greatest contribution to the feminine world from chapter 35 onwards of her autobiography. Her experiences, as described from her life after coming to Calcutta, is of the greatest appeal to us world due to the honesty and sincerity of those naked revelations. The society that has beautified itself with a veil of sophistication compels a woman to suppress most of the victimizations towards her to have an outwardly peaceful life. Even if she reacts at a moment of intolerance, the society will label her as perverted or immoral. It is in such a situation that Das makes an open and sarcastic criticism about the cocktail parties of the rich in chapter 35 "The Government servants drag their foolish wives to such parties hoping that their comeliness and charm will impress the rich. The rich......And after the girl had had a drink... the rich man gets closer, overpowers the girl with the unfamiliar smell of exotic shaving lotions...while her husband will be lying on a sofa, passed out, after a dozen free drinks, dreaming alcoholic dreams".

It was this nude truth about the party games that made Das lose her faith in the essential goodness of human beings. This is a very common situation in the present social set-up where parties and official get-togethers have become a fashion. The mean-minded husbands expose their innocent wives as a showpiece and they are victimised by the onlookers. Some husbands show their loyalty to their bosses by leaving their wives alone to give company to their bosses. An innocent girl fallen into such an adjustment trap prepared by the husband and his boss finds it extremely difficult to get out of the predicament.

In chapter 36, Das mentions about how she used to get frustrated at her husband's indifference when she talked about her unhappiness. Mr. Das might have his own reasons; still a lot of patient listening to the partner can minimize the problems in marital life. Though he was very caring, loving and understanding, Das confesses that they had no mental contact with each other.

This lack of deeper emotions and her aversion towards what she considered artificial about her husband's over-caring and over-protective attitude might have been the main cause of her search for love outside her marital bond.

The biggest hypocrisy of Das was the way she encouraged the kisses and hugs of the elderly men for selfish motives, and complaining to her husband about the corrupted men around her. However corrupt men are, a woman of decency can check him; but women who are in a world of fancies and over-expectations like that of Das will definitely have a miserable life as she had as a puppet at the mercy of gross men and women. With so many lovers and admirers around, life for Das was a wonderful experience. She writes, "I was like a poor girl who found herself rich all of a sudden. I was drunk with power" (145). For the first time in her life, she had the feminine urge to look beautiful. She visited beauty parlours, changed her hairstyle and tried to look modern. She was a new self "ripe for the sexual banquet."

Sickness is a teacher. She clips the wings of fancies and brings out the reality. This is a stage of self-awareness in everybody's life. Das also realized the same truth when she became lonely and still as a statue due to her illness. It must have been in room number 565 of Bombay Hospital that Das realized the real value of family or the meaning of family relations and the deeper meanings of life. She experienced the sacrificial love of her husband, children, brother, sister, doctors and many hospital people sincerely praying for her recovery. Das was changing there. She says, "Disease and pain matured me. I forgot the art of localizing my love ...I had shed my carnal desire as a snake might shed its skin....I found it easy to love nearly all who came to see us" (200, 201).

The women who once led a perverted life can be seen undergoing a complete metamorphosis in their life and general outlook at a particular stage in their life. The threats of war in Bombay life, the bed-ridden life, deadly disease, the adolescent problems of her son, the divine experience of self-awareness, the meaninglessness of the carnal love etc. made her return to her Nalapat house as the mistress of the house. Any person who leads a life forgetting herself will later sometime in her life get filled with remorse and disgust. Das says, 'Why did I not get my peace in the arms of my husband? Subconsciously I hoped for the death of my ego. I was looking for an executioner whose axe would cleave my head into two" (180). But our society won't leave such women to correct their mistake and lead the peaceful life of a 'pativrata'. If she doesn't yield to her previous love mates, they'll turn out to be the bitterest critics spreading the worst scandal against her. That was what Das experienced when she showed her disgust to her previous acquaintances. Usually in such situations the whole society would be against the woman giving her no way to escape other than to remain in the same mud pool of mistakes. But for Das her extraordinary will-power and the support of her husband helped her to resurrect. All her frustrations came to a control when she occupied herself in poetry writing. She was fully engaged and had no time to brood upon anything.

At the beginning of chapter 45 Das points out one of the most serious issues of the present homes which are really mere houses. She says, "As a marriage, in the conventional sense, mine was a flop. There were silences between the two of us that seemed to me interminable, although at times I broke them by a word or two about our little son or about the grocer's bill." It shows how many of the unsatisfied marriages force the husband and wife to live as strangers within the four walls of the beautiful mansions. Harold Pinter reveals this fact of the modern families more beautifully in his play. There the husband and wife have nothing to communicate. The silence becomes so dreadful that the wife makes some meaningless utterances to fill the gap of silence between them. This often happens when there is no mental contact between the husband and wife.

A mind that runs after lust and luxury finally comes to rest with a self-realization. Das says, "I was physically destroyed beyond resurrection. But while my body lay inert on my sick bed, my mind leapt up like a waking greyhound and became alert....Not even the best-looking man in the world would any longer arouse in me an appetite for love....What did I finally gain from life?" (220). The question "What did I gain from life?" haunts and torments the person at this stage.

In chapter 48 Das says, "Some of my Communist friends ask me what I have done in my life for the common man. Should I not have written with a social conscience? Should I not have written solely of the poor and the downtrodden? I remain silent." But she reveals her inner mind, a mind very much different from what she had revealed in the early chapters. Yes...the mind of a philanthropist...a mind that yearns for a better earth... a mind that sees the inner goodness of human beings... a mind that cries for the poor and the abandoned ones... a mind that wants to do something good for the suffering.

Das is basically a good person aspiring for the goodness of mankind. But her contribution to the Kerala women is incomparably praiseworthy. The highly conventional and orthodox society of Kerala had confined its women in a framework of norms and regulations. Assigning the honorary designation 'Grihalakshmi', she was ill-treated and exploited by the male-dominated society. Her basic nature of shyness and timidity made her suppress all the tortures and humiliations she underwent. In the course of time the society moulded her into a mute animal who like a slave accepted all the injustice towards her without a word of protest. She neither knew how to react nor to express what she had in her mind. For her even the thought of sex was a taboo. So, as Sharad Srivastava, says, "In this pseudo-moral system of male-dominated society a woman has been the victim of male-hypocrisy, exploitation and violence since the earliest times but she could not freely narrate or openly discuss these experiences...the emancipated women started freely discussing such experiences...and they would be more uninhibited in their writings." With extraordinary freedom and courage Das narrates in her autobiography how when she got engaged, her fiancé "...pushed me into behind a door and kissed me sloppily near my mouth. He crushed my breasts with his thick fingers. Don't you love me, he asked me, don't you like me touching you...I felt hurt and humiliated" (85). To the female society Das's *My Story* was a thunderbolt, a shudder. Later each of them could identify a Das in them. They realized that what Das aspired for, what she got, what she felt, how she reacted and how the society treated her are all realities because they all had the same in their inner self which they could never reveal. The whole of womankind could identify their hidden feelings, experiences and aspirations with that of Das with a cathartic effect. It helped her to be alert, and also to be confident and independent. Thus *My Story* has a revolutionary effect among the women of Kerala. The real greatness of *My Story* is that it costs Das many things that she held dear; still with a sacrificial mind she ripped open herself without a speck of hypocrisy, with utmost sincerity and honesty for the downtrodden fellow women to resurrect; and of course she succeeded.

## Works Cited

Das, Kamala (1978), *My Story,* New Delhi: Sterling Publishers.

Das, Sangeeta "The Predicament of Women", *Indian Women Writers,* Dhawan, (1994), New Delhi, R.K. Prestige Books.

Eliot, T.S. (2003), *The Waste Land and Other Poem,* Ed. Kermod, Frank, Penguin Books.

Simon de Beauvoir (1964), *The Second Sex.* trans. H.M. Parshloey, New York: Bantom.

Pinter, Harold (1981), *The Birthday Party,* London: Metheun & Co Ltd.

Srivastava, Sharad (1996), *The New Woman in Indian English Fiction: A Study of Kamala Markandaya, Anita Desai, Namita Gokhale and Shobha De,* New Delhi: Creative Books. pp.1,140.

# 7

# Kamala Das's *My Story*: A Confessional Feminist Modern Autobiography

Malshette Yogesh Trimbakrao & Shete Sonali Shivraj

> I am different; I am an entity.—*Kamala Das*

Call her Kamala Das, Madhavikutti or Surayya, Kamala Surayya (the name means Saptarishi or the Ursa Major, in Persian) took the literary world by storm in the mid-sixties. She has created a permanent place for herself in the contemporary Indo-Anglian poetry. "But the woman by any name"—her introduction is given by herself in the poem '*An Introduction*':

> I am Indian, very brown, born in
> Malabar, I speak three languages, write in
> two, dream in one. ('An Introduction')

Kamala Das was barely six, when she started writing her poetry. There is a vivid description of her childhood days in her autobiographical novel *My Story*. She wrote tragic poems about her dolls that lost their heads and limbs, and confesses that "each poem of mine made me cry".

Kamala Das is one of the most distinctive female writers of her time. Her autobiography *My Story* (1976) is one of the bold, uninhibited self-revelations seen in recent times. *My Story* is an attempt at redefining male-female relationship. It is a challenging account of the writer's mental as well as physical urges. Through her life-story she has redefined her personality. It is an account of a woman who tries to live traditionally but is forced to break the social rules in order to satisfy her instincts.

Das's childhood was spent like a common Indian girl. Her mother was from the royal Nalapat family. Her father was a peasant Nair, who, 56 years, later became a Managing Director with a British concern. In the very beginning of her life narrative Kamala Das confesses that there was no bridge of communication between the parents and the kids. Kamala and her brother were always treated indifferently. She remarks:

> They took us for granted and considered us mere puppets moving our limbs according to the tugs they gave us. They did not stop for a moment to think that we had personalities that were developing independently, like sturdy shoots of the banyan growing out of crevices, in the walls of ancient fortresses.

Das was born into an aristocratic Nair Hindu family in Malabar (now Kerala), India, on March 31, 1934. Her maternal grandfather and great-grandfather were Rajas, a caste of Hindu nobility. Her love of poetry began at an early age through the influence of her maternal great-uncle, Narayan Menon, a prominent writer, and her mother, Balamani Amma, a well-known Malayali poet. She was also deeply affected by the poetry of the sacred writings kept by the matriarchal community of Nairs. Das's father, a successful managing director for a British automobile firm, was from a peasant stock and favoured Gandhian principles of austerity. The combination of "royal" and "peasant" identities, along with the atmosphere of colonialism and its pervasive racism, produced feelings of inadequacy and alienation for Das. Educated in Calcutta and Malabar, she began writing at age six and had her first poem published by P.E.N. India at age fourteen. She did not receive a university education. She was married in 1949 to Madhava Das, an employee of the Reserve Bank of India, who later worked for the United Nations. She was sixteen years old when the first of her three sons was born; at eighteen, she began to write obsessively.

Although Das and Madhava were romantically incompatible according to Das's 1976 autobiography, *My Story,* which describes his homosexual liaisons and her extramarital affairs, Madhava supported her writing. His career took them to Calcutta, New Delhi and Bombay, where her poetry was influenced by metropolitan life as well as by her emotional experiences. In addition to writing poetry, fiction and autobiography, she served as editor of the poetry section of *The Illustrated Weekly of India* from 1971 to 1972 and 1978 to 1979. In 1981 she and her husband retired to Kerala. Das ran as an Independent for the Indian Parliament in 1984. After her husband died, she converted to Islam and changed her name to Kamala Suraiyya. She later lived in Kerala, where she wrote a syndicated column on culture and politics.

Kamala Das, being bilingual, wrote easily in Malayalam (under the name Madhavikutty) and English. Her autobiographical novel, *My Story*, shocked mainstream Kerala with its candid accounts of her encounters with men. As an artist, her paintings included nudes.

In 1999 she converted to Islam, an action she said she had been contemplating for many years. She said:

> Two plain reasons lured me to Islam One is the Purdah. Second is the security that Islam provides to women. In fact, both these reasons are complementary. Purdah is the most wonderful dress for women in the world. And I have always loved to wear the

> Purdah. It gives women a sense of security. Only Islam gives protection to women. I have been lonely all through my life. At nights, I used to sleep by embracing a pillow. But I am no longer a loner. Islam is my company. Islam is the only religion in the world that gives love and protection to women. Therefore, I have converted.

She is also known as a feminist writer. She says:

> I don't think any genius can survive caught in the machine of formal education.

Indian critics have disagreed about the significance of Das's choice to write of her experiences as an Indian woman in English; some scholars suggest that, in her shunning of traditional aesthetic form, she has created a new language for the expression of colonial contradictions. Despite disagreement over the aesthetic qualities and consistency of Das's body of poetry and autobiography, scholars agree that Das is an important figure whose bold and honest voice has re-energized Indian writing in English. Her book *My Story* created some controversy for its frank discussion of her search for love inside and outside marriage. She writes critically of the traditional conservative society in which she lives.

Much of the world's literature has been dominated by a canon that nearly dismissed women's writing more than two centuries ago. The counter-canons that have emerged as the result of this exclusion have helped to establish women's writing in mainstream culture, but still in some ways fail to acknowledge women's literature coming from non-white countries. This essay is an attempt to highlight some of the works produced by women in India over the ages.

Although India has a history of ancient civilisations such as the Harappa and Mohenjodaro, and of matrilineal societies in the south, no written records of women's literary prowess exists predating the sixth century BC. The emergence of the first body of poetry by women in India could be attributed to the advent of Buddhism. Perhaps it was the freedom offered by the religion, the way of life it offered to women, and the principle of equality that it propagated which allowed women to pen their thoughts for the first time.

Among the women who wrote was Janabai, the Varkari saint poet of the low caste Shudra community of Maharashtra, who in defence of her lower-caste status lowered the position of God to that of a fellow sweeper who aids her when she is tired and doesn't mind shovelling dirt for her. The same trend was observed with other lower-caste women who wrote to criticise the Hindu caste system which the Bhakti tradition had failed to eliminate.

This was also the period in India's history that witnessed invasion and gradual settlement by the Persian empire. The rise of Islam, not only as a religion but also as the framework of the Mughal dynasty that ruled India for almost three centuries thereafter, brought a new set of experiences and influences to women's literature in India. Muslim women had to be literate to comply with the requirements of the *Holy Quran* which made it mandatory for every Muslim, male or female, to pray. Women made use of this rule of the religion to write about themselves and their experiences. One of the earliest to write was Princess Gul-Badan Begum who in 1587 completed the *Humayun Nama* which details the life and history of one of India's most powerful Mughal kings. She wrote so 'beautifully' in Persian that when translated into English in 1898, her translator, Annette Beveridge, described it as the first novel-biography ever written by an Indian woman.

In ca. 1730, Maddhupalini, a courtesan in the kingdom of the Nayaka kings of Thanjavur in south India, was born. Since the rulers of the Nayaka dynasty were scholars and poets, lovers of music and literature, and patrons of the arts, they granted extensive patronage to women educated in the art of dance and music. There were other distinguished women poets and scholars in their courts, who were recipients of this patronage. One of them, Ramabhadramba, writes about women in the Thanjavur courts who composed poetry in eight languages.

Maddhupalini's *Radhika Santwanam* consisted of five hundred and eighty four poems about the relationship between Krishna and Radha. In an unusual third section, Krishna complains that Radha insists on making love even though he doesn't want to. According to K. Lalita, no other Telugu poet, man or woman, has written about a woman taking the initiative in a sexual relationship. Her compositions created a stir in the literary world when they were published almost two centuries later. The erotic poems in her most reputed work, *Radhika Santwanam*, stunned even the most liberal of readers and critics.

Traditionally the only women who had access to scholarships and the arts of literature and dancing were courtesans. Their status in society was of high standing, and because of the wealth they accumulated due to patronage, their property endowed them with the ability to choose their lovers and friends.

Another courtesan who was raised within the Asaf Jahi Sultanate in the Mughal Empire was Mahlaqa Bai Chanda, who received an 'elaborate education and composed beautifully' as a court poet and song writer. Her poetry was collected and published after her death in 1824 as *Gulzar-e-Mahlaqa* (Mahlaqa's garden of flowers). According to Afeefa Banu most of her poems are composed in the ghazal form which originated in Iran.

Around the eighteenth century, however, a combination of factors led to the decline of women writing in India. The East India Company, established in 1600, whose initial purpose had been to trade, gradually took over as rulers, and thereafter the British government established its rule in India. As a result of princes and kings losing their kingdoms, and being restricted by a small privy purse, there was loss of patronage to women in courts. Since these were women with education, the association of educated woman with 'bad' women became common. This led to the loss of education for women, and the production of women's literature almost came to a standstill.

The trend of educating women began again in the late nineteenth century with the rise of the reformist movement in India which saw more women's participation in rebelling against British rule. This led to a new stage in the development of women's literature in India. The body of work produced was often related to the freedom struggle and the reform and nationalist movements. Although there were still women such as Bhabani and Jogeswari whose writings in the early nineteenth century questioned the patriarchal dominance of their husbands, the majority concentrated on the freedom struggle.

The earliest woman writing during the reformist period was Savitribai Phule, who along with her husband championed the cause of women's education. She was the first woman teacher in modern Maharashtra, and together with her husband started the first school for girls. Her writing carries the mark of an activist and scholar who wholeheartedly believed in the cause of the untouchables.

Among the women writers who followed was Pandita Ramabai Saraswati who was educated both in English and in Sanskrit. In her *The High Caste Hindu Women* she argues against the patriarchal reading of the Hindu scriptures and early scholarly works of learned Brahmins which encouraged a repressive and demeaning interpretation favouring the suppression of women.

Sarojini Naidu, dubbed the nightingale of India, published her first set of poems at the age of sixteen and went to England where she was educated at King's College in London, and later at Cambridge. Her writings as an activist and as the governor of Uttar Pradesh reflect her honest and heartfelt concerns about the situation of her country.

Towards the mid-nineteenth century more and more women began to write in English. Some of them, such as Rokeya Sakhawat Hossain, created a world of feminist ideologies. In *Sultana's Dream* she talks about a world dominated by women; a world which has imprisoned men in a male equivalent of *zenanas* (women's quarters). She creates a world that is much better than the one men managed. In her woman's world, there are no wars and there is constant scientific progress and love for the environment.

Women's writing in the twentieth century moved towards a medium of modernism in which womanist and feminist statements were combined with political messages. The writings of women such as Hamsa Wadkar conveyed an honest impression of a world of professional women whose careers in television and stage segregated them as a class apart, yet subjected them to the same brutality and force of patriarchy. In her autobiography, Hamsa Wadkar talks about her life as an actor from the age of eleven, her marriage to a suspicious and abusive husband, the birth of a daughter, her life after eloping with another man, the imprisonment she faced at his home along with two of his other wives, and her rape by a justice of peace.

Women writers such as Mahasweta Devi combined women's causes with political movements. In Draupadi Mahasweta Devi creates a world of tribal rebels whose fight against a political system of enforced capitalism has driven them to become Naxalites (supporters of a Chinese-style Communism). Others such as Shashi Deshpande build a platform of universal female experiences. In *Binding Vines* she examines the experiences of women coming from different echelons of society.

Over the years and throughout the political instability which affected Indian society at large, along with a myriad of other influences which have affected culture, language and social patterns, women's literature in India has evolved to show common experiences, a sense of sisterhood and a range of female experiences that question the recurring face of patriarchy.

> *The Vedas* cry aloud, *The Puranas* shout:
>
> "No good may come to a woman."
> I was born with a woman's body
> How am I to attain truth?
> "They are foolish, seductive, deceptive—
> Any connection with a woman is disastrous."
> Bahina says, "If a woman's body is so harmful,
> How in the world will I reach truth?"
>
> (Bahinabai Chaudhari, 1682-1700)

*My Story* is to date the best-selling woman's autobiography in post-independence India. *My Story* is a chronologically ordered, linear narrative written in a realist style. It follows Kamala's life from age four through British colonial and missionary schools favoured by the colonial Indian elite; through her sexual awakening; an early and seemingly disastrous marriage; her growing literary career; extramarital affairs; the birth of her three sons; and, finally, a slow but steady coming to terms with her spouse, writing, and sexuality.

Over the years Kamala has proffered several contradictory accounts of the genesis of *My Story*. In her preface to the autobiography, she claims that she began to write the text in the mid-1970s from her hospital bed as she grappled with a potentially fatal heart condition. She wrote the autobiography, she states, "to empty myself of all the secrets so that I could depart when the lime came, with a scrubbed-out conscience" and in order to pay mounting hospital bills. Since the publication of her autobiography, she has repeatedly changed her stance on this topic in interviews and essays.

Das confesses that she had a very nice humpty-dumpty childhood at Nalapat house. For a few years she studied at a European school in Calcutta. While giving contemporaneous account, she observes that in those days it was quite normal for a British family to have friendly relations with Indian families. Her father worked at a private firm selling cars. He also had British friends who often visited their house. They had intimate British friends. Nevertheless, at school they were treated quite indifferently by the British and the Anglo–Indian classmates. She has depicted a heart-wrenching account of the brown children discriminated in a European school. She narrates that her brother was the cleverest in his class, yet he had been treated very rudely by the British counterparts. Once, a fellow student named William refrained:

> Blackie, your blood is red.

Kamala scratched his face in a mad rage but another Anglo-Indian supported the white man. Thus, Kamala and her brother always confronted the tortures of the British fellow students. Recollecting her schooldays, she narrates that the Britons were treated with a sense of partiality while the Indians always had a secondary lot.

Once, a girl called Shirley Temple was asked to read a poem composed by Kamala Das in an assembly. When the visitor asked who wrote it, the principal said that it was written by Shirley. The Governor's wife offered her a special kiss considering her to be a beauty with brains.

Child psychology is much influenced by parental bondage. It appears that Das's parents did not encourage her poetic sensibilities. In her tender childhood, she was not only aware of the colour discrimination meted out by the Britons but also about the fact that they encouraged arts and literature unlike their Indian counterparts. She remarkably declares:

> I wondered why I was born to Indian parents instead of to a white couple, who may have been proud of my verses....

Thus, Kamala felt alienated. At school she was a brown child humiliated by the European teachers.

Kamala Das describes her relations with her husband before their marriage. It is clear that she admired him but we do not find glimpses of her love and affection for her hubby as a man or as a lover. In My Story she has expressed her romantic ideas of an ideal lover. She writes:

> I had expected him to take me in his arms and stroke my face, my hair, my hands and whisper loving words. I had expected him to be all that I wanted my father to be and my mother. I wanted conversation, companionship and warmth. Sex was far from my thoughts. I had hoped that he would remove with one sweep of his benign arms, the loneliness of my life.

She has presented herself as either too bohemian to care about revealing her sexual adventures and her periods of mental breakdown or, conversely, as the submissive wife following the dictates of her husband who was apparently more eager than herself to cash in on a spiced-up and heavily fictionalized account of her life. And yet, at every opportunity Kamala reverts to the convention that she is India's most unconventional woman writer with no regrets about her work or her foci.

Kamala chose quite explicit and titillating titles for most of the 50 short chapters that make up the autobiography. Chapter headings for 38 of the 50 chapters are quite clearly sexual or at least hold the promise of some sexual content.

> She was half-crazed with love and hardly noticed me.

Kamala describes her experiences as a nine-year-old in an all-girl boarding school where she shares a room with three other girls. The eldest and prettiest of her roommates is 15-year-old Sharada who has many admirers among the young schoolgirls. The chapter ends with the following passage that also provides the title:

> The lesbian admirer came into our room once when Sharada was away taking a bath and kissed her pillowcases and her undies hanging out to dry in the dressing room. I lay on my bed watching this performance but she was half-crazed with love, and hardly noticed me.

Kamala was warned against associating with an 18-year-old college student. Of course she goes on to describe how in spite of (or because of) the warnings, she felt

> instantly drawn to her....
> She was tall and sturdy with a tense masculine grace...
> When her eyes held mine captive in a trance,
> for a reason that I could not fathom, then I felt excited.

In the summer of her sixteenth year, Kamala's father arranged for her to make an overnight journey by train to her grandmother's house, in the company of a group of professors and students.

As luck would have it,

Kamala writes, the "girl who was different from others" is part of the group. Kamala describes the seduction on the train:

> I hate the upper berth, she said. She looked around first to see if anyone was awake. Then she lay near me holding my body close to hers. Her fingers traced the outlines of my mouth with a gentleness that I had never dreamt of finding. She kissed my lips then, and whispered, you are so sweet, so very sweet, I have never met anyone so sweet, my darling, my little darling.... It was the first kiss of its kind in my life. Perhaps my mother may have kissed me while I was an infant but after that no one, not even my grandmother, had bothered to kiss me. I was unnerved. I could hardly breathe. She kept stroking my hair and kissing my face and my throat all through that night while sleep came to me in snatches and with fever. You are feverish, she said, before dawn, your mouth is hot.

A friend of Kamala's family meets the group at the station where they have to change trains, and another family friend invites the whole group for lunch. The college student coaxes Kamala to bathe with her and to allow herself to be powdered and dressed by her:

"Both of us," Kamala writes, "felt rather giddy with joy like honeymooners." By the time they join their group, the meal is well underway, and their host, Major Menon, Kamala wryly says, "seemed grateful to me for having brought into his home a bunch of charming ladies, all unmarried."

Kamala continues in the same passage to blend this romance with the girlfriend into the romance with her husband-to-be. In the next paragraph, she begins describing her courtship with a male relative. She learns from her grandmother that the family wants them to marry.

This chapter ends a page later with this description of their first kiss:

> Before I left for Calcutta, my relative pushed me into a dark corner behind a door and kissed me sloppily near my mouth. He crushed my breasts with his thick fingers. 'Don't you love me? 'he asked me, don't you like my touching you?' I felt hurt and humiliated. All I said was 'Goodbye'.

The chapter in which Kamala meets and is courted by her future husband is titled:

> She lay near me holding my body close to hers.

In the next chapter (titled "His hands bruised my body and left blue and red marks on the skin"), Kamala writes of the visit of Madhav Das, her cousin, and now her fiance, to her home in Calcutta, during their engagement:

> My cousin asked me why I was cold and frigid. I did not know what sexual desire meant, not having experienced it even once. Don't you feel any passion for me, he asked me. I don't know, I said simply and honestly. It was a disappointing week for him and for me. I had expected him to take me in his arms and stroke my face, my hair, my hands, and whisper loving words. I had expected him to be all that I wanted my father to be, and my mother. I wanted conversations, companionship and warmth. Sex was far from my thoughts.

Right after the passage Kamala says:

> I did not know whom to turn to for consolation. On a sudden impulse, I phoned my girlfriend. She was surprised to hear my voice. I thought you had forgotten me, she said. I invited her to my house. She came to spend a Sunday with me and together we cleaned out our bookcases and dusted the books. Only once she kissed me. Our eyes were watering and the dust had swollen our lips. Can't you take me away from here, I asked her. Not

> for another four years, she said. I must complete my studies she said. Then holding me close to her, she rubbed her cheek against mine. When I put her out of my mind I put aside my self-pity too. It would not do to dream of a different kind of life. My life had been planned and its course charted by my parents and relatives. ... I would be a middle-class housewife, and walk along the vegetable shops carrying a string bag and wearing faded chappals on my feet. I would beat my thin children...and make them scream out for mercy. I would wash my husband's cheap underwear and hang it out to dry in the balcony like some kind of national flag, with wifely pride....

We never hear of this girlfriend again, either in the autobiography or in any meaningful way in the many critical responses to this text.

In Chapter 22, titled "Wedding night: Again and again he hurt me and all the while the Kathakali drums throbbed dully," what Kamala records in this chapter is her initiation into heterosexual intercourse via marital rape, unsuccessful attempts at first and then, after a fortnight of attempts, successful. She becomes pregnant almost immediately and by the time her first son is born, she has few illusions about her relationship with her husband. The consequence is that now, aged 17 or 18, she decides

to be unfaithful to him, at least physically.

Chapter 27 begins:

> During my nervous breakdown there developed between myself and my husband an intimacy which was purely physical ... after bathing me in warm water and dressing me in mens clothes, my husband bade me sit on his lap, fondling me and calling me his little darling boy....I was by nature shy... but during my illness, I shed my shyness and for the first time in my life learned to surrender totally in bed with my pride intact and blazing.

She writes:

> He (the fiance) talked about homosexuality with frankness. Many of us pass through that stage, he said.

In Chapter 32, Kamala writes of her trouble with a "woman's problem" for which she requires hospitalization. Here she is tended to by a woman doctor who saves her from bleeding to death when she haemorrhages after surgery. Kamala falls in love with her and keeps going to see her in the clinic, kissing her, watching her, smelling her. She writes:

> I kept telling my husband that I was in love with the doctor and he said, it is all right, she is a woman, she will not exploit you.

She began writing seriously in her 20s, and for years afterward, as she recounted in *My Story,* sat night after night at the dining table, long after her husband and three sons had gone to sleep, writing:

> until it was 5 and the milkman clanked at the gate, with his cycle and his pails.

Kamala Das declared in the preface to the book *My Story,* it is my autobiography". She began writing it during her first serious bout with heart disease. She observes:

> the doctor thought that writing would distract my mind from the fear of sudden death and besides there were all the hospital bills to be taken care of.

After the publication of *My Story,* when she went to her home for a short vacation; she was not welcomed with warmth. *My Story* as well as several others of her past sins began to haunt her. She had to confess that *My Story* was not a truthful account but a mix-and-match effort.

The critic, Meena Sodhi, opines that the autobiographical form of writing helps to bring into focus "the search for self delineation" through the "lifelines'. The journey into the past can be proved cathartic and is a catalyst for healing. My Story is one such autobiographical journey which helped Das in coming to terms with herself and proved extremely cathartic:

> I have written several books in my lifetime, but none of them provided the pleasure the writing of My Story has given me. I have nothing more to say.

An autobiography is a never ending dialogue with the self. It is a depiction of the self by the writer himself. Das's dialogue with the self reveals her urges, yearnings and her inner longings. She knows that:

> One's real world is not what is outside him. It is the immeasurable world inside him that is real. Only the one, who has decided to travel inwards, will realize that his route has no end.

In the rest of the autobiography, we see her accounts of extramarital affairs, sexual flings, and desire for spiritual consolation. After her breakdown and her grandmother's death, Kamala Das becomes a different sexual person. She is no longer a passive object of her husband's actions and victim of the rapes of various strangers; she is now able to take pleasure and desire. She discovers her sexual self. A woman's desire becomes dominant.

The theme of female victory continues with the narrative of extramarital affairs. From Das's autobiography and her poems, it is understood that she is in an open marriage. Her husband accepts her love affairs. He does not prefer divorce. However, it seems that being sexually powerful does not satisfy her. She even puts a poem in her autobiography that does not accept the equation of liberated sexuality with satisfaction of female desire:

> We lay On bed,
> glassy-eyed, fatigued, just
> The toys dead children leave behind,
> And, we asked each other, what is
> The use, what is the bloody use?
> That was the only kind of love,
> This hacking each other's parts
> Like convicts hacking, breaking clods
> At noon.

There is a certain kind of magnitude in an autobiography. The writer has to maintain an interrelation between his past and present and offer a creative and consistent draft of his life. In the autobiography, the author himself is the thesis of his book but he writes as if he were another person. The journeying into the past is a very tiresome process where the author has to be very careful in articulating those special incidents of his life which shaped his personality. Many a time the writer has to withdraw himself from the society, temporarily to reconstruct his past. While recollecting the past the writer discovers the past "I" to be different from the present 'I'.

Das's autobiography is a marvellous example of the life-story where the past events have played a vital role in making her what she presently is. Here we constantly feel that though she is the thesis of her book, she views herself as a different persona. The magnitude of the autobiography depends upon the writer's skill to arrange the past and present of his/her life in an organic whole. *My Story* has no dates. The great critic Shirley Neuman opines that a woman's autobiography has

> discontinuity and fragmentation...
> as opposed to chronological,
> linear and coherent narrations by men.

The narration of *My Story* moves back and forth in time. In one episode we find the Vannery children's dramatic society at Nalapat and in the other Das takes us inside a boarding school where her father admitted her to be a disciplined child. Later in Calcutta, her father employed an art-tutor for her, who was a young Bengali and she often admired his pink ear lobes. This was her first encounter with a man who could attract her.

Kamala Das's physical relationship with her husband and his obsession with her body shocked many conservative readers. Right from her childhood a woman is taught to be docile and reserved about her instincts. Kamala Das also observes that women of good Nair families never mentioned sex. Nevertheless she is very candid in expressing her relationship with her hubby. She observes:

> The rape was unsuccessful but he comforted me when I expressed my fear that I was perhaps not equipped for sexual progress. Perhaps I am not normal, perhaps I am only a eunuch, I said.... Again and again throughout that unhappy night he hurt me and all the while the Kathakali drums throbbed dully against our window and the singers sang of Damyanti's plight in the jungle.

Kamala Das has been termed as an exhibitionist by critics because of her frank and confessional tone. In her teens she had viewed marriage through the glasses of romance. She opines:

> I thought then that love was flowers in the hair, it was the yellow moon lighting up a familiar face and soft words whispered in the ear...

> At the end of the month, experiencing rejection, jealousy and bitterness I grew old suddenly, my face changed from a child's to a woman's and my limbs were sore and fatigue.

Further, Kamala Das notes that she was a plaything for her husband. At the time of her marriage she was so much deeply in love with him that she was ready to undergo any tortures made by him. However her body was not ready for love-making. On the other hand, her husband had rowdy ways of sex which he had practised with the maids working at his home. Furthermore, whenever came to Nalapat house he was offered bathing water in the dark bathrooms by the working maids. Kamala Das also relates the fact that her husband had a spicy homosexual affair with one of his friends from Y.M.C.A. Thus, the age difference between the couple played a major role in turning them into an incompatible pair. After the birth of her first son her life took a new turn completely. She had found a toy to play with. Her world became full of colours. She disliked the idea of leaving her hubby to have her first child at her grandma's place. Nevertheless, the husband had grown weary of her temperament and decided to send her to Nalapat. She observes:

> Tearing myself away from the man who did not ever learn to love me, I went back to Malabar with an uncle who had been sent to take me home.

She was yearning for love. When her hubby was unable to give her the love she was searching for she decided to seek it 'Outside its legal orbit'. She made up her mind "to be unfaithful to him (her husband) at least physically." She wished to assert her individuality. If her husband could satisfy his sexual urges elsewhere, then why could not she? Nevertheless, she was conventional and God-fearing we as readers feel that she deliberately brought in the religious aspect. In one of her poems 'Radha' she becomes Radha worshipping her ideal lover:

> O Krishna, I am melting
> Melting, Melting
> Nothing remains but you....

In one of her interviews Kamala Das declared that her love-poems are based on love of Krishna and Radha and they are not at all obscene. The lover that she sought after was Lord Krishna, the God of Love for whom Mirabai left her husband and family.

As an autobiographer Kamala Das caters to both these factors and becomes the victim of criticism. She projects herself as the passive female, incapable of action, and relapses into hysteria when the surroundings become intolerable for her. She compares herself with a house with its lights put out. The same lecherous husband gave her complete liberty to go to any extent. In one of her poems entitled 'compositions' she remarks:

> When I got married
> My husband said,
> You may have freedom
> As much as you want.
> My soul balked at this diet of ash.
> Freedom became my dancing shoe,
> How well I dance,
> And danced without rest,
> Until the shoes turned grimy
> On my feet and I began to have doubts.

The husband who was so liberal and caring, can he ever be so indifferent towards her kids to shut them in another room to have a peaceful sleep?

Kamala Das's search for independence in sex and other subjects is exceptional in the tradition of Indian writing in

English, whether written by women or men. She explains female desire in the Indian context:

> In the Indian context, female desire, because it breaks social conventions of marital and sexual property and propriety, is inherently illegitimate and therefore doubly exceptional. Marilyn French explains this as "Indian women's primary duty, a duty so emphatic as to override their children's well being and certainly their own, is to "make the marriage work." This means that a woman must adjust to her husband. Whatever he is or does – if he is cold or cruel, if he is never home, or does not give her money, if he drinks or gambles or has other women, if he beats her – is her lot. She is expected to submit, serve, and produce a son. (360)

## Conclusion

Das's life-story concludes with the hopeful note. Nevertheless we can't say that it is the ultimate conclusion. An autobiography, like other forms of literature does not have a conclusion. It is never complete. We get more information about Das while going through her interview with eminent scholars, published after the publication of *My Story*. She attacks patriarchal constructions that show the male as superior and the female as passive. While doing this, she also attracts the Western readers who only know the stereotypical representations of Indian women. Nevertheless, the greatest contribution of Das to her own society is to encourage women to write for empowerment. Finally, it must be kept in mind that by writing, women will be able to express themselves freely and they will find a chance to speak the unspeakable. She has been considered as a writer who fought for the rights of women. Thus, she comes to the forefront with the innermost doubts and wishes of the modern Indian woman. The most remarkable point of her life-story is her confessional tone. She is at her best in the exploration of the female self. Her autobiography is the collective repository of woman's experience that would ordinarily be treated as superfluous. She has exhibited a unique courage and frankness in exposing the urges of the flesh in her autobiography. Her confession of her sexual experiences displays her candidness in being true to herself and denying masks. Nevertheless, she has subverted patriarchal stereotypes by externalizing her innermost self. So far as truth in the autobiography of Das is concerned one can say that is more of an imaginative rather than factual.

*My Story* has received mixed reactions from the readers and the critics. Her life has been a long drawn battle against a religious and cultural orthodox that frowns upon the somewhat uninhabited lifestyle of its apparently forthright persons.

The conclusion will experiment the broader implications of Indian autobiography by new techniques of perceptions. Keeping in a view the factors such as aesthetic and autobiographical, contemporary social pleasure, a theoretical research framework, creative interpretative, expounding controversies and a value-judgment, the research has been devised. In a nutshell, the practical study is carried out chiefly in terms of artistic, thematic and critical categories to bring out the precise implications of Kamala Das's *My Story* as a confessional, feminist, and modern autobiography.

## Works Cited

Bhatnagar M.K. *Indian Writing in English*, Vol.–VII, Atlantic Publishers, 2001, p. 183.

Delmar, Rosalind, Mitchell, Juliet and Ann Oakley, eds. *What is Feminism?* Oxford, Blackwell, 1986, 8.

Dwivedi A. N. *Kamala Das and Her Poetry*, New Delhi: Atlantic Publishers, 2000.

————"Quest for True Love in Kamala Das's Poetry", *Journal of Alternative Perspectives in the Social Sciences.*

Eccleshall, Robert; Geoghegan, Vincent; Jay, Richard, Kenny, Michael eds. *Political Ideologies: An Introduction*, 2nd edition, London: Routledge, 1994.

Fritz, Blackwell. "Krishna Motifs in the Poetry of Sarojini Naidu and Kamala Das", *Journal of South Asian Literature*, 13. Nos. 1-4 (1977-'78). p. 13.

Folkenflik, R. *The Culture of Autobiography : Constructions of Self-Representation*, Stanford: Stanford University Press (1993).

Innes, C. L. *The Cambridge Introduction to Postcolonial Literatures in English. Cambridge*: Cambridge University Press, 2007: 140.

Iyengar, *Indian Writing in English*, New Delhi: Sterling Publishers, 1983

Das, Kamala, *My Story,* New Delhi: Sterling. 1976, p. 191.

————, *Next Indira Gandhi, only the soul knows how to sing,* D.C. Books, Kottayam, 1996, p.118.

Kohli, Devendra, *Kamala Das*, Delhi: Arnold Heinemann, 1975, p. 25.

Mittapalli and Pier Paolo Piciucco, *Kamala Das: A Critical Spectrum*, New Delhi: Atlantic Publications, 2001.

Peeradina, Saleem, *Contemporary Indian Poetry in English*, Madras: Macmillian, 1972.

Sodhi Meena *Indian Writing in English, The Autobiographical Mode*, Creative Books, New Delhi, 2004, p. 103.

# 8

# Kamala Das's *My Story*: A Compendium of Confessions, Convictions or Contradictions?

**Abhilash Nayak**

The life stories of women crafted by the male writers, in spite of the exhibition of their commitment and sincerity, have been set aside by the feminist critics as unrealistic and in authentic on the ground that since they do not live the life of women, they cannot recreate a woman's life in their fiction. All such writings are alleged to be doubly distanced from the truth. The attempts of the male writers at documenting the female stories have either been lop-sided or exaggerated, negative and false because the male perspective on women's issues have been either distant or concocted, thus failing to portray the travails of women in their private and public domains. On the other hand, when women write their own stories, it is treated as women's writing, not as a document of human creation and is given a lower status in the literary cannons.

Women writers round the world, irrespective of the differences in their problems and perspectives, share an unspoken agony, the agony of being branded as women writers, notwithstanding what they produce and how they produce it. Their gender becomes more prominent than their genres; their sympathy for their own folk is misinterpreted and branded as 'feminism', not humanism.

This indifference, inequitable or nonchalant attitude of the male critics and litterateurs notwithstanding, women writers wield their pens to voice their views and raise their voice against the repressive and unacceptable social conventions. The more the oppression, the more audible is the voice. Maybe for the same the reason autobiographies by women in the developing countries are more poignant and pronounced than that of their counterparts in the developed world. The predicament of women in general, especially in the Third World countries, despite sporadic signs of development, leaves much to be desired. Hence women have to dispose of the 'exaggerated, negative, and false images', take the onus of scripting their own stories to create their own 'self-images', in ways they find suitable to them. Harris beautifully justifies why and how black women have shouldered this responsibility:

> It has become necessary, for many reasons, for Black women to dispose of these exaggerated, negative, and false images of themselves and to create their own self-images. One major reason is that the previous sources of these images were unreliable and based their constructions on stereotypical, prejudiced, and distorted representations and ideologies. The redefinition of the self through the writing of autobiography places power into the hands of the writer to define who she is and to share her self-identity with the readers (2005, 38).

The process of writing autobiographies has been a purgative experience for these writers as it pre-empts them to think critically about their lives, free themselves from the stereotypical and derogatory images' inflicted on them historically (Bracks 1998; Davies 1994 as quoted in Harris 2005: 44) and project their perspectives in the right manner.

While writing an autobiography, the author is expected to tell everything about his life, including the revelation of some secrets of life which have hitherto remained hidden from the public and this may often cause embarrassment, debasement or loss of pride in one's own self. The orthodox autobiographers prefer to keep their secrets confined to themselves whereas the modern autobiographers with an open mind prefer to bare their heart before the readers. Bracks corroborates this in the following words:

> When producing autobiography, the author must be open to the revelation of things that are usually kept secret, and that may even be so buried that they are nearly completely forgotten. However, the choice to fully reveal themselves and admit their vulnerabilities to an openly hostile world requires lack of shame, as well as pride in who they are. (as quoted in Harris 2003 56).

After the revelation is done, the authenticity of the tone, text and technique are often questioned, the authorial intention is challenged and attempts are made to denounce the autobiography as an output of an emotional wreck. Some critics at the other extreme are of the opinion that the presentation of life in its real sense, the sense their authors hope their lives make is more important than historical accuracy and authenticity of the facts (Spacks as quoted in Cisar 1996).

It is a general belief that there is absolutely no difference between the ways in which men and women write as they both deal with the same stuff as their ingredients. But some critics, like George Henry Lewes, view that a woman's literature "promises a woman's view of life, woman's experience: in other words a new element". He differentiates the writings of men and women on the basis of their focus: in men's writing the focus is more on intellect whereas in women's writing the focus shifts to emotions. To quote him:

> Masculine mind is characterized by the predominance of intellect and the feminine by the predominance of emotions.... Woman, by her greater affectionateness, her greater range and depth of emotional experience, is well fitted to give expression to the emotional facts of life... (Lewis 1971).

For men writing autobiographies is just another act of portraying their perceptions of the world outside, but for women it is much more than that: it is more the portrayal of the world within, the world hitherto hidden from the rest of the world, than the world outside. Often the focus is neither the world within, nor the world outside but the conflict between the two, between the individual and society, between tradition and modernity, between fact and fiction. Cisar explains this beautifully in the following words, "Studying women's autobiography fixes our gaze on the dichotomies between inside and outside, the community and the individual, patriarchy and feminism, history and fiction" (Cisar 1996). This dichotomy in their existence requires them to make multiple adjustments at every phase of their life and when the extent of adjustment crosses the limits of forbearance, it leads to revolt. This revolt is often orchestrated either through emotional turmoil or physical inertia, thus jeopardizing all healthy sexual relationships and targets either the multiple layers of subjugation encoded in a patriarchic family set-up or the religious practices, social conventions and traditions perpetuated by such a set-up.

In the Third World countries, especially India, this miserable condition of women is magnified by multiple socio-cultural constructs like caste, class and religion, and results in their multiple fissured colonized identities. And women writers in India, instead of imitating their male counterparts, have always tried to create their own identities and establish a tradition of their own. The tradition of women writing autobiographies dates back to the late nineteenth century and early parts of twentieth century when the voice of the autobiographer was more or less in consonance with that of their male counterparts. The autobiographies written during this period lack an authoritative voice and focus mainly family or religion (Thakore 2010, 40). In the later part of twentieth century, we find their voice gaining prominence through the writings of autobiographers like Amrita Pritam, Kamala Das, Shobha De, Dilip Tiwana, Sharanjeet Shan, Mrinal Pandey and Bangladeshi writer Tasleema Nasreen. Their writing is distinctly separate from the earlier writings because it is blunt, non-conservative and aggressive in the expression of innermost feelings and intimate experiences of women. All the autobiographies from Sunity Devee's *The Autobiography of an Indian Princess* (1921) to Mrinal Pandey's *Daughter's Daughter* (1993) and Taslima Nasreen's *My Girlhood Days* express the inner search of women from a woman's point of view and project their predicament in realistic ways. Some radical writers are bold enough to defy the established norms of conduct and ethics whereas the rest make the autobiographies political or social documents, documenting the events in life in a journalistic matter-of-fact style. But how do we read them? Do we read them as compendiums of confessions, convictions or contradictions? Many modern writers use the confessional mode, some of them tell about their convictions about life and the socio-political ideologies they follow and some others maintain different modes of expression at different junctures of life so that they turn ambivalent and often confuse the readers. One would often notice that there are contradictions either within the text or between the text and the life of the author concerned. In some the contradictions are prominent and in others it is hidden or camouflaged.

*My Story* by Kamala Das is less a replica of the autobiographical stories written before than a modern one.

Though it shows a little resemblance to many of the autobiographies written before her, it also exhibits a clear divergence in terms of its audacity, candidness and, most importantly, ambivalence. The admiration and the admonition, the compliments and the complaints on and about her poetry and life are often confusing. But her ruthless exposure of the fallacies of the patriarchal system and the hypocrisies of the high class society in this book deserve approval and appreciation. Rosemary brilliantly brings out her achievement as a writer of autobiography:

> The standard Indian literary feminist reading of Das's work commands her for her determined protest against patriarchal norms and practices that oppress women and for her courage in continuously mining her own life experiences for material. Thus, much of this feminist championing of Das was intended as a corrective to the mainstream, masculinist reading of *My Story* as titillating trash. (George 2000 )

*My Story*, like any other piece of creative writing, is replete with multiple layers of meaning. The readers response across the years in regard to tone, technique and texture of the book have been varied. Some have been carried away by the candidness in her confessions, some others have been impressed by the conspicuous convictions and the rest have been lost in the mire of contradictions. Satchidanandan, while writing the Preface to *My Story* writes:

> Like all women's autobiographies, Kamala's too is a polyphonic text and the reader has to listen closely to hear its different voices and discern the diverse layers of its meaning (Relocating *My Story*, X, 2009).

*My Story*, though an autobiography, is a narrative written in a realist style, moving back and forth in time. It records Kamala Das's growth from that of a child of four to a sexually awakened middle-aged woman, from a naïve Nair girl to a mature woman, from a nonentity in Nalapat to a woman of international repute. The trajectory of her life through the British colonial and missionary schools, Nalapat House, Mumbai Calcutta, favoured by the colonial Indian elite is both interesting and intellectually stimulating. Her sexual progress through homosexual experiments in the convents with her English teacher, with Dr. Karunakaran and Shirley at later dates, her early marriage and the frustration out of it, her brush with and quest for love in and outside marriage, her growing literary career, the birth of her three sons, her bout of illness and subsequent refuge in spiritualism, and, finally, a slow but steady coming to terms with her spouse and social service find focus in the autobiography in varying degrees.

While describing these multitudinous experiences of her life, she has shown utmost sincerity and bravery. Her voice is feminine to the core, often confessional in vein, speaking uninhibitedly about woman's desire and her unending search for true love. But many critics believe that she has created an amalgamation of fact and fiction, personal experience and romantic imagination to make the reading breathtaking. To quote Karim's words, "She melted her personal experiences in the red-hot fire of her romantic imagination and remoulded them into memorable, evocative imageries without any inhibition of the genteel kind of feminine writers" (2009).

When things from the past are presented in an autobiography, it is usually rooted in the individual memory of writer and the collective memory of the family or society. The density or complexity of the text depends upon the quality and extent of events being referred to in the text and the extent of information received from others. Irrespective of the varying degrees of memory power that the authors are blessed with, there is every chance of its being second hand and hence distanced from the truth. This is particularly true of the events from childhood when an author was too young to remember anything systematically:

> The depiction of childhood has been a favourite theme for the autobiographers. As a matter of fact, the childhood memories are often second-hand. Generally, parents and grandparents narrate incidents from early life. Thus depiction of childhood is an indirect experience. What is offered as recollections of childhood is generally no more than what the writers have heard about themselves from others (Thakore 2010).

Hence it can be surmised that all the incidents related to childhood days are either expansions of faint memories or reconstruction of the tales told by others. They are either imaginary or concoctions out of the fag memories which cannot be construed as the final truth. In *My Story,* out of the fifty chapters, nearly one-third of them have been devoted to childhood days or events of present life referred to these days. Many of the experiences in the childhood are enjoyable, some are painful but all of them are memorable.

When *My Story* was serlialised in *Matrubhumi* it attracted the attention of the public who enjoyed reading the sensuous stuff being provided to them in their platter. Her family members and relatives were embarrassed at this revelation. Annoyed over this her father even asked the editor to suspend its publication but Kamala did not give in. After the publication of the book, she said in one of her interviews that she did not have any regrets for writing the book. In order to clarify her stand before the public she wrote in the Preface to *My Story*:

> *My Story* is my autobiography which I began writing during my first serious bout with heart disease. The doctor thought

> that writing would distract my mind from the fear of a sudden death and, besides, there were all the hospital bills to be taken care of.... Between short hours of sleep induced by the drugs given to me by the nurses, I wrote continually, not merely to honour my commitment but because I wanted to empty myself of all the secrets so that I could depart when the time came, with a scrubbed-out conscience... The serial had begun to appear in the issues of the journal which flooded the bookstalls in Kerala. My relatives were embarrassed. I had disgraced my well-known family by telling my readers that I had fallen love with a man other than my lawfully wedded husband...This book has cost many things that I held dear but I do not for a moment regret having written it. (Preface, *My Story*)

The spiritual impulse for a 'scrubbed out conscience' and the commercial intention of paying the hospital bills clash and confuse the readers. As Shirley Geok-lin Lim states, "the spiritual impulse and the commercial intention are both evident in the dialogic, ambiguous, and contradictory features of the text" (350). The phrase "scrubbed-out conscience" induces an expectation in the readers for representations of sinful or immoral subjects as the verb 'scrub' is always associated with 'dirt' or 'stain', something undesirable. Besides, with a commercial intention one would always be ready to make compromises with truth to add sexually stimulating, forbidden events to make it marketable and get as much money as one could. On the other hand, one is also forced to question the authenticity of a description when it is done between the slots of sleep induced by drugs. Initially she defended everything written in the book, saying that it contained nothing but the truth but later on she declared that it was just a "wish-fulfilling fantasy", an alter-life she had created for herself. To quote Satchidanandan again:

> Her father, the powerful V.M. Nair who was the Managing Director of the *Mathrubhumi group*, asked the editor to suspend its publication, but the proud author would be the last to yield.

> The readers were drawn into a charming and threatening life of love and longing, of desire and disloyalty. Her readers, in the typical Malayali fashion, lapped up the story of forbidden delights and then condemned her "moral aberrations". And she, the eternal Sphinx, kept them tantalised by dropping contradictory hints, first confessing that it was nothing but truth and then declaring that it was just a wish-fulfilling fantasy, an alter-life she created for herself. (Satchidanandan 2009)

While telling her story, Kamala Das has not left anything untouched and has not spared anybody: her friends, readers, her teachers, her parents, her grandmother, her relatives and her husband, everyone has been under the camera of her critical genius. In regard to her parents she is brutal in her description. She has simply brought them into picture when it is imperative. She describes her father as a man always busy with his work and not very affectionate. On the other hand, she describes her mother as a vague and indifferent woman who spent her time "lying on her belly on a large four-post bed, composing poems in Malayalam". In an environment like this, both Kamala Das and her brother grew up neglected. In the middle of the book, she uses bitter words to describe her parents who were least bothered about their children:

> She never asked any questions. My father too was entirely without curiosity. They took us for granted and considered us mere puppets, moving our limbs according to the tags they gave us. They did not stop for a moment to think that we had personalities that were developing independently like sturdy shoots of the banyan grew out of the crevices in the walls of ancient fortresses. (71)

In one of her poems that she wrote on the death of her father she described him as an "occasional visitor who came with banana chips and abuses". In another poem she describes him as one of the best persons on earth. The readers are forced to oscillate between one truth and another truth, and are not able to decide upon the ultimate truth. Her words and actions show a radical divergence, perplexing the readers altogether. Frustrated over her loneliness inside the house after her mother went away to Malabar with her brothers and sisters and his elder brother went to Madras to read medicine, she lost interest in her lessons and wanted to escape from this desolate life. Her father was there with her but she felt lonely. To quote her own words, "Every morning I told myself that I must raise myself from the desolation of life and escape, escape into another life and into another country" (73).

After her engagement with Madhava Das, she had a painful experience. Whenever they were alone, Madhava Das pleaded her to bare her breasts and turned brutal if she did not, and left blue and red marks on the screen. He also delightfully shared his sexual exploits with the maidservants in his house in Malabar. Kamala Das painfully but boldly recollects this experience, "The poor women born of a peasant stock were accustomed to a clumsy rapid mating like that of the birds, for their men had very little time to spare for niceties of any kind since all the incomplete chores waited for them, the hoeing, the ploughing, the chopping of firewood and the feeding of livestock" (79-80).

She is full of venom for her husband who, like a lecher, went for sexual exploits with anybody he found accessible, including maidservants and decides to be unfaithful to him, at least physically. But interestingly enough she prefers to keep an 'extremely handsome' bricklayer as a pet, when her husband turns unfaithful. Her obsession with the body is also discernible in her attraction towards this man whom she had been watching at work since long and finally sent her maidservant to him with a gold coin to summon him and keep him as a pet (90). Fortunately or unfortunately, the man had left before the message reached him but she promised her maidservant that she would give her a gold chain to her if she got him in a week as she was "ready for love. Ripe for a sexual banquet" (90) and the poor husband "faded into an unreal figure, became a blush on the horizon after the sun had set" and she had stopped loving him (90-91). Which decent woman would think of doing such things inside a marriage? Any woman unhappy in her marriage, especially a woman of her repute, has the liberty to easily walk out of marriage instead of challenging her husband in such filthy ways, to be at least 'physically' 'unfaithful' to her husband. One fails to imagine how sensible it is to describe the love among the people in the lower wrung in this manner and brand it as 'rapid mating'. Do we have right to denigrate others to tell the truth of our lives? What kind of a confession it is?

When she got married, she had expected conversation, warmth and companionship from her husband; she had wanted her husband to be like his father or mother but what she got in the first night was brutal physical assault and "unsuccessful rape" (80). She alleges that she went through the agony of cruelty, negligence and selfishness in the hands of her husband, who simply wanted her body but did not understand her emotional needs. He continued such sexual assaults even when the scars of the operations spoiled the beauty of her abdomen and her breasts had a slight sag (185). But she did have a special attraction for the body. She had a mischievous and notorious tendency of desiring a man who was "wicked" and had "ruined the lives of several girls" and "disgraced some of the best families in India." Warnings of her teacher did not have any impact upon her. On the contrary she said that she liked his looks (56) and wanted to be his mistress when she grew up as if she found pleasure in doing things forbidden by others.:

> It was the first time that I had seen somebody who was notorious. I felt that I ought to meet him when I grew up, and perhaps become his mistress. All the wisdom of early adolescence told me that it would not do to marry a wicked man. Being a mistress to him meant pain in a bearably moderate dose and plenty of chances to forgive the sweet sinner. (57)

Only Kamala knew why she preferred to be the mistress of the most wicked and notorious man. Do we call it a fantasy in a child's mind or the crooked design of a grown-up woman to win cheap popularity? What kind of confession or conviction it is? At the age of thirteen again, she wanted to ensnare a student leader in her love but he did not reciprocate as politics was his only interest. This time also her grandmother, looking at her 'infatuation' with the boy, had warned against developing any relationship with this boy as he had 'serpent eyes' and was not to be trusted. But she did not pay heed to her and wore flowers in her hair to woo him. However, the boy still did not give in and advised her to read Marx and Engels (59-61). Subsequently, she had also fallen in love with her Art teacher who was mature, understanding and not exploitative. He was gentle enough to take out the wet tunic from her body, wring the water out of it and put it back on her body without making any sexual advances. In this case as well, it was not the amicable behaviour or sweet voice of the gentleman that endeared her, it was once again his body, the 'startlingly beautiful' 'serene' mouth and 'pink ear lobes' that drew her towards him. She considered herself a fool for having resisted the temptation to kiss his mouth (67-69).

Her mischievous erotic errands did not stop here. A friend of her family had warned her against associating with a particular girl in the college hostel but she befriended the girl. She was very excited when the girl's eyes held her eyes in a trance. Besides, she permitted her to sleep in the same berth and allowed her to hold her body close to hers, trace the outlines of her mouth with her fingers and kiss her lips. The same girl also coaxed her to take a bath when everyone had gone away for lunch, sprayed her body with Cuticura and dressed her. Both of them "felt rather giddy like honeymooners". Even at her grandmothers place she was haunted by the voice and smile of the same girl (75-76). Even after marriage, being upset with the sudden arrangement of marriage and not being able to forget her homosexual experience with her friend, she called her to her house where they got only one chance to kiss each other. Kamala also pleaded with her friend to take her away from her home. She painfully recollects this experience, "Our eyes were watering and the dust had swollen our lips. 'Can't you take me away from here?' I asked her. Not for another four years', she said. 'I must complete my studies', she said. Then holding me close to her she rubbed her cheek against mine" (80).

With Dr Mrs Karunakaran also she had a brief amorous relationship. Her body which had gone chilled after illness got warmed with Dr Karunakaran's touch and her ears filled with her gentle voice telling her that she was saved (130). She also shared this experience with her husband who laughed it away saying that since Mrs Karuanakaran was a lady there was no fear of being exploited.

Besides these preferences for abnormal and mischievous amorous errands, she also had the audacity of inviting a drunken man to her bedroom late in the night when her husband was away to Assam on official work. This incident also raises questions about the kind of love Kamala had been looking for in others. The point to note here is that the man came to her room after getting her consent. The words of her ayah are worth noticing,

"This is the man I talked to you about, the one who used to ask often about you. He wants to talk to you...(100). Kamala was in shock and "dazed with horror". The ayah left the man in her room and closed the door. The man threw himself down upon her, attempted an unsuccessful rape, then rolled off her body and lay inert at her feet. After sometime he kissed her toes, begged her forgiveness and asked her not to talk about this to people. The next day morning when she talked about this to the ayah, she muttered aloud and said, "Child, you are mad....(101). Was it a real incident or a simple nightmarish dream? How does one know? If it was not a real incident, what pleasure Kamala might have derived by narrating such a cooked up nightmare? If it was a real incident, how did she justify it?

Immediately after the death of her grandmother she fell in love with an 'extremely handsome' man from the Khar gymkhana where she had gone in the evening to play tennis. She was mesmerised by his grey eyes, lit up by the evening sun, and the gloss of his skin and the beauty of his smile made her feel all of a sudden so awestruck, so humble (107). She let the gentleman come and sit at her feet, hid his face in the folds of her sari, dress her hair with scented while flowers and do with her as he would, make love to her but the gentleman did not want to 'dishonour' her body (109). But her quest for lust/love continued unabated. She still looked for the 'bodiless one' in the brilliance of the bodies of her suitors and lovers:

> I was perhaps seeking a familiar face that blossomed like a blue lotus in the waters of my dreams. It was to get closer to that bodiless one that I approached other forms and lost my way. I might have gone astray, but not once did I forget my destination…'(112)

What destination is she talking about here? She was aware that she had 'lost her way' and had 'gone astray'. Is it possible for someone who has 'lost her way' and 'gone astray' to remember the destination? If the person was able to remember the destination, how did she lose her way and go astray? These questions baffle the readers so much that they infer the incident to be a concoction of the imagination created for entertainment and nothing else, not even fiction, let alone truth.

Now it was the turn of Carlo, her pen-friend from Italy, whom she had stopped writing to after her marriage. His 'hooded eyes' gave him enormous sex appeal but she did not feel physically attracted to him but let him kiss her right cheek and hold her hair in one hand (113). Carlo proposed to marry her and take her to his country but she was not willing to divorce her husband and leave her sons. When she wrote to Carlo seeking his advice, he came personally to meet her and was staying in a hotel. One day after being heavily drunk in a cocktail party thrown by a cousin in honour of a novelist who was a relative of her husband, she decided to go to Carlo as she did not think it appropriate to go to her children in that condition (148). One day she had a fulfilling experience with Carlo in the hotel and could recreate her happiness from the Nalapat days when she used to sun her face and her growing limbs on the banks of a pond:

> But he offered himself as a soft drink, he offered to help me forget and in the afternoons I lay in his white arms, drowsily aware that he was only water, only a pale green pond glimmering in the sun. In him I swam, all broken with longing, in his robust blood I floated, drying on my tears. Carlo reminded me of the pond at Nalapat where I used to lie sunning my face and my growing limbs. He reminded me of the ancient Nirmatala tree which had at one time a string hammock tied onto its branches where I lay listening to the gentle sounds of the summer afternoons (152).

Another gentleman who happened to be a friend of her husband, a participant for the Seanza course, visited her house every day to have evening meal with them. Gradually the gentleman developed an infatuation for her. One day he massaged her with his nimble fingers, kissed her, taught her dancing and danced with her, bought all strings of jasmines on sale at Churchgate and decorated her hair. Her husband watched all these but did not take it seriously as the man was old enough to be her father and she was not exactly for hard up for male attention (138-139).

Kamala herself admits that there were at least "a dozen men deeply infatuated" with her but she feared Calcutta and longed to escape from it (144). Her vulnerability to amorous advances might have been at the root of this desire to run away from Calcutta. Immediately after she fell in love with another visitor from Bombay who had invited them for breakfast in his hotel room. The gentleman stroked her legs and caressed her hair while having a conversation with her. Though she was a little disturbed initially, she took pleasure out of it, stood acquiescent when he kissed her on her mouth and nearly fell in love with him (144). When she asked him if he loved her, he replied that he liked her. No reader with his sense intact will accept these activities as demonstrations of liking for somebody, particularly a married woman. And no woman, with a minimum sense of decency will allow someone to stoop so low. She was so free with her husband that she could share this incident with him. He simply warned her to be careful while choosing her playmates because he never wanted her to be hurt in life. To quote her own words:

> 'He is not capable of loving anyone except himself,' my husband said. ' You are always a child in my eyes, Amy,' he said, ' you may play around with love but be choosy about your playmates. I do not want you ever to get hurt in your life.' (145)

What did she want to say? At one point she accused her husband of being brutal and insensitive and at the other point she showed him to be open-minded and understanding. If this was not freedom, then what was it? What more liberty did she expect from her husband? In one of her poems ('Invitation'), she even blames him to be a 'coward' and a 'ruthless watcher'. If someone does not object to his wife going on amorous errands (or sexual escapades?) with others, what do we call him? Only she knew what she wanted to convey through the description of these events.

Still there was more to come. Her search for love in relationship with fatherly figures did not end. One of the old persons who used to visit her on Sundays had a face that resembled Stan Laurel's whom she admired. The old man delighted her and her children with his mimicries, took them out when her husband was out on tours. He often slobbered kisses on her cheeks. She felt guilty of encouraging him but could not help it as she wanted someone to take her children out and give them some good time. But she snapped the friendship when the old man gave her a pornographic book (150). Does every mother who does not have someone at home to take her children out allow others to 'slobber' kisses on her cheeks only to give them 'good time'? Is the Indian society ripe enough to endure such extrovert codes of conduct? She alleges that she had to bear the lecherous hugs and leering of old uncles who used to be related to her husband's business or happened to be her father's friends (151). She wanted to run away from Calcutta but her husband paid no heed to her.

What does Kamala Das try to tell by describing such incidents? Was it really the fault of people who made such advances? Didn't she encourage them with her encouraging gestures? She herself admits with pride that her oily skin made her look younger than her years and endeared her to old people. Moreover, she was 'drawn' to old people for they seemed harmless and they had charm. They smelt clean. They knew how to put a girl at ease just by paying her a simple compliment (150). Does it happen with every lady who lives in Calcutta?

During her bout of illness in New Delhi, she had promised God that she would live an exemplary life if she was spared but immediately after recovering she was back in her previous mischievous amorous self, seeking love from all corners. Her infatuation with Shirley notwithstanding, she painted her lips up with pink lipstick and wanted to be loved again. To quote her own words:

> Like the phoenix I rose from the ashes of my past. I forgot the promises that I had made to God and became once more intoxicated with life. My lips had without rest uttered the sweet name of Lord Krishna while I lay ill, but when I recovered my health I painted them up with pink lipstick. On moonlit nights once again I thought wistfully of human love. (164)

She now looked for an ideal lover, as if the list of lovers was still not complete. This time she sought cruelty that lay in the depth of a man's heart:

> I was wanted in those days, loved as men love their women, but I yearned for a change, a new life. I was looking for an ideal lover. I was looking for the one who went to Mahtura and forgot to return to his Radha. Perhaps I was seeking the cruelty that lies in the depths of a man's heart. Otherwise why did I not get my peace in the arms of my husband? (165).

As she wrote more and more, she became lonelier and lonelier in the intimate circles. Gradually she withdrew into the cave she had made for herself where she wrote stories and poems and became safe and anonymous. There were books all round her, but no friend to give her well-meaning advice, no relative telling her of her discrediting her family name by her unconventional way of thinking (170). She was a victim of her own making. But she still had the desire to make more of life, fill life with the pleasantries of love. When she was in Bombay hospital she found to her dismay that her body's contours had changed and her skin had turned gross, and she was afraid of not being able to charm others until she came across the handsome dark one with a tatoo between his eyes. To quote her words:

> What was happening to me? Was it no longer possible to lure a charming male into a complicated and satisfying love affair with the right words, the right glances, the right gestures? Was I finished as a charmer? Then with the force of a typhoon he conquered me, the last of my lovers, the most notorious of all, the king of all kings, the bison among animals, the handsome dark one with a tattoo between his eyes (171).

Here was her ideal lover, the lover she had been looking for in others. Though she identified him with Krishna, he was a prototype of the wicked man she had desired to marry in her childhood days, the "dark god of girlhood dreams". The use of imagery in the above passage is noticeable: the words and phrases "conquer", "force of a typhoon" and "bison" relate to aggression and physical violence, which Kamala seemed to dislike in her husband. There is nothing spectacular about the description of his voice or behaviour. It was his "dark limbs" and "eyes glazed with desire" that made her restless and finally she fell into his arms:

> Health has its own anointments. When I recovered from my serious illness I grew attractive once again. Then at the airport I collided with the elderly man who had once fascinated me just by turning back to glance darkly at me. I had heard of his fabulous lusts. He drew me to him as a serpent draws its dazed victim. I was his slave. That night I tossed about my bed thinking of his dark limbs and his eyes glazed with desire. Very soon we met and I fell into his arms (174).

Here again we come across the words and phrases like "dazed victim" and "slave" which usually indicate a "master-slave" or "powerful-powerless" relationship, indirectly suggest a physical relationship, with the body at its centre. This love experience was so fulfilling that she stands out on the verandah of the man's house and tells the sea, the only witness of their love "Oh, sea, I am at last in love. I have found my Krishna...'(175). She frankly admitted that she loved him but her love for him was "guided both by the wisdom of *her* body" and by "that of *her* mind". She even declared that at the first touch of his body all her past infatuations were obliterated (178). Is this the bodiless love she was talking about? If she did not believe in the existence of body in all the love relationships, where was the scope for 'infatuation'? In all relationships, her body was the channel through which she initiated the relationships, either homosexual or heterosexual. The ambivalence of her preferences for both men and women bewilders the readers and they are not able to brand her as 'lesbian', 'hetero' or 'hermaphrodite'. Towards the end of the book, she herself confesses that she had "carnal desire" earlier and now she had shed it "as a snake might shed its skin". Because of this shedding of the carnal desire, she was no longer "bed-worthy" and "a charmer of lecherous men" (186). She declared that she "was never a nymphomaniac" and sex did not interest her except as a gift she could grant to her husband to make him happy (186) but her love relations were deeply rooted in the bodies.

She blames her husband for not being communicative and maintaining an interminable silence. She confesses that as a marriage, in the conventional sense, hers was a flop as there were silences between the two of them that seemed to her interminable, although at times she broke them by a word or two about their little son or about the grocer's bill (187). If this is the truth, what about the evening walks they did together? What about the advice she sought from him from time to time about her paramours, both men and women, from her acquiescent husband? It really surprises the readers when they see a woman suffering so much in the hands of her husband instead of looking for a solution. Some are tempted to even surmise that it suits her to move from one partner to another when there is no restriction from her husband, irrespective of the kind of person he is.

She sought shelter in the arms of more than a dozen men and women to find true love but was it necessary to stray so much just in order to find love? Which husband would tolerate a wife straying so much? She blamed her husband for being insensitive, selfish and cruel as he failed to understand her needs but the same lady was full of praise for her husband at a later stage and calls him the "best friend" who was "very understanding". He was also very proud of her and encouraged her to associate with people of her own age. It is to be noted that in September 1971, Kamala Das published a short prose piece in *The Illustrated Weekly of India's* "Love and Friendship" series. Eunice de Souja records that the piece titled "I Studied All Men – I Had to" is an account of Kamala Das's early marriage, her husband's admiring talk about easy women, sluts and nymphomaniacs. Kamala Das narrates as follows:

> Last week the Editor of a *Kerala Weekly*, a well-known capitalist, offered in return for my autobiography, a month's holiday at the most expensive hotel... I was thrilled. My husband said: "Why not take K. along with you as diversion? You seem to find him attractive. After working hard, I shall not, grudge you a bit of relaxation." This is what I mean by friendship. It is hard to find a friend as good as my husband. (quoted in De Souza, 1977)

Though he was sick for three years before he passed away, his presence brought her tremendous joy and comfort. She stated that there "shall not be another person so proud of me and my achievements" (Warrior interview). During her psychological breakdown, her husband took her to Lonavala where he dressed her in his woollen trousers and a blue sweater, fed her hot chicken soup, and she lay for hours with her head against his chest, "listening to the unpredictable rhythm of the monsoon" (104). Will an insensitive husband ever behave like this? But this too she could not accept. She calls this affectionate treatment of his as lust, "I accepted with gratitude his tenderness which was but lust, loud and savage, for it seemed like a good substitute for love. I was by nature shy" (104). She only talks about her rights but hardly ever bothers about her responsibilities. What did she give him in return for his care, understanding and admiration for her achievements? She strayed so much in search of so-called lust in the cloak of love in the arms of many but she was not able to forget her husband for a single moment. Pathak, (2012) very bluntly brings out the dichotomy in her definition of love:

> Despite seeking comfort in the arms of different men the image of her own husband lurches in the background. This ghostly shadow seems to be pursuing her each time she seeks an extra-marital affair and perhaps this shadow curtails her enjoyment. Das therefore remains torn between her own unfathomable longings and the restriction of belonging to only one. (Pathak 2012)

After the birth of her second son, the gap between Kamala and her husband widened and their marriage survived in spite of being on the brink of collapse. She did not dare to go back to Nalapat as the two families had had goodwill for three generations which she did not want to ruin. She was concerned about the reaction of her parents to such a broken marriage which, they considered, was as horrible as an attack of leprosy. Bust for a lady of her calibre and guts, was it really so difficult for her to snap off the ties with her husband? When a person can brand her husband as a homosexual and provide graphic details of pre-marital, post-marital and extra-marital sexual escapades, is it really impossible for her to divorce a husband who has tolerated so many things? One doubts the sincerity of her intention in getting a divorce and the commercial intention, albeit in a camouflaged manner, seems to be dominating over her mind here as well. She seems to have been torn between her desires for longing for sexual pleasures and belonging to her husband, her family and her tradition. Pathak, (2012) sums this up in the following words, "Indeed Das's traumatized experiences are like the fissured wounds of the cracked earth, the dry gashes shrieking out for an answer that could help her to solve the dichotomy between longing and belonging".

She hated her husband for being too much obsessed with sex but she herself was so much obsessed with the body that she got into physical relationship with many in her search for love in the disguise of lust. After her illness, she felt that she was physically destroyed beyond resurrection but her mind leapt up like a greyhound and became alert. As all the ancient hungers that had once tormented my little body were fulfilled, she had no regrets. "Now the body was so incapacitated for love that not even the best looking man in the world would arouse in me an appetite for love" (204).

Her spiritual concerns, convictions and commitments also seemed to be superficial and exhibitionistic. She was the same person who saw Ghanshyam in every person she loved, the Ghanshyam she had been in love with since her childhood, the Ghanshyam whom she had promised to love all along her life and had proudly said to Him, "Only you will be my husband, only your horoscope will match with mine..." (87). It is to this Ghanshyam she turned to in times of crisis as she had done when her son was terribly ill (98). But she forgot all this and converted to Islam for reasons best known to her as she gave different reasons on different occasions in justification of this act. Weisboard records that Ms Das had developed a romantic and physical love for a young married Muslim man when she was 65. The consequent unrealised promise of marriage is supposedly the reason for her apostasy (Suneeetha). Some viewed it as an opportunistic measure to please her Muslim doctor friend whom she wanted to marry but desisted from it on the suggestion of Weisbord as it would have deprived her children of her property. Some others say that she did this when there was violent criticism from Hindu corners for her unholy and anti-religious writings.

Even after her conversion to Islam, she ridiculed Hindu religious practices but did not have guts to displease her Muslim brothers and sisters: she refused to meet Taslima for the same reason. Neither did she have the courage to play with the sentiments of Muslim fraternity by making fun of Islamic religious practices. Her commitment to any ideology or religion, like her commitment to her lovers, was transitory and subject to change in times of need. One is prone to judgmental fallacy if one construes her comments on anything as the final one.

Every religion is unique in its own ways and it is wrong to make fun of its age-old practices. Despite the age-old orthodox rituals and institutions, Hinduism allows the flexibility to its followers to attend to the religious practices as per their will and pleasure which is mandatory in other religions. Moreover, how is it going to benefit the readers? Reading such unpalatable things against their own religions, the devout practitioners will be outraged, the young will be encouraged to take up such habits of mind and the future generations will look at their own religions with despise. The remarks of Satchidanandan, a very close friend of hers, are worth reading:

> Kamala, now Surayya, again confused them by attributing different reasons at different times to her conversion, from a friendship misunderstood as love to the indifference of the Hindu scholars who never introduced her to the scriptures even while criticizing her and a desire for ultimate peace. She, however, continued to be what she was but for occasional compromises so that she might not hurt her Muslim sisters and brothers (like refusing to meet Taslima Nasreen when she visited Kerala) and declared that god is one for all religions and women receive no respect in any religion (Satchidanandan, 2009)

*The Love Queen of Malabar: Memoir of a Friendship with Kamala Das* by Merrily Weisbord, a Canadian film maker and writer, tells how she dealt with her life after apostasy. Hounded by demands for constant public appearances and confused about the decision that she once celebrated with pomp, Ms Das is shown as ill and helpless. The author quotes, "Religion cost me too much, cost me dearly" (Balakrishnan 2011).

Like European women authors, Das seized control of the society's own cultural codes, particularly those formed by dominant religious ideologies. She used, for example, the terrifying religious image of Kali, the goddess of war and destruction, in her defiant reaction:

> I hung a picture of Kali on the wall of my balcony and adorned it daily with long strings of red flowers, resembling the intestines of a disemboweled human being. Anyone walking along the edge of my paddy field a furlong away, could see the Goddess and the macabre splash of red. This gave the villagers a fright.
>
> Kamala Das often uses traditional religious imagery to sustain and dignify herself. She reaches into her own religious tradition to find support for her defiant individuality (Landoow 1989).

As regard her views towards the poor of India in concerned, we find her contradicting herself at different parts of the book. In one place she wants to be a rich woman, walk in the midst of royal arrangements and at the other place she declares herself and her son as socialists (189) and has 'delicious anticipation' that one day the 'locust' of the poor people will 'devour' the riches of the wealthy. On her visit to Shantu's pleace, she gets so much attracted to the riches in her house that she prayed God to make her rich enough to live in an old mansion full of statuettes and silver and old lace. She also wanted to marry a rich man, zamindar, and live on in the city of Calcutta as she wished to be a snob (53). There does not seem to be any occasion where she has performed any exemplary act of generosity doing anything significant for the poor. Towards the end of the book, in the section on "Indian Poverty" she plans to organise a campaign to collect a rupee from every middle class to build lowcost tenements where the slum dwellers can be housed so that we might see "their children grow up healthy and without that utter hopelessness deeming their eyes" (206) but she engaged seven servants to attend to their needs when they visited Nalapat (191). Such dichotomies in her word and action nullify her convictions that she really thought for the poor and sincerely wanted to do something for them.

Her views regarding her grandmother are equally ambivalent. The lady who permeated her life and worked all along did not escape the venom of her criticism. Kamala writes, "I was a burden and a responsibility neither my parents nor my grandmother could put up with for long. Therefore with the blessing of all, our marriage was fixed" (22). After the death of her grandmother she had a mixed response. Though she loved the amicable side of her grandmother's personality, she never appreciated her dictatorial decisions in consonance with the family traditions:

> She was orthodox, and very puritanical. I did not wish ever to cause her unhappiness by my unconventional way of thinking. So when I heard that she had died, a part of me rejoiced at my new found freedom, while another felt only a deep desolation (107).

Finally when she reached Malabar after the autobiography had been serialised in a Malayali journal, her relatives looked askance at her and were not able to know what had forced her to go back to Malabar, alone without her husband. People could not guess whether it was a separation from her husband and their 24-year-old marriage was on the rocks (190). Although she was a favourite with the students of her home state who supported her plea of a new kind of morality but she was an eye sore to her relatives who thought her to be a threat to their respectability (195).

Kamala writes that her relatives were afraid that she would write of their misdeeds, of the accidental deaths in the locality and of the true immorality which takes shelter nowhere else but in the robust arms of our society (195) but she did not do any of them. She was clever enough to focus her story on her husband and her volatile love relation with more than a dozen lovers. Some of her relatives took their grievances to her parents who were embarrassed but were totally helpless. She bragged of her commitment to writing out the truth:

> It had become clear to them that I had become a truth-addict and I loved my writing more than I loved them or my own sons. If the need ever arose, I would without hesitation bid goodbye to my doting husband and to my sons, only to be allowed to remain what I was, a writer (195).

The remarkable thing to note here is that she called herself a 'truth-addict' but she herself seemed to be confused about the definition of truth as she constantly contradicted her own stands from time to time and took different pleas to escape from the crises. At one time she called her story as only truth and at the other time she called it a "wish-fulfilling fantasy". Sensitive readers of any age would always be able to understand she wrote controversial things to be in the news, to gain cheap popularity and to attract the attention of the western readers looking for writings divergent from Indian cultures and in consonance with new notions of morality. They would be able to discern between her confessions and nightmares, between facts and fantasies, between her pronouncements and performances. She cunningly used her loquaciousness to convince the other person that she had revealed her inner self; yet, she lived behind a veil of words, at all times.

Ms Weisbord's recent book on Kamala Das is the most authentic treatise on her as it records the intimate discussions between the two and contains some revelations but one wonders why these "revelations" are necessary, especially when the "discussed" are not all around to defend. In her interview with Weisbord, Kamala had wanted her to clear the misconceptions of her country people regarding her. The author has kept her word, and the book is honest in tone, but one remembers that the book is after all about Kamala Das, the woman who has been known to "celebrate beautiful lies" about herself (Balakrishnan 2011).

Despite her efforts at projecting herself as a woman libber, she ended up as a woman who was a slave to her desires for man's love. Sahu's remark in this regard is noticeable:

> She questions the traditional role of woman as good wife, mother and householder. But she is not a woman libber, for after all questionings and probing, she realizes that man's love is the last resort even though it may be crushing her own being and personality (Sahu 257, 2008).

She took pride in writing things which she knew well would create ripples in the familiar circles. She repented for her thoughtless writings when Mohan, a young poet, came to meet her and told her that he was 'at a loss for words'. She told him, "With words I had destroyed my life. I had used them like swords in what was meant to be a purification dance, but blood was unwittingly shed" (198). She used her freedom to expression to an unlimited extent, so that there was resultant rupture and anarchy everywhere. Her commercial intention in writing the book has succeeded but her spiritual purpose has failed, as the autobiography has sustained her in the domains of literature as a controversial writer, with limited or no commitment to her convictions, hence falsifying majority of the pronouncements that she called confessions. Nayak poignantly sums up the impact of her writings on the readers:

> The youth find little in them to emulate, the old cherish in them by recollecting their youthful days and the libertines find in them the strength and inspiration to flout the age-old traditions. On the whole, they can be read as the manifestos of a spirit struggling for freedom, but freedom, like anything offered free, can lead to anarchy, if not put under proper checks and balances (2010, 74).

Writing out the dictates of the inner self is welcome but informed readers will prefer not to be misled by nightmares, in the name of so-called confessions or convictions. But as readers we will always be there with the authors, requiring her to dance to our tunes and humming her tunes once they are composed. To quote her own words:

> I have no secrets at all. Each time I have wept, the readers have wept with me. Each time I walked to my lover's house dressed like a bride, my readers have walked with me. I have felt their eyes on my right from my adolescence when I published my

first story and was called controversial. Like the eyes of an all seeing God they follow me though the years (202).

## Works Cited

Balakrishnan, 2011, Balakrishnan, 2011. "Remembering Kamala Das." http://www.business-standard.com/india/news/remembering-kamala-das/436618/ May, 2011.

Bracks, L.L. (1998). *Writings on Black Women of the Diaspora—History, Language, and Identity.* New York and London: Garland.

Butterfield, S. (1974). *Black Autobiography in America.* Amherst: University of Massachusetts Press.

Cisar, Mary. "Mennonite Women's Autobiography: An Interdisciplinary Feminist Approach." *Journal of Mennonite Studies,* Vol. 14, 1996. p. 143

Das, Kamala. *My Story.* New Delhi: Harper Collins, 2009.

De Souza, Eunice. "Kamala Das." *Osmania Journal of English Studies,* 1977.

Geok-lin, L. S. (1992). "Terms of Empowerment in Kamala Das's My Story". In *De/Colonizing the Subject: The Politics of Gender in Women's Autobiography.* Ed. by.Sidonie Smith &Julia Watson. Minneapolis: Univ.of Minnesota Press.1992.346-370.

George, Rosemary Marangole Calling Kamala Das Queer: Rereading My Story. *September, 2000.* http://www.highbeam.com/doc/1G1-76558452.html

Harris, Meta Y. *Black Women Writing Autobiography: Autobiography in Multicultural Education,* 2005.

Karim, NA. Tribute: Kamala Suraiya—Femme Fatale of Indian Literature. *Mainstream,* Vol. XLVII, No 26, June 13, 2009 http://www.mainstreamweekly.net/article1439.html

Landow, Shoshana M. "Kamala Das: Creating a Voice by Seizing and Reinterpreting Religious Tradition" '91 (Anthropology 302, Princeton University, *1989.* http://www.postcolonialweb.org/india/literature/sml4.html

Lewis, George Henry. The Lady Novelist" in *Women's Liberation & Literature,* ed. by Elaine Showalter. New York: Harcourt Brace Jovanovich, 1971, p. 174.

Nayak, Abhilash. Revisiting My Story as the Lullaby of Lust: A Comparative Study of Kamala Das's My Story and Poetry. *Creative Forum,* 23(1-2), 2010, p. 49-75.

Pathak, Neelanjana. Longing and Belonging in Kamala Das' Love Poetryhttp://www.the-indian-subcontinent.org/content/longing-and-belonging-kamala-das%E2%80%99-love-poetry-0 2012

Satchidanandan, K. "*Beyond the body*".http://www.hindu.com/fline/fl2613/stories/20090703261311400.htm

Sahu, Nandini. Between Lust and a *Tender* Love: *The Poetry of Kamala Das. Recollection as Redemption*. Authorspress: New Delhi, 2004.

Thakore, Sheetal Y. *Select Women's Autobiographies: A Study*, Saurashtra University, PhD Thesis, 2010.

# 9

# A Critical Study of Autobiographies: Kamala Das's *My Story* And Shobhaa De's *Selective Memory—Stories From My Life*

Mayur R. Agravat & Rita Dabhi

The title of this work is "A Critical Study of Autobiographies-Kamala Das's My Story and Shobhaa De's Selective Memory—Stories from My Life", wherein as the title itself suggests that the discussion is about autobiography. In order to understand the genre one must know the difference of its nature from the other literary forms like novel, drama, poetry, biography etc. if we look at these genres and try to see the nature of autobiography then autobiography is a form more personal and subjective in nature than the other literary forms, because it is written about the life of the author himself, or it is valid to call it the life of the author himself.

When we use terms such as 'Literature' or 'Author' then certain questions arise in our minds that, "Is Autobiography Literature?" that we are looking at the comparison of its nature with the nature of other literary genres?" If it is 'Literature' then "What place does it occupy among the other literary genres? "Is it 'Fiction' or is it 'Fact'?" If it is 'Fact' then "How does it differ from 'History'"?

If it is 'Literature' then the distinguishing factor of literature is as Northrop Frye calls it, "Radical Presentation, shape, texture, and mode of presentation are important to determine the form." It is easy to differentiate drama from an epic, or a lyric from a work of fiction but when it's autobiography, it becomes difficult to come to any conclusion, on one hand a reader is tempted to put it in proximity with non-fictional forms like history or biography, as it is nothing but a narration of the factual events which are a part of an individual. On the other hand one is drawn to place it in a section called fiction, this inherent quality of autobiography, as it falls very much on the border line of fact and fiction, makes difficult to categories the form.

If one looks at the dictionary meaning of the word then it is divided in the simplest manner, which provides the reader with surfacial meaning of the term, it is made up of three Greek words,

*'Autos'—Self*

*'Bios'—Life*

*'Graphein'—Write*

Murray defines the word autobiography in his *New English Dictionary* as:

> The story of a person's life written by that person.

The *Compact Oxford Reference Dictionary* defines the term as:

> An account of a person's life written by that person.

To think of autobiography then, in its modern context one would find an almost all inclusive definition of the form in *Autobiography and Psycho Analyses,* by Bruce Mazlish, for it covers some of the main aspects of autobiography in the contemporary sense, Mazlish defines the term as:

> A literary genre produced by romanticism which offers us a picture from a specific present viewpoint of a coherent shaping of an individual's past, reached by means of introspection and memory of special sort, wherein the self is seen as a developing entity, changing by definable stages, where knowledge of the self links with the external world and both together provides us with a deep and true grasp of reality.
>
> (Mazlish, *Autobiography and Psycho Analyses: Encounter,* Vol. 35, Oct. 1970, 28)

Thus, from these definitions of the term 'autobiography', one can form a picture that it is a work of art written or narrated by that person, where the writer passes and grows through the definable stages of his life to present the real picture. It is not a form completely new for the world, as it has always existed in the form of journals, letters, diaries, memoirs etc. Like other genres this form also contains ebbs and flows, as it was written for self-exaggeration and self-glorification in the days of antiquity.

## Comparing *My Story* and *Selective Memory—Stories from Life*

> *Truth* naked and unblushing truth...must be the sole recommendation of this personal narrative.
>
> —*Gibbon*

> The best autobiographies seem to suggest a certain *power of personality* over circumstances.
>
> —*Roy Pascal*

> Autobiography is *collusion between past and present;* its significance is indeed more the revelation of present situation than the uncovering of the past.
>
> —*Roy Pascal*

> The presentation of the past is controlled by the *character of the man writing.*
>
> *Roy Pascal*

> Autobiographer must rigorously select from his life and perhaps the chief task is to make the *line linking past and present* far too exactly continuous and logical.
>
> —*Roy Pascal*

> Autobiography is not just reconstruction of the past, but *interpretation*; the significant thing is what the man can remember of his past.
>
> —*Roy Pascal*

Truth, power of personality, present situation and collusion of past and present, character of the autobiographer, his experiences, interpretation, search for the true self. All these given fragmentary definitions of autobiography lead a reader towards confusion, rather than leading him to a coherent idea of the form autobiography.

Some have tried to group them according to the attitude of the author, or his motivation in writing, for instance, the desire to chronicle, to confess, or to expound. These different motivations are mixed in autobiographies. Autobiography is the only least affected a form by national characteristics, it is a distinctive product of, Western and post-Roman civilization, and only in modern times has it spread to other civilizations. It is a form which holds the balance between the self and the world, the subjective and the objective, its purpose is to search one's inner standing, it is an affair of conscience, and its main reason behind being written is the metaphysical urge of the autobiographer.

The life represented in an autobiography is not something established but it is a process; it is not a narrative of the voyage but the voyage itself. Remembering a voyage is itself a creative act, and the recording and ordering of memories even more so. Autobiography therefore has a function far beyond the pleasure of reminiscences or reflection on an interesting set of experiences.

Considering all the above aspects, a definition can be derived that,

> It involves the reconstruction of the movement of a life, or part of a life, in the actual circumstances in which it was lived. Its centre of interest is the self not the outside world, though necessarily the outside world must appear so that, in give and take with it, the personality finds its peculiar shape.
>
> —*Roy Pascal*

Then does the definition mean that truth in autobiography can be taken for granted? No, not only the readers expect truth from autobiography, but autobiographers themselves make more or less successful efforts to get at the truth and they try to stick to it.

The truth used in the autobiography won't be an objective truth, but it will be a truth used for a purpose, a purpose as the specific quality of the writer, grown of the author's life. The purpose affects the choice of events and the manner of autobiographer's treatment and expression. One can call it the 'biographical approach' to autobiography that has led us to think that the chief test is the factual truth, because in biography, a biographer writes about someone else, and his account is thus, naturally needs to be objective for which he needs the factual details about the life of the person concerned. Whereas an autobiographer makes a selection, or selects events which have shaped his conscience, not everything, which is true, needs to be mentioned in an autobiography.

By experiences, we don't mean the age factor, but experiences which shapes human beings. As, for instance, Kamala Das wrote her autobiography at the age of forty seven, and says, she wants to die "with a scrubbed out conscience" whereas Shobhaa De, for instance, starts her *Selective Memory* at the age of fifty and feels it an inappropriate time for writing an autobiography. According to her, seventies is the age when one looks back. Shobhaa De is a novelist and perhaps that is the reason behind her autobiography's 531 pages, and Das, on the other hand, is a poet, and for sure that is the reason behind her story running into only 195 pages, full of imagery, symbols and a language that is so thoroughly poetic.

There are autobiographies in which the author seems to be candidly giving us himself, dropping no clues as to reticence or bias, and bringing his life and actions into a consistent harmony with his personality. Kamala Das is one amongst them. Initiation of her autobiography is quite different from that of Shobhaa De's account. Both of them begin their prefaces with, how the idea of autobiography initiated. Poet Kamala Das uses the term 'Preface' often used before writing a prose, whereas Shobhaa De a novelist prefer the term 'Prologue' for the introduction of her Selective Memory, it is a term generally used by the poets for their poems.

It was Das's serious heart disease, her hospital bills, and a need for distraction which made her initiate the autobiography, she says in the preface of her work:

> From that moment the book took hold of me, carrying me back into the past rapidly as though it were a motor boat chug-chugging through the inky waters at night.
>
> *My Story*—Preface

Whereas, for *Selective Memory*, David, Shobhaa De's friend, made her think, she till then felt that a person has enough material and time for an autobiography, when he touches his seventies. In the beginning she refutes the idea of writing an autobiography altogether, but when her father gave her, her 50th birthday gift, one month in advance, fearing his death, at that time she realized the futility of human existence and started writing the book, she says in the prologue:

> In my preoccupation with the present I'd lost touch with my past. The book served as an excuse.

After writing it De felt better, comfortable and at peace with her self, the impatience, restlessness, irritation, all these negative emotions left her to give the 'best shot'. Kamala Das on the other hand, wanted to "scrub out her conscience, by emptying herself of all the secrets", and then prefers to die. Being a daughter and a wife of reputed family, she was not supposed to express, what she has put forth in her autobiography. She has paid for writing her story, so openly, still without regret she says in the preface of the work that

> This book has cost me many things that I held dear, but I do not for a moment regret having written it. I have written several books in my lifetime, but none of them provided the pleasure the writing of *My Story* has given me.
>
> *My Story*—Preface

If one pays attention to the tittles of both the autobiographies then, Shobhaa De selects events and experiences to be expressed publically, and therefore the name of her autobiography is *Selective Memory—Stories from My Life*. Trollope in his autobiography *An Autobiography* opines that:

> It will not, I trust, be supposed by any reader that I have intended in this so called autobiography to give a record of my inner life.

De too responded something similar when asked by an interviewer, "Why did a writer who is known for her forthrightness choose to be 'Selective' when it came to herself?" she answered:

> I don't have to tell everything. It is not obligatory for a writer to do the full Monty in public.
>
> *Indian Express*, (Bombay), Annu Kumar

While in contrast to Shobhaa De and Trollope, Das calls her work *My Story*, depicting each incident and experience which made her the Kamala Das her readers know today, as she has already expressed her heart in the preface that, she wanted to 'empty herself of all the secrets' before death. She writes her story from an inner necessity; the weight of experience is burden that cannot be borne until it is composed in autobiography, that too not in the form of history of her life, history deals with facts only. An autobiographer can, and he should be inaccurate to make his work a piece of art. History books were, and never will be, appreciated for its aesthetic value for it has no aesthetic value at all.

Das, while writing her autobiography, is sometimes accurate, but to give a touch of art to her work, she describes the smallest experience, which has made her the Madhavikutty. For instance, she talks about the 'Sanyasi' who once had visited her home and through him she got the knowledge that she is a 'Hindu' girl. She talks a lot about her grandmother, grandmother's sister, her great grandmother who played a vital role in shaping her conscience and personality. Even the South Indian rituals are also described to give us an outlook to Keralian society. De too talks about a certain rituals, in the preface itself she mentions the 'pooja' her father has organized for her on her fiftieth birthday. It was 'Satya Narayan Katha' but instead of directly talking about the effect of the incident on her personality she mentions "the light eyed, bare chested, fair skinned Brahmin, the silk 'Dhoti' her husband wore, and the nine yard 'Pathani' sari", In the first chapter of her birth she even mentions that she went home from the hospital in a 'Blue Buick', and that too a 'borrowed one', the school timings for which they had to wake up 'at 5:30 am' the list is long and unending. These incidents are of no significance in making her the novelist she is today.

If one looks at the works of both the authors, through the criteria as depicted in *Design and Truth in Autobiography* written by Roy Pascal, then Shobhaa De's *Selective Memory* can be called a memoir or reminiscence, but certainly not an autobiography. It is 'Selective' as De herself has confessed, and fulfils all the qualifications a memoir or reminiscence requires. An autobiography, according to Pascal, is a mirror of the personality of the writer. It gives a clear view of the psyche of the person writing; the character of the writer peeps through the work; it's all about the inner actions and interpretations of the life experiences. It focuses on the self of the writer while a memoir or reminiscence focuses on other outer things. It loses its purpose when the mass of reminiscence makes the reader lose trace of the distinctive personality of the author.

The usual pattern of writing an autobiography is that it begins with the childhood and moves towards youth, but as the autobiographer enters into the complex outer world and if the autobiographer is well established in his or her vocation then, the focus gradually turns and moves around the vocation only, leaving the autobiographer aside.

Das also moves through the usual pattern of writing the narrative, but unlike the established personalities, who are indulged too much in their profession, her autobiography moves around her life, around the unconventional incidents and experiences, which has shaped her personality and character.

She does mention her poetic career, but it doesn't over shadow the pain that she was undergoing at each moment of her life, and with De it seems as if she has decided to write the narrative just to discuss her career as a model, journalist, a columnist, a TV soapwriter and a novelist.

She moves according to the usual pattern and gives us her childhood accounts, but after her modelling as a vocation her memoir is a lot about each details of modelling world, then journalism. There too she mentions each interviews taken and given as a celebrity. As a journalist she has not spared a single Bollywood star or a celebrity from other diverse fields, whom she's ever met, had a conversation with, or interviewed.

It becomes unbearable for the readers who have expected something worth reading, when De allots complete chapters for the trivial gossips of film stars and celebrities. Her autobiography displays a power of circumstances over her personality but with Das circumstances do affect her but her personality over powers the dark gloomy circumstances of life. There are moments in her life when she thinks of committing 'suicide', but this pain is also transformed into the form of poetry and she writes:

> Wipe out the pain, unmould the clay.
> Let nothing remain of that yesterday...
>
> (*My Story*, 94)

In De's life too, a time came when she was neck deep in debts of '*Celebrity*', the magazine which affected her physically and mentally but then this critical situation never resulted in a novel or in the form of something creative. Each profession she has ventured in was an accident, she never thought of becoming a model, a journalist, a columnist or a novelist, yet she possesses all the titles around her name.

According to Roy Pascal, there are four general kinds of, or ways of writing an autobiography

1) Story of a profession or calling

2) Story of theoretical understanding of the world

3) Essayistic autobiography

4) Autobiography of childhood

If we try to evaluate both the women autobiographers on these four general ways, then De's autobiography falls under the first kind, as her autobiography depicts what her profession offered her or the steps by which she has reached the public achievement. *My Story* of Kamala Das seems a mixture of first, second and fourth kind, as her life story has a childhood, which still is the most important aspect of her personality. Her story establishes her as a poet embellished with poetic skills and poetic language, and her taking refuge to poetry is the ultimate theoretical understanding of the world around.

Shobhaa De does begin her initial chapters with the childhood accounts but it seems as if her childhood is curious and eager to transform itself into the youth, while Das is still the Madhavikutty, the poet, and short story writer, only because of the childhood that she had in Malabar, in the lap of grandparents, and amidst their love and care.

De's narrative is a bit illusive, as it can be defined as a memoir, reminiscence, and a diary too. *Selective Memory*, like a memoir, hovers around the profession of the author, or for her it's her profession and the outer world which is significant as opposed to the self. It seems like a diary, as a diarist notes down an account of a meal, or his changing moods throughout a day, De doesn't go beyond these kinds of trivial prattles. It's only once that she narrates something significant, when she feels guilty on her mother's death, she describes the incident of 'Delhi Darbaar Chicken', she is quite natural describing the incident which is truly poignant otherwise she fills pages with,

> When Mandakini (her elder sister) brought home her first 'earnings' (she did a short stint as a tourist guide with the Maharashtra State Tourism Board), I provided a useful tip: 'Take my advice—buy yourself a lipstick' and she did. She hasn't stopped wearing lipstick since.
>
> (*Selective Memory*, 21

Her children's friends call her "Evil Empress" ($E^2$) and its beyond one's endurance when she even remembers the whole of the conversation of two models on a flight.

> "Hey... what have you done to your eyebrows?"
> "I decided to bleach them, Nice, no?"
> "Umm, I'm not sure, I liked your old ones better."

Vanity crosses the limits when she calls it 'nauseating self-indulgence'. Pascal calls it the most frequent cause of failure in autobiography, when autobiographer lies or hides things or character to appear admirable. When De expresses her obsession for her children, or when she mentions her pregnancy, without referring to her marriage, then it feels as if she deliberately skips the chronology, readers wonders, "when did she get married and to whom?", why doesn't she mention it at least the way she mentioned the model's conversation? Das, on the other hand, is all set to tell her 'whole' story. It is only, almost towards the end of the narrative that, Shobhaa De, gives a hint of her divorce and in the twelfth chapter she elaborates the incidents and mentions her ex-husband Sudhir's second wife Smita.

Even the photographs showing De from her childhood to the fiftieth birthday, doesn't contain anything of her first marriage, not a single photograph of her ex-husband. When she is judging or putting whole of her life on paper for her readers, then this kind of significant event missing dubs her as a partial woman or a woman without nostalgia, but if she is not a nostalgic woman then why does she put Nari Hira's and her modelling photographs just in the middle of the narrative? Even the core chapters of her autobiography are sans the details of her first marriage, the ceremony and all about her being Mrs. Shobhaa Sudhir Khilachand.

Roy Pascal supports De and terms this kind of omission a result of the conflict of fact and feelings. It is perhaps the memory which performs the shifting process, as memory plays a powerful unconscious part in shaping the past according to the will of the writer, but then if she can remember the religion of her father's colleagues, then it seems impossible that there can be a case of memory failure when it came to mentioning her ex-husband and the first marriage.

There are some significant similarities between the two-poles-apart writers, and that too regarding their marriages only. Both the women are of significant literary potentialities, and both were unsatisfied with their marriages. Shobhaa De blames her career, a 'celebrity', the magazine, for her failed marriage and with Kamala Das it was the age factor—her husband Das and Kamala were romantically incompatible, he was much older than her, he was her father's friend and of his age. Das was born in an age and family where even the thought of divorce was not allowed, whereas for De living in the later part of the twentieth century, it was a bit easy to call it quits. For both the women writers, their children are their world; if they have sustained then their offsprings are the important reason.

The significant theme of their writings is women's physical relationships and its consequences. All the novels of Shobhaa De invariably show a modern woman as the central character and her sexual encounters. Das, on the other hand, has already written her 'poetic autobiography' long before she wrote *My Story*, each of her verses is the experience which she has gone through. Critics have dubbed her 'vulgar' when she is depicting her life experiences in poetry. De is abusive even in her autobiography. Both the women are darlings of critics, as they get plenty of material to criticize. In fact critics love to hate them.

Kamala Das unlike Shobhaa De comes from a reputed family of Malabar her maternal grandparents were *Rajas* and her maternal uncle *Narayana Menon* was a well known Malayali writer. Das's mother Ballamani amma was also a well established Malayali poetess. It was this familial background which Kamala Das inherited and expressed in her works. While Shobhaa De's father was a government servant and mother a housewife, siblings were also in sharp contrast to this youngest child of Rajadhyaksha family, who had a modern bent of mind. Both the writers have ventured in more than one field, but at the end settled as a poet and a novelist.

The quality of a personality is perhaps most rapidly detected in style. Style is of course as varied in autobiography too, as in any other form of literature. The great autobiographies are works that stand by themselves, and are appreciated without reference to the actual lives and works of the authors. This quality of truth must emerge from the work itself. Vanity and triviality show themselves immediately, and style in general is the most revealing element in any autobiography.

De's memoir represents a distinct style in chapterizing her life in the narrative. Rather it is a bit confusing for the readers to shape a coherent idea of her life because though she starts the memoir from her birth, and gives every single details regarding incidents and events but skips all her child births, and first marriage, in the last chapter, she mentions each child birth chronologically. Photographs also contradict her views on modelling and her humour on her looks, because in one of her chapter she's found expressing her contempt for modelling, and celebrity, hood, and still her autobiography's front page and first page bear her super model images given in the middle of the work. These more than thirty photographs prove that she is a self-indulgent woman.

Das, being a poet, shows a rare kind of subtleness. Not a single unnecessary element is visible in her *My Story*. Being a poet herself, she cannot escape poetry at the beginning of some of her chapters and language that naturally turn poetic.

Das's My Story is partially an 'autobiography of childhood'. In half of her chapters she talks about her life as a child. There she explicitly expresses her innocent likeness for girls and boys alike, and there were many whom she loved. 'Velu', 'Govinda Kurup', her lady teacher, an elder girl. For 'Velu' she says, "I was infatuated with his charm", about 'Govinda', it was his wickedness which affected her. She says "her voice was strange...itwas easy for me to fall in love with her" for her lady teacher. She even felt love for a senior girl. She expresses herself and says, "She lay near me holding my body close to hers." Autobiographies of childhood are thus all about growing up. Half of Das's autobiography consistently talks about these love affairs with boys and girls alike, and when she was hardly a teenager her parents married her off to a man of her father's age.

These kinds of childhood autobiographies, when linked with an elder's life, proves itself best, while if the writer treats the childhood without reference to what he has become, it tends to be in many parts irrelevant to the story he is narrating. All good autobiographies are in some sense a story of a calling, but in some cases, like De's, the inner calling merges into a profession and a public personality is grown out of the private.

Pascal, in the chapter called *'The Autobiography of the Poets'* says that a poet's imagination, his love of words, and literary dexterity can lead him to the problem of over-writing. A poet autobiographer can only evoke scenes and characters properly, can make more delicate self-observation of obscure urges, and thus can make his autobiography a skilful and penetrating account. In this respect Kamala Das is a true poet, while De, being an imaginative writer, evokes scenes and characters properly but fails at observing her obscure inner urges. As a result whole chapters are allotted to unnecessary things, and the true past is forgotten. There are times though when she is reflective on issues like modelling, parenting, life, writing, family etc. and these are her views which give the readers a glance of her true potentiality not the pages full of trivial descriptions. If the writer like Shobhaa De simply tries to establish herself as a 'personality' her work tends to be vain and crude. It is the ability to fuse the past and the present in an artistic whole, which proves that the work is of an imaginative writer.

There are writers who deviate from the usual chronology and produce a fragmentary works like *Selective Memory* but then the writer has to be conscious and curious about the attitude and the special subject. The fragmentation also needs an artistic arrangement by the autobiographer, and then it can appeal to the general reader.

Autobiographers, in general, unconsciously or consciously represent their generation and age in which they have lived. De time and again compares her time and the times of her children. She often compares herself with her mother as a mother, and her husband with her father. The modelling career, in which she ventured successfully, is also quite different from the point of time she is writing. Das, on the other hand represents the age in which she has lived but doesn't compare the past and present. *My Story* and *Selective Memory* are autobiographies distinct in themselves, but when a researcher has to compare them with each other from the yardstick of a set of rules, then it is obvious that Kamala Das wins the race. Das possesses the naturalness of Malabar, whereas Shobhaa De is the modern Mulgi of Mumbai, having all the characteristics of Mumbai, the metro city.

Her book lacks the quality of a great autobiography, because she writes it to inform and not at all for her own sake. It should have been, as Gottfried Keller says, when he uses his autobiographical material for his autobiographical novel, that:

> Not because it is mine, but in spite of the fact that it is mine.

Das's work is a true autobiography not only because of her brilliant insight, but also because we are intimate with her from the beginning of her life. Readers find a historical consistency of character which satisfies them. Here it needs to be mentioned that, when it is about the truthfulness of the author then it needs to be noted that the reader could not and did not want to know everything about the author, but only what is distinctive and essential.

Autobiographies fail if the autobiographer lacks an insight or seriousness, wholeness of character, but they frequently fail too because they do not create the significant meeting place between the individual and the outer world.

There can be no final or complete truth about man. So, the man also changes as he writes his autobiography. Montaigne rightly said once:

> I have not made my books more than my books has made me.

This is why, beyond factual truth, beyond the 'likeness', the autobiography has to give that unique truth of life as it is seen from inside, and this kind of unique truth can be produced only by men and women pledged to their innermost selves.

## Works Cited

*Compact Oxford Reference Dictionary.*

Bose, Manjula. *Autobiography as a literary Form: Studies In the Autobiographies of Edwin Muir, Stephen Spender and C. Day Lewis.* 1st ed. Ahmedabad: Gujarat University. 1992.

Bruss, Elizabeth. *Autobiographical Acts—The Changing Situations of a Literary Genre.*

Das, Kamala. *My Story*: 1st ed. New Delhi: Sterling, 1976.

______ *"I have not Glorified Lust."* Rediff.com (http://www.rediff.com/)

______ Interview with George Iype. *"Allah told me in order to be effective, you should have Political Power."* Rediff.com (http://www.rediff.com/). 16th July. 2000.

______ *The Many Journey of Kamala Das,* Unnikrishnan M.S., 26th June. 2008.

______ *The Old Playhouse and Other Poems.* 2nd ed. Mumbai: Orient Longman, 1986.

De, Shobhaa. *Selective Memory—Stories from My Life.* 1st ed. New Delhi: Penguin, 1998.

______ "Life in the De of Shobhaa: Some Selective Quotes", Kumar Annu, *Indian Express News Paper.* Bombay Ltd.

______ *"Shobhaa De: From Incredible to Unstoppable."* Headlinesindia.com India. 03rd June, 2008.

______ *Shooting From the Hip.* 1st ed. New Delhi: UBS 1994.

______ *Starry Nights,* 1st ed. New Delhi: 1991.

Harish, Ranjana. *Indian Women's Autobiographies,* Translated in Gujarati by Thakar, Bela. *"Bharatiya Strioni Atmakathao" revised* ed. Ahmedabad: Gurjar Granth Ratna. 2007.

Pascal, Roy. *Design and Truth in Autobiography.* 1st ed. London: Routledge & Kegan Paul, 1960.

Headlines India (http://www.headlinesindia.com/)

Hindustan.net (http://www.hindustan.net/)

Indiatoday.com (http://www.indiatoday.com/)

## 10

# Kamala Das's Bold Confession of Premarital Life in *My Story*

Anita Mudkanna

An autobiography of any writer is the mirror of his/her life. It doesn't hide any matter, incidents and experiences of writer. A writer has an ambition to present his life story before his reader as it is. But sometimes I think that some writers don't want to highlight the dark shades of their life. As a human psychology anyone feels shy to open the matters related to sensuality, sexuality and man, woman relationship but a writer like Kamala Das has dared to express it through writing without hesitation. The present article is a little attempt to focus on her bold confessional note of premarital life with reference to her autobiography *My Story*.

*My Story* articulates the writer's personal experiences as well as the incidents in her life which force her to think about the condition of women in the society. Women are humiliated and neglected everywhere. A woman discovers through her life that she is a thing of attraction and seduction. In her autobiography she describes all the details of each and every situation which impacts on her mind.

Kamala Das was born on 31 March, 1934 in Malabar, Kerala. As her autobiography tells that her maiden name was Madhavikutty. She first attended a European school in Calcutta, then the elementary school at Punnayurkulam, and then a boarding school run by the Roman catholic nuns, but in each of them she stayed for a short while.

Kamala Das was proud of her ancestral home in Malabar which was called Nalapat House. She had never forgotten her glorious childhood which she had spent in Nalapat House with the lovely family members, aunt Ammini, grand uncle Narayan Menon who was a "poet philosopher", her great grandmother and her two sisters. The members of Nalapat family were steeped in Indian epics, the *Mahabharata* and the *Ramayana*, and had a belief in Lord Shiva and Lord Krishna, whose stories are naturally impressed on the innocent mind of Kamala Das in her childhood. Her grandmother always told her about the purity of their ancestral blood.

In her childhood Kamala Das was very fond of her great grandmother who was the only daughter of a wealthy chieftain, the Raja of Punnathore Kotta. She was married to the Raja of Chiralayman, came to Nalapat House and became a good wife, good mother and a good grandmother.

Her grandmother was good caretaker, psychologist and adviser who guided Kamala Das and took care of her personality. She taught her the manners of their ancestors. She was the dearest person of the poetic persona who understood the psyche of Kamala Das and helped her to make it stable. All the secrets which she had were shared with her great grandmother. The repetition of the adjective "great" regarding her grandmother suggests Kamala Das's feeling of gratitude and the place of the grandmother in her life. When her grandmother died, she felt a vaccum in her life and felt alone in the world. The Nalapat House, its memories and of her grandmother use continuously mentioned by Kamala Das many times. It symbolizes her attachment of the Nalapat family and her past glory.

While speaking about her parents Kamala Das was not so happy. They are not ideal for her because they were a mismatched pair. Her mother Balamani Amma, a renowned poet in Malayalam, was always lying on bed and busy in writing. Her father belonged to a traditional Nair family who never loved Balamani Amma. It had a negative effect on her.

Kamala Das was married at the early age of fifteen to Mr. Madhava Das, an Executive Director of the Reserve Bank of India, Bombay. Her married life was unhappy. He was experienced in sex with his maidservants. It compelled her to enter into extra-marital relationship in search of true love. But it was unsuccessful and fruitless. The result was that she became frustrated. It stimulated her to write her own story and coloured her poetry. It was filled with different shades of her life.

Kamala Das lived in many metropolitan cities such as Bombay, Calcutta and Delhi, and written about them. She has contributed to Malayalam literature and Indian English literature.

She was awarded prestigious awards like P.E.N. prize in 1964, Kerala Sahitya Akademi Award for her insightful Malayalam short stories in 1969, the Chaman Lal Award for Journalism in 1971 and Asian World prize for Literature in 1985. She was awarded an Honorary Doctorate by the World Academy of Arts and Culture, Taiwan, 1984 and the Indira Priyadarshani Vrikshamitra Award in 1988. She published a full length autobiography *My Story* in 1976 which was first serialized in *The Current Weekly* of Bombay from January to December, 1974.

According to Kamala Das any language doesn't any matter. She also said that caste, religion, language and geography to which the writer belongs is not important. While replying to P. Lal she says:

> I do not like to classify writers as Indians, English or Indo-Anglians. The language one employs is not important. What is important is the thought contained by the words.[1]

Kamala Das's writing is considered as autobiographical and confessional. Her work is not to be separated from the moments of her life. Whatever she felt and experienced, is put before the world. It is her sincere attempt to describe everything that happened with her.

Her poetry is an honest appeal. It is her revolt against the social norms and her assertion of right to exist as an individual with a distinctive identity.

She designed her humiliated and neglected personality through the media of writing. Her writing is the weapon to struggle with society. She brings the vivid pictures and focuses on her own self as a woman. She is rebellious in nature which is highlighted in her poetry. She has a tremendous courage to demand all the feminine needs.

Kamala Das is certainly the most considerable Indian woman poet writing in English today. She has created a permanent place for herself in the contemporary Indo-English poetry through her bold writing. Poets like A. K. Ramanujan, R. Parthasarathy, Arun Kolatkar, K. N. Daruwalla, Jayanta Mahapatra, Shiv K. Kumar, Nissim Ezekiel have written about the subject of childhood, alienation, love, sex, sensuality, as well as on political, social, mythical issues. But among them she has her own range, popularity and feminine sensitivity. The thematic concern may be the same in their writing but Kamala Das's autobiographical and confessional touch in her writing makes her different. Her writing is based on the realistic approach to her own life. It is her honest description about her own life dealing with her lesbian relationships, homosexuality, extramarital relations, and her husband's brutality and his indifferent nature.

### Initial Hetrosexual Attractions

Kamala Das had a sensuous personality from her childhood. In her autobiography, *My Story*, she writes explicitly about her sensuous experiences. When she was a student of the elementary school, she fell in love with Govinda Kurup, a student of eighth standard. While speaking about him she says:

> He was handsome and had dimple on his right cheek which appeared only when he smiled. I could hardly take my eyes off his face. I was so infatuated with his charm.[2]

She never had any clear idea of love but had physical attraction towards the male friends. She told her grandmother about her attraction towards Govinda and her ambition of marriage to him. She was not able to control her feelings of attachment towards the opposite sex. She never kept aside any secrets of her life regarding her love affairs and her physical attraction.

A Syrian Christian spinster was one of her tutors who was a short and aggressive lady. One day when she was at Kamala Das's home to take her tuition, she stood at the window watching from behind that curtain and she suddenly felt restless. The reason behind it is that she had a sight of that man who had ruined her life and that of many other girls. Kamala Das looked at him and felt him attractive. She told her tutor that "I like his looks".[3] Her lady tutor warned her that the person had ruined the lives of several girls. Even after the knowledge about his wicked personality Kamala Das thought:

> I ought to meet him when I grew up, and perhaps become his mistress.[4]

This incident clearly indicates the irresistible temptation that sex was for her throughout her youth. Further she describes about her another male attraction at the age of thirteen when she went to Malabar for the summer vacation. She fell in love with a student leader who had been jailed for his revolutionary activities. He was interested in politics. He never had any attention towards Kamala Das. But she was interested in him. Her grand-aunt tried to keep her away from these affairs. As she describes:

> She must have deduced from my behaviour that I had become infatuated with his charm. I tried to spend as much time as I could get in his company, but he did not once touch my hand or show any particular fondness to me.[5]

It was the nature of Kamala Das that she could not control her craze for the opposite sex. At the early age of her life she was interested in physical satisfaction before knowing the meaning of love. In her hunger for physical attraction / satisfaction she had forgotten the age limits. At the age of fourteen she fell in love with the art tutor, and never thought about the age difference and the relationship between the teacher and the student.

The art tutor came to teach her every Wednesday. She was crazy about him. She watched his face with intense feelings of physical attraction. Every Wednesday she had a good make-up and was busy to make herself attractive. Her parents noticed the changes in her personality and the tuition was discontinued. She had never forgotten the last rainy day of her life when she went to the art tutor's home to express her emotions to him. She was totally drenched due to the sudden rain. He raised his eyes and invited her in. He said:

> 'You are wet, you must change your clothes,' he mumbled. He pulled my tunic over my head and wrung the water out through

> the window. His fingers were warm on my skin. Then with a handtowel he dried my hair and put the tunic on my body again. And without another word he took me by taxi to my house and shook my hand at the gate.
>
> . . . that was the last time I saw him. But off and on I remembered the tenderness with which he pulled aside my dress and dried my body.[6]

However, she continued to crave for the physical satisfaction through encounters like this:

> Why did he not kiss me? Why didn't he make love to me? I asked my friend in school why my first adult meeting with him gave me only disappointment.[7]

## Her Initial Lesbian Attractions

Her immature physic and psyche was continuously searching for physical satisfaction. She also had some of the experiences of lesbian relationships when she was a teenage girl of twelve years. She was living in a hostel where she had friendship with Sharada Menon, Raji, Meenakshi and Annie. Sharada Menon was the prettiest among them. One of the lesbian admirers from Goa fell in love with her and kept watching the beauty of Sharada Menon. But Sharada Menon was not interested in all these things. She lost her temper and shouted at her. One day Kamala Das observed the behaviour of that admirer. She writes:

> The lesbian admirer came into our room once when Sharada was away taking a bath and kissed her pillowcase and her undies hanging out to dry in the dressing room. I lay on my bed watching this performance but she was half-crazed with love, and hardly noticed me.[8]

Kamala Das took an interest in these things and also had a habit of reading the love letters of other girls and their love stories. She had always accompanied Annie who had a boyfriend. She had enjoyed the gossips with Annie. Once Sharada Menon warned her to keep her away from these gossips. But Kamala Das's sensitive mind was not ready for it. It was her nature that she was easily attracted towards these things.

Once Annie showed Kamala Das the letters of her lover who wrote about her attractive figure and desired to touch her breasts. Kamala Das was shocked when she read it. Annie too became angry with him and shouted:

> Didn't I tell you he was a worthless lecher? He does not love me. He only wants my body.[9]

and then next morning she showed Kamala Das a bruise on her upper lip and whispered:

> ... he climbed over the wall and came to my bed last night when all of you were asleep.[10]

But during the third term Annie was expelled from the boarding school. Later on, Sharada Iyer told Kamala Das that all the letters were written by Annie herself. It was the nature of Annie that she liked to live in a world of fantasy. It proves that all the hidden desires of the girl are to be fulfilled through imagination. It underlines the fact that girls can't openly express their sexual needs and have to suppress them. They are caught in a dual psychology, the desire of enjoy the sex and hide them smoothly from the world.

Once Kamala Das got a love letter from her schoolmate Devaki. She had the intention of reading that letter but her grandmother found the letter in her bag, read it and became upset. She was angry with Kamala Das. But there was no change in her personality. Again she fell in love with her Austrian teacher. As she describes:

> Her voice was strange, fractured in the middle and I thought it beautiful. It was easy for me to fall in love with her, for I had at that time a need to squander, but there were no takers. I wrote a poem addressed to my teacher in which I likened her to a rose.[11]

She had an interest to discuss physical secrets with the elders. Mr. and Mrs. Kunhappa were one of the couples who always visited her house when she was in Calcutta. One day Mrs. Kunhappa visited her and had a very frank discussion with Kamala Das. Kamala Das writes:

> She was frank with me and to my frank questions she gave frank answers although at that time I did not even believe all that I heard. I could not for a moment believe that all the dignified couples coming to my house to discuss politics and literature with my parents, could in the dark perform sexual acrobatics to get what my dear friend called the great orgasm. She made me laugh in disbelief. Was every married adult a clown in bed, a circusperformer?[12]

Once Kamala Das had enjoyed a lesbian attraction towards a young girl who lived in the college hostel. Kamala Das's mother had professor friends of that college. A family friend warned Kamala Das against accompanying that hostel girl who was different from others. Kamala Das wished to meet her but she did not wish to displease her mother's friends.

One day her mother went to Malabar. After some days Kamala Das's father decided to send her home for vacation with a batch of professor friends and students. She describes the sensuous lesbian encounter which she had enjoyed with that college girl.

> She looked around first to see if any one was awake. Then she lay near me holding my body close to hers. Her fingers traced

> the outlines of my mouth with a gentleness that I had never dreamt of finding. She kissed my lips then, and whispered, you are so sweet, so very sweet, I have never met anyone so sweet, my darling, my little darling.[13]

In the same journey this college batch and the professors visited Major Menon's house, who was the family friend of Kamala Das's parents. Again the poet and her girlfriend enjoyed a bath together. She said, "Both of us felt rather giddy with joy like honeymooners."[14] The affair left a deep impression on her mind. As a result even after her unwilling engagement she phoned the same girl, invited her home and wished to give her company.

The description throws light on the intense feelings of love and sex that she had. In her discussion with her relative Mr. Das before her marriage, she mentions that Oscar Wilde was her favourite writer. When she speaks about him she says:

> My favourite author at that time was Oscar Wilde and my favourite poem the 'Ballad of Reading Goal.' He talked about homosexuality with frankness.[15]

Regarding her interest in Oscar Wilde as well as the lesbian and homosexual relations, Mr. Das says: "Many of us pass through that stage."

Kamala Das was afraid that her grandmother might hear her frank discussion which was not suitable for a girl of the Nair family, where the women of Nair family never mentioned the word 'sex'. On the contrary, Kamala Das was very opposed to that situation. After a frank discussion with Mr. Das as they walked to the hedge, she had a shocking experience.

> At the hedge, beside the Damson tree, he embraced me, and puzzled by his conduct I ran back to my house.[16]

Later on her marriage was fixed with Mr. Das. Before he went to Calcutta he pushed her into a dark corner and tried to crush her body. It was a sudden shock for her which she never imagined about her future husband. While telling the truth about her husband's nature, she had also accepted another truth—that she could not control her lustful nature even after the engagement and marriage.

One of her family friends arrived in Malabar with her daughter and an 18 year-old son with whom Kamala Das enjoyed same sensuous moments. She liked to give him a company.

> I felt beautiful when he was with me, arranging my limbs shyly with a blush pinking his cheeks. He was stocky and fair-skinned.[17]

He was unhappy when he heard that she was going to marry in the month of February. She would like to give him company but she was not ready to marry him because he had no job. He came to attend her marriage, expressed his feelings through his eyes and went out.

To confess all personal matters is not easy for a girl or a woman but Kamala Das confesses it very frankly before us. A writer needs courage to say her life story. As a woman she takes more risks to sketch her premarital life and confesses it before a conventional Indian society. But she did it sincerely and uncovered all the pages of her life in *My Story*.

## Works Cited

1. Lal, P. *Modern Indian Poetry in English* (ed.) P. Lal, Writers Workshop Selection, Calcutta: 1969, p. 102.
2. Das, Kamala. *My Story,* New Delhi: Sterling Publishers, 1977, p. 21.
3. Ibid., p. 40.

4. Ibid., p. 61.
5. Ibid., p. 65.
6. Ibid., p. 75.
7. Ibid., p. 74.
8. Ibid., p. 47.
9. Ibid., p. 46.
10. Ibid., p. 84.
11. Ibid., p. 72.
12. Ibid., p. 82.
13. Ibid., p. 83.
14. Ibid., pp. 88-89.
15. Ibid., p. 84.
16. Ibid., p.84.
17. Ibid., p. 77.

# 11

# Truth in Autobiography: Rousseau's *The Confessions* and *My Experiments with Truth*

Rajnish Mishra

Pontius Pilate asked Jesus a question when he claimed to be a witness to truth: "Quod est veritas?" (John 18:38). His remark has been interpreted in various ways through the ages, but the fundamental question remains: "What is truth?" It is also from where the present paper originates. Unless one addresses to this question satisfactorily, it'd not be possible to graduate to our next question: Do biographies and autobiographies reveal the truth? Therefore, the present paper will deal with the problem in hand in two parts: one dealing with the nature of truth and the other with truth in the historically located narratives of human beings called auto/biographies. To avoid further complications, an auto/biography will be accepted as one based on the intention and explicit mention of the fact that the narrator/writer/protagonist happens to be a real life, historically placeable, sentient entity.

Defining any abstract quality has always been very easy. Only proving the definition right before the barrage of exceptions complicates the matter. Provisionally, just as a point of departure, truth may be defined as "that which is accepted by everyone to be correct or right". It's simple enough; deceptively so. The solar system (ironically, or was it called the earth system then?)

was accepted to be geocentric before Copernicus (just to take a name) took the risk of proving otherwise. Was it true before he proved it otherwise and false afterwards? Does truth have a solid foundation, or it stands on a slippery base. Is it eternal, objective and "real", or just a social construct that is relative, temporary and subjective? Our knowledge of truth is a part of the total body of knowledge that we possess which is our database on whose basis we judge whether what we know is true or not, following an abstract, semi-conscious and nearly automatic process at the back of our mind. The process is called semi-conscious because its steps are so fast at times that it appears to go on without any conscious effort. Yet, it's not totally unconscious, as our dreams prove. Until the dream ends, one's unsuspecting self remains in a world constructed by the conscious mind on the input affected by the unconscious part.

One believes it to be true and realizes that it was not so on reflection after returning to a conscious state, provided one remembers the dream's "untrue" part and also provided there is such a difference. If the dream state is taken as an analogy, sans the benevolent God that Descartes posited, one's existence with the truths of sleeping and waking worlds is at an equal ease and effortlessness. Moreover, there is no way of knowing one state, or one truth, from the other as long as one remains in the unknowing or dream state. Thus, ignorance does turn out to be bliss. Therefore, an ignoramus's truth will not be the same as that of someone who knows comparatively more.

Socrates had spoken so eloquently in his apology about how by his knowing of his ignorance he knew more than others: "for he knows nothing, and thinks that he knows; I neither know nor think that I know" (Plato). Yet, he had to drink hemlock. Despite Socrates's demonstrating very clearly how he was falsely accused, at least for the time being, truth was shown as falsehood, and most people believed the opposite to be true. Both Jesus and Socrates died martyrs in the name of truth; but what is truth?

Relativism will not accept any claims truth makes at absoluteness. Linguistic determinism will prove that truth is a construct, and not something existing objectively. Pragmatism will simply scoff at such a wasteful hair-splitting expenditure of time. Yet, the one working definition without which no progress can be made here is that of truth. A brave attempt is all that is required to reach truth. In "What is Enlightenment", Kant asserts:

> Enlightenment is man's emergence from his self-imposed nonage. Nonage is the inability to use one's own understanding without another's guidance. This nonage is self-imposed if its cause lies not in lack of understanding but in indecision and lack of courage to use one's own mind without another's guidance. Dare to know! (*Sapere aude.*) "Have the courage to use your own understanding," is therefore the motto of the enlightenment.

Enlightened to the core, and awaken from his dogmatic slumber, Kant did dare to use his "own understanding without another's guidance" and to know. More than that, he also dared to convey the truth about what he knew through his *Critiques* and his *Prolegomena.* So, was truth found or defined finally, conclusively and unquestionably? Not at all, if the history of philosophy is to be believed. Plato, an idealist, had proven through his various myths that there was something like Truth. He had claimed that the philosopher (as in a lover of wisdom and truth) had an access to that Truth through his use of reason and the poet through inspiration. He remained uncharacteristically subtle and elusive when it came to defining and describing what that final point of convergence was. So did the footnotes to him, i.e. his successors in the Western philosophical tradition. It was like: you know it when and if you reach there; it can't be taught, shown or explained. The moment one attempts to grasp truth, one is at the farthest remove from it, says the Zen philosophy. *Sansara* is all *maya*, says the Indian classical thought. So there remains no question of fixing the point called truth in the world of mundane elements and events, unless, of course it is absolutely essential.

"The truthfulness or not of autobiography is essentially a matter that must be left to biographers and philosophers. The plausibility of an autobiography however must find its authentication by the degree to which it can correspond to some approximation of its context" (Drabble 53). As we have chosen to focus on the truthfulness, and not just plausibility, of the text this paper will make one more attempt at fixing the working boundaries of truth, but only in one specific instance. It is the truth in an account of the events of a character's life—fictional or real—written by the person himself or by someone else, in what we are interested. This definitely makes the task less complicated by narrowing down the number of possible exceptions and objections.

To play a game, one must compile a set of rules that all players abide by. If any attempt is to be made to test the *veritas* quotient (let's call it VQ) of a biography or autobiography – literary or otherwise, one must first define the scale. The beginning must be the conventional zero, i.e. totally false and proven to be so; and the end of the scale may be any convenient number greater than zero that denotes total truthfulness. The falseness or truthfulness of the text under question has to be assayed against some objective and external indicator. That indicator happens to be history in case of texts that claim to be "real" life events, psychology helps partially in testing the validity and truthfulness of the mind processes revealed after introspection, and philosophy in the form of theory if the text claims to be fictional and literary, or at least "factional".

History, psychology (or philosophy of mind) and philosophy intersect to form the kind of litmus for a text whose VQ must be tested in order to reach any satisfactory conclusion regarding the trustworthiness of the narrative. Even this approach, scientific it may sound, is not fool-proof. There are factors that any objective test cannot test, e.g. facts can be tested against externally existing and recorded history, the emotions, intentions and interpretations presented by the auto/biographers can never be proven correct or otherwise with one hundred percent certainty. Out goes VQ then. Concreteness is the element missing in this predominantly abstract discussion. Examples will be used in the lines that follow to make the task easier.

All fiction is autobiographical and hard determinism will claim the same for all writing. The Brontë sisters, Dickens, Tolstoy, George Eliot, D.H. Lawrence, Maugham, Joyce, Fitzgerald, Proust, Hemingway, Miller, Ellison, Rand, Kerouac, and the list is interminable, all presented autobiographical elements in their fiction. Yet there is a consensus of sorts on the genre wise compartmentalization of texts and auto/biography is a commonly accepted and recognizable genre in English at least since Wordsworth's *The Prelude*. St. Augustine's and Rousseau's famous autobiographies, both called *The Confessions*, are classics and pioneering attempts made before the word was ever used. Saint Augustine starts his autobiography with:

> In *God*'s searching presence, Augustine undertakes to plumb the depths of his memory to trace the mysterious pilgrimage of grace which his life has been—and to praise *God* for his constant and omnipotent grace. In a mood of sustained prayer, he recalls what he can ... [and] concludes with a paean of grateful praise to *God* [emphasis mine] (13).

The one central trait of his autobiography is its, and his, holding and propagating an intense kind of theocentricity that finds all things mundane and material totally inconsequential. Rousseau's *The Confessions* is more egocentric than theocentric. Keeping with the tradition, Rousseau makes his intention clear in the very beginning of his autobiography:

> *I* mean to present my fellow-mortals with a man in all the integrity of nature; and this man shall be *myself. I* know my heart, and have studied mankind; *I* am not made like any one *I* have been acquainted with, perhaps like no one in existence; if not better, *I* at least claim originality... *I* may have supposed that certain, which *I* only knew to be probable, but have never asserted as truth, a conscious falsehood [emphasis mine] (7).

The various times he refers to himself in the very first paragraph will act as a fair indicator of the real subject of his work. Closer home, Mahatma Gandhi's autobiography is an example that can be picked by virtue of its, and his, being most widely known. Moreover, it also conforms to the commonly accepted definition of autobiography as "the author.... declares that he is the person he says he is and that the author and the protagonist are the same" (Anderson 3). Gandhiji does not declare his intentions as he begins; instead, he jumps straight into introducing his parents and background. Intentions come later, that too, as side observations. If the truth of writing is tested against that of the world and judgement is passed to declare the faithfulness of the text to truth, Ganhiji intended to present only truth and made a valiant and thorough effort too. He knew that being truthful would not be easy. In the chapter on his child marriage he writes: "Much as I wish that I had not to write this chapter, I know that I shall have to swallow many such bitter draughts in the course of this narrative. And I cannot do otherwise, if I claim to be a worshipper of Truth" (5). The intention is clear in both the cases and they intend to report the events of their lives truthfully. They assume their truth to be our truth too, as they see truth as something objective, absolute and external to the subject.

The way they recount their past and the people they came in contact with presents two different modes of autobiographical writing. Rousseau reports how his father used to read the books of his mother's collection at night, with him alongside. He presents that fact as strong force writing on the *tabula rasa* of his mind. While mentioning his parents Rousseau writes that since their very childhood there was a: "natural sympathy of soul [that] confined those sentiments of predilection which habit at first produced; born with minds susceptible of the most exquisite sensibility and tenderness" (8). Abstract ideas abound in the description that are unverifiable too. In contrast to Rousseau, Mahatma Gandhi writes of his father as: "To a certain extent he might have been given to carnal pleasures. For he married for the fourth time when he was over forty. But he was incorruptible and had earned a name for strict impartiality in his family as well as outside" (3). The qualities mentioned in the account are either objectively verifiable or logically reached at. The similar kind of treatment of persons and events may be seen in their respective autobiographies.

Rousseau's idea of truth was given out as generalizations interspersed with facts in the text. Moreover, unlike Wordsworth, his egotism was not sublime. It bordered on self-aggrandizement at times: "We suffer before we think; it is the common lot of humanity. I experienced more than my proportion of it" (7). His assumptions and his hidden sense of importance come to the fore very frequently in his autobiography. Gandhiji, on the other hand, presents another kind of introspection. He keeps as close to the externally observable fact as possible and gives an analysis of emotions, feelings and other abstractions generally when they are his own but tries to keep the focus away from himself as a person. Self-effacement is what he attempted, and nearly succeeded too. He sometimes does stray from the path of objectivity but much less than Rousseau. The following lines do have a hint of self-importance, but unlike Rousseau's, it is very dry and ungloating in nature: "Since then I have twice been to Kashi Vishvanath, but that has been after I had already been afflicted with the title of *Mahatma* ... People eager to have my *darshan* would not permit me to have a *darshan* of the temple. The woes of *Mahatmas* are known to *Mahatmas* alone" (128). All is not rotten with Rousseau's introspection and self-presentation. His critical glimpses of his nature succeed to shed light on human nature in general, especially of his age, with emphasis on purity of sensations and sentiments:

> An infinity of sensations were familiar to me, without possessing any precise idea of the objects to which they related—I had conceived nothing—I had felt the whole. This confused succession of emotions did not retard the future efforts of my reason, though they added an extravagant, romantic notion of human life, which experience and reflection have never been able to eradicate (7-8).

His introspection and his special facility in presenting his psyche as on a postmortem table after the autopsy, make the text full of deep insights in the individual's, and by corollary, general psychology. He does generalize and it happens to be one of his weaknesses, yet, it makes him and his story interesting for a modern reader. It'd have definitely had more attraction for his contemporaries. Although absolute statements are his weakness he uses them very artfully, as in his comment regarding his relation with his cousin Bernard when he claims that "a similar example among children can hardly be produced" (15). The

Mahatma's generalizations are not personal in nature. His purpose is different as he affirms: "I must reduce myself to zero. So long as a man does not of his own free will put himself last among his fellow creatures, there is no salvation for him. Ahimsa is the farthest limit of humility" (Gandhi 269). There's a clear resonance of Christianity, especially the New Testament, and even in that Jesus's Sermon on the Mount on his ideas. Nietzsche wouldn't be very pleased with Gandhiji's attempt at strengthening of the ideal of meekness, sacrifice and selfless service. Yet, that is what he does throughout the autobiography. A devout worshipper of Truth that he saw as God, Gandhiji tried to reach it through his honest introspection. Whatever he found out was reported without any kind of polishing. Self-purification was his aim and he attempted to purify others who came in contact with his ideas too—personally or through printed words. That's why his sole attempt was to present unadulterated truth because nothing else would solve his purpose. It is his content that lends his plain and totally utilitarian style an aura of its own. Rousseau, on the other hand, sees pride as a positive and uplifting trait: "but if this pride is not virtue itself, its effects are so similar that we are pardonable indeceiving ourselves" (325). The Gandhian humility must neither be expected nor met with here. Yet truth can be present in various forms in various places. So it's in *The Confessions* too. The reader has to sift through a lot of chaff before reaching the grain of truth. Patience and empathy, always the virtues for a communicator, are demanded especially of the reader looking for an objectively verifiable truth.

History, psychology and philosophy come to the rescue of the unsure reader who is trying to reach truth in the two autobiographies. First of all, as far as history is concerned, the chronological data is definitely correct in both the texts, yet *The Confessions* depends less on and uses smaller proportions of such information because it is generally an account of the processes of the author's mind and not just plain recounting of events. Gandhiji, on the other hand, kept scrupulously close to the historically verifiable facts. Moreover, he kept the level of revelation of his subjective self relatively low. Therefore, more historical truth is to be found in his autobiography in comparison to that of Rousseau. The proportion of the analyses of mind processes is more in Rousseau's than in the other text. Thus the psychologically verifiable truth (and ironically, for the same reason, falseness) is present more in Rousseau's work. The most difficult part of ascertaining the truth claim is when one reaches philosophy. Both the texts have rich philosophical content, as both are the autobiographies of deep and original thinkers who affected the minds of millions and even determined the flow of history of their times. Their thoughts continue to affect the posterity. Content-wise, Rouseau's work focuses more on presenting his personal views and beliefs, whereas, the other focuses more on facts. Yet, there are parts that intensely and pithily present the Mahatma's philosophy so effectively that its comparative absence is made over. As far as the plausibility is concerned, both the texts pass the test, as the reader believes the writer-protagonist but then, so do many fictional autobiographies.

As far as the truth factor is concerned, it's difficult to pass any final judgement. Both the autobiographies have their share of historical, psychological and philosophical truths. Thus both are true. At the same time, in some respects, both are false or inadequate too. The same may be applied as a generalization on the whole auto/biographical genre.

## Works Cited

Anderson, Linda. *Autobiography*. Routledge: New York, 2001. Print.

Augustine, Saint. *Confessions and Enchiridion*. Tr. Albert C. Outler. ccel.org. N.d. Web. 22 January 2012.

Gandhi, M. K. *An Autobiography or The Story of my Experiments with Truth*. Tr. Mahadev Desai. Ebookee. N.d. PDF. Web. 26 December 2011.

Kant, Immanuel. "What is Enlightenment?". N.d. Html. Web. 22 January 2012.

Plato. *Apology*. Archive.org. N.d. TXT. Web. 26 December 2011.

Rousseau, Jean-Jacques. *The Confessions*. Tr. Edmund Wilson. Vol. 1. Knopf: New York, 1923. Print.

*The Oxford Companion to English Literature*. Ed. Margaret Drabble. 6th Edition. OUP: Oxford, 2000. Print.

## 12

# Note of Confession in Gandhi's *The Story of My Experiments with Truth*

G.B. Shelkikar

M.K. Gandhi was a humanist and a man of religion more than a nationalist and patriot. By nature he was a free and frank personality. He never tried to hide any private or public information from his followers. Actually, he worked for the liberation of the Indians from the British rule but his heart was not cruel for the Britishers. He hoped that the Indian might one day become lingua franca of the country, but he continued to write and speak in English, and was fully sensible of the advantage of a knowledge of that great world language.

As a writer of Autobiography M.K. Gandhi stands in the front rank. "*The Story of My Experiments With Truth*". says Mohinder Singh, "is not an ordinary experiment in-self portrayal, but the product of a life wholly dedicated to truth as understood in its widest connotation and an outstanding creation standing apart in its lonely grandeur on the Indian autobiographical scene".[1] The revelation of truth has been Mahatma Gandhi's main aim in writing his autobiography. The narration of his experiences and experiments with truth aims at the moral and spiritual enrichment of the readers of his autobiography.

Indeed, it is a beacon to poor mortals, drifting like a rudderless boat on the pathless sea of life. Gandhiji himself writes explaining the purpose of writing his autobiography. He says, "But it is not my purpose to attempt a real autobiography. I simply want to tell the story of my numerous experiments, it is true that the story will take the shape of an autobiography. But I shall not mind, if every page of it speaks only of my experiments. I believe or at any rate flatter myself with the belief, that a connected account of all these experiments will not be without benefit to the reader." (*Autobiography*, 9)

According to *Everyman's Encyclopaedia* the term 'confession' in the ancient time was quite different means it was strict, A confessor was required punishment. "The main difference between the ancient and the modern confession is that formerly great sins were to be if not verbally confessed in public yet publicly atoned for whereas no much emphasis is aid on the seal of secrecy".[2] The paper tries to highlights over the Gandhiji's revelation of confession in his earlier life.

Mahatma Gandhi's autobiography *The Story of My Experiments with Truth* occupies an important place in Indo Anglian literature and ranks very high with the greatest autobiographies of the world : Rousseau's *Confessions* (1781-88), Cardinal Newman's *Apologio Pro Sua Vita* (1964), Helen Keller's *The Story of My Life* (1903). Anna Robeson Burr's *The Autobiography* (1909), E. Stuart Bate's *Inside Out* (1936), Anton T. Boisen's *The Exploration of the Inner World* (1936), and De Quincey's *Confessions of An English Opium Eater* (1921). "Autobiography is literature of personal revelation".[3] The main interest of an autobiography resides in a conscious or unconscious self-portrayal by the author. It may be called a connected narrative of the author's life. In an autobiography great stress is laid on introspection, or on the significance of the author's life against a wider background. Autobiography, defines, *Encyclopedia Britannica*, "is the biography of a person written by himself. Its motivations are various among others self scrutiny for self-edification, self justification, as Cardinal Newman's beautifully writeen *Apologia Pro Sua Vita*, a nostalgic desire to linger over enchanting memories, as Selma Lagerfof's *Marbacka*, belief that one's experiences may be helpful to others, as Helen Keller's *The Story of My Life*, an earnest attempt to orient self amid a world of confusion, as the *Education* of Henry Adams, the urge for artistic expression, or the pure commercial desire to capitalize on fame or position".[4] Thus, the aim of autobiography has been to give truth about oneself. It may be the truth about ones moral, spiritual and religious beliefs, or the truth of worldly or material achievements, or the truth of one's profession. It may also reveal one's outlook. An autobiography contains comments on crucial incidents and personages one comes across. "Gandhi was no writer, properly so called, nor was he at any time particularly interested in the art of writing, but he had to write or talk a great deal, even as we have to walk or eat or breathe".[5]

Mahatma Gandhi's famous autobiography *The Story of My Experiments with Truth* unfolds the various stage of the development of his personality. In it we see how a shy Kathiawar boy evolved into one of the greatest men of modern times. His various roles as a householder, as a social and political leader, as a spiritualist and confessor emerge before us after reading his autobiography.

Mahatma Gandhi, the Titan of the modern age, was of "sluggish" intellect and "raw" memory in his childhood. He was a mediocre student. From his early childhood, he loved truth and hated falsehood. He writes: "I do not remember having ever told a lie, during this short period, either to my teachers or to my school mates" (*Autobiography* 3). He saw the play *Harishchandra*, which strengthened his love for truth. Shravana Pitribhakti Natak strengthened his love and obedience for his parents. Both Harishchandra and Shravana became his ideals. His father's charitability and his mother's "saintliness" and "deeply religious" nature left an indelible impression on him. He imbibed the qualities of truth and saintliness impression on him. The qualities of truth and saintliness he imbibed in childhood were the foundation of his future when he became Mahatma Gandhi from M.K. Gandhi.

His love of truth made him confess his mistakes frankly. He stole money from the servant's pocket in order to purchase cigarettes. At the age of fifteen he stole a bit of gold out of his "meat-eating" friend's armlet. He made a written confession to his father who wept at this. But "those pearl-drops of love cleansed my heart, and washed my sin away". This was for Gandhiji "an object-lesson in ahimsa". "Then I could read in it nothing more than a father's love, but today I know that it was pure ahimsa." His father was wonderfully peaceful and this was due to his clean confession. A clean confession is the purest type of repentance. Thus love of truth, ahimsa, confession of mistakes and repentance were the cardinal characteristics of Mahatma Gandhi since his boyhood. As time went on, he made new experiments in the sphere of truth and ahimsa and ultimately became the apostle of truth, ahimsa and peace in a war-battered world.

A relative and Gandhi became fond of smoking not because they found any good in smoking but they were enamoured of the smell of cigarette. They wanted only to taste the smoke of it. Because his uncle had that habit, Gandhi always used to observe him while smoking. At that time they had no money. So they began to steal the sturbs of cigarettes thrown by his uncle. So at that time he started stealing coppers. He says in chapter I, 'Stealing and Atonement', "so we began to steal coppers from the servants' pocket money in order to purchase Indian cigarette. But the question was where to keep them. We could not of course smoke in the presence of elders. We managed some how for a few weeks on these stolen coppers. In the meantime we heard that the stalks of a certain plant were porous and could be smoked like cigarettes." (*Autobiography* 45)

He was endowed with a religious bent of mind. To him religion meant 'self-realization or knowledge of self'. The *Ramayana* and the *Bhagavad Gita* were the main fountains of his inspiration. In his boyhood days he acquired faith in morality. He writes: "But one thing took deep root in me the conviction that morality is the basis of thing, and that truth is the substance of all morality. Truth became my sole object. It began to grow in magnitude every day, and my definition of it also has been ever widening." (*Autobiography* 25)

As a husband Mahatma Gandhi was 'faithful but lustful'. He was very anxious to teach his wife, Kasturba, but "lustful love" left him no time. He was a severe husband but his seventies were all based on love. "I wanted to make my wife an ideal wife. My ambition was to make her live a pure life, learn what I learnt, and identify her life and thought with mine" (*Autobiography* 8). He suffered lifelong regret and shame because he found himself lustfully approaching his pregnant wife at a time when he should have been holding his dying father in his arms, he writes in the chapter, "My Father's Death and My Double Shame". He scrupulously managed to retain the faithfulness of a husband and, therefore, spurned all opportunities of sexual contact with other women.

With perfect candidness Gandhiji describes how he dissembled to be a bachelor in England. Indian students in England dissembled to be bachelors. Gandhiji too caught the contagion. He writes. "I did not hesitate to pass myself off as a bachelor though I was married and the father of a son. But I was none the happier for being a dissembler" (*Autobiography* 4). This was his great mistake and confession too.

His wife, Kasturbai, adjusted with the saintly ideals and dictatorial manners of her husband. But once they fell out because to clean the posts used by a Panchama was too much for her. Recalling this incident Gandhiji writes. "I was a cruelly kind husband. I regarded myself as her teacher, and so harassed her out of my blind love for her" (*Autobiography* 207). In 1906 Gandhiji's thought on brahamacharya which took definite shape and he began to practise it. The practice of brahmacharya brought peace and happiness to his domestic life : "... with the gradual disappearance in me of the carnal appetite, my domestic life became and is becoming more and more peaceful. Sweet and happy." (*Autobiography* 208)

Mahatma Gandhi loved his sons and was proud of his capacity of handling and educating them but his methods were more suited to adults. He was so busy that schooling had to be done during his morning walk to office with children. He could not impart the necessary literary education to them. He frankly admits his mistake: "My inability to give them enough attention and other unavoidable causes prevented me from providing them with the literary education I had desired, and all my sons have had complaints to make against me in this respect." (Autobiography 150)

Here Gandhi confesses one of his bigger mistakes. When he was married his father was suffering from a fistula, and was bed-ridden. His condition was very serious. Gandhi and his mother were regular attendants for his father's nursing. His father's health was getting worse every day. As a son he had to take care of his old bed-ridden father. Actually his father was given various kinds of treatments at that time. Gandhi used to massage his fathers legs but his mind was hovering about the bedroom, thinking about sexual intercourse with his wife during this difficult period which he admits very frankly in the chapter 'My father's Death and My Double Shame.'

"The shame to which I have referred in a foregoing chapter, was this shame of my carnal desire even at the critical hour of my father's death which demanded wakeful service. It was a blot I have never been able to efface or forget, and I have always thought that, although my parents knew no bounds and I would have given up anything for it, yet it was weighed and found unpardonably. Wanting because my mind was at the same moment in the grip of lust. I have therefore always regarded my self as a lustful, though a faithful husband. It took me long to get free from the shackles of lust, and I had to pass through many ordeals before I could overcome it" (*Autobiography* 16). Here he never lost any opportunity to give advice to the married and to those who were going to be married to take lessons from his own example.

Mahatma Gandhi emerges as a saintly figure who had no allurement for worldly possessions. Therefore his role as a householder has been underestimated. Indeed for a long period he worked as a successful householder. A few months after his arrival in London he hired expensive rooms, got new and fashionable clothes, took lessons in ballroom dancing, elocution, French language and violin playing. But soon he realized that the slavish imitation of English style of living was doing him no good.

He says, "That period of infatuation was not unrelieved by a certain amount of self introspection on my part" (*Autobiography* 38). He took to simple living. Plain living saved him plenty of time and he passed the examination. After returning to India once again the European style of living fascinated him and he completed the Europeanization by adding the European dress. Soon the external glitterings of life disillusioned him. In Durban he functioned as a successful lawyer earning large sums. He lived in a fashionable bungalow and his family was presentably attired. But under the influence of Ruskin and Tolstoy he comprehended the futility and wastefulness of a life of pomp and show. His own inner promptings also inspired him to adopt simplicity in life and thereafter a drastic change came in his life.

In his autobiography Gandhi emerges as a Mahatma who is the incarnation of purity, unselfishness, detachment, universal love, truth and ahimsa. He is an emancipated soul who sacrifices himself for the betterment of humanity. To him politics devoid of religion is immoral. Romain Rolland calls him a religious man: "To understand Gandhi's activity, it should be realized that his doctrine is like a huge edifice composed of two different floors or grades. Below is the solid groundwork, the basic foundation of religion. On this vast and unshakable foundation is based the political and social campaign in other words, Gandhi is religious by nature, and his doctrine is essentially religious. He is a political leader by necessity, because other leaders disappear, and the force of circumstances obliges him to pilot the ship through storm and give practical political expression to his doctrine."[6] He hated violence in politics. Gandhiji writes in his autobiography, "The see the universal and all-pervading Spirit of Truth face to face one must be able the meanest of creation as oneself. And a man who aspires after that cannot afford to keep out of any field of life. That is why my devotion to Truth has drawn me into the field of politics; and I can say without the slightest humility, that those who say that religion has nothing to do with politics do not know what religion means". (*Autobiography* 383)

M.K. Gandhi attained infinite spiritual and moral power, and exercised and is still exercising immense influence on wavering humanity because there was a concord between his philosophy and his daily conduct. Gandhiji was imbued with the quintessence of the East and the west. He was dedicated to morality and spirituality but his devotion to social and political work was no less. He was "the rarest combination of an oriental sage and a modern man." Summing up Mahatma Gandhi's personality Dr. B. Pattabhi Sitaramayya says: "By Gandhi's teachings, the inebriate has become abstenious. Through is benediction the inebriate has become abstenious. Through his benediction the harlot has become a housewife. Under his direction the drone has become a labourer. His one act of renunciation has ennobled poverty, his one whisper has emancipated the slave. His one breath has transformed woman from goods and chattel into a sentient being and a responsible member of society. He is a cosmopolitan but is primarily a Hindu. He is a social reformer but is essentially a conservative. He is for rural resuscitation but is not a pilgrim back to primitive faith. He loves the village but does not hate the town. He battles with Britain but befriends the Britisher. He abhors all sin but never antagonizes the sinner."[7]

In this way Gandhiji put forth his experiences with confessional mode of writing before his readers. And the readers also have accepted very nobly the greatness of the great Mahatma.

## Works Cited

1. Mohinder Singh "Truth in Autobiography in Gandhi's" *Experiments with Truth*", *Gandhi Marg*, 1980, 739.

2. *Everyman's Encyclopaedia*: Carbine-Culdees, p.335.
3. Shipley Joseph T. *Dictionary of World Literary Terms*, Londan, George Allen and Unwin Ltd. 1955, p. 32.
4. *Encyclopedia Britanica.*
5. K. R. S. Iyengar & Prema Nandakumar, p.248.
6. Roman Rolland: *Mahatma Gandhi*, pp.17-18.
7. Dr. B.P. Sitaramayya: *Gandhi and Gandhism*, Allahabad Kitabistan 1943, p.29.

# 13

# Reflections on the *Confessions of Jean Jacques Rousseau*

J. David Livingston & Sophia Livingston

Jean Jacques Rousseau, a noted French philosopher and thinker, was an advocate of the Romantic ideology. His book *The Social Contract* is a wonderful testament of the rules and regulations that governed monarchy in France. The Louis kings were known for their despotism and tyranny. Their principles were governed by the "Divine Right" theory.

Jean-Jacques Rousseau was born on June 28, 1712 in Geneva, Switzerland. His mother died shortly after his birth. When he was 10 his father fled from Geneva to avoid imprisonment for a minor offence, leaving young Jean-Jacques to be raised by an aunt and uncle. Rousseau left Geneva at 16, wandering from place to place, finally moving to Paris in 1742. He earned his living during this period, working as everything from footman to assistant to an ambassador. His thoughtful insight can be found in almost every dash of modern philosophy today. Somewhat complicated and vague, his general philosophy tried to grasp an emotional and passionate side of man which he felt was left out of most previous philosophical thinking.

Rousseau begins his *The Confessions* by claiming that he is about to embark on an enterprise never before attempted: to present a self-portrait that is in every way true to nature and that hides nothing. He begins his tale by describing his family, including his mother's death at his birth. He cogitates on his earliest memories, which begin when he was five, a dawning of consciousness that he traces to his learning to read. He discusses his childhood in the years before his father left him and his own decision to run away to see the world at the age of sixteen. He often dwells for many pages on seemingly minor events that hold great importance for him. He talks about the persons who left an indelible impact on him. Mademoiselle Lambercier made a lasting impression on Rousseau though she was extremely strict and astute in morals and ethics.

> Just as Mlle Lambercier felt for us: the affection of a mother, so too she had a mother's authority, which she sometimes exerted to the point of inflicting common childhood punishments, on us, when we had deserved this. For a while, she restricted herself to threats of punishments which were quite new to me and which I found very frightening; but after the threat had been carried out, I discovered that it was less terrible in the event that it had been in anticipation, and what is more bizarre, that this punishment made me even founder for the woman who had administered it. Indeed, it took all the sincerity of my affection for her and all my natural meekness to prevent me from seeking to merit a repetition of the same treatment; for I had found in the pain inflicted, and even in the shame that accompanied it, an element of sensuality which left me with more desire than fear at the prospect of experiencing it again from the same hand. (*Confessions* 14)

Throughout *The Confessions*, Rousseau frequently discusses the more unsavoury or embarrassing experiences of his life, and he devotes much of the early section to these types of episodes. In one section, he describes urinating in a neighbour's cooking pot as a mischievous child. He also discusses the revelatory experience he had at age eleven of being beaten by an adored female nanny twice his age—and desiring to be beaten again, which he analyses as being his entry into the world of adult sexuality.

Rousseau continues to describe his life and eventually reaches adulthood. The narrative continues in a similar vein in the later sections, with Rousseau focusing less on places travelled and jobs held than on his personal trials, unrequited loves and sexual frustrations. He speaks at length of his significant relations with women, including his rather unremarkable long-time companion Thérése le Vasseur and the older matron Madame de Warens, at whose home he often stayed as a young man. In the last of the twelve books that make up the work, he speaks about his intellectual work, his writing, and his relations to contemporary philosophers. He concludes *The Confessions* in 1765, when he is fifty-three. At this point, all his major philosophical works have been published, and his fears of persecution are growing.

> As I write this, I feel my pulse beginning to race again; these moments would always be fresh in my mind, even if I lived for a thousand years. This first experience of violence and injustice has remained so deeply engraved in my heart that any idea that is at all associated with it brings back the emotions I felt at the time; and these feelings, originally excited on my own behalf, have acquired their own integrity. (*The Confessions* 19)

Although Rousseau states that *The Confessions* should not be read as an infallible version of dates and events and admits that most likely he often gets such factual data wrong when his memory fails him, dates and exact events are not the point of the work. He says that though he may mix up the dates of specific accomplishments, he will never get wrong his feelings about them, and his feelings—and what his feelings have led him to do—are the subject of his story. He does not engage in the comprehensive unburdening of his whole self, with all its frailties, prurient desires, and natural failings, as an act of pure humility and self-deprecation. Rather, he does it as a way of saying that, even with all his weaknesses, he is, as we all are, fundamentally a good and honest being. This principle is at the heart of his entire philosophy, and it connects *The Confessions* to the rest of his work. *The Confessions* is key to understanding Rousseau's work as a whole.

> Constant scoldings and beatings on the hand, continual secret and unsuitable reading on the other, all of this began to have a bad effect on my character and temper, and to make taciturn and unsociable, a real misanthrope. Every night, after supper, we read some part of a small collection of romances [i.e., adventure stories], which had been my mother's. My father's design was only to improve me in reading, and he thought these entertaining works were calculated to give me a fondness for it; but we soon found ourselves so interested in the adventures they contained, that we alternately read whole nights together and could not bear to give over until at the conclusion of a volume. Sometimes, in the morning, on hearing the swallows at our window, my father, quite ashamed of this weakness, would cry, "Come, come, let us go to bed; I am more a child than thou art. (*The Confessions* 39)

The influence of *The Confessions* reaches well beyond philosophy. As a work of literature, it launched the modern genre of autobiography and impacted narrative technique in the great novels that would appear in the following century. Rousseau's prominence on the effects of childhood experiences on adulthood, especially in relation to the development of sexuality, foreshadows the revolutionary psychological work of Sigmund Freud. *The Confessions* is also the work considered most accountable for Rousseau's recurrent certification as the father of the romantic movement, for the degree to which he emphasizes the importance of subjective, exclusive, and sensory experience of the world.

A few distinguished autobiographies existed in Europe before Rousseau published *The Confessions*, but his work in many ways symbolized an entirely new literary form. Although works such as St. Augustine's own *Confessions* (A.D. 397) had previously been widely read and celebrated, religious works of that kind differed greatly from Rousseau's own, since they sought to put across an inspiring story of religious genius. By contrast, Rousseau's *The Confessions* sought to bare the entire life of its author subject, detailing all his imperfections, virtues, individual neuroses, and formative childhood experiences as a means of explaining and justifying the views and personality of his adult self. Thus, a new system pertaining to autobiographical traits was forged through. This mode became quite popular and paved way for authors penning autobiographies in times to come. John T. Scott remarks in this context:

> How *The Confessions* manages to combine these two (history guided by either the imitative standard of moral utility or the philosophic standard of general principles of human nature) very different possibilities, how it manages to put the truth in an agreeable and useful form without distorting it, can be determined only in the course of the interpretation of the work. The somewhat different question of why Rousseau would wish to write a philosophic autobiography can be addressed prior to that interpretation. The possibility of an enterprise does not prove its desirability. What *The Confessions* adds to these works can be considered in the following ways. First, it gives fuller treatment to themes that are touched on in other works. Viewed in this light, *The Confessions* complements Rousseau's other works by filling in gaps in his philosophic system. Secondly, it directly addresses one question of crucial importance for Rousseau's system, or indeed any philosophic system. Viewed in this way, the Confessions can be said to be necessary for the justification of Rousseau's entire system. (Scott 491-492)

Any other autobiographer would have suppressed unflattering incidents, and Rousseau chides Michel de Montaigne, famous for his honest self-portrayal in his *Essays*, for having included nothing comparable. If Rousseau's facts are not always verifiable, his frankness is certainly genuine. He wrote out of a sense of his uniqueness, not of his greatness. Indeed, he believed in the uniqueness of all humans; it is simply that he knew his own story and his own self best. This conviction that the individual—good or bad—is worthy of description represents one of the author's major contributions to forward-looking social and political thought. His narrative skill and attractive informal style have been as much responsible as his frankness for his authority. Susan M. Levin comments on Rousseau's outspokenness:

> Rousseau writes an epic about himself, insisting that nothing is too shameful or commonplace to be included if it helps to show how he developed into the individual he is. Twentieth century readers have fixed on Rousseau's *The Confessions* as perhaps the text in discussing the construction of a self in language. The vocabulary and procedures of structuralist and post-structuralist works on Rousseau inform the vast field of contemporary autobiographical criticism. (Levin 4)

Rousseau's contribution to the shaping of the worldview of the French peasants and in a subtle way geared them for revolution. Rousseau was highly concerned about the civic life. He projected a deep sense of the discernment of public and private lives. His value-system shaped his opinions to a great extent. Being a liberal humanist, he advocated the cause of the downtrodden and the afflicted.

*The Confessions* deals with leading personages and transactions of a significant epoch, when totalitarianism and feudalism were joining forces for their last struggle against the modern spirit, chiefly represented by Voltaire, and Rousseau himself—a struggle to which, after many turbulent quarrels and internal wars throughout Europe and America, has succeeded the prevalence of those more open-minded and rational principles by which the statesmen of our own day are actuated. Margaret Ogrodnick accentuates:

> Enraptured by the satisfactions of intimacy but also propelled by republican concerns, Rousseau does not distinguish so sharply the sentiments and values of private and public realms. He draws upon our intimate experience with sharing, authenticity, affection and romantic love to cultivate the civic self. Thus, as opposed to the public dimension of the liberal rights bearing self, Rousseau suggests the possibility that through the resultant civic identity. We may be thickly constituted selves not only in private but also in public. (Ogrodnick 187)

Rousseau's life was one full of conflicts, first when he was apprenticed, later in academic circles with other Enlightenment thinkers like Diderot and Voltaire, with Parisian and Swiss authorities and even with David Hume. Although Rousseau discusses these conflicts, and tries to explain his perspective on them, it is not his exclusive goal to justify all of his actions. He chastises himself and takes responsibility for many of these events, such as his extramarital affairs. At other times, however, his paranoia is clearly evident as he discusses his intense feuds with friends and contemporaries. And herein lays the fundamental tension in *The Confessions* Rousseau is at the same time trying both to justify his actions to the public so that he might gain its approval, but also to affirm his own uniqueness as a critic of that same public:

> I would be interested to know whether the minds of other men are troubled by puerile notions that sometimes pass through my own. In the midst of my studies, of a life as innocent as

> any that could be led, and inspite of everything that had been said to reassure me, I was often still troubled by fears of hell. I would ask myself what state I was in, and whether if I were to die at that moment I would be damned. (*The Confessions* 237)

On the whole, we can assume that Rousseau attempts to put forth truth in an agreeable form. His ruminations on the various stages of his life have helped him delve deep into the mechanics of the human mind. As he lays bare his self in *The Confessions,* he manages to trace a sympathetic audience to put forth his ideas on life in particular and philosophy in general. His work is notable as one of the first major autobiographies. Prior to his writing *The Confessions*, the two great autobiographies were St. Augustine's own *Confessions*, and Saint Teresa's *Life of Herself.* Both these works, however, focused on the religious experiences of their authors. *The Confessions of Jean-Jacques Rousseau* was one of the first autobiographies in which an individual wrote of his own life mainly in terms of his worldly experiences and personal feelings. Rousseau recognised the unique nature of his work; it opens with the famous words:

> I have resolved on an enterprise which has no precedent, and which, once complete, will have no imitator. My purpose is to display to my kind a portrait in every way true to nature, and the man I shall portray will be myself.

## Works Cited

Levin, Susan M. *The Romantic art of Confession: De Quincey, Musset, Sand, Lamb, Hogg, Fremy, Soulie Janin,* Columbia, Camden House, 1998.

Ogrodnick, Margaret. *Instinct and Intimacy: Political Philosophy and Autobiography in Rousseau,* Toronto, University of Toronto Press, 1999.

Rousseau, Jean Jacques. *The Confessions of Jean Jacques Rousseau,* Oxford, Oxford University Press, 2000.

Scott, John T. *Jean-Jacques Rousseau: Politics, Art and Autobiography,* Oxon, Routledge, 2006.

# 14

# *Against All Odds*—A Spiritual Autobiography

S. Jeyachandra

## Autobiography and Its Features

Autobiography writing has been included as one of the literary genres in the late eighteenth century. Until then the style of writing has given us glimpses of the early history, through journals and diaries kept by individuals. Robert Southey coined the term in 1809 to describe the work of a Portugese poet (Anderson, 17). E. Stuart Bates defines it is a narrative of the past of a person by the person concerned (Bates 8 ). It is defined as a retrospective prose narrative produced by a real person concerning his own existence, focusing on his individual life, in particular on the development of his personality. The remarkable thing is a crowded life that is most easily remembered. A life full of turns, achievements, disappointments, surprises and crises, it is a life full of landmarks which will be an effective autobiography.

## Spiritual Autobiography and Its Objectives

The features of autobiography include identity of self, self-reflection and introspection. Benjamin Franklin in his introduction quoted eleven reasons. Some of them are revelation of truth, expressing your perspective, purpose or the objective of writing and knowing your audience, and choosing a direction.

Among this one important factor is to search for a meaning and reveal it to the world. Truth must be told, whatever happened must be portrayed. In this regard a category has been evolved, as spiritual autobiography. John Raphael states that "Autobiographers may write to teach, advise, convert or warn others, particularly the next generation" (Staude 254). That kind of didactic autobiography is spiritual autobiography.

Staude defines it as a history and interpretation of a person's life written by a person who experienced it, considered in relation to its spiritual foundations" (Staude 250). He continues to explain that as the personal experience of connectedness relationship to transcendent. This might take a form of "religion or it could manifest itself through love, art, music, poetry, nature" (Straude 251). The objective of the spiritual self-narrative is to convince others about ones spiritual experience. Diane Bjorklund says that "religious autobiographers concentrate on their transformations" (Bjoklund 62). C.S. Lewis very plainly says that he strictly means his business of writing his spiritual experience, omits everything irrelevant. (Lewis VIII)

*The Confessions* the experience of St. Augustine, is the first of its kind, dealing mainly about his relationship with God. Since its publication such autobiographies have come into vogue with the 'four pattern' as defined by Staude. He outlines that as the "description of the individuals life before spiritual awakening, an account of the events leading upto the individual's encounter with god, a description of actual encounter with God and the impact of this event on the narrator, a celebration of new life following the event" (Staude 258). All these four elements are present in the book 'Against all odds' and makes it as a spiritual autobiography.

## *Against All Odds* and Its Author Wendy Alec

The author and pastor Francis Frangipane in the foreword of the book says, "In every generation there is a song rises in the redeemed toward God. It is a hymn of praise, of thanksgiving to God for all He has accomplished in their lives. Yet there is a unique song .... 'The song of the Lamb'. I hear this song of the lamb, in the soul of God TV". (Alec 19)

The book, *Against All Odds*, written by Wendy Alec, is an autobiographical account of how she and her husband Rory brought this wonderful song of the Lamb, 'GOD TV', into existence. She shares her experiences, her struggles, her travelling and her tears and anguish to birth the first European daily Christian channel God TV. It is subtitled as the story of GOD TV'S pioneers Rory and Wendy Alec. In her narrative she has beautifully portrayed her inner turmoil as she was wrestling against her own sinful past which was transformed through the love of Christ and the dream and the supernatural word of knowledge she received to launch a new daily Christian channel in Britain.

Wendy is the author of the Chronicle brothers – a series in which she has penned down three volumes which comes under genre of spiritual fiction through which she is reaching out the young readers who are rebellious and who will never sit to read the books for edification and the *Bible*. Her efforts did not fail as her first book was shocking to see the portrayal of Father God's love for humanity which would make a reader weep. Her book, *The Unknown Prophet* relates her insight and vision received from God regarding this age and era. Her talent as a story-teller is amazing and the simple way of explaining God's love is really exciting.

As Jean Quigley says in *The Grammar of Autobiography*, "As soon as we are asked about ourselves, to tell our autobiography, we start tell stories. We tell what happened what we said, what we did" (Quigley 144). The third edition of the book adds the story of GOD TV in America along with the story of Wendy and Rory and the head-start in England. Wendy Alec describes her happy childhood memories with her parents in South Africa in the chapter 'Roots'. Then she narrates her own story of rebellion and redemption, story of dramatic transformation and restoration in a powerful way. This autobiography proves to be a spiritual autobiography, autobiography of a revolution in Christian media and a motivational or inspirational autobiography.

### Before Spiritual Awakening and Confessions

When the teenage years began she started rebelling and behaving so badly that she was demoted in school. Things went downhill and she degenerated into night clubs and music and singing her pop songs. Her worst condition didn't give her hope and she went on and on. At the same time there was another kind of thirst and emptiness eating her soul and she told," during all my rebellious years I was hungry for God" (Alec 27). Her quest for spiritual awakening brought her many Christians. Her spiritual journey turns out to be the most individual dimension of life. Once when one strict (straitlaced) Christian cornered her in the ladies room she glared at her. "With tears brimming in her eyes, she confronted me: What are you doing to Jesus?"( Alec 29). Despite the immediate anger she was alone facing her own reflection. That moment revolutionized her destiny, "Suddenly the room was filled with the presence of God and very slowly I looked up into the mirror and I saw the Lord Jesus Christ.... Jesus looked at me and oh, how he loved me. ... It was His eyes. They were filled with such tender mercy and compassion....all the while tears running down his eyes" (Alec 29). She surrendered her life. A few days-after her Damascus road experience in the hostel revival broke out as she started teaching and sharing to those who were hopeless and beyond redemption. A strong desire was forming or created in her heart to reach out the lost especially whom the Christians, church and the so-called religious organization forgot, through their own means of music, TV and media. She received God's word or prophecy" And you shall be raised up as a forerunner of creative evangelism in this generation." (Alec 31)

The life story of Rory Alec was written in an incredible way of a biographer. Rory's troubled childhood made him commit to the Lord and after his conversion Wendy met him according to God's blueprint. God brought together two young Christians who loved each other and the Lord Jesus with all their hearts, with a vision to reach out to the world through creative evangelism. They had absolute assurance conviction that God could use them as a 'little David' to impact media (Goliath). They were married in 1987 and by this time they were into musical projects which won them money and name.

## Discovering the Identity

Rory and Wendy wrote lyrics and Rory and Nikki arranged the musical tracks. But within three months the strife set in among the producers and the project was disintegrated. In the maze of shattered dreams, they had the conviction from God that He was going to help them and train them for this vision. They were in a secular media as they had to generate a living. Soon their advertising career began. This has been a seed for equipping themselves for the future endeavour. In her words, "God took us from concentrating on just musical gifting that he placed us and started to expand our creative talents in a very secular world." (Alec 40)

The birth of a TV channel began when Rory became an agency radio producer, and she became a copywriter. They were promoted to middle management, working on national campaign across as South Africa for clients with highly creative concepts to gain universal appeal. Then came the introduction of television in the form of the production of agency television commercials. For the mammoth task ahead they learnt to combine audio and visual together. Thus having God's vision for the media still burning in their hearts they encompassed television, film and music.

God confirmed their calling through a wonderful momentary success. Music video from their Christian music project had been nominated in the secular Tele Top Music Video of the year awards. Rory Alec was awarded the top one and this led them into the wilderness of the television commercial production industry.

Any biographer will often be "enlarging on special aspects of his life, such as the influences that moulded him.... or the services that he rendered to what he most cared about ....the way he organizes and arranges the events of the story shows what the author considers important" (Bates 3). Like this Wendy Alec narrates the story of developing the Christian channel and how that vision grew instead of narrating the story of her and her family in detail. This book thus becomes the biography of God TV.

In its history the next stage was the power and the glory in advertising. One commercial led to the other and very soon they were being viewed as the up and coming, the newcomers to watch, and the production house of the nineties. Their life was in luxury and all of a sudden the disaster struck and because of the South African political situation big businesses started to cut their advertising budgets. All the clients went out and they were devastated. She openly admits that "we would admit that our aim had now become a desire to get to the top and to make as much money as possible while getting there, rather than to honour God in the industry. Pride comes before destruction" (Alec 47). When she identified her weakness which caused this kind of mighty fall was really a self-discovery, this book turned out to be to be the book of spiritual journey through self discovery and processing to a spiritual perfection.

There was destruction all around them and however they worked "to rescue the sinking ship", nothing worked. They lost everything including the house, car, the equipments and even clothes. They arrived in desperation at Rory's parents' house. They had lost everything. She was seven and a half months pregnant with no knowledge of what the next month held. "The dream was shattered". Still they had this spark that whispered "and now the will of God'. (Alec 49)

## Onward Spiritual Journey

The spiritual journey towards perfection was progressing and Rory had to go through the struggle as he was going on a tour of programmes which lost a lot of money. Humorously she revealed Rory's hard heart and the consequences thus: "So he returned to England, still fighting with God, but with his back against the wall. In fact… I would say that God slammed his nose full face into the wall" (Alec 53). But God saw this and He opened a door to join the staff at Cornerstone Centre in Kent. There came a chance to look out for an outlet for Christian programmes that they were making at church. It was a total shock to realize that there was literally no daily Christian television in Europe.

The seed is now sown in a different way altogether. Rory has a strong conviction:" Launch Christian TV into Europe". Rory's spiritual journey doesn't end there. He was tempted to do business of getting a land full of gold mining. This sparkled their eyes and the deal progressed. Meanwhile he started to know the prophet Kwame and he grew in fear of God. A supernatural impartation took place and he became a new man. He was transformed and it was evident for all to see. He became the associate minister of the church in Bromley. God through difficult and many disasters taught them humility and both were brought to the same level in their spiritual journey.

At the beginning of January 1995, with no assets but led by the voice of God, they decided to go for ASTRA – the satellite system, the most highly sought–after in Europe, beaming its signal into over 22 million houses and 24 nations across Europe. The task was impossible still they were determined to go. After many months of negotiating they felt dejected as nothing happened. Still deep in her heart she knew that "they could not give up now and that is what pioneering is about. It would take every bit of courage we possessed to continue". (Alec 71)

## Motivational Autobiography

This autobiography could be called as an inspirational and motivational one for those who have shattered dreams. Even when they lost everything they didn't give up. With a three-year-old little girl and a four-week-old baby they struggled for food and clothing and their daily survival. They were faced with a dashed gold deal and the cable operators were sitting on a fence and they had not even a glimmer of light for their future. Everyone in the ministry said that it was impossible and they had tried already. The book says that impossible is possible with God. Among all odds, oppositions they had a destiny to fulfil. Wendy realized that their role in this was very important. God's attention was riveted on Europe and the part the TV would play in this end times. God has a timetable and His timetable cannot be pushed forward by man.

Her following words serve many people and build their images: "God's chosen, appointed vessels may not to the natural eye, be the most established or most learned.... This is an answer to questions like, where's your god amongst all these filth and violence. Where is this God that so many of you in the UK and US say you serve?" Their faith had a reward. A light broke through the darkness. The biggest miracle happened. BSkyB – a bigger channel—came for discussion. BSkyB was ready to enter into negotiations with a condition that they received the ITC licence (to broadcast courtesy of the Independent Television Commission).

## Narrative Style

The book is an exciting one and in places it reads like a fictional novel with twists and suspense. It would seem a novel if anyone would not believe the facts and this effect is achieved through the narrative style and her incredible story-telling. Her remarkable way of narrating the story makes the readers have a ride to know what happened to ITC. Everything hinged on this decision. If they didn't get ITC license they would be no Christian channel and no deal with BSkyB. At last the first daily Christian channel got its license for 10 years and the agreement was signed with BSkyB. The legendary first channel was operating out of the kitchen table, the whole house becoming a work area.

BSkyB informed them after a week that the needed the morning hours 8-00 to 9-00 and instead they would offer 5 to

8-00 am. Still with no money they struggled to prepare the programs and they were not sure what and how they would fill those time slots. Again God in his supernatural way opened a door. Benny Hinn wanted to meet them in London immediately. Their meeting with Benny Hinn was fruitful and they got 'This is your Day' twice a week and also he invited them over to America to be a guest, to introduce him to many people. With a faithful gift of support very month Benny Hinn sustained them through the worst of times.

Wendy Alec was able to write the great saga of Christian media and the fight to bring about the Christian media revolution. They had to encounter a lot of hurdles immediately on signing the agreement. SkyB applied for approval for Channel Europe from BT, ASTRA and the government of Luxembourg. They thought that the approvals were a mere formality. Money could not be released without approvals. It was early September and they had less than 20 days to launch.

They were in a hard dilemma and they had no assurance that this program would continue. They had a question should they delay their launch yet again a month to November. They were in prayers and they felt God's answer was 'Launch'. And so they worked day by day towards the launch by faith, with no budgets knowing that in the natural, the house would come crashing down. Their waiting ended when they received the fax on the late afternoon. It was on Wednesday 27 September 1995 they gathered in front of the national press. London. The presentation was made. All the newspapers and the radio like BBC, VIVA and many others announced the news of the impending launch of Christian channel. When it was launched on the first of October they had a scathing criticism. Some said, "Do not convert your dish! Tele evangelism comes to Britain".

One stated, "Young gifted fanatical, the Alecs are perfect exemplars of religious revival". Many were excited to have such a channel.

## Historical Autobiography

With all dates and news paper criticism she narrates the incidents with realism and tries to make it as a historical document of God TV. The following are some excerpts and samples:

> BBCI crew filmed their progress in the next few days the documentary Miracle channel was aired on 28 January 1996. That created havoc and from every frontier comments came. The verbal war had to be fought with the media and their harsh criticism.
>
> *The Financial Times:* "Keep your head down, lock the doors and pull out the TV plug—the telly evangelists are at the door.... And it was frightening."
>
> *The Times,* Rory and Wendy were brain dead." (Alec 114)

The crew struggled and they were able to air the programmes with all opposition. The struggle faced to cover the cost of production was yet another story of faith and miracle working power of God. In short, the history of media revolution in the name of Miracle TV—later to be God TV—is given as facts. The importance of factual accuracy and chronology superseded, often authenticated by quotes from newspapers is evident in this book. So it not only tells Wendy Alec's story but also to document the story of their times and the story of the induction of God TV and its growth.

1991 – Rory and Wendy arrived in UK.

1996 – GOD TV dedicated to God.

1997 – On October first God channel launched breaking down religious barriers and political correctness.

1997 – Programmes increased to 7 hours a day.

1999 – Programmes increased to 24 hours a day.

2002 – Headquarters moved to Jerusalem, launched to Africa, reached 20 million homes.

2004 – First Western broadcaster in Hong Kong.

2005 – Launched in Australia.

2006 – In USA with the largest satellite platform.

Their obedience to the call of God made them leave Britain to US to prepare the groundwork for God TV. The hard work the couple put in, the sacrifices they made, even at the cost of their children education make the reader to have a glimmer of hope and the trust to obey God at any cost. The last chapter, 'Personal Miracles', is again an inspiring, inducing chapter to everyone, who has faith and who doesn't have. When they dared to live on the edge depending on God alone, God works miraculously and helps them settled in Plymouth. The launching of God TV from Jerusalem was another proof of God's faithfulness.

## Objective Fulfilled

It is appraised by R.T. Kendall in his foreword of this book, "On the whole this book is a story of rags to riches, riches to rags and back again, of a couple who almost gave up again and again had not God stepped in" (19). "This autobiography will make one laugh and cry but most of all 'increase your faith that God works on behalf of those who wait for Him" (19). The events are retold in a dramatic style in the best narrative, as the story of supernatural, inspirational, spiritual biography, making the readers alive with climaxes and suspense. Anyone who has a dream will find similar emotions and struggles and they will be a part of the story. *Against All Odds* is a complete history of God TV up to 2006, a fulfilment of prophecies uttered to Rory and Wendy. There is no doubt that it would ignite same kind of fire burn in the hearts of the readers towards their God-given vision. This autobiography is a fantastic read for those who are oppressed and suppressed, who need to be encouraged. As Rory and Wendy Alec have overcome with perseverance, humility and unshakable faith in God and His word, anyone could also overcome the adversities and succeed through the love of God.

## Conclusion

Such autobiographies of spiritual journeys or growth as a human being are written to teach en essential truth or a concept to the reader. The author finds compelled or forced to share something special happened to them. All the transformational encounters which are shared by authors like John Bunyan, Augustine, C.S. Lewis etc., make their writing didactic. They are written to influence the world and make a powerful impact upon the readers' lives. When a person writes an autobiography, it is transformed. It is no longer the writer's own experience: it becomes everyone's. (Staude, 117). This is the reality of *Against All Odds*, which will become the readers' experience.

## Works Cited

Alec, Wendy. *Against All Odds*. War Boys Publishing. London, 2006.

Bates, Stuart. *Inside Out: An Introduction to Autobiography*. New York, Sheridan. 1937.

Bjorklund, Diane. *Interpreting the Self.* Chicago: Univ. of Chicago Press, 1998.

Lewis, C.S. *Surprised by Joy*. New York: Harcourt, Brace & World, 1955.

Staude, John-Raphael. "Autobiography as a Spiritual Practice." *Religion, Spirituality, and Aging: a Social Work Perspective*, Vol 45(3), 2005, 249-269.

Quigley, Jean. *The Grammar of Autobiography: A Development Account*. Mahwah NJ: Lawrence Erlbaum Associates Inc. 2000.

# 15

# Perspectives on Nehru's *An Autobiography*

**Bhaskar Roy Barman**

As the title itself suggests, I have picked on Jawaharlal Nehru's autobiography to discuss in this paper. We shall search for literary merit in this autobiography, because Nehru wrote this autobiography at the time when he involved himself in the freedom movement in its full-fledged swing, and it reflects his thoughts and actions surrounding the freedom struggle. During the pre-Independence period other activists like Mahatma Gandhi, Maulana Abul Kalam Azad wrote their autobiographies to tell their readers how they involved themselves in the freedom struggle, but Nehru's is considered the best in that genre.

Autobiography is a metaphor of the self, a journey from the known to the unknown and contains in itself a history. Hence an autobiography is considered a genre linked to literature. The most widespread and flourishing methods of studying literature concern themselves with its setting, its environment, its external causes. These intrinsic methods are not limited to a study of the past, but are equally applicable to present-day literature which concentrates on its change in time, and is centrally preoccupied with the problem of history.

Autobiography is undoubtedly a work of art and the most obvious cause of it is its creator, the author himself / herself. We cannot deny its importance as a study of the man of genius. We expect that the man of genius writes an autobiography or has his biography written by another man who takes his genius for granted. Though biography and autobiography are akin in textures, there is a nuance of difference between them: an autobiography is infused with the personal feelings of the author and his personal prejudices, but a biography is shorn of these. Yet, I shall use in this paper biography in the sense of both biography and autobiography, for both tell of the man of genius, because biographers draw upon a series of public documents, interviews and personal reminisces, and even are granted access to private documents of the man of genius

Biography can be judged in relation to the light it throws on the production of a particular work. It is universally conceived of as a study of the man of genius, of his moral, intellectual and economical development which carries a hint of intimate interest, and is finally thought of as affording materials for a systematic study of the man of genius and his literary and poetic process. Biography, an ancient literary genre, is chronologically and logically a part of historiography, and makes no methodological distinction between a statesman, a general, an architect, a lawyer and a man who plays no public role. Coleridge somewhere said that any life, however insignificant, would, if it were told truthfully, be sound enough. But many biographers are of the opinion that the man of whom to write a biography, be he a poet, a novelist, a social activist, is just another man whose moral and intellectual development, external career and emotional life can be reconstructed and evaluated as well by reference to standards, usually drawn from some ethical system or code of manners.

I shall treat Jawaharlal Nehru's *An Autobiography* in the light of the concept of biography discussed above. It is doubtful how much his autobiography influenced the writing in English. But his autobiography acts as a mirror to reflect his personal image, the image of his family and the image of other individuals who happen to have established relationship with his family, and tells of his association with the freedom movement. He hints in his autography published in 1980 by Oxford University Press at how the familial atmosphere hovering around him paved the way for him to get involved in the freedom movement.

> My childhood was...a sheltered and uneventful one. I listened to the grown-up talk of my cousins without always understanding all of it. Often this talk related to the overbearing character and insulting manner of the English people as well as Eurasians towards Indians, and how it was the duty of every Indian to stand up to this and not to tolerate it. (Ch. II. 6).

The question of how the Nehru family imbibed the spirit of protest is likely to raises itself. The first chapter tells of this. Nehru belonged to a Kashmiri Pundit family and this sense of belongingness always persisted in his mind, even though his ancestor, Raj Kaul, who was a great scholar in Persian and Sanskrit, had migrated from the fair valley of Kashmir is about the year 1716. The erudition of Raj Kaul attracted the attention of Emperor Farrukhsiar which resulted in an invitation being sent out to Raj Kaul to reside in his capital, Delhi. Raj Kaul accepted the royal invitation and the family stayed in the capital, basking in the royal patronage until the break-out of the Sepoy Mutiny in 1857 and the consequent suppression of the Mutiny by the Government of the East-India Company. Jawaharlal informs the reader how his family name got to Nehru, as in the following passage.

> A jagir with a house situated in the banks of a canal had been granted to Raj Kaul... and, from this fact of residence 'Nehru'

> (from nahar, a canal) came to be attached to his name. Kaul had been the family name; this changed to Kaul-Nehru; and, in later years, Kaul dropped out and we became simply Nehrus. (P. 1)

The Sepoy Mutiny put an end to his family connection with Delhi, and all his family papers and documents were destroyed in the course of it, and, shorn of all their possessions they moved to Agra. His father, Motilal Nehru, was not born then. The scanty knowledge of one of his two uncles and some other members of their family saved them from "a sudden and ignominious end". While they were living in Agra, Motilal Nehru was born, a posthumous child, on 6 May 1861, as his father, Jawaharlal Nehru's grandfather, had died three months earlier. His English-knowing uncle "attached himself to the newly established High Court and when this court moved to Allahabad from Agra and family moved with it."

Apropos of his father who grew up under the sheltering care of his uncle, Nehru says:

> ...my father was going through school and college in Cawnpore and Allahabad. His early education was confined entirely to Persian and Arabic and he only began learning English in his early teens. But at that age he was considered to be a good Persian scholar, and knew some Arabic also, and because of this knowledge was treated with respect by much older people. (3)

A bit further down the same page in the following passage he refers to his father's capriciousness and hauteur which he may have inherited:

> He got through various university examinations without any special distinction, and then he appeared for the final, the B.A. He had not taken the trouble to work much for it and he was

> greatly dissatisfied with the way he had done his first paper. Not expecting to pass the examination, as he thought he had spoiled the first paper, he decided to boycott the rest of the examination and he spent the time instead at the Taj Mahal. (The university examinations were held then at Agra).

Later his professor scolded him by saying that he had done well in the first paper. "Anyhow this ended my father's university career. He never graduated" (4).

However, after having served his apprenticeship for three years in the district court of Cawnpore, Motilal Nehru moved to Allahabad to work in the High Court.

In the footnote to the last line of the first chapter, "Such was our home in the early days of my childhood" (5), says Jawaharlal Nehru: "I was born in Allahabad on the 14th November 1889, or according to the Samvat Calendar, Margshirsh Badi 7, 1946".

It was Motilal Nehru who contributed a great deal to his becoming what he was. A nationalist, Jawaharlal Nehru admired him tremendously and regarded him as an embodiment of strength and courage and cleverness, "far above all the other men I saw" (Ch. II, 7). His advent to Indian politics could be compared to Prince Siddhartha's renunciation of the world. On the eve of his going out to London with his parents and his baby sister to study at Harrow and Cambridge, when he was just fourteen, the spirit of nationalism budded forth, as he says: "Nationalistic ideas filled my mind. I mused of Indian freedom and Asiatic freedom from the thralldom of Europe. I dreamt of brave deeds, of how, sword in hand, I would fight for India and help in freeing her" (Ch. III. 16). On returning from England, a cultivated flower of Harrow and Cambridge, he cast his lot, though the son of an affluent father, with the humble and the lowly, and dedicated the rest of his life to achieving complete freedom of India,

He was extremely delighted when Gandhiji announced his decision to plunge into direct action against the Rowlatt Act. When he read about the decision in the newspapers, "my reaction was one if tremendous relief. Here at last was a way out of the tangle, a method of action which was straight and open and possibly effective." (Ch. VII, 41). Afire with enthusiasm, he had decided to join the Satyagraha Sabha. But his father, Motilal, was dead opposed to his decision and requested Gandhiji to come over to Allahabad to talk Jawaharlal out of his decision Gandhiji accepted his invitation.

> Gandhiji came to Allahabad at father's request and they had long talks at which I was not present. As a result Gandhiji advised me not to precipitate matters or to do anything which might upset father. I was not happy at this, but other events took place in India which changed the whole situation, and the Satyagraha Sabha stopped its activities. (Ch.VII, 42)

Bit in course of time and there were many factors that contributed to tilting the scale heavily in favour of Nehru's joining politics, though. Added to his own innate pride that rebelled at the subordination of his people to an alien and unsympathetic authority, he inherited his father's attitude towards men and women. Motilal Nehru was not wont to bow his head to anyone in obeisance. He experienced the nature of his father's temper in his childhood. For a venial fault of taking one of his pens lying on the table when his father was not home, he gave him a "tremendous thrashing" (Ch. II, 7). He did not bear any grudge against his father for having thrashed him unjustly, for he felt that "it was a just punishment, though perhaps overdone,"

Politics always fascinated him, but in his time there was nothing in politics to stimulate his enthusiasm, The Nehru family was distinguished for its pugnacity; but Jawaharlal Nehru knew not how to take on the adversary, He saw the futility of an armed insurrection, for the bulk of a disarmed and dispirited people were weighed down by grinding poverty. Nehru gathered a first-hand knowledge of the peasantry of India, while wandering among peasants. His wandering among them feeding with them and talking to them confirmed the futility of an armed insurrection and terrorism was, in his view, equally futile. But he did not give at the same time an absolute allegiance to the doctrine of non-violence propagated by Gandhiji, nor did he accept it for ever. Even Congress politics appeared to him insipid and dull.

Though he admired Gokhale and felt to a great extent attracted to the great institution, the Servants of India Society, he did not desire to join his partly because its politics were too moderate for him to embrace and partly because he had no idea of giving up his legal profession.

Congress was still controlled by men who not only believed in the good intentions of Britain in the matter of India's political enfranchisement but also in the doctrine of the inevitability of gradualness. When Gandhi gained the leadership of the Congress and transformed it into a vital organization, most of them left it to form a separate party and called themselves Liberals, and Jawaharlal Nehru on every opportunity lashed out at them. He targeted his attack at V.D. Srinivas Shastri, one of the most illustrious sons of India. Shastri shocked "him in a matter quite unconnected with politics. Mr. Srinivas Sgastri, however," says he, "gave me a great shock in a little matter unconnected with politics. He was addressing a students' meeting in Allahabad, and told them to be respectful and obedient to their teachers and professors and observe carefully all the rules and regulations laid down by constituted authority. All this goody-goody talk did not appeal to me much; it seems very platitudinous and somewhat undesirable, with all its stress on authoritarianism." (Ch. V, 30)

Jawaharlal Nehru found himself enthused for a while by Dr Annie Besant's All-India Home Rule League founded in September 1916. When she visited Allahabad in October of the following year after his internment, she was accorded a cordial welcome by the people of Allahabad. Though she was doubtless a dynamic personality, her leadership was only confined to the urban elite. India's salvation lay in the support of the masses. The intellectual classes could give effective leadership, but they would never deliver the goods. In the early years of the British rule the framers of India' educational policy put forward what came to be known as the filtration theory meant to enlighten the masses group by group on Western arts and sciences, This attempt was doomed to an utter failure, In politics, too, mass action alone would bring forth the desired results.

Nehru found in Gandhiji the true leader who could marshal the masses and their irresistible power to the cause of winning the Swaraj. He met Gandhiji for the first time at the Lucknow session of the Congress during Christmas 1916. Apropos of his first meeting with Gandhiji, he says: "My first meeting with Gandhiji was about the time of Lucknow Congress 1916. All of us admired him for his heroic fight in South Africa. He seemed very distant and different and impolitical to many of us young men. He refused to take part in Congress or national politics then and confined himself to the South African Indian question. Soon afterwards his adventures and victory in Champaran, on behalf of the tenants of the planters, filled us with enthusiasm. We saw that he was prepared to apply his methods in India also and they promised success." (Ch.V. 35)

In this connexion it deserves to be mentioned that over the thirty years Nehru stayed in close and active association with Gandhi, he had never wavered in his allegiance to Gandhiji, even though he had had many occasions to dissent from Gandhi's approach to certain aspects of the Country's political, economic and social problems. To the close relationship between Gandhi and Nehru a hard-hearted civilian who rose to distinguished positions both in British and free India testified in the following words:

> I have seen him (Nehru) at the end of a long day – tired, feeling harassed and looking careworn – drive over to see Mahatma Gandhi.; and I have seen him come out full of buoyancy and eager to work for several more hours when all Delhi was asleep. On one occasion towards the end of 1947 the Prime Minister said to me; "I do not think I could have carried on if Gandhiji had not been in Delhi. Bight after night I went to see him ; and he gave me hope, courage and strength." (Quoted by V.B. Kulkarni in *The Indian Triumvirate*, published 1967 by Bharatiya Vidya Bhavan, Bombay on p. 460 from 'Intimate Glimpse of Panditji by "One who worked with him'", published in the Nehru Supplement dated 14 November 1949 in the defunct English daily, *Bharat*, Bombay).

The year 1921 turned out to be a turning point in the political life of Jawaharlala Nehru, for it was characterized by a strange mixture of nationalism and politics and spiritualism and mysticism and behind all this were an agrarian upheaval in villages and rising working-class movement in big cities. Nationalism and a vague but intense country-wide idealism sought, in the words of Nehru, "bring together all these various, and sometimes mutually contradictory, discontents, and succeeded to a remarkable degree" (Ch XI, 75) Yet this nationalism proved to be composite force encompassing, as it did, Hindu and Muslim nationalisms partly looking beyond the frontiers of India. The two separate and distinct nationalisms commingled into an Indian nationalism in consonance with the spirit of the times. For the time being they overlapped and pulled together. Referring to the commingling of these two separate nationalisms, says Jawarharlal Nehru:

> It was Hindu-Musalman ki jai everywhere. It was remarkable how Gandhiji seemed to cast a spell on all classes and groups of people and drew them into one motley crowd struggling in one direction. He became, indeed (to use a phrase which has been applied to another leader), "a symbolic expression of the confused desires of the people." (Ch. XI, 75)

All freedom fighters, particularly those who leadered different movements, were keen on political imprisonments with a view to boosting up the morals of their followers. Jawaharlal Nehru also voluntarily courted imprisonment. He had already paved the way for the government to imprison him, suffice it to say. Imprisonment was not a new thing in the year 1921. Since the time of the Bengal partition agitation there had been a continuous stream of men and women flowing into prison, sentenced often to long terms. About his imprisonment and that of other leaders Nehru says:

> We had come to prison of our own accord, many of the volunteers indeed having pushed their way in almost uninvited. There was thus hardly any question of any one of them trying to escape. If he had any desire to go out, he could do so easily by expressing his regret for his action or giving an undertaking that he would refrain from such activity in future. An attempt to escape would only bring a measure of ignominy, and in itself was tantamount to a withdrawal from political activity of civil resistance variety. (Ch. XIII, 91)

In course of time down through his personal history Nehru tells us of how he got appointed as secretary of All-India Congress at its annual session. In his speech Maulana Mohamad Ali, then president of the All-India Congress, delivered at the annual session held in December 1923 at Coronada in the South. He 'traced the growth of political and communal feeling among the Moslems and showed how the famous Moslem deputation to the Viceroy in 1908, under the leadership of the Aga Khan, which led to the first official declaration in favour of separate electorates, was a command performance and had been engineered by the Government itself." (Ch.XVII, 107)

On the heels of assuming his office, he tried to synthesize the communal identities and this testifies to his true nationalistic feeling. He had introduced in the A.I.C.C. office "a practice of addressing all our members by their names only without any prefixes or suffixes, honorific titles and the like." But he could not adhere to this practice for long, for Maulana Mohamad Ali directed him on the strength of his office to "revert to the old practice".

Early in 1924 Gandhiji fell ill, while in prison, and was removed to a hospital and underwent an operation. As he was convalescing in the hospital the government remitted the rest of his sentence. He had just served about two years out of the six years he had been sentenced to. He went over to Juhu, by the seaside near Bombay, to recuperate. Nehru's family trekked over to Juhu and stayed for a while in a cottage with a view to talking Gandhiji into at least passively cooperating with them in the Swarajist movement. The talks Motilal Nehru had had with Gandhiji was doomed to a failure, as is evident in the following passage.

> The Juhu talks, as far as the Swarajists are concerned, did not succeed in winning Gandhiji, or even in influencing him to any degree. Behind all the friendly talk, and the courteous

> gestures, the fact remained that there was no compromise. They agreed to differ, and statements to this effect were issued to the Press. (Ch. XVIII., 124)

Jawaharlal Nehru returned a little disappointed from Juhu, for Gandhiji had not resolved any of his doubts, As was usual with him, he sort of disdained looking into the future and laying down any long-distance programmes. Says Nehru: "We were to carry on patiently 'serving' the people, working for the constructive and social reform programme of the Congress, and await the time for the aggressive activity, The real difficulty, of course, was that even when that time came, would not that incident like Chauri Chaura upset all our calculations and again hold us up? To that he gave no answer then. Nor was he at all definite in regard to our objectives. Many of us wanted to be clear in our own minds what we were driving at. Although the Congress did not then need to make any formal declaration on that subject. Were we going to hold out for independence and some measure of social change, or were our leaders going to compromise for something much less?" (Ch. XVIII, 124-125).

These doubts gave rise to conflicts of opinions and attitudes within the Congress. While Nehru and other like-minded leaders wanted to make the issue of independence clear in the Congress, the Liberals had drifted so far that "they publicly gloried in pomp and power of the Empire, although that Empire might treat our countrymen as a doormat, and its dominions keep our countrymen as helots or refuse them all admittance." (ibid. 125) This drifting away in course of time contributed to toning down the Swarajist movement. Some Swarajists became ministers, some executive councillors in the provinces. Even some congressmen who had been to prison with Jawaharlal Nehru did not feel any hesitation to become ministers and hold high offices in the government.

Another conflict appeared between Gandhiji and the Swarajists at a meeting of the All-India Congress Committee held at Allahabad some time in the middle of 1924. Gandhiji proposed at the meeting a fundamental change in the Congress constitution, changing the franchise and the rules for membership; he insisted on limiting membership to those who gave a certain amount of self-spun yarn instead of the four annas which the Swarajist would pay to become members. This was a serious limitation of the franchise and the AICC was not competent enough to agree to this proposal. The Swarajists mounted pressure on Gandhiji to repeal the proposal. Though Gandhiji did not bow down to their pressure, he adjusted himself to them by agreeing to accept the spinning franchise as an alternative form, the old four-anna franchise remaining. The conflict, though temporarily patched up, contributed to the drifting of some Swarajists away.

I should not elongate the elasticity of the reader's patience; I shall conclude my discussion by dwelling upon the Hindu-Muslim conflict which culminated in the partitioning of India. There was during this time a progressive deterioration of Hindu. Muslin relations, in north especially. In the bigger cities a number of riots "brutal and callous in the extreme" took place. There hovered an atmosphere of distrust and anger which bred causes of distrust which "most of us had never heard of before". The following passages are worth quoting to illustrate how the Hindu-Muslim relations deteriorated.

> Previously a fruitful source of discord had been the question of cow sacrifice especially on the Bakr-id-day. There was also a tension when Hindu and Muslim festivals clashed as, for instance,, when the Moharram fell on the days when the Ram Lila was celebrated. The Moharram revived the memory of a past tragedy and brought sorrow and tears; the Ram Lila was the festival of joy and the celebration of victory of good over

> evil. The two did not fit in. Fortunately they came together once in about thirty years, for the Ram Lila is celebrated according to the solar calendar at a fixed time of a year, while the Moharram moves round the seasons, following a lunar year. (Ch. XIX., 134-135)
>
> ..............................
>
> It seems amazing that a question which could be settled with mutual consideration for each other's feelings and a little adjustments should give rise to great bitterness and rioting. But religious passions have little to do with reason or consideration or adjustments, and they are easy to fan when a third party in control can play off group against another. (ibid. 135)

The communal conflict over the Hindu and Muslim festivals that synchronized with each other foreboded the partitioning of India close on the heels of India's achieving freedom. Before plunging into the freedom struggle the Swarajists and their followers need to have reoriented themselves to the needs of India when it achieved freedom and to what they were actually aiming for. Jawaharlal Nehru himself confessed to his inability to fit in with the developments leading to this communal discontent (Ch. X IX, 134). He seems to have reconciled himself to the developments paralysing the communal harmony inch by inch. Perhaps it was beyond him to check the developments surging forward. Earlier on, while speaking of Gandhiji's personality, Nehru said: "As is usual with him, he refused to look into the future, or lay down any long-distance programme" (Ch, XVIII, 124).

The biography reveals Jawaharlal Nehru as a true nationalist.

## Works Cited

Jawaharlal Nehru, An Autobiography, Bombay: Allied. Publishers Limited, 1962.

# 16

# Taslima Nasrin's *My Girlhood*: An Autobiography of a Known Architect

Indrani Singh Rai

Childhood is the state of life that holding the hands of recollections carries to the innocent blessed realm where everything seems to be sheltered within a celestial beam. But to a few, childhood remains as a testimony of blistering, anguished and traumatic phase that is not apparelled with divine glow. The exception is Taslima Nasrin, the fiery female voice from Bangladesh who angered the Muslim clergy in her country by questioning the *Quran*. *My Girlhood* is the eternal memoir of childhood days of the writer. The loutish and tender glum of the past days leave a pleasing pain of nostalgia in her heart events, and she is compelled to tell a brutally honest and brave harrowing memoir of her voyage from birth to adolescence.

*My Girlhood* is an insightful retelling of Taslima's growing up in Bangladesh and erstwhile East Pakistan. The memoirs float like the waves, and standing on the shore, a woman can still hear the silent cry of a girl. The pictures emerge like flashes from a colourful screen, creating a sparkling image as the author travels back and forth between her own life and that of the horizon of her nation. A candid innocence and freshness pervades her sharp observations of Bangladeshi society with its class discriminations and bias, its transparent gender discrepancies, and growing religious orthodoxy and fanaticism. Nasrin along with a handful of fearless hearts have challenged the existed norms decided by the patriarchal society. She dares to utter the truth that all traditions are not venerable to trust and all long-standing doctrines are not always worthy. She witnesses the fastidious wave of passion taking hold in post-war Bangladesh.

*My Girlhood,* Nasrin's autobiography, opens with violence, blood and suffering. It reminds the events occurring in Taslima's life during the 1971 War of Independence, when she was only nine years old. The drama of the nine-year-old girl and her family is unfolded against a background of cruelty and hostility. She was born at the time of the transitional phase of Bangladesh. The shadow of war reached each and every life. The child Nasrin was a thorough witness of events within and without her periphery; she was a keen observer of changing values around her.

> ...in daylight and after dark, clutching children and bundles of belongings under their arms or on their shoulders. Running, they were running away, from cities to villages, from Mymensingh to Phulpur, Dhobaura, and Nandail. Rushing to the other side of the river, they left behind the buildings, schools, theatre, and shops they knew so well. On they swarmed to the rice fields, barren lands, the forests, anywhere to get away. Even those who had never once imagined they would leave their home became keen to pack their belongings and get out. (*My Girlhood* 4)

Things were falling apart and in the gulf of pain she was trying to create an identity or confer a voice to the silence. Along with the traumatic experiences due to impending war, Taslima questions the prevailing sexual discrimination and abuse against women in her country. She refuses and rejects the rigid patriarchal norms of a society that is reluctant to acknowledge the liberty of a woman.

She remembers the breathless tension of war time. The numb, brutal military force left deep scars in almost everyone's life. It was a common hell felt by all continually. The girl shares the dark night, she faced:

> Not that I was asleep. I was simply pretending to be asleep, as if travelling the land of dreams, playing there with fairies, winging on a high swing, no longer a part of this world, as if I did not know that men wearing heavy boots had entered the room and were walking about, a rifle dangling from every shoulder. (18)

Nasrin unfolds the cold-blooded primitivism of those butchers in whose hands, people were killed casually or snatched forcefully to the camp, where they were whipped unremittingly, tortured with a bayonet till all the bones of the body were crushed. It is unbearable to even imagine those dark nights which like a python ingested the humanity. She was tormented mentally when she was asked:

> So, little girl... you must continue to sleep...when they look at you, lust and desire pouring from their eyes, they will shoot flames out of their mouths as they speak in a language you cannot understand. Keep absolutely still when they flash a light on your face, your chest, your thighs. They must see that you are not yet fully grown.... Their eyes and tongues—dripping lust and fire—swept slowly over my hair-eyes-nose-ears-neck-chest-stomach-thighs-legs-feet. A cold, slippery snake slid down the men's bodies, crawled all over me, sniffed my back, stomach, and genitals, then entered my flesh, my bones, and settled deep in the marrow. (18)

The unprovoked and malicious gift bestowed upon the girl by repugnant 'snakes' is just as appalling as the blood-spattered manoeuvre of war being played out in the nation at large. The book's magnifying gaze searches the social, religious, cultural ethos, and each is diagnosed prolifically.

Taslima had a gloomy and poignant childhood. The most aching thing in a child's life is injustice and she was forced to accept the wrong. Her mother was her world around which she grew like a creeper. Her mother was married at the time of blooming of a girl's dream. She aspired for continuing her study but advised to accept the confinement of a home by her father-in-law. When her first child started going to school, she demanded that she be granted to go too. Her husband agreed but her father-in-law had strong objections. "Your job is to raise your children and stay at home and take care of your husband. There's no need for a girl to think of education." (30)

Her mother was not an exceptional beauty and so she was always felt an insecurity about her husband's attentions. She discovered him in bed with the wife of another man. The husband and wife had an unfortunate conjugal bond that not only affected their lives but distressed the lives of their children. Nasrin could feel the emptiness of her mother's life, the loneliness created a dependency between the mother and the daughter. Taslima suffered for her mother but could do nothing. "...she pulled me closer and held me to her breast. 'Tell me, my love, if I die, will you cry for me?' she asked. I shook my head firmly. 'You won't die. If you do, I will die too.'" (27)

The little girl became a shadow of her mother. When the mother chopped vegetables or stuffed fuel into her clay oven, her eyes watering with the smoke. The baby slept on her lap, woke up time to time by the smell of onion, garlic, turmeric, pepper, the sweat on her mother's body, or a noisy dog or crow. When the mother went for her bath, she sat alone in the courtyard in the dust, amid dry leaves, when her brothers returned back from school they carried her about in the courtyard. With the passage of time, she grew up, often held and petted and caressed at times and ignored and abandoned at others. When she was eleven, she was informed the true nature of her father who did use but never revere her mother. A woman was forced to lead a subjugated life, make assure that her body boundary enclosed her into tears. She confessed her daughter that she never proved herself as a good and conscientious mother because she was always in a battle, constantly in a struggle to accept her fate.

> Ma told me something else, staring absently out of the window. That sad and depressing afternoon, she said to me: "I was not myself at that time. I kept crying all day. Your father had fallen in love with Razia Begum. Nearly every day when I took his shirt to wash it, I found a love letter from her in his front pocket. You were still a baby, sometimes rolling off your bed and falling down. When you cut your head, I did not pay you any attention. I could not concentrate on anything at all. Each night, your father came home late." (28)

Taslima's father was a puzzling person who wanted his children to study secular subjects, did not want them to be dragged to the 'baba' for religious instruction and wanted his wife to look after the children but he was a womanizer too. He remained dutiful to his family economically but could never seem to understand his wife or his daughter.

A feeling of injustice started gathering in young Taslima's heart against her father, and the smoke did not take much time to turn into a blaze against her communal norms which she thought, was insensitive and unfeeling. It treated women like cutting the wings of a bird and left it for living. Taslima always considers her society in Bangladesh as a closed one that only grants confinement, estrangement and disgrace to a woman. She strongly believes and makes people trust that not every word written in any holy book is indeed holy, and not every attempt to bring renaissance to the hearts of darkness, radiance to the shadows of unawareness can be sent back home considering as 'cultural imperialism.'

She feels for and with all those socially confined women whose lives are restricted within four walls, who take their pain for granted as their fates and gives the message that men and women are identical. Women can never be inferior to men. She gives the voice to the voiceless to reject the rigid patriarchal norms of a society which is reluctant to acknowledge a woman expressing her opinions on male exploitation and oppression.

The unseen, unheard and unfathomable loneliness created a pool between mother and daughter. Taslima could understand her mother more than any other. She saw her mother's ecstasy when her father transferred to Pabna. Her mother who was in as much pain as a sinner scorching in Hell, found herself in the seventh heaven because for long she had dreamed of a home of her own and she discovered her on the edge of it. She extracted happiness by dusting her husband's books but she was always in a sea of fear that he would flee from her magic-casement," It was this thought that made her turn blue with fear and prompted her to powder her dark face white, and line her small eyes with kohl to make them appear larger, so that she would not look entirely ugly" (30). It is correct that fancy cannot cheat so well, reality has much stronger weapon to hurt. All the dreams and desires of the lady were blown away by a sudden dust storm named Razia Begum, her husband's woman and she was obliged to return to the old house. This power relationship of dominance and subordination is apparent in male controlled society and emphasizes women's dependency on men. Patriarchy reins the family, the smallest unit of social organisation, and the ruler is always the father, the patriarch.

Taslima witnessed her family falling apart bit by bit. Being frustrated by her father's apathy, her mother tried to find refuge from domestic discord. She started involving herself by going to the cinema every afternoon, abandoning her children after school to their uncles and aunts. Probably she revolted in that silent way. Her loneliness introduces a marginal crowd, limited within the walls of their tears, unable to do justice to themselves and one thing they can do only, is to wait. She felt her mother's agony for being cheated by her own man. "Every night she would stay up, waiting for Baba to come back home. Crickets chirped, dogs howled, the night got deeper and darker. Afraid that the sound of her own breathing might drown the sound of Baba's knock on the door, Ma would hold her breath" (32). This is a common scene of that society where women are prohibited to question. Women are needed to veil the shame of their counter parts and to clothe their injuries at the same.

The rage that sparks from the writer has a deep root. Taslima was molested twice in her childhood by her uncles. She did not protest then because she could not. She was scared, tormented and felt very alone. The adult Taslima's anguish at this incident is real; the pain comes through quite clearly.

> Nor could I guess why uncle Sharaf and uncle Aman wanted to climb over me. Uncle Aman had told me not to tell anyone else. I started to think he was right. It was not something one talked about. At the age of seven, suddenly a new awareness rose in my mind. It told me that whatever had happened was shameful, it would not be right to talk about it, it had to be kept a secret. (92)

An innocent girlhood was parted into two. One half was convincingly mingled with all the other children, played games and ran around. The other half was imprisoned, depressed and alone even in the middle of a crowd. It seems there was thousands of miles' distance between this lonely girl and all the others. She needed shelter, but could not find anyone, not even her mother and she could achieve only emptiness. If a sensitive soul feels with her, it will go through the same inferno and burn by the same felling of shame and injustice. Childhood speaks of the ease and natural glee in things that one is accustomed to right from it. These are the rightful staple of existence of every child. To rob one of these is to quash one's entity.

Not only a single girl, but there were so many Taslimas in Bangladesh, all are wounded by an insensate and unfeeling butchery. Another tale of a victimized girl is told by the writer. Fajilatunnisa, one of Taslima's aunts was selected as a bride groom when she was a school going girl by Amirullah, a teacher in a Madrasa for his son Musa. Neither the girl nor her mother had the dare to protest. So the girl was hunted down, captured, brought back home from school, draped a red saree around her, and she was made to sit down and got married. In another three years, she would have passed her matriculation and could have gone to college but her flight was stopped instantly. Amirullah built a high wall around his house so that no one from the outside world could see his pretty daughter-in-law. He compelled a sportive girl to read out from several holy books and most strangely she was informed that it would please Allah to see a woman spend her life obeying and looking after her husband and his parents. But Fijli did not ready to follow the ethnicity which turns a woman into a slave. When she was punished for dancing with her friends by her father-in-law, she revolted:

> "Yes, so I am. So what? I shall do exactly what I want. If you try to stop me, I will kill you. I'll chop you to bits with a knife. You don't know me!" Aunt Fajli began thrashing her arms about. Now, Amirullah gripped his stick and raised it. The more his daughter-in-law thrashed her arms, the harder he

> brought it down on her back, neck, even her head. Never before had she been beaten like this. (103)

How can a community grow by ignoring, torturing or suppressing its partakers? Why should a culture prosper when it considers women's culture as sub-culture? Culture must not be used against humanity.

The little Taslima was forced to step into the cage of the burqa when the maturing body robbed her freedom she enjoyed as a girl. So she had a strong disgust against it though she was informed:

> It is to protect our chastity; Allah has said that any man from the outside world who is not a close relative of woman must not see any portion of a woman's body. If any man see, then it's a sin for the woman...You *must* learn to obey what Allah has said. He has ordered women to wear burkhas. He said nothing about men. You must accept that without question. It is a sin to question, and to doubt. (138)

Taslima criticises her religion by questioning its teaching. She was revolted against the social taboos which restricted women lives. She noticed that her frustrated mother starting depending on a Hazrat baba, a sort of Muslim guru with huge women followers. Some of the practices followed by the baba were quite perverse. It is really a shock to hear *Quran's* teaching which was explained and valued by uncle Siddique, la *ehellu lakannisau meen vayadu ola al tabadalla bihinna* that means it is perfectly legitimate to have sex with a female servant. All devotees followed their religious Guru blindly without questioning. They feared that any enquiry might have the potential for hurting or perturbing the peer. Taslima's mother too just waited for the next directive and accepted it without protest when it came. She was instructed to give up wearing sarees because Peer Amirullah had told them quite clearly that no one was allowed to grow their hair, all women must dress the way the Prophet's wives did and moreover Muslim women were taught that the sari belongs to Hindus and to wear it, is just like kissing hell like a kafir. Taslima's mother was convinced and she reflected the darkness of her community, "I will never wear sarees now...that is what Hindus wear. It is a garment worn by kafir. If I wear one now, it will be a sin!" (134) Taslima expressed her heart frozen to fear to read a page of *Quran* as it teaches, "The moon has its own light, it said. The earth always stands still. If it does not lean on one side, it is because all the mountains, acting like nails, are holding it in place" (145). Where does logic or science stand? How can a society move forward holding the hands of so blind superstition? The moving memoir attempts to exhibit how it is possible for young women to reach within themselves and rear their own spiritual life in spite of the physical and emotional pain that men and tradition bound societies can impose upon them.

Taslima becomes a prey in the eyes of orthodox Muslims of her country because male members of society have been enjoying the privileged position in the name of religion. Her writings must be extremely good, must be enormously prevailing, and must be awfully frightening to the existing institution of male domination and patriarchy. So Muslim women are taught persuasively:

> Man's female companion has been created out of one of his ribs. One of the bones in a woman's neck is crooked. That is the reason why no woman thinks straight, or walks on a straight path. Women are like a field for growing crops, the men are totally free to cultivate whenever they like. If a woman is disobedient, her husband has the right to drive her away from his bed, then he may try to talk some sense into her, but if she remains disobedient. he can beat her. Women can claim only

> one-third of any property owned by their fathers. Men can claim two-thirds. Men can take one, two, three, even four wives. Women have no such right. Men can divorce their wives simply by uttering the word 'talaq!' three times. Women are not allowed to seek a divorce at all. When acting as witnesses to an event, two women are counted as one witness, whereas every single man is seen as a complete witness. (146)

There is no logic why should anyone need two women to act as *one* witness, when the word of a single man is considered sufficient. Do not women speak the truth? Only men are honest and truthful? Human being should not allow barbarism, humiliation, inequality or injustice in the name of culture. *My Girlhood*'s bravery, vividness and ground breaking subject matter make it a remarkable achievement, and one that will live. Taslimais one of the most important Bengali writers of contemporary times who moving away from flamboyant and bejewelled rhetoric, orchestrates language that is direct, even ruthless. Her sexual explicitness is heroic and blatant. Her voice is loud enough to cause sufficient distress to the religious leaders of Bangladesh and the result to speak right is expulsion from her own native soil. She becomes a stranger in her own homeland. A hatred against injustice and inequity flows underneath her veins. A pain penetrates her heart for being away from home. *My Girlhood* is the window through which Taslima can revisit her past and through it again she can send a message to the world to embrace humanity.

## Work Cited

Nasrin, Taslima. *My Girlhood: An Autobiography*. New Delhi: Kali for Women, 2001.

# 17

# *Autobiography of a Yogi*: A Study of the Tradition of Guru-Disciple Relationship

Archana Bhattacharjee

*Autobiography of a Yogi* is one of the world's most acclaimed spiritual classics. It is an autobiography written by Paramahansa Yogananda (January 5, 1893-March 7, 1952) in which he discusses his life story, and which introduced many Westerners to meditation and Yoga. In 1999, it was designated as one of the "100 Most Important Spiritual Books of the 20$^{th}$ Century" by a panel of theologians and luminaries convened by Harper Collins Publishers. The work is enduringly popular because it introduces millions of readers to Eastern spiritual thought.

Yogananda's masterly story-telling epitomize the Indian oral tradition with its wit, charms and compassionate wisdom. "The Yogi begins by showing how his childhood experiences in turn-of-the century India produced a spiritual youth in search of an enlightened teacher, continues with an account of his years of training in the heritage of a revered master, and concludes with the highlights of a period, beginning in 1920 during which he lived and taught in America" (Rudley James 1997).

Initially published in 1946 to widespread critical acclaim, *Autobiography of a Yogi* quickly gained recognition as a literary masterpiece as well as a seminal work in the field of Eastern philosophy. A perennial bestseller, it is one of the most widely read and respected books ever published on the wisdom of the East, and is used as a text reference work in colleges and universities throughout the world.

The *Autobiography of a Yogi* is such a book that it could be quoted in its entirety for various purposes such as exemplary pieces of literature to illustrate some specific point such as the history of India, or on guru-disciple relationship. This paper makes an endeavour to examine the time honoured tradition of guru-disciple relationship as portrayed in the text which is universal to all spiritual paths and tradition. The guru-shishya tradition, lineage, or *parampara*, denotes succession of teachers and disciples in traditional Indian culture and religion such as Hinduism, Sikhism, Jainism and Buddhism. It is the tradition of spiritual relationship and mentoring where teachings are transmitted from a guru "teacher" to a "disciple".

As Sri Swami Shankaranda so aptly quoted:

> This God-created universe runs by orderly cosmic law, and the guru disciple relationship is rooted in that law. It is divinely ordained that he who seeks God shall be introduced to Him through a true guru. When a devotee sincerely desires to know God, his guru comes. Only one who knows God can promise the disciple: 'I will introduce you to him'. A true guru has already found his way to God; therefore he can say to the Chela, 'Take my hand. I will show you the way'. The Guru-disciple relationship encompasses the discipline and principles of right action which the disciple must follow to prepare himself to know God. When the disciple with the Guru's help, perfects himself, the divine law is fulfilled and the guru introduces him to God.

The story of Yogananda's meeting and relationship to his guru, Sri Yukteswar, is highlighted throughout *Autobiography of a Yogi*, along with the importance of the guru-disciple relationship. Chapter 12 "Years in My Master's Hermitage" is the longest in the book. The importance that Yogananda gave to that relationship is made clear by the very first paragraph of his autobiography:

> The characteristic features of Indian culture have long been a search for ultimate verities and the concomitant disciple-guru relationship.
>
> My own path led to a Christlike sage; his beautiful life was chiselled for the ages. He was one of the great masters who are India's truest wealth. Emerging in every generation, they have bulwarked their land against the fate of ancient Egypt and Babylonia." (Yogananda, Paramahansa, *Autobiography of a Yogi*, 1985. 1)

## Early Spiritual Quest

Yogananda writes openly about his intense desire, even in childhood to know what lay behind all the experiences of life and death. As a child he asked, "What is behind the darkness of closed eyes?" (*Autobiography of a Yogi* 1985. 9)

The death of his mother when he was 11 to whom he was deeply devoted, greatly intensified his personal search for God. He states, "I loved Mother as my dearest friend on earth. Her solacing black eyes had been my refuge in the trifling tragedies of childhood." (*Autobiography of a Yogi* 1985. 13)

While still a student in high school, Yogananda with three friends, attempted to run away from home and find his long-sought guru amidst the Himalayan Mountains. But it was not until after his graduation from high school, which he had promised his father he would finish, that he was to meet Swami Sri Yukteswar Giri.

## Spiritual Lineage and Influences

Lahiri Mahasaya was the guru of Yogananda's parents and also the guru of Sri Yukteswar, Yogananda's guru. At the age of eight, Yogananda was instantly healed of cholera after his master's insistence that he pray to Lahiri Mahasaya. Beginning with chapter 31 of his autobiography, Yogananda spends the next five chapters interweaving the life of Lahiri Mahasaya with that of Lahiri Mahasaya's guru Mahavatar Babaji. Using the stories and biographical facts collected on his return trip to India in 1935 from various disciples of Lahiri Mahasaya (including the wife of Lahiri Mahasaya) as well as Yogananda's own personal testimony, he pays tribute to the three individuals whose life and collective influence became inseparable from his own life and teachings: Mahavatar Babaji, his chief disciple Lahiri Mahasaya, and his own guru Sri Yukteswar.

## The Essence of Guru-Disciple Relationship

Yogananda's lifelong search for his guru ended when he met Swami Sri Yukteswar. Even though he describes many saints and people who claimed to be miracle workers in his book, his relationship with Sri Yukteswar was unique. He spent several years being trained by Sri Yukteswar for the ultimate mission of spreading the science of yoga to the West. The wisdom of Sri Yukteswar, and the many spiritual lessons that Yogananda learned at his guru's feet are described in the chapter 12 "Years in My Master's Hermitage". His guru also bestowed on Yogananda the experience of samadhi, the ultimate goal of the Yogi, as described in the Chapter 14 "My Experience in Cosmic Consciousness."

Yogananda explains the importance of his relationship with Sri Yukteswar, and the eternal bond between guru and disciple:

> Retracing my steps as though wing-shod, I reached the narrow lone. My quick glance revealed the quite figure, steadily gazing in my direction. A few eager steps and I was at his feet.
>
> "Gurudeva!" The divine face was none other than he of my thousand visions. These halcyon eyes, in leonine head with pointed beard and flowing locks, has of peered through gloom of my nocturnal reveries, holding a promise I had not fully understood.
>
> "O my own, you have come to me!" My guru uttered the words again and again in Bengali, his voice tremulous with joy. "How many years I have waited for you."
>
> We entered an oneness of silence words seemed the rankest superfluities Eloquence flowed in soundless chant from heart of master to disciple. With an antenna of irrefragable insight I sensed that my guru knew God, and would lead me to Him. The obscuration of this life disappeared in a fragile dawn of prenatal memories.
>
> Dramatic time! Past, present, and future are its cycling scenes. This was not the first sun to find me at these holy feet! (*Autobiography of a Yogi* 1985. 88-89)

Yogananda then spent the better part of ten years under his guru's strict discipline. Excerpts from Chapter 12: "Years in My Master's Hermitage":

> Discipline had not been unknown to me; at home Father was strict, Ananta often severe. But Sri Yukteswar's training cannot be described as other than drastic. A perfectionist; my guru was hypercritical of his disciples, whether in matters of moment or in the subtle nuances of behaviour.
>
> (*Autobiography of a Yogi* 1985. 118)
>
> "If you don't like any words, you are at liberty to leave at any time." Master assured me, "I want nothing from you but your own improvement stay only if you feel benefited."
>
> (*Autobiography of a Yogi* 1985. 119)

> "I am hard on those who come for my training", he admitted to me. "That is my way, take it or leave it. I will never compromise. But you will be much kinder to your disciples. This is your way. I try to purify only in the fires of severity searing beyond the average toleration. The gentle approach of love is also transfiguring. The inflexible and the yielding methods are equally effective if applied with wisdom. You will go to foreign lands, where blunt assaults on the ego are not appreciated. A teacher could not spread India's message to the west without an ample found of accommodative patience and forbearance." (I refuse to say how often in America, I have remembered Master's words!)
>
> (*Autobiography of a Yogi* 1985. 120)

At his master's feet Yogananda fully discovered the cleavage between spiritual realism and the obscure mysticism that pass as a counterpart. He seldom discussed super physical realms or subtle laws. While others talked of miracles but could not manifest it, Sri Yukteswar seldom mentioned it but secretly operated them at will. He was the embodiment of a perfect spiritual Guru.

## Conclusion

Part of India's religious system, the guru-disciple relationship was surrounded by a set of cultural ideals that supported mutual trust and intimacy. The guru's role was to skilfully guide the disciple's development and always act with his best interest and highest welfare in mind. The disciple's role was to adopt a reverential attitude towards the guru, study and practice the teachings, diligently and follow the guru's personal guidance without doubt or hesitation. The guru was duty bound to find and successfully mentor at least one disciple able to carry on the lineage. This is the essence of the guru-disciple relationship which is beautifully portrayed in *Autobiography of a Yogi* leaving a permanent impression in the heart, mind and soul of the readers. This spiritual text is truly a masterpiece, and paves the path to perfection in the spiritual journey of each individual.

## Works Cited

Dudley, James. *Library Journal: Autobiography of a Yogi*. Cahners Magazine Division of Reed Publishing, 1997.

en.wikipedia.org/wiki/Autobiography_of_a_Yogi

*Harper Collins' 100 Best Spiritual Books of the Century*. www.liberatything. com/ .../Harper Collins+100+Best+Spiritual Books+...

The Autobiography of a Yogi-eNotes.com reference.

The Autobiography of a Yogi. En.wikipedia.org/wiki/ The Autobiography-of-a-Yogi.

Sankarananda, Swami, *The Guru-Disciple Relationship*, (swamisankarananda. blogspot.com/.../guru-disciple-relationship.html

www.enotes.com/topic/ The Autobiography of a Yogi.

Yogananda, Paramahansa, *Autobiography of a Yogi*, Bombay: Jaico Publishing House. 1985. Print.

## 18

# Lal Behari Day's *Recollections of My School Days*: A Case Study of the 'Childhood'

Rajiv Kumar

The simplest definition of autobiography as recorded in *Encyclopedia Britannica* is "the account of an individual human life written by the subject himself" (854). As a literary genre, however, autobiography tends to evaluate critically the history of one's past in the light of one's present and mature state of mind. According to D.G. Naik, in his *Art of Autobiography*, "Autobiography is primarily subjective. It is built from within outward. The invisible world within the individual is revealed to the readers and that too by no less an authority than the individual himself. It is, therefore, first-hand and direct information and no guess work" (12-13). Autobiography, as is clearly evident, is a critical history of one's own life. The autobiographer is himself the protagonist of his work. He frequently mentions other persons or even incidents not directly related to him but the only purpose that they serve is to throw light on the development of the central figure. An autobiography loses its intensity and its quality if the subject gets lost in the description of the world around him.

The autobiography is a firmly established genre with a long history ranging from masterpieces such as the *Confessions* of St. Augustine to Gide's *Si le Grain ne meurt*, with Rousseau's

*The Confessions*, Goethe's *Dichtung und Warheit*, Chateaubriand's *Memoires d' Outre-Tombe*, and Newman's *Apologia* in between.

The growth of autobiography in India has been phenomenal since its initiation on the Indian soil with the autobiographical letter of Raja Rammohun Roy which appeared in the *Athenaeum and the Literary Gazette* in 1832. It is not that autobiographies were never written before 1832. There are examples of autobiographical sketches much before Raja Rammohun Roy's endeavour. R.C.P. Sinha, in his pioneering work, *The Indian Autobiographies in English*, states:

> The Indians managed to find some sort of an outlet for their autobiographical impulse; a fact not yet brought into prominence. The examples of such autobiographical expressions, though fragmentary in nature and small in number, still possess an irresistible charm and their worth as autobiographical document is undeniably great. (12)

These literary efforts were never strong enough for this powerful mode of expression to find general acceptance. Moreover, the doctrine of *karma* and the importance of fate in the Hindu society undermined the significance of individual life. Autobiography is the outcome of intense individualism. Hence, with the lack of self-consciousness and an absence of the significance of an individual, autobiography, as a literary genre, could not be expected to germinate and grow in the traditional Indian society. The arrival of the British in India and the impact of English education brought about a renaissance in the Indian society. There was a radical change in the orthodox ideas which prompted a wide range of social reforms. With the break from the traditional beliefs and the inculcation of the liberal western ideas, the growth of individualism was bound to occur in renascent India, which, in turn, facilitated the growth of autobiography.

Raja Rammohun Roy has been called the father of modern India. His untiring endeavours for many social reforms were responsible for a great many social changes. Raja Rammohun Roy, with his autobiographical letter written to his friend, Mr. Gordon on his request, laid the foundation of this new literary genre and once again proved himself a pioneer. He knew that the traditional Hindus did not look favourably upon a Hindu revealing his own life. But he was a revolutionary and set about to give an account of his own life to one of his English friends. Similarly, Kasiprasad Ghose (1809-1873), an Indian English poet, gave a brief account of his life to the Rev. James Long. It appeared in 1834, soon after that of Rammohun Roy.

Though these two autobiographical letters marked the birth of this genre in English in India, yet they were brief sketches of the lives they dealt with. The first full-length autobiography appeared in 1854 when Lutfullah published the exciting and interesting experiences of his life. It is interesting to note that though this was the first full-length autobiography ever written by an Indian it became instantly popular in Europe and was liked both by its English and Indian readers. M. Garcin De Tassy states this fact in his *Histoire De La Litterature Hindouie Et Hindoustanie* (238).

The next autobiography was written by Rev. Lal Behari Day. His account of his early life, *Recollections of My School Days* was serialised in the *Bengal Magazine* from February, 1873 to May, 1876. Born in a small village of the Burdwan district of Bengal in 1824, Day moved to Calcutta for his school and higher education. He was converted to the Christian faith after completing his education in the General Assembly Institution which had been founded in 1830 by Rev. Alexander Duff. Before writing his autobiography he had already written and published a novel, *Govinda Samanta,* in English. His popular work *Folk Tales of Bengal* was also being serialised in the *Bengal Magazine* at approximately the same time. Thus, when his *Recollections of My School Days* was published, Lal Behari Day had already established himself as a zealous writer in English. Apart from this he was well known among the enlightened as a dedicated missionary and academician.

As the title of the autobiography suggests, it is limited to that early part of Day's life which he spent at school. Day, for this restricted account of his life, has a particular motive which he makes clear at the very beginning of his work: "Gentle reader! . . . I am about to relate to you at length the story of my education . . ." (PS 447). Education is largely responsible for the shaping of a man's personality. The period of education in a man's life is the most important part of that which he spends in this world. John Stuart Mill has expressed a similar motive for writing his autobiography. The account of his "unusual and remarkable" (Mill 1) education would serve, according to him, as an example to others. It is an important motive which has not yet lost its currency and popularity. Out of four books into which Nirad C. Chaudhary's *Autobiography of an Unknown Indian* is divided, the third one dealing with his education makes his motive explicit. R.C.P. Sinha, while discussing Chaudhary's autobiography states that the main theme of this autobiography is the making of a scholar's mind, ". . . it is the story of the author's education" (166). To Day the 'remarkable' education was the newly-introduced system of English education. He has striven to show that English education was far superior to the Oriental method of teaching, and, after giving a complete account of his school life, he puts down his pen.

It may appear that *Recollections of My School Days* is a partial, even incomplete autobiography. But the truth is that it is a full-length autobiography complete in itself. It comes under an independent genre which has acquired popularity over the past hundred and fifty years. It is the autobiography of childhood and adolescence or, more appropriately, according to Richard N. Coe, 'Childhood' (Coe, Preface xi). The 'Childhood' is not an incomplete or partial autobiography. It is a standard autobiography with a clear motive for taking up the account of the early life:

> The Childhood . . . narrates the development of the hero (who specifically *is* to be identified with the author) from a point of non-awareness to a point of total awareness of himself as an individual, and particularly as a writer and as a poet, who will produce, as evidence of his mature poet-identity, the Childhood which he has written (Coe 09).

The first ever example of a Childhood is *Page disgracie* which was written in 1642 and is a "sparkling autobiographical portrait of adolescence" (Coe 24) of the author, Tristan l' Hermite. After this initiation, the Childhood was caught in a chaotic turmoil in the eighteenth century and the beginning of the nineteenth century. There were a number of productions but they lacked the true characteristics of the genre. It was finally retrieved in 1835 by Stendhal when he wrote his autobiography *Vie de Henry Brulard.* This was a perfect example of Childhood.

Lal Behari Day is a pioneer in that he is the first Indian to write a Childhood in English. He begins his journey in his Childhood "from a point of total non-awareness" that is, from a time of which he has none or very little personal recollections. He ends the journey of his Childhood when he reaches the point of total awareness, that is, when he completes his school education and achieves maturity and is ready to go out in the world and prove his worth.

Day begins his autobiography by stating his identity humbly which shows his respect for and acknowledgement of his roots. He says: "As to who I am, I may tell you at once that I am my father's son. . ." (*PS* 447). This acknowledgement of the roots is characteristic of oriental culture. Even Raja Rammohun Roy states that his 'ancestors were Brahmins of a high order' (Collet 496) and Kasiprasad Ghose asserts in his autobiographical letter: "In caste I am a *Kayastha*, of the order called *Kulin*, or the high born, a descendent of Makranda Ghose. . ." (Shaw 506).

Day's recollections of his father are fond and affectionate. His father was a bill and stock broker in Calcutta. Brokers are usually supposed to be dishonest in their dealings. Day's father, however, was of a different sort, strictly honest and straight forward in his business. Day, with pride and reverence, informs us that his father "was an orthodox Hindu of the old Puritanic stamp, was strictly honest in his dealings; and it was because he was strictly honest that he did not get on well in the world, in the worldly sense of getting on well" (*PS* 447). One of the reasons why he did not get on well in the world, as he knew, was his ignorance of English. That is why he wanted his son to have an English education for, in his opinion, "a knowledge of English . . . was necessary to earn a competence in life" (*PS* 461). Nirad C. Chaudhary's father shares the same opinion regarding his son's education. We learn from Nirad C. Chaudhary's autobiography that his father wanted him to "acquire some ancillary qualification in the field of art which would lend grace to our life" (Chaudhary 151). Though Day's father was not as educated as Chaudhary's father, he just desired that his son should gain 'a decent livelihood' (*PS* 461). However, this decision of his father was responsible for Day's future education.

Day's father belonged originally to Dacca where he lived with his wife and two sons. In a sudden misfortune he lost his wife and sons to death. Heart-broken, he migrated to Sonapalasi, a small but picturesque village in West Bengal. However, Day mentions Talpur as his native village. These errors are found rampant in autobiographies as the present often tends to cast a shadow over accurate recollections. George Misch is of the opinion that "our most ordinary recollections are impregnated in our own minds by distorting influences. . ." (11). Day, having some personal reasons, would have altered the name of his native village. The bitter experience of his wife on her first visit to his native place might have prompted him to commit this deliberate error. However, this is not a significant error autobiographies 'are not to be regarded as objective narratives' (Misch 11). The mere change in the name of the birth place of the autobiographer does not have any impact on his personality.

The autobiography of Lal Behari Day is primarily the 'story of his education' (*PS* 447). He, therefore, speaks very little of his early childhood. In the first chapter only, he speaks of his childhood of which, he says, he remembers very little. However, he writes at length about an incident which, though it may appear trivial, had remained vivid in his memory all his life. One afternoon, without the knowledge of anyone, he had climbed up and gone to sleep on a high window-sill. After some time, when his absence was felt by the members of his family, they started looking frantically for him in the house as well as in the neighbourhood. He was finally discovered by one of his cousins, a fourteen-year old girl, who instantly took him in her arms and covered him with kisses and tears. This incident, which emphasizes the passionate feeling of belongingness, moved Day so much that it surfaced many years later in his novel in the form of the description of the missing of a small girl, Yadumani, whose body was found in a pond, murdered by robbers. In the case of Day, too, people of his village feared that he was drowned in a nearby pond. "As there was a small tank within a hundred yards of my house, most people supposed that I had strayed on its banks, dropped into it and had got drowned" (*PS* 449).

As there was a wide gulf between the views and beliefs of Lal Behari Day and that of his father – the son exposed to the radical world of Christianity and the father an orthodox Hindu—one may expect a certain amount of tension between the two. However, Day's recollections of his father are full of love and respect for his beliefs which are evident from the manner in which he speaks of his father's daily observations as a devout Hindu. "...my father was a strict Hindu of the orthodox stamp. He never ate any other than vegetable food in his life. Keep meat aside, he never ate fish. Of drinks, he took nothing but water and milk. He was diligent in the practice of all his religious duties" (*PS* 450).

As the purpose of Day's autobiography is to narrate the story of his education, he launches into it in the very second chapter of his work. Day was initiated into the realms of learning in 1830 at the age of five. His education began in the village *pathshala*. As is usual in an orthodox Bengali family, his initiation was accompanied by a religious ceremony. Astrologers were consulted and on an auspicious day he was taken to the village *pathshala* and the *gurumahasaya* who, with a simple ceremony admitted him to the school.

Lal Behari Day goes into detail in describing the school, the *gurumahasaya* and the mode of teaching. Irony and ridicule play an important part in his description of this 'House of Reading' and its owner. Upon the *pathshala* he remarks: "The *pathshala*, literally 'House of Reading', of the village of Talpur, had no house of its own. It met under the open sky on a spot of ground in front of a temple of Siva, which was situated in exactly the middle of the village. On two sides of this spot of ground there were six banyan trees, three on each side standing in a line: under these trees, ranged in rows sat the boys. There were of course no benches; each boy sat on a little mat or a gunny-bag which he brought every day from his house along with his writing materials" (*PS* 451). Day's description of the *gurumahasaya*, Gopi Kant Mukhopadhyaya, is marked both by ridicule and praise. While recounting his physical appearance Day becomes humorous:

> The presiding genius of this hall of learning was Gopi Kant Mukhopadhyaya. At the time I sat at his feet he was about thirty years old. He was about five feet nine, rather thin looking, had a fine head of hair which fell considerably below his neck, and which gave him a somewhat feminine appearance, an ample forehead, and a splendid pair of moustaches, which he kept continually twirling with his fingers. He was dressed in a simple *dhuti*; having no jama or chadar either. He always walked to school without shoes, at least I don't remember having seen him with either shoes or slippers on. What struck anyone who saw him was his snow-white *paita*, Brahmanical thread, which consisted of a great many threads and shone over his left shoulder and across his chest like the Milky Way in the heavens (PS, 453).

Regarding his merits as a teacher Day remarks ironically that though he was a school teacher and a Brahmin he was ignorant of Sanskrit. He was even unable to make proper use of many of the Bengali letters of the alphabet. He was the village schoolmaster simply because it was his family occupation and he had inherited it from his forefathers. Gopi Kant Mukhopadhyaya was, however, not without qualities. According to Lal Behari Day:

> ...the *gurumahasaya* was an arithmetician of the first force. All the rules of Subhankara, the Indian cocker, were at his fingers' ends. He could mentally go through intricate processes in the

> double rule of three without the use of slate and pencil or pen paper, and solve in a trice difficult questions in mensuration. And as to his penmanship, nothing could be more exquisitely beautiful. It was, as his pupils expressed it, *devakshara* – the penmanship of the gods (*PS* 453).

Though there was a single teacher in the village *pathshala* and the boys assembled 'under the open sky' without the provision of rooms, the students were arranged in four classes. This arrangement was, however, different from that adopted in English schools. The boys were arranged on the basis of material they used for writing.

> The last class were called the 'floor boys', because they traced the letters of the Bengali alphabet by means of ochre on the floor or on the ground; the third class were called the 'palm-leaf-boys', because they wrote on palm leaves with pens of reed; the second class were called 'plantain-leaf-boys', because they wrote on plantain leaves; and the first or highest class were called 'paper boys', because they wrote on paper (*PS* 452).

Day, then, goes on to speak in detail about the mode of teaching in the village *pathshala* and his progress in the realms of knowledge. He was in the paper class when he had to leave for Calcutta because his father wanted him to receive better education, particularly the knowledge of English.

The journey from his village to Calcutta marked a turning point in Day's life. It was a journey from rural life to urban life, from ignorance to enlightenment, from darkness to light. It is because of this that he narrates this journey in detail. He also describes his guide, the Kasid or the courier-messenger who bears the credit, according to Day, for giving him the first lesson in geography by "teaching me to distinguish a river from a tank" (*PS* 465).

Day, however, found it difficult in the beginning to adjust to the unhygienic environment of a city life. It was not unusual for a young boy who was used to the fresh healthy air and the openness of countryside. Day fell sick before he was able to get an admission into an English school. "I had scarcely been a month in Calcutta when I had a violent attack of diarrhoea, from which I had hardly recovered when I was laid prostrate by severe form of fever" (*PS* 465). It was only after he recovered that he could be admitted to an English school.

Before recounting the story of his education in Calcutta, Day gives, in Chapter IV, a short history of English education in Calcutta before 1834. It may be argued that this historical account interrupts the flow of the narrative. But this deviation is justifiable in that it has, unlike Lutfullah's autobiography, a solemn motive. Day wants to apprise the reader of the importance and impact of English education in India. For this he finds it necessary to pinpoint the causes which led to the popularity and progress of English education on the Indian soil. Moreover, his style is so elevated and captivating that one hardly feels the interruption. Equally interesting is his anecdote regarding the first English scholar – who was, in fact, a *dhobi* or washer man – among the Bengalis. It so happened that towards the end of the seventeenth century, an English ship sailed up and anchored at Hooghly. The captain of the ship requested the local businessmen to send a *dobhasia* or interpreter. This word was used mostly on the western coasts of India and was unknown to the Bengalis. As a result they misunderstood the term and sent a *dhobi* instead. This *dhobi* came into regular contact with the Englishmen on the ship and gained a little knowledge of English words.

In this chapter, Day discusses two landmarks in the history of English education in India. The first was the setting up of

Hindu College in 1817 and second was the founding of the General Assembly Institution in 1830. The former was founded by the joint efforts of David Hare, a watchmaker by trade and a dedicated educationist and Sir Edward Hyde East, the then Chief Justice of the Calcutta Supreme Court. The latter was the result of the endeavours of the Church of Scotland and the Rev. Alexander Duff, a missionary educationist. As Day was admitted to Duff's Institution, he gives a brief sketch of the opening of General Assembly Institution. Duff's name as a devoted missionary had spread widely among the Hindus of Bengal.. It was believed that Duff's main aim was to convert the Hindu youth to the Christian faith. It is interesting to note that Day considered it a 'serious drawback' at this later stage of his life when he himself had embraced Christianity:

> . . . there was one serious drawback. Dr. Duff (he was then simply Mr. Duff) was a most zealous missionary. He made no secret of it, but publicly avowed, that his chief object in setting up the Institution was to initiate the Hindu youth into the principals of the Christian religion. He had already appeared as a Public Lecturer on Christianity, and his lectures had taken Calcutta by storm. Those lectures had not only created a great sensation in the Hindu community, but had brought to the Christian faith some of the brightest and most intelligent youth of the city (*PS* 474).

One such young man was Krishna Mohan Banerjee whose conversion had unsettled many of the orthodox Hindus.

In view of Duff's missionary zeal and the subsequent conversion, many of the friends of Day's father tried to dissuade him from sending Day to Duff's school. Day's father was, however, adamant and he gave two arguments to ward off the dissuaders. The first was that:

> though Dr. Duff was a very zealous missionary he never baptized young boys who were unacquainted with the Christian religion, but baptized those only who had studied English for at least seven or eight years; that he did not intend to make me of me a learned man, but to give me so much knowledge of English as would enable me to obtain a decent situation; and that long before I was able to understand lectures on Christian religion, he would withdraw me from the Institution. . . (*PS* 474).

The second was the argument of a staunch fatalist that his father was. He said: .

> If it is written on Kala Gopal's forehead that he will not become Christian, then he will not become Christian, let Duff sahib do what he can, but if it is written on Kala Gopal's forehead that he will become Christian do what I can (*PS* 475).

These two arguments clinched the issue and Day was admitted to Duff's General Assembly Institution in the year 1834 – the date and the month not remembered by the author. Lal Behari Day continues the story of his education in a lively manner though it lacks compactness and order. The story is not narrated in a chronological order and is marked by many interruptions. These interruptions are so frequent that they sometimes threaten to destroy completely the sense of order which is an important aspect of an autobiography. They, however, serve to show the system of English education in Duff's institution which was by far one of the most popular schools not only in Bengal but in the whole of India.

The method of teaching adopted in General Assembly Institution was aimed at bringing out the hidden talent of the student. Day writes that at the time of his admission he was so ignorant of English that he was unable even to distinguish between the letters of the English alphabet. But the method of teaching was such that he soon acquired not only a perfect knowledge of the alphabets but could read monosyllabic words and simple sentences in English as well. This outstanding method of teaching which was called the Socratic or the interrogatory method was the backbone of Dr. Duff's system of teaching. According to Duff:

> Education. . .is, as the etymology of the word shows, the bringing out of whatever is in the mind, that is to say, the development of all its powers and susceptibilities, intellectual, moral, social and religious. In most systems of education knowledge is communicated to the pupils (*PS* 507).

The General Assembly Institution did not merely communicate knowledge, it aimed at bringing out of students "whatever they had by a process of close questioning; criticised that imperfect knowledge; subjected it to the crucible of investigation, and thus purified it; and last of all added to its stores" (*PS* 507). Day, then, proceeds to give a detailed description of the interrogatory method, through examples. The method was highly successful and students benefited immensely from this method adopted by Duff in his institution:

> The ideas of the pupils were greatly encouraged; their powers of thinking were developed; they were encouraged to observe; their stock of knowledge increased not in an arithmetical but in a geometrical ratio; and as learning was made pleasant to them, their affections were drawn towards the acquisition of knowledge (*PS* 509).

Another aspect of the education system in General Assembly Institution was the teaching of science in addition to literature. It is fascinating to note that while in the fourth decade the teaching of science had not properly permeated into the education system of the Indian schools, the General Assembly Institution had already started teaching a course which included Physical

Science, Mechanics, Hydrostatics, Pneumatics, Optics, Astronomy, the steam engine, Chemistry, Geology, etc.

The most important feature, however, was the teaching of literature and science with their bearing on morals and religion. It was not unusual as the institution itself was founded with religious aim. But this complete impregnation gave a new outlook even to the teaching of modern science. Day writes in his beautiful style: "Literature and Science were animated, vivified, hallowed and baptized in the spirit of true religion" (*PS* 510).

Day soon adjusted to this new system of education. Of his achievement Day speaks but little as a modest person would do. He received the highest prize in the eighth class. He was not satisfied with a single promotion and applied for treble promotion to Dr. Ewart who was the head of the institution as Duff was away in Scotland on account of illness. As he was the youngest pupil in the class, Dr. Ewart refused to comply with his wishes. However, on the request of Lal Behari Day Dr. Ewart examined and found him fit for the fifth class. Dr. Ewart began to take a keen interest in this young boy who had so much of talent in him. Self-praise is not an easy task for a humble man. Day requests his readers not to consider him vain for his being truthful about himself:

> I shall be glad if I am only thought ridiculous, for I much fear that the reader will think me a great deal worse when he hears what I have to say about myself, he will probably think me vain. But gentle reader! Don't ascribe vanity to me. Vanity is the besetting sin of youth; but as an OLD BOY I have passed the age of vanity. Attribute it rather to garrulity, which the besetting sin of old age (*PS* 491).

Day's early life was not a bed of roses. He had to encounter several hardships in his school days. The trouble began when he was granted treble promotion. Some of the boys began harassing him to the point of even beating him up in the streets after school hours. He, however, overcome this difficulty by turning the public opinion of the class against them. It was at end of the same year 1837 that Lal Behari Day's father passed away. As Day was very fond of his father, this came as a great shock to him. Though he attended his father day and night in the last few days, he expresses regret for not being present at his father's bedside at the time of his death.

> I saw my father's lifeless body stretched on the *khat*. I gave a shriek and wept bitterly, and reproached myself for having been quietly sleeping while my father was struggling with the last enemy" (*PS* 496).

Gandhi, too, had the same regret when he failed to serve his dying father. But in his case it arose not from sleep but from lust (Gandhi 43).

With his father was gone what little support Day had of his never-buoyant exchequer. Had it not been for a cousin of his who gave him shelter, food and clothing and to whom he pays his grateful tribute, he would have to abandon his studies and leave Calcutta. Beside this kind cousin there were others who lent a helping hand to the author during his period of distress. Though they did not have any direct impact on his intellectual growth, yet they had an emotional and affective relationship with him. Day feels indebted to these characters and portrays them in his *Recollections* with an overwhelming sense of gratitude. One of these characters was Kunjo's mother, the cook in the house of his cousin. She was a cripple and could not stand on her legs. It was she who, despite her handicap and several other difficulties, used to get up early in the morning and prepare breakfast for Day to enable him to go to school on time. Day was so touched by kindness that he remembers her after the lapse of so many years and writes almost one full chapter of his *Recollections* in her memory. Speaking about Kunjo's mother he remarks:

> That she exercised self-denial on my account will appear evident when it is remembered that no orthodox Hindu woman ever cooks before bathing. When I recollect that this poor deformed cripple got up from her bed some two hours before sunrise, that she rowed downstairs with the help of her hands, that she bathed at about five o'clock in the morning in the weather, that she did all this only to enable me to go to school at the proper time – when I remember all this, I cannot but feel grateful to her (*PS* 518).

Another character who helped him considerably in his pursuit of studies, though not directly, was a hawker of books whom Day used to address as *Pagla Chacha* or the mad uncle. He was half-witted but was very fond of Day. As Day's financial state was never (even when his father was alive) strong enough to enable him to buy new books as he had an unquenchable thirst for books, he turned to this half-witted though kind dealer of old, half-torn and dilapidated books. As he had very little to invest, he used to return a book after reading it and get another one in place of it. Day, therefore, felt greatly indebted to his *Pagla Chacha.*

There were other minor characters to whom Day pays his debt by way of mention. One was Lazim Mandal, a strong youth and schoolmate of Day who had given him physical support and defended him many times on the street from his tormentors, the students who were against his treble promotion.

Day's autobiography is the story of his education. It is, therefore, quite natural for him to pay his respect to those teachers who helped him in the making and shaping of his intellect. In the last chapter titled 'My Instructors – In Memoriam', he writes in detail about three of the five teachers to whom he was "indebted for the unfolding of my intellectual and moral being" (*PS* 548).

One of these missionary teachers was the Rev. William Sinclair MacKay – a scholar in the real sense of the term. He was well read in Greek and Latin literature and contributed to various magazines of the time such as the *Calcutta Christian Observer* and the *Calcutta Review*. Apart from his literary exploits he was a mathematician and an astronomer. He was probably the first astronomer in India having his own observatory. Day attended his lectures on astronomy for three years. He not only discussed the theories of astronomy but demonstrated its application to navigation. It was Dr. MacKay who familiarised the students of the Institution with the principles of the steam engine long before the system of railway was introduced in India. Besides literature and science, Dr. MacKay also lectured on the Evidence of Christianity which had a great impact on Day's mind:

> I seemed to be introduced into entirely a new world of thought, and the impressions I then received have never been effaced from my mind, though there have been from time to time new and fresh ideas on those subjects (*PS* 552).

Another missionary teacher to whom Day offers his respect is the Rev. David Ewart. Though he was not as talented as Dr. Sinclair William MacKay, he excelled as a kind and loving teacher. The Rev. Ewart was a benevolent teacher who sympathized with his students and was always eager to help them whenever there was a need. Lal Behari Day gives a pen-portrait of the Rev. Ewart in the following words:

> The perfect equanimity of his temper; his freedom from all prejudice; the philosophic coolness of his judgment; his frankness which was even visible in his countenance, the rigid uprightness of his character, never swerving in the slightest

> degree for a moment from the path of rectitude; his gentleness which more resembled that of a woman than of a stout, stalwart man upwards of six feet high; his wonderful patience, in bearing on his shoulders the cares of a large educational establishment and listening to the complaints of his pupils; his kindness to poor students, assisting some with books and others with means of livelihood from his own pocket; the lively interest that he took in the welfare of those who had at any period of their lives sat at his feet, readily giving them letters of recommendation, and endeavouring to get employment for them; and above all his charity which led him never to think evil of any men, Hindu, Mohammedan or Christian – the exhibition of these virtues in the daily life and conversation of David Ewart was to me more instructive than a course of lectures on Ethics or a whole body of Divinity (*PS* 554).

Another missionary father who left an indelible mark on the mind of Day, was the Rev. John Macdonald, who, though he had gained proficiency in classical literature, philosophy and mathematics, had been sent to the General Assembly Institution to impart to the students the teachings of the *Bible*. The contribution of this theologian was great, as Day remarks:

> He took me through nearly the whole of the *Bible* from Genesis to Revelation excepting some of the minor Prophets, expounding the sacred writings with great clearness and power, pouring a flood of light on difficult passages, and removing infidel and rationalistic objections with singular logical acumen. And his lectures on Christian theology, of which I took copious notes, were to me of the utmost value. It was from those lectures that I first obtained a systematic view of all the doctrines of Christianity (*PS* 555).

Beside these teachers, Day mentions briefly the impact on him of Dr. Thomas Smith who was mainly responsible for the flowering of his literary genius and the shaping of his style. Dr. Smith taught English composition in the Institution. He was a master of English composition and favoured plain Anglo-Saxon style. Among his several pieces of advice on the style of writing, he firmly discouraged preface-making. "Dr. Smith . . . impressed on us the principle of directness of thought, clearance of language and downrightness of manner – qualities absolutely necessary to all good composition" (*PS* 551-552).

These missionary teachers had their everlasting impression on Day and were definitely responsible for his shaping as a good human being, as a devout Christian and, above all, as a literary genius. But the greatest impression was cast by Dr. Alexander Duff, the founder of the General Assembly Institution. Dr. Duff's life and his influence on Lal Behari Day have been discussed in a separate chapter of this thesis.

Keeping in view the influence of these highly qualified and devoted teachers and their pronounced emphasis on the doctrines of Christianity, it is not surprising that by the time Day completed his studies, he was fully prepared to embrace Christianity.

One of the motives of Day for writing his *Recollections of My School Days* is to show the superiority of the English system of education over the oriental or native system of education. His sense of irony and ridicule in portraying the village school master, Gopi Kant Mukhopadhyaya, when contrasted with his eulogistic portrayal of the missionary teachers, proves the same. In a similar vein he portrays some native teachers of the General Assembly Institution. We find most of the traits of the *gurumahasaya* in them.

Three pundits who taught arithmetic, Bengali and Sanskrit were ill-tempered and cruel and never hesitated to use the rod which Duff so vehemently opposed. One of these pundits even used filthy language and abusive words with his students. Another teacher who taught Urdu stood on the other extreme. He was so submissive as to be bullied by the students who wanted to have their own way. The native teachers were total misfits in the new milieu.

The motive that impelled the writing of this autobiography becomes explicit as we go through it from beginning to the end. Day follows the course of his education from the village *pathshala* to the General Assembly Institution and at the end he pays a glowing tribute to his mentors. This narrative is interspersed with many of his comments on various aspects of English education. There is, however, many a time when he interrupts the flow of the narrative with a digression which, apparently, has nothing to do with his education. For instance, he includes a chapter in which he narrates how he had to carry the dead body of a child to the cremation ground which was three or four miles away from his house. The only explanation that justifies its inclusion in his autobiography is that this horrifying experience had made a firm imprint on his mind and lay suppressed in him since its occurrence. He found this narrative as an outlet to unburden his memory.

In another chapter he tells us about one of his journeys from Calcutta to Talpur. It has already been mentioned that his journey from Talpur to Calcutta was very significant as it marked a turning point in his life. Therefore, its description was inevitable. The mention and detailed description of the journey from Calcutta to Talpur is significant, too, as it reveals another part of his personality – his love for the countryside, particularly his village. He hated Calcutta for its busy life, stink and sickness, and, whenever he had an opportunity, he visited the countryside to enjoy fresh air, natural beauty and simplicity of life. He usually spent his winter vacations in his native village. He gives an almost poetic description of early morning natural landscape of the countryside:

> . . . after washing my mouth and eyes I went out to the outskirts of the village for a stroll. O! How I enjoyed those strolls in the prime hour of 'incense-breathing morn'! The sun is not up yet, but the glowing east behind yon mango top heralds his speedy approach. The grass is yet studded with pearly dew, and gives out a fresh and peculiar fragrance. That umbrageous and beautiful *vakula* tree, on the branches of which hundreds of birds found shelter last night, is not yet emptied of all its feathery lodgers; they are now flying away, sometimes singly and each pair by itself but often in bevies. All nature seems fresh as if just awakened from repose. What pomp of vegetation is here displayed! The gigantic *vata* with its smooth foliage and its crimson berry, the stately *aswatha* around which cluster a thousand associations, the sturdy tamarind tree remarkable alike for its strength and its beneficence to man, the graceful *kadamba* with its beautiful flower, diffusing fragrance all around, and the tall Palmyra towering over all with its tufted crown – all this presents a scene of fascination which it is impossible to describe (*PS* 536).

Lal Behari's love for nature is also reflected in his novel, *Govinda Samanta.*

It is the same love for rural folk which makes him recount the festivities of the Durga Puja. Though he criticises severely the puja on grounds of idolatry, he knows that this is one of the few occasions which bring happiness to the poor in whose life sorrows and sufferings are regular visitors. "It is the season of universal festivity, the rich and the poor, the high and the low, the *raja* and the *raiyat*, the Brahman and the *Chandal*, alike welcome it with exultant hearts" (*PS* 539).

*Recollections of My School Days* is the autobiography of Day's childhood. However, Day interrupts quite a few times to tell the reader something about the system of English education in India, to relate some of his unusual experiences and to acquaint the reader with Indian festivals. But he stops when his school life comes to an end. Day could have continued his story even beyond it. He, however, abstains from it since his primary aim is to present the story of the making of his mind. His actions, feelings and experiences of his later life were a direct outcome of what he had learnt in school. That was the most important part of his life.

The style adopted by Day to tell the story of his life is quite eloquent. It is marked by humour and irony which give life to the pen-pictures that he has drawn in his work and also serve to reveal his lively temperament. He has adopted both narrative and descriptive methods to fulfil his motive. It can be concluded with R.C.P. Sinha's remark in his *Indian Autobiographies in English* regarding the style of Lal Behari Day:

> The strength of the writer lies, however, in his power to describe with extraordinary vividness the incidents and experiences of his life. Both Lutfullah and Lal Behari Day survey the outward course of their career but they differ widely from each other in their approach and intention. The former is concerned with the simple narration of exciting episodes of his life and it is not the manner of relating the incidents but the incidents themselves that make his account interesting. The latter, however, is a greater master of style, and can, by his manner of writing, make even trivial incidents exquisitely interesting. A pervasive sense of wit and humour adds to the intrinsic beauty of his narrative (54-55).

## Works Cited

Saha Mahadevprasad (ed.), *Lal Behari Day: Bengal Peasant Life, Folk Tales of Bengal, Recollections of My School Days*, Calcutta, 1969, Print

[*NB:* The above work has been cited in the paper as *PS*, i.e., Primary Source]

Chaudhary, Nirad C. *Autobiography of an Unknown Indian*. London. 1951.

Coe, Richard N. *When the Grass Was Taller: Autobiography and the Experience of Childhood.* Yale University. 1984.

Collet, Sophia Dobson. *The Life and Letters of Raja Rammohun Roy,* edited by D. K. Biswas and P. C. Ganguli. Sadharan Brahmo Samaj. Calcutta. 1962.

De Tassy, M. Garcin. *Histoire De La Litterature Hindouie Et Hindoustanie.* Paris. 1870. Vol. II.

*Encyclopedia Britannica.* Vol. 2. Edition 19.

Gandhi, M.K. *An Autobiography or The Story of My Experiments With Truth.* Ahmedabad. 1948.

Mill, John Stuart. *Autobiography.* London. 1882.

Misch, George. *A History of Autobiography in Antiquity.* Vol. 1. London. 1950.

Naik, D.G. *Art of Autobiography.* Poona. 1962.

Shaw, John Farquhar. *The Rev. James Long's Handbook of Bengal Missions.* London. 1848.

Sinha, R.C.P. *The Indian Autobiographies in English.* New Delhi. 1978.

# 19

# Feministic Study of Doris Lessing's Autobiographies *Under My Skin* and *Walking in the Shade*

**Brajesh Sawhney & Ajit Kumar**

> In five years time, I'll be saying, my god, what a fool I was. I really do feel this way about every two years—what a fool I was two years ago.
>
> —*Doris Lessing*

In the postmodern literature, all the writers, who are more explicitly committed to feminist politics and more formally adventures in their engagements with the postmodern, are equally resistant to the indiscriminate aestheticization, or idealization of female experience and identities. Women's autobiography, once acknowledged as an inferior and devalued genre, has now achieved a significant place in literary writing and criticism. The publication of anthologies on the subject has increased over the past few decades. Also, well-known authors have written numerous autobiographies.

For Carter, Byatt and Drabble began writing in the shadow of that earlier generation of women writers, Lessing, Spark and Murdoch, who had come of age during World War II. After Nazism, it had seemed evident to them that the projection of Promethean desire beyond the controlled realm of art had, as often as not, realized a hell of violence rather than an

"Aestheticized Utopia" (Singleton 194). The counter-cultural and situationist slogans which fed into the liberation movement of the sixties, of taking one's desire for reality, even more than the technocratic state, could be seen to invest in a potentially destructive aestheticization of experience. Women writers of this generation therefore were often both cautious about utopian politics and also anxious to explore the issue of female authorship in the context of broader ethical and political commitments. Autobiography also has a healing power enabling both the writer and the reader to cope with the wounds of the past. Hence, women find a chance to speak the unspeakable by writing their life stories and they hold mirrors to the lives of other women. Writing biographies have become the vehicle of revelation of truth making confessions of self rather than pouring emotions and feelings only.

The most prolific of contemporary British writers and the recipient of more than twenty literary prizes and awards, Doris Lessing, one of the most important writers in British literature, as a woman autobiographer presents her life story and experience in *Under My Skin: Volume One of My Autobiography to 1949 and Walking in the Shade: Volume Two of My Autobiography, 1949-1962.* The first volume recounts the first thirty years of Lessing's life, from her birth in Persia in 1919, through her childhood and young adulthood in Southern Rhodesia (now Zimbabwe), to her departure, in 1949, for London, where she would make her career as a writer with the typescript of her first novel, *The Grass is Singing.* Briefly, in this volume, she describes how her mother loved her younger brother, Harry, but not her; how she was not in love with her first husband, nor he with her, "though such were the intoxications of the time it was easy to think so" (Lessing, *Skin* 206); how she left him with their two young children, intent on making the world a better place for them how she then married

Gottfried Lessing, a German refugee and comrade, "but only because in those days people could not have affairs, let alone live together" (Lessing, *Skin* 293). She has focused on all the hidden aspects of life. She describes the political scene of wartime Salisbury, where she joined a group of Communists, selling their newspaper, *The Guardian*, to locals. A portrait of the developing writer, in love with books, can be seen in this volume. If we do not know what is important in our memories, as Lessing states, we have to create our lives and our memory. In our daily lives, we make up our pasts. We can actually watch our minds doing it, thinking a little fragment of fact and then spinning a tale out of it (Lessing, *Skin* 13). This making up of past is seen in the first chapter, where Doris Lessing introduces her parents and her grandparents. Here, she even writes about the days before she was born. The devastating impact of the First World War on her parents is her main focus. Alfred Cook Tayler, Lessing's father, loses a leg in the trenches and marries the nurse who helped him in his hard times; already thirty-five, she herself loses her lover in the war. After giving information on how her parents met and married, Lessing tells the story of her birth as if she remembers all the details:

> I was born on the 22nd October 1919. My mother had a bad time. It was a forceps birth. My face scarred purple for days. Do I believe this difficult birth scarred me—that is to say, my nature? Who knows. I do know that to be born in the year 1919 when half of Europe was a graveyard, and people were dying in millions all over the world—that was important (Lessing, *Skin* 8).

It is generally seen in women's autobiographies that writer relates herself with others. Doris Lessing identifies herself with her father and mother, because of this she prefers to talk about the days before she was born. And Doris Lessing hides no feelings related to this period of her life.

Doris Lessing expresses another reason why she wanted to write this autobiography. Her parents' decision of migrating to Southern Rhodesia has been a question. But Lessing answers it through her first attempt of biographies *Under My Skin*. She tells that Southern Rhodesia has become a symbol of prosperity. She reveals:

> It is believed that when the whites arrived in the area that later became Southern Rhodesia, there were a quarter of a million people. By about 1924, there were about half a million...In 1993 they think they are twelve or thirteen million. Some demographers there will be a thirty million by 2010. It is currently thought by most experts that the continual increase of population since the whites arrived is because Portuguese introduced maize which is easily grown, abundant, easily stored and nourishing. (Lessing, *Under My Skin* 420)

In fact, thorough this fact, Doris Lessing want to present that she has been a daughter of a socially, economically wise parents. At the same time, she seems to praise the whatever place she lives in. When she migrates to London. She says, "I held my little boy and said, 'Look, there is London...wooden walls and beams, cranes, tugs, little and big ships'" (Lessing, *Walking* 3). She wants to say that this autobiography is also an alternative history of the end of British colonialism:

> One reason for writing this autobiography is that more and more I realize I was part of an extraordinary time, the end of the British Empire in Africa, and the bit I was involved with was the occupation of a country that lasted exactly ninety years. People no longer know what that time was like, even those who live in Southern Africa. My own children can be surprised when I tell them this and that, are perhaps disconcerted at the roughness of those times....The sometimes paternalistic, sometimes brutal relations between white and black then have changed. African friends, white friends, may be infuriated or amused at my father and Old Smoke philosophizing for hours

> sitting on either end of a log while they watched the "boys" at work. Whites will refuse to believe in the brutalities of Cyril Larter or Bob Matthews, or that white adolescents were not rebuked by their parents for pretending 'as a joke' to run down a black man or child in the car along the track, or that the more stupid white men played cruel jokes on their employees. (*Skin* 160-61)

Truly, pointing at some facts of life to the whole world is like an attempt to bring a new picture which is improved and may be not accepted openly. Belinda Bozzoli describes Doris Lessing's work as "more therapeutic than confessional" (2). Even Joanne Frye discusses the therapeutic nature of much diary writing or self-representational writing. He provides an examination of Anna Wulf's diary writing in *The Golden Notebook* and comments of Lessing that "part of her complex effort is to erode the boundaries between writing and living one's life"(2). She has been terribly poor, always in trouble for a small place to live in, in her life. She reveals this through her discussion with Joan:

> 'What you doing?'
> 'Cleaning my house,' she said.
> 'But it isn't your house.'
> 'Yes it is.'
> 'You'd better have documents to prove it, then.'
>
> (Lessing, *Walking* 20).

However, she faces with the first problem of the self-chronicler; 'truth'. She feels a true sense of consciousness and has a new paradigm to think and initiate a new journey in her life. She says:

> I left Southern Rhodesia in 1949, because there are few people left who can be hurt by what I say; I have had to leave out, or change mostly a name or two—very little. So Volume One is being written without snags and blocks of conscience. But Volume Two, that is from the time I reached London, will be

> different matter, even if I follow the example of Simone de Beauvoir who said that about some things she had no intention of telling the truth... I have known not a few of the famous, and even one or two of the great, but I do not believe it is the duty of friends, lovers, comrades, to tell all. The older I get the more secrets I have, never to be revealed and this, I know, is a common condition of people of my age. And why all this emphasis on kissing and telling? Kisses are the least of it.
>
> (*Walking* 11)

According to Doris Lessing, the problem of shifting perspectives is a bigger problem than telling the truth or not telling it. It is not the end of tragic tales in her life, Doris shares the hard time when she lacks money in her life for stay and food:

> I survived from cheque to cheque. Joan did not mind my weekly rent being paid two weeks or three weeks late. Once, the debt ran on until it was five weeks, and this made me sick and worry, because she did not have much money either...I was walking down Church Street, having dropped the child at school, and I was crying because I could not buy food...I sold my mother's jewellery. (Lessing, *Walking* 124)

She asserts that people see their lives differently at different stages. Lessing resembles this like climbing a mountain while the landscape changes with the every turn in the path. She says:

> ...am at once submerged in a hot struggle of emotion, justified by thoughts and ideas I now judge wrong. Besides, the landscape itself is a tricky thing. As you start to write at once the question begins to insist: Why do you remember this and not that? Why do you remember in every detail a whole week, month, more, of a long ago year ... How do you know that what you remember is more important than... (*Walking* 12).

The second volume of Doris Lessing's extraordinary autobiography covers the years 1949-62, from her arrival in war-weary London with her son, Peter, and the manuscript for her first novel, *The Grass is Singing,* under her arm to the publication of her most famous work of fiction, *The Golden Notebook.* She describes how communism dominated the intellectual life of the 1950s and how she, like nearly all communists, became disillusioned with extreme and rhetorical politics and left communism behind. Evoking the bohemian days of a young writer and single mother, Lessing speaks openly about her writing process, her friends and lovers, her involvement in the theater, and her political activities. *Walking in the Shade* is an invaluable social history as well as Doris Lessing's Sentimental Education. Doris Lessing offers an account of this incident which happened when she was staying with the novelist Naomi Mitchison. "Naomi asked me to take a certain inarticulate young scientist for a walk. And for goodness' sake, get him to say *something* – his tongue will atrophy" (Lessing, *Walking* 113).

> His name was James Watson. For about three hours we walked about over the hills and through the heather, while I chatted away, my mother's daughter: one should know how to put people at their ease. At the end of it, exhausted, wanting only to escape, I at last heard human speech. "The trouble is, you see, that there is only one other person in the world I can talk to." I reported this to Naomi, and we agreed that it was as dandified a remark as we could remember, even from a very young man. (*Walking* 113).

What is striking in this narrative is not so much the distance Lessing establishes between herself and the awkward young scientist, as the connections which she also points towards: While he is working on the scientific mechanisms of human inheritance, she too presents herself in terms of patterns of descent, as her mother's daughter, behaving like her mother in spite of herself. Lessing responds to and interrogates the models of inheritance developed by twentieth-century science, in the context of her own longstanding preoccupation with questions of motherhood and inheritance.

Through her autobiography, she wants to draw attention to the terrible war and its consequences. She tries to say that in such a bad condition, her birth becomes a sign of hope for future. In 1990 which is the year she began to write *Under My Skin*, Lessing is still under the influence of World War I. What she has tried to do is just to put light on the hidden aspects of her life and atmosphere around her. She says, "All over Europe, in every city, town, and village is a war memorial, with the names of the dead of World War I…" (Lessing, *Skin* 9). She believes, "her generation was made by war: I used to joke that it was the war that had given birth to me, as a defence when weary with the talk about the war that went on-and on-and on. But it was no joke. I used to feel there was something like a grey cloud, like poison gas, over my early childhood (Lessing, *Skin* 10). But later she feels, "I found people who had the same experience. Perhaps it was from that war that I first felt the struggling panicky need to escape, with a nervous aversion to where I have just stood, as if something there might blow up or drag me down by the heel" (Lessing, *Skin* 10). As it is seen above, in Doris Lessing's autobiography, war plays an important role. The experience of war deeply affects her. Another striking theme in this personal narrative is the relationship between Lessing and her mother. It is not surprising to see this relationship in the centre of an autobiography written by a woman. As Brodzki asserts, mother is the pre-text for the daughter's autobiographical project (157). She continues as follows:

> Indeed, these autobiographical narratives are generated out of a compelling need to enter into discourse with the absent or

> distant mother. As the child's first significant Other, the mother engenders subjectivity through language; she is the primary source of speech and love. And part of the maternal legacy is the conflation of the two. Thereafter, implicated in and overlaid with other modes of discourse, the maternal legacy of language becomes charged with ambiguity and fraught with ambivalence. In response (however deferred), the daughter's text, variously seeks to reject, reconstruct and reclaim—to locate and recontextualize—the mother's message (157).

Doris Lessing has got her ideas all indifferent towards her mother. She describes her mother "as always doing the best as she saw it, a good sort, a good sport" (*Skin* 26). She is always in a state of accusation against her mother.

Doris Lessing's mother wants her to be a proper daughter. She puts a rigid system of rules and hygiene at home. Both mother and daughter had different perspective of living the life. In her autobiographical project, Doris rejects the role that is given by her mother. She, in fact, has almost opposite opinion to her mother towards life. Once, Lessing reveals her thoughts about her mother as:

> All you need is love. Love is all you need. A child should be governed by love, as my mother so often said, explaining her methods to us. She had not known love as a child, and was making sure we would not be similarly deprived. The trouble is, love is a word that has to be filled with an experience of love. What I remember is hard bundling hands, impatient arms and her voice telling me over and over again that she had not wanted a girl, she wanted a boy. I knew from the beginning she loved my little brother unconditionally, and she did not love me (*Skin* 25).

In *Under My Skin*, Doris Lessing generally refers to the memories about her mother that filled her with hatred. She is as if taking her revenge from her mother. One of these memories is about the day which she starts to wear a bra. It is a very embarrassing situation for Doris. Her mother calls her father and her brother to expose Doris's breasts. She is "consumed with rage and hatred" (*Skin* 171). Neither her father nor her mother like displays of emotion. Her father is affectionate but he is not tender. If her mother's daughter had been like her, of the same substance, everything would have gone well. However, according to Lessing, it is her misfortune to have an over-sensitive, always observant and judging, battling, impressionable, hungry-for-love child. Lessing feels that her mother has never allowed her to live her life the way she wants. Lessing hates when her mother kept insisting, "I always came first, because I had a good memory. You are just like me." Her so frequent "You are just like me" made her white-hot with rage (*Skin* 150). Years later, the relationship between Doris Lessing and her mother is still the same. They face with the same problems when she is a grown up and married woman.

She has had her own way of living the life. That is why, sometimes she finds her mother standing in the way of her life style what she had desire to live like. Lessing sees her as a threat in her life although her mother is old and has to look after her father: What was going on in her life was certainly more than she could bear. My father was now permanently ill. She reveals:

> His liver...bowels...stomach...his good leg was so thin now he could hardly walk. There she was, alone with him on the farm, and he could no longer safely drive. She was always appealing to neighbours for lifts in to town, and she hated being dependent. Why did she not learn to drive? She did later, in town. Her letters to me were, in the current idiom, cries for help. To me they were threatening. She was a threat: half an hour with her reduced me to exhaustion. After a visit from her I would go to bed and sleep (*Skin* 223).

However, her individual way of living a life is sometime blamed as selfish. Once more, Doris Lessing and her mother's traumatic relation is seen above where they have their own perception towards life. This time, her mother blames Lessing for being selfish and not to think of no one just herself. Actually, her mother is the one who is selfish. She is cold and remote to her children but she expects warmth from her daughter. Only when Lessing becomes a mother herself, she feels sympathy and pity for her mother. In the following chapters, Lessing tells her experiences in the school. Like most of the girls living in colonies, Doris Lessing attends the Convent school. She describes the atmosphere in the Convent as "unwholesome" (*Skin* 93), a favourite word of her mother's. Lessing tells the story of her Convent days as:

> I was at the Convent for four years. Or for eternity, I used to wake up in the morning with the clang of the bell and not believe I would live through that interminable day until the night. And, after this endless day would be another...then another. I was in the grip of homesickness like an illness. It is an illness... I wanted to be home. I wanted my mother, my father, and my little brother, who until he was eight was still at home. I wanted my dogs and my cat. I wanted to be near the birds and animals of the bush. I did not believe it would ever end. I have exchanged recollections with men who were sent to schools in England aged seven, and some remember this weight of misery. There must be by now hundreds of memoirs, autobiographies, testifying to the misery of small children sent too young to school. (96)

It was really difficult for Doris Lessing to understand how parents send small children to boarding school knowing the fact their children would suffer as they did once upon a time. She claims, "This says something pretty important about human nature. Or about the British" (*Skin* 96-97). By the time Doris Lessing leaves the Convent, she knows how to set a hen, look after chickens and rabbits, worm dogs and cats, pan for gold, take samples from reefs, cook, sew, use the milk separator and churn butter, go down a mine shaft in a bucket, make cream cheese and ginger beer, paint stenciled patterns on materials, make peppier Mache, walk on stilts, made from poles cut in the bush, drive the car, shoot pigeons, and guinea fowl for the pot, preserve eggs—and a lot else. Doing these things she is truly happy. Few things in her life have given her greater pleasure. Lessing says, "That is real happiness, a child's happiness: being enabled to do and to make, above all to know you are contributing to the family, you are valuable and valued" (*Skin* 103).

In 1926 Lessing was sent to a convent school in Salisbury (now Harare), where she experienced extreme homesickness:

> I was at the Convent for four years. Or for eternity. I used to wake up in the morning with the clang of the bell and not believe that I would live through that interminable day until the night. And, after this endless day would be another. Then another. I was in the grip of homesickness like an illness (Lessing, *Under My Skin* 96).

At the school, the Roman Catholic teachers perpetually tried to convert the girls of the Protestant faith. Lessing went through rapid changes concerning her own faith:

> I had a sudden conversion to Roman Catholicism. This was regarded by all the Protestant girls as bound to happen at some point...My submission was sudden and total....my mother saw the holy water and the rosary under my pillow and exploded into reproaches. This marked the beginning of a rejection of my mother... she began on a history of the crimes of Roman Catholicism. The inquisition figured as the chief wrong, but others were cited, for instance the way Catholic missionaries converted the Africans they thought to their religion. ...

> listening, full of cold loathing for what I saw as illogic masquerading as virtue. I lost religion in a breath; ... I had become an atheist. (Lessing, *Under My Skin* 123-125)

Due to the convent school and her mother, Lessing removed herself from religious beliefs, but in the 1960's Lessing is yet again drawn to another religion, and she becomes a Sufi. Doris Lessing dropped out of an all-girls high school in Salisbury when she was fourteen; "My fourteenth year was a make or break year, a sink or swim year, a do or die year, for I was fighting for my life against my mother. That was how I saw it. That was how it was" (*Under My Skin* 155), and she moved away from home at the age of fifteen to get away from her mother, to work as a nursemaid, a telephone operator and clerk. She continued to read and write, and at the age of seventeen she tried to write a novel:

> ...my first novel, on the mountain of a typewriter sent all the way from Johannesburg. It was a short satirical novel, mannered, stilted, making fun of gilded youth, the young whites whose ways I had after all only glimpsed. I would become one of them within a year. Their pretensions, their privileges were contrasted with the lives of the blacks. I did not know enough to write it. This production too was later torn up in transports of embarrassment (Lessing, *Under My Skin* 191).

Although Lessing's first published novel did not appear until 1949, she made numerous attempts beforehand to become a published author:

> I was also writing short stories, and sold two to smart magazines in South Africa. Coming on these in some drawer years later I so burned with shame that I had to tear them up on the spot. I had written to suit a market. I had succeeded. But later I could not do it, even when I badly needed money (Lessing, *Under My Skin* 181).

At nineteen Lessing married Frank Wisdom and had two children, John and Jean, but they divorced in 1943, and the children stayed with their father.

She remembers the day when she goes home for the holiday and her mother sees the holy water and the rosary under her pillow and explodes into reproaches. Lessing accuses her mother about the change in her thoughts about religion. She has differed her mother not only on personal but religious aspects too. She tells her story:

> This marked the beginning of a rejection of my mother, like a slamming of a door. She called me out to sit with her in front of the house, set her chair opposite mine, and began on a history of the crimes of Roman Catholicism...By now I was listening, full of cold loathing for what I saw as illogic masquerading as virtue. I lost religion in a breath; Heaven fled from me on the wings of Reason, when I said that everything she said was true of the Protestants, who had burned Catholics at the stake, just as Catholics had burned Protestants... I had become an atheist, but what I really did was to put an end to the conflict of being a Protestan in a Catholic school. (*Skin* 124-25)

From the passage above, it is understood that Lessing's mother is a very influential figure in her life. In the first volume of her autobiography, apart from her mother, she only mentions about Ivy. She was her first husband Frank Wisdom's friend, Tommy Wolton's wife. Ivy is pregnant like Doris and she becomes her special friend. She is her first real woman friend, only because they were having the same experiences at the same time (*Skin* 213).

She has been a great mother who has proud being mother and does share this with her known. Lessing believes that a woman friend is essential for balance if not for survival. Ivy and Doris sit for long morning hours comparing their sensations. Lessing's relationship with her mother was complicated, as Emily wanted and expected a boy rather than a girl, and Lessing was left feeling unloved: "What I remember is hard bundling hands, impatient arms and her voice telling me over and over again that she had not wanted a girl, she wanted a boy. I knew from the beginning she loved my little brother unconditionally, and she did not love me" (*Under My Skin* 25). Her relationship with her mother colours Lessing's work as an adult, as we see when we study *Memoirs*, where the matter of mother and daughter relationship is one of the central issues. They insist that their babies respond them energetically when they dance or make love with their fathers (*Skin* 214). Most of the women who give birth to a child like to tell the stories of pregnancy and birth. Here, Lessing tells the reader her gynecological history:

> I was in a mood of triumphant accomplishment, and looking forward to the birth. I did not believe it would be as painful as they said, because I was so healthy and at ease with myself. My gynecological history would be appropriate for that fabled peasant woman who has never had anything wrong with her. I had my first period when I was fourteen. My periods lasted two or three days and were never excessive. They were sometimes mildly painful. As for premenstrual tension, no one had heard of it. I gave birth three times normally, was never torn, stitched, forcepped, caesared. I have never suffered from thrush or herpes. My periods ended in my early forties, as is common for women who smoke. The dreaded menopause did not happen: my periods ended and that was it. I do not see how I could have been more fortunate. Women with this kind of history—quite a lot of us—are sometimes made to feel guilty, as if womb troubles are the proper fate of females. (*Skin* 216-17)

Doris Lessing's telling of her gynecological history makes this autobiography typically women's. These are very private details from her life Lessing argues that the women of her generation feel more confident and in control than new generation. Her generation is lucky because they are not bombarded with bleak information from television, radio, newspapers, women's magazines. She says; "If girls are told, from very young, that they can expect bad times of every sort from pre-menstrual tension to menopausal miseries, it is not possible that they are attracting bad times?" (*Skin* 217). In *Under My Skin,* Lessing's entry into political life and Communist movement takes great place. With the happiness of belonging to a group, she makes very radical decisions. She divorces from Frank Wisdom and leaves her two children with their grandparents. Then, she tries to justify her abandoning children by saying that they will be brought up with much concern and love with their grandparents. Lessing explains the reasons of becoming a Communist:

> People became communists because of cynicism about their governments—that, first. Because they had fallen in love with a communist—as Gottfried Lessing did. In my case it was because for the first time in my life I was meeting a group of people (not and isolated individual here and there) who read everything, and who did not think it remarkable to read, and among whom thoughts about the Native Problem I had scarcely dared to say aloud turned out to be mere common places. I became a Communist because of the spirit of the times, because of the Zeitgeist. (*Skin* 259)

Doris Lessing feels herself very powerful with these people. She even thinks that she can change this ugly world and they would live in a beautiful and perfect world where there will be no race hatred, injustice and so forth (*Skin* 262). For her, their group was a real Communist group. She says, "real" because they have nothing in common with real Communist parties in Communist countries or established Communist parties in Europe.

About her joining the communist party, she first says, "Although I was not a member of communist party, I was accepted by the comrades as one of them." (Lessing, *Walking* 22) What do they believe and what are the ideas that fuelled them are the questions have to be answered. Lessing makes a list in order to answer the questions:

> First, that, within ten years, well fifteen then, whole world would be Communist, from free choice, because of the manifest superiorities of Communism. There would be no race prejudice, oppression of women, exploitation of labour—no snobbishness or contempt for others. This paradise would follow a brief period of resistance by reactionaries, only a minority, after all, because by then "the State would have withered away" (Lessing, *Skin* 281).

She keeps on telling, "Paradise, then, was on the world's agenda, and soon. Who would lead the world thither? Why, we would, people like us, Communists, the vanguard of the working class, destined by History for the role" (Lessing, *Skin* 281). Secondly, "...that there was no way to paradise but by Revolution. We despised anyone who did not believe in Revolution—that is; with a few exceptions...We were united with each other by superiority of character, because we were revolutionaries and good. Our opponents were bad" (Lessing, *Skin* 281). People who did not believe in socialism were not credited with good intentions. She reveals, "Thirdly, we were a part of a family that covered the world. A Communist can arrive in any country anywhere and at once be at home, with people who think the same, with same ideals" (Lessing, *Skin* 281). And then, "Fourthly, a Communist should always be better than everyone else, work harder, study more, look after people, always be ready to do the dirty work, both as a human responsibility and to attract people into the Communist Party, which embodied now, and would embody in the future, all the best qualities of humankind" (281-282).

Doris Lessing and her friends believe there would never again be nationalist wars or religious wars. Nationalism is obviously a thing of the past. So is religion. They used to congratulate each other: at least they can never have a religious war again, or a nationalist war. She lives on "heroic myths and fantasies" (*Skin* 287). However, this does not last long. Lessing admits that she is never committed with all of herself to Communism. So, the loss of faith does not hurt her so much. Forher, the loss of faith happens when the Soviet Union invaded Finland and Hungary and when Stalin makes a pact with Hitler. Influence of World War I, Lessing's relation with her mother, education and politics are the central themes explored so far. While reading an autobiography by a man or a woman, it is important to expose the reasons of writing. In the second chapter, Doris Lessing tries to explain why she chooses to write her autobiography. She confesses that the reason for writing autobiography was a "self defence" (*Skin* 14). She did not want to let other people write about her life. She explains it as:

> In the year just finished, 1992, I heard of five American biographers writing about me. One I had never met or even heard of. Another, I was told by a friend in Zimbabwe, is "collecting material" for a biography. From whom? Long dead people? A woman I met twice, once when she asked me carefully casual questions has just informed me she has written a book about me which she is about to get published.... Probably interviews, too, and these are always full of misinformation (*Skin* 14).

To prevent her life from any misinformation, Doris Lessing decides to write her autobiography. It is clearly seen that her intention is not to convey a message to people.

After having personal aspects of life, then she comes and shares a few of the facts related to her fiction which had great relation to her personal life. She tells, "she had written *The Grass is Singing*, which she had caused her mother some anguish and shame, because it was so hated by the whites" (Lessing, *Walking* 33). She has shared many a discussion which took place between her and Joan. She reveals, "...gossiping with Joan over the kitchen table is my one of the pleasant memories. We both cooked well...gentle competition went on...which I later shared in The *Golden Notebook*" (Lessing, *Walking* 43). Peter, Doris Lessing's son, has been a companion in her life whom she always considers a good reason of living. She tells, "And so I had made a life for me and for Peter. That was an achievement and I was proud of myself. The most important part was Peter..." (Lessing, *Walking* 31). Later, she felt the need of her husband only because of Peter. She points out, "He is very important man. He sends you his love. He is not my husband. I would say, it is Peter, who needs his love" (Lessing, *Walking* 50). In the last part of *Walking in the Shade*, Doris opens her heart saying:

> But usually, when I hear someone talking nostalgically about the sixties-'If you remember it, you were not there'—what comes into my mind is a line from a poem I wrote when I was very young not more than a girl: *when I look back I seem to remember singing*' Well, yes, that seems to be about it (369).

Doris Lessing believes that one's experience plays very vital role in its writing. Her fiction brings us to the question of relation between autobiography and fiction. There is no doubt from the evidence of Mrs. Lessing's interviews and non fictional works that her early writing (till the last volume of *Children of Violence* 1969) is autobiographical. Fact and figure blur together: it is quite difficult to detangle them. So, the female characters in her fiction are autobiographical, at same time, they are the part of this world those help Lessing to present a true picture of the society. So, she is a woman novelist whose antennae sensed the crucial issues of feminism and wrote about them. That is why *The Golden Notebook* has *autobiographical* layers: the character Anna reflects elements of author Doris Lessing's own life, while Anna writes an autobiographical novel about her imagined Ella, who writes autobiographical stories. The structure of *The Golden Notebook* also intertwines the political conflicts and emotional conflicts in the characters' lives.

So, Doris Lessing in *Under My Skin* (1994), the first of a proposed three-volume autobiography, follows Lessing from her birth in 1919 to 1949, the year she left Southern Rhodesia for London and her life as a single mother and aspiring writer. *Walking in the Shade* (1997), the second volume of the autobiography, covers Lessing's life in London from her arrival in the to the publication in 1962 of *The Golden Notebook*. In her Psychoanalysis, psychotherapy, and self-representational writing, all provide opportunities to reach the past, analyse past experiences, and perhaps re-invent them by experiencing them again, while living in the present.

During a session with a psychoanalyst or a psychotherapist, an individual attempts to reconcile her or his present feelings and existence with the past which she or he may have suppressed. Doris Lessing is able to recreate past selves and commune in an inner dialogue with earlier and necessarily fictive selves while constructing a coherent text that represents a healed and unified self at a particular instant in time (Chodorow 2).

According to Chodorow, Lessing's autobiographical writing resembles a therapeutic session because she invests herself with authority and distance through the literary positioning of herself as "author"(13). She is able to use power and command over the text. At the same time she allows her own silent past to be recreated. *Under My Skin* helps her to maintain a dialogue with herself and her past. Here, Doris Lessing makes an effort to create a unified self; that is an effort generally made in men's autobiographies. In autobiographies, the text becomes the dream-space in which to re-live your life and relationships in the way that you think you did or wished you had. Chodorow asserts that the autobiographical act is a result of pre-text:

> The autobiographer's own life occurs before the text and then the autobiographer and the reader read as the text. Autobiography also becomes the pre-text for the construction of a self-image by the autobiographer and the reader, the latter reading the autobiographical text while considering her or his own life-text. The self-conscious and careful selection of events, people, and memories within an autobiographical text either fictive or re-orders the past and can generate more memories. (3)

Consequently, with her autobiographies *Under My Skin and Walking in the Shade*, Doris Lessing does not let anybody to write about her life and manages to prevent her life from any misinformation. She also tells the story of end of British colonialism from an alternative perspective. For Lessing, writing about her mother helps her to restore and heal the traumatic relation. She manages to heal the wounds of the past. Doris Lessing finds a chance to speak the unspeakable while writing her autobiography. She holds a mirror to the other women's lives. The years spent in Africa influenced Lessing deeply, both as a maturing woman and as a writer. "Africa belongs to the Africans", she wrote in 1956. Undoubtedly she is one of 'those' who feel at home in it, to the extent that ever since she left Africa, she has regarded herself as an exile. She is, after all, "an expert in unsettlement" (Sage 11), or, in Judith Gardiner's words, "a colonial in exile", whose work is characterized by "a fruitful unsettledness that makes... her both an inheritor...and an antagonist...to imperialism.... The English literary tradition is the reassuring heritage of a mother tongue, but it is also somewhat alien" (Gardiner 13). In doing so, "Lessing puts it, the myth of a white bourgeois hegemony in Southern Rhodesia" (116), that "intensely race and class-conscious colonial society" (Thorpe 6). And Doris Lessing's background has been a powerful influence on her fiction.

## Works Cited

Bozzoli, Belinda. 'Marxism, Feminism and South African Studies'. *Journal of Southern African Studies* 9.2, 1983. Print

Brodzki, Bella." Mothers, Displacement, and Language". In *Women, Autobiography, Theory: A Reader.* Ed. Sidonie Smith & Julia Watson. Madison: The University Of Wisconsin Press, 1998. Print

Chodorow, Nancy.(1978). *The Reproduction of mothering: psychoanalysis and the sociology of Gender.* Berkeley: University of California Press, 1978.

Friedman, Susan Stanford. "Women's Autobiographical Selves". *The Private Self: Theory and Practice of Women's Autobiographical Writings.* Ed. ShariBenstock. Chapel Hill and London: Univ. Of North Carolina Press, 1988. Print

Frye, Joanna. *Living Stories, Telling Lives. Women and the Novel in Contemporary Experience.* Ann Arbor: University of Michigan Press, 1989. Print

Gardiner, Judith Kegan. *Rhys, Stead, Lessing and the Politics of Empathy.* Bloomington: Indiana UP, 1989. Print

Gikundi, Simon. "Lessing, Doris." *Encyclopedia of African Literature.* Ed. Simon Gikundi. London: Routledge, 2003. Print

Heilbrun, Carolyn G. *Writing Woman's Life.* Istanbul: Yapi Kredi Yayýnlarý, 1992. Print

Hunter, Eva. 'Marriage as Death: A Reading of Doris Lessing's *The Grass is Singing*'. *Women and Writing in South Africa: A Critical Anthology.* Heinemann: Marshalltown, South Africa, 1989. Print

Karl, Frederick R. 'Doris Lessing in the Sixties: The New Anatomy of Melancholy'. *Modern Critical Views Doris Lessing.* Ed. Harold Bloom. New York: Chelsea House Publishers, 1986. Print

Lessing, Doris. *Under My Skin, Volume One of My Autobiographies, to 1949.* London: Flamingo Publishers, 1995. Print

______ Walking in the Shade, Volume Two of My Autobiography, 1949-1962. London: Flamingo Publishers, 1995. Print

Maslin, Elizabeth. *Doris Lessing.* Plymouth: Northcote House Publishers Ltd, 1994. Print

Rigney, Barbara Hill. 'Hysteria *as Sanity in The Four-Gated City'. Madness and Sexual,* Politics in the Feminist Novel: Studies in Bronte, Woolf, Lessing, and Atwood. London: U. of Wisconsin Press, 1978. Print

Sage Lorna, *Doris Lessing,* Methuen, London and New York, 1983. Print

Singleton, Mary Ann. *The City and the Veldt: The fiction of Doris Lessing.* Becknell: University Press, 1977. Print

Thorpe, Michael. *Doris Lessing's Africa.* London and Ibadan: Evans Brothers, 1978. Print

# 20

# Revelation as Divine Truth in St Augustine's *Confessions*

Chung Chin-Yi

In the autobiographical *Confessions* of St Augustine, a journey is made from darkness and a life of sin and debauchery to light and gradual acceptance of divine truth. St Augustine pursued a life of lust and hedonism as a youth, taking on a mistress out of wedlock with whom he fathered a child and engaging in affairs outside marriage. He also pursued rhetoric and perpetuated lies and injustice therein. He consulted astrology rather than God about his future. It was a gradual journey however towards light and divine truth when he realized how spiritually barren and lost he was, and how he needed the sanctifying grace of Christ to redeem himself from the cesspool of sin he was mired in.

Indeed the entire autobiography is a movement from lies to truth. A rampant thief when he was young, Augustine was not an honest person in his youth. He loved sin, darkness, indulged in carnal affairs purely for pleasure, and became a professor of rhetoric, mastering the art of disseminating lies and persuading people away from objective truth by twisting and manipulating language. Gifted in the liberal arts, he accumulated a wealth of knowledge which he was eventually to find empty and worthless when compared to the light and truth of knowing Christ as saviour. He was well versed in philosophy, but eventually discovered that the endless quarrels of the philosophers and infighting amongst themselves led people away from, rather than closer to the truth. He was steeped in materialism and greed and pursuing the empty and hollow things of the world, which he eventually deemed worthless in comparison with knowing the light of Christ.

Augustine as a youth was steeped in the ways of the world. He pursued wealth, fame, women and prestige. He sought to be esteemed by those around him in the world, and to be measured by worldly standards. He rose high by these worldly standards, acquiring the status of a professor of rhetoric and living with a mistress out of wedlock with whom he fathered a child for many years. Upon dissolving the relationship out of hopes for marriage, he engaged in a loveless affair with another woman out of wedlock. He mastered the art of rhetoric, which involved manipulating language and distorting the truth. He gained a wealth of knowledge in philosophy and the liberal arts, which was secular rather than spiritual, and which he eventually found empty and barren. Indeed he was esteemed highly by the world's standards, but found that he was spiritually destitute and barren. This was changed after his conversion, in which he exchanged wealth, riches and prestige for the truth of God, in which he finally found fulfilment and his spiritual home.

Augustine indeed describes his early life as a famine. While on the surface he seemed to have gained the world by rising to a professor and indulging in wine and women, he found that spiritually he was lost. He was a master of lies, perpetuating deceit in his discipline of rhetoric and teaching students how to perpetuate deceit. He found himself repeatedly falling into sin by being dishonest and stealing. He had gained the world but lost his soul. His long term relationship with a woman out of wedlock did not come to a good end either, because it lacked the sanctity and legitimacy of marriage. He found himself unfulfilled at the end of rising and conquering fame, wealth, women and prestige because he was living a deeply sinful and decadent lifestyle. Spiritually, he was destitute and lost.

Augustine describes his conversion experience as realizing that the riches of the world lie not in sin and conquering wealth and women but in turning to God. He describes the passage that converts him as a passage which instructs him to turn away from the hedonistic ways of the world and the paths of sin, debauchery and lust and forsaking these things for Christ. He realized that a beggar was infinitely richer than him because while he did not possess the world, he was a child of God. Thereafter he realized how hollow his previous pursuits and material conquests had been. He realizes to truly be a child of God, he has to forsake his life of sin and pursuing material wealth and prestige, which mean little in God's kingdom.

Augustine then heeds Christ's injunction to sell all his material possessions and ultimately pursue the life of serving God. In his riches gained in the ways of the world he was infinitely poorer than when he had taken up the yoke of serving God as a theologian and minister. He realizes that it does not benefit a man to gain the world but lose his soul. He then takes up Christ's injunction to forsake a life of sin, materialism and debauchery and to become a theologian and minister.

Augustine then moves from a life of deceit and lies to truth. His journey is one in which he exchanges the lie of worldly glory for the truth of God. While to be a child of God is to be esteemed lowly by the world's standards, Augustine discovers in his pursuit of Christ riches that are infinitely greater than the wealth and prestige he had gained by becoming a professor of rhetoric and indulging in wine and women. From a heartless thief and perpetuator of lies through his practice and teaching of rhetoric He moves towards the truth of Christ as saviour and redeemer. He then charts a journey from darkness to light, forsaking his worldly ways for the truth and light of knowing and serving God. While this meant forsaking his sinful and adulterous lifestyle, he found it infinitely more rewarding to know and serve God. Though he had been esteemed well by the world's standards, Augustine found that he was spiritually dead. He then charts a journey of exchanging the lie of worldly glory for the truth of God in his autobiographical *Confessions*.

## Work Cited

Augustine, Saint. *Confessions*. New City Press. New York. 1997.

21

# Amrita Pritam's *The Revenue Stamp*: A Journey of the Artist's Mind

Varsha Gosavi

An autobiography is an affirmation or analysis of a person's life. It is creation of the self. It is a journey of human life that depicts a way from childhood towards a mature human being. Rather than collection, it is a collection of experiences that an individual undergoes, shaded with varied emotional expressions and intellectual outlines. It is a mirror of the inner self. Previously, the form autobiography was written in the form of letters, diaries, journals etc. With the educational opportunities and with the use of innovative techniques in literature, it acquired a kind of shape.

Till the nineteenth century, women's autobiographies did not get published in the significant numbers in India. It was with the publication of Amrita Pritam's *The Revenue Stamp* and Kamala Das's *My Story* the readers understand how women have urge for freedom, self-assertion, autonomy and a longing for establishing one's own identity. Avrom Fleishman while trying to explain the concept of autobiography, comments:

> It is not conterminous with the narrated historical I; the autobiographical act itself takes place in dramatic and discursive present that is neither continuous with nor divorceable from the experiential time of the subject. Autobiographical writing

> now confirms, now suppresses these and other philosophical problems. One means of developing a coherent account of self is to choose a metaphor of the self and develop it in a narrative or other myth. (Gilhead 1988:60)

The present paper is an attempt to view the inside of the writer's mind. It is an effort to recognize the bondage between the creativity of the artist and the reality of life, art and experience. It tries to study *The Revenue Stamp* as a discovery of the mind of the artist; Amrita Pritam. The book was published in 1976, when Amrita Pritam was fifty-seven.

Amrita Pritam with the publication of *The Revenue Stamp,* is still as an autobiographer ruling the hearts of the readers. As the critics analyse, it was not for getting fame or prestige or to grab any award, She wrote her autobiography, but it was in the form of inner outlet, the confirmation of her vision of life. As Claire Martin (1976: 34) comments on the women autobiography:

> In case of women, autobiography does not spring from a common intention to assess the past and define it as do men. Instead it springs from women autobiographers deep sex-awareness of their marginalized existence in the world dominated by the male culture.

Amrita Pritam in her preface of *The Revenue Stamp,* explains that it was suggestion that she got from the senior writer, Khushwant Singh, that she should stamp the experiences of her life in the form of autobiography. She felt he was right. Even she felt, what she had to express, she expressed through her novels and poems but her autobiography would place the revenue stamp upon the accounts and experiences of her life. It was the manifestation of her private self, her inner self. It was presentation of a true account of her life. It was purely the individual personal experience that is the revelation of truth.

*The Revenue Stamp* is an exploration of the self-development. It not only deals with the emotional growth, but it also is an exploration of the intellectual and spiritual emerging. It is also a tale of suffering and isolation of a woman. Besides, it is an expression of the rebellious soul and a true woman's mind. It expresses the spiritual reality through the experiences of the physical world. It also expresses the changes and the transformation Amrita Pritam has undergone as a woman, a poet and a writer. It pictures the experiences of her childhood and youth, her marriage, her social spiritual, intellectual world, her private self, her womanhood and her poetic vision. It is a beautiful combination of art and life, her urge for dreams and vision of reality.

*The Revenue Stamp* is a transparent and a perfect text of self-revelation, where Amrita Pritam has nowhere tried to hide the facts or the truth of life that makes a way to hypocrisy in society. It is like the sea which, sometimes is filled with Milky Way, sometimes with the violent rebellious waves. Her autobiography is an example of the honest commitment. It is also the finest example where the writer gives great importance to the human values.

Amrita Pritam was born in 1919 at Gujranwala. The place was found in Pakistan after partition. Both her parents were teachers. The period when she was born was violent one in India, in the same period the mass assassination at Jallianwala Bagh took place. Raj Bibi was Amrita's mother, and her father's name was Kartar Singh. She was named as Amrita Amrita Pritam (1994: 03) and claims "since he wrote poetry, he has also taken on a pseudonym – *Peeyookh* – the santskrit word for nectar. Ten years later when I was born, he named me 'Amrita', the Punjabi equivalent for *peeyookh*. Really like *peeyookh*". Her mind was also filled with nectar, her thoughts and emotions were also sprinkled like nectar. Amrita Says: "I did not then think of the world or of what the world thought of me.... I am not in the least mindful of what others think of me. My only desire is to be at peace with my innermost self"(4). It is the love of spirituality, the importance of the innerself that provides spiritual shades to Amrita's autobiography. It is also an autobiography of the poetic mind, which is filled with love and devotion of the writer as an artist and also as a true and transparent human being. As she was the only child of her parents, she felt a kind of loneliness in her life. Her mother passed away, when she was only eleven years old. Due to the loss, she lost faith in God and gave up prayers and meditation. This sense of the loss and loneliness of the past haunted her mind throughout her life, that is reflected in her writings. It shows how human mind, cannot escape from the shadows of the past experiences and reflections of the childhood.

Amrita Pritam's writing is voluminous in number. She has written around forty philosophical treatise in prose, nearly eighteen collections of short stories, thirty-eight novels, and fifteen anthologies of poetry. She also has two autobiographies and three self-narrative collections of prose articles to her credit. She has been honoured and awarded with number of awards, degrees, titles and prizes. Most of her writings are in Hindi, many in Punjabi, her mother tongue, and innumerable are translated in English and in more than thirty-four languages. Her fiction was also filmized and she was also interviewed on television. More than fifty articles are contributed by her to foreign anthologies. Some of her novels are translated into Russian, French, Spanish, English, Japanese and Urdu languages.

In the sixteenth year, Amrita started writing love poetry, but afraid of her father, she tore them up. She describes it as the beginning of the uneven road of life. It was in the same year she built a rebellious spirit within. At the age of sixteen, she married Pritam Singh of Lahore, with whom she was engaged at the age of four. Since 1935, the name 'Pritam' was added to her and remained with her forever. For her it was not a good experience of life, she felt lack of fulfilment. It was for some twenty years or so. It was in 1960, she got divorced from her husband. She had a daughter Kandla, and a son Navraj, with whom she stayed independently in Delhi. In her autobiography, she didn't provide much space for her husband or her domestic life. It seems, when she wrote the autobiography, she was for away from those events, hence, rather than growth of the family, it describes the growth of the selfhood, of spirit and of an artist. Rather in the notes of the diary which is included in her autobiography, Amrita writes:

> It was on the night of the wedding ceremony forty years age. I went up to the terrace and wept my heart out in the pitch-black dark. Father knew about my state of mind and followed me. I kept on telling him again and again – "I do not want to be married" (144).

Amrita's silence means much in not mentioning about her husband. She thinks by marrying she has paid debt of the society, but she says, "All I know is, some day I will have to render accounts. How many more women will I cannot say…. but speaking for myself, I sorely feel the weight of that debt" (28). Regarding separation from her husband she says that it was the truth that was accepted by both and was larger than that of the court. Even regarding her motherhood, she writes that motherhood was longing and she remembers how much she longed for a baby till it was born. But she thinks motherhood has given her a kind of satisfaction of being a woman. For Amrita, it was a rebellious step of breaking her marriage with her husband

and living with an artist like Imroz without marriage. The same step brought social and religious criticism to her. He reached his heights as an artist and acquired national and international recognition. It's true of a human being and especially of a woman, i.e., "gaining something is losing of the other".

Since *The Revenue Stamp* opens various inner avenues of Amrita Pritam's life, her autobiography gives an expression to emotion of love. In her girlhood Amrita created an image of an ideal lover in her mind. She states: "I can remember.... the face of my ideal lover, and mine, that I imagined growing wiser, stronger, and more mature" (14). Since she was a poet with a very sensitive mind, she longed for true and ideal love, which is also reflected in her literature. In the mid of her life she happened to meet the poet, Sahir Ludhianvi, in whom she visualized the image of her ideal lover. She cherished him through her collection of poems *Sunehare*, which grabbed her the Sahitya Akademi Award in 1957. Through her character in fiction, she has revealed her feelings for him. He was as an inspiration for her male portrayal. P. Lal (1973:43) comments: "Like an expert ballerina, she played simultaneously with the realities of her life of imagination." Regarding her relationship with Sahir, Amrita recalls: "No words came between our friendships. It was a beautiful relationship in silence. The beginning of this tale was silence and the intensity of it too was carried out in silence" (154).

Another lover in her life who cared for her was Imroz, with whom she shared her loneliness. "In the years that followed, I had Imroz, he has had only loneliness. Fate has also been all too frugal in giving him anything that gives life a meaning"(30). She has also mentioned a friend Sajjad, who lived in Pakistan; it was he who had some misunderstanding with her. It was this emotion of love that made her to write. Her disillusionment and realization of love is fictionalized in her novels, *Ek Thi Amrita* and *Akharee Khat.* Amrita Pritam in complex socio-cultural ethos, struggles for her freedom and self-identity.

It is always criticized regarding women's autobiographies that women deal more with their personal lives than about the world and public life. Amrita's *The Revenue Stamp* is an exception to it. The socio-political, historical and cultural ethos is highlighted more in her autobiography than her personal and domestic life. Her personal life is reflected, but it is more reflected as a writer's life than a woman's life. Despite that, it contains an aesthetic shade. She describes how she was disturbed by the partition and the religious riots. She writes:

> At the time of the partition of the country in 1947, when all social, political and religious values came crashing down like glass smashed into smithereens under the feet of people in flight.... Those crushed pieces of glass bruised my soul and my limbs bled. I wrote my hymns for the suffering of those who were abducted and raped (13).

Amrita Pritam, by expressing herself freely, provides an exclusive meaning to the autobiography. A letter by Indira Gandhi stands as a testimony to it. Indiraji reflects: "It is you and yet there is something universal.... Most people bury their real selves in some unfathomable depth of their being and just skin the surface of life. It is the privilege of the artist and the poet to be more poignantly aware" (151). Her autobiography is an example of the self-truth, or self-loyalty. It expresses her loneliness, her isolated childhood, her quest for sharing her self-consciousness, her love for freedom, her longing for self-identity, her anger against injustice. Despite these aspects, her autobiography is not self-glorification, but it is journey of her mind that tries to discover herself. As Amrita claims, it is self-acceptance. On the cover page of the *Rasid Ticket,* she admits that life is a strange book that is constructed by letters which combine and break, to scatter away and change. She confesses:

> Only I keep wondering if I have accepted myself for what I am. That is why perhaps I have written all my life – So that whatever I could not accept in me, I would in time not reject altogether (4).

While writing, she has also maintained a critic's attitude all through the text. In her fiction too she described her vision regarding women. But she lived with a rebellious spirit. Rather than living as a woman, she kept the artist within her alive. As an artist, she is great, but she is greater as a thinker and philosopher. Sometimes she transcends the boundaries of gender bias and maintains the human attitude. She is a woman devoted thoroughly to her art, her work, and who seeks knowledge, and that is why her autobiography has an aesthetic foundation. *The Revenue Stamp* is a record of her creativity. Besides it possesses a beautiful combination of intellect and emotions. It is an exclusive contribution to the women's autobiography and women's literature in the world. It will definitely spread fragrance in the universe until the doom of the world.

## Works Cited

Claira, Martin. 1976. *In Angron Glove: An Autobiography,* trans. Strafford Philip. Montreal: Harvard House.

Gilhead, Sarah. 1988. "Immigrant Selves: Narrative Strategies in Three Women's Autobiographies" *Criticism,* Winter. Vol xxx. No.1.

Lal, P. July 1973. "Tragic contents in Amrita Pritam's Two Faces of Eve", *Journal of Indian Writings in English,* Vol.1, No.2.

Pritam, Amrita. 1994. *The Revenue Stamp.* trans Krishna Gorawara. New Delhi: Vikas.

## 22

# Perspectives on Nirad C. Chaudhuri's *Autobiography*

J. Ravindranath

The twentieth century has witnessed a titanic struggle in the name of liberty and equality between capitalism and socialism. The life and rights of an individual have been sandwiched in this conflict of different social systems and ideologies. This has made many intellectuals, including writers, suspicious of any collective entity such as "nation" or "class." Salman Rushdie, in his *Midnight's Children* writes: "Religion, region, class, ideology are poisons poured into the minds of children" (306).

Twentieth century has been called "the most murderous century" in human history by Hobsbawm, a prominent historian (1995, 13). It has taught us an invaluable lesson that rejects the sacrifice of an individual at the altar of any collective entity. The phenomenon of nationalism is so knotty that the terms such as 'nation', 'nationality', 'nationalism' have proved difficult to be defined, let alone be analysed (Anderson 13). Nationalism has become a site of contention between individualists and collectivists, universalists and localists, religious chauvinists and the left wing revolutionaries. In this backdrop, this article examines the nationalist context, the intricate relationship between history and autobiography, the contemporary relevance of

Chaudhuri's autobiographical works and offers a variety of critical perspectives on Chaudhuri's autobiographical trilogy.

In the conflict between nationalism and universalism in the era of globalization, 'universalism' has come to be seen as an inescapable destiny of many nations. Still, nationalism is powerful although it is labelled as "a very old fashioned idea" (Seabrook 73). Western countries have gone through a nationalistic phase for centuries and have attained a high degree of cohesion. But the newly independent countries are being advised to renounce nationalism within half a century after their independence in the interests of the globalization. Culture never entails absolute borrowing or lending but of appropriations, common experiences, and interdependencies of all kinds among different cultures (Said 262). The passion of the people of the newly industrializing countries to nationalist ideology is quite understandable. But the people of developing countries like India would only be offering their markets as hunting grounds for the advanced countries, in case they accept "universalism" uncritically. In fact, one has to find a way out of the devil of invading universalism and the deep sea of exclusive religious nationalism.

In our country, the terms such as "Nation," "India," and "Indian" have become contentious in terms of ideology and practice. There are contextual similarities between the late 1940's and recent times which have seen the rise of the hydra-headed religious fanaticism and its hostility to religious and political minorities, the anxiety over the future of nationalism vis-à-vis globalization, a necessity to appreciate our freedom struggle characterized as merely 'Hindu xenophobia' by Nirad C. Chaudhuri. In this context, his autobiographical works are significant as they offer a debatable historical interpretation of Indian civilization in general and of Indian national movement in particular.

Chaudhuri's autobiographical trilogy epitomizes the saying "Style is the man." If the historian Gibbon's autobiography can be read for his literary style, the writer Chaudhuri's can also be read for his sense of history. In fact autobiography gives vivacity to history, (and this is more so if the autobiographer is an active participant of historical movements) compared to history based merely on documents and other historical works. Although Chaudhuri was a spectator to the national movement, his account gives the reader a vicarious joy in watching that panorama unfolded by his pen. Thus, both autobiography and history can be read from alternative vantage points and perspectives to arrive at different conclusions. As J.V. Gunn writes, "reading takes place at two moments of 'autobiographical situation'— by the autobiographer who, in effect, is 'reading' his or her life and by the reader of the autobiographical text" (8).

## History and Literature

For a very long time history and literature have been closely associated with each other and history has remained a part of literature. Indian *itihasa* in the form of legends, myths and traditions offers a lot of information related to life, manners, moral and social conditions of the people. The epics of Homer such as *The Illiad* and *The Odyssey* could act as sources of history of ancient Greece and Sparta (Ali 1). While in ancient Greece, historical literature grew out of ballads and songs, historians in Elizabethan England used to copy the style of Italian drama resulting in art but no history. In the hands of Herodotus, Thucydides, Livy, Tacitus, Hume, Macaulay, Trevelyan, and Gibbon, history exuded the fragrance of literature (Ali 81) while Scott, Hugo and Tolstoy are prominent novelists who dealt with historical themes artistically.

While history is based on facts, literature actively mirrors and negotiates with those facts of life. The concern with the past and the use of imagination are common to both history and literature, especially the form of autobiography. Literature uses imagination more liberally whereas history is more factual. It does not mean that history is dry-as-dust or literature is completely fictitious.

## Nature and Function of Autobiography

Literature is one of the forms of human consciousness. Autobiography, a literary form is a study of the way that one's own experience is transformed into literature, creative process, and the ways of men and the forms of human consciousness (Olney 10). The autobiographies of Gandhi, Nehru, Bose and Nirad C. Chaudhuri reveal the vast worlds of social consciousness in pre-Independence India.

Gusdorf sees autobiography as a "late phenomenon in Western culture which appeared when the Christian contribution was grafted onto classical traditions" (Olney 29). It is a history of the human mind reflecting man's rise from dogma to greater individuality (Howarth 363). Autobiography is also not a mere list of chronicles or memories but a narrative or self-portrait historically. It can be experienced as something that constrains or directs the acts of reading and writing (Forguson 148). The core of its value lies in the roles played by an author and a reader, the uses which the text is being put to (Bruss 5).

Autobiography is a compound of the words "auto," "bios" and "graphie." It means the story of one's life and provides order in the place of chaos, significance in the place of anonymity and literary immortality in the place of mortality. An autobiographer wants to share his feelings, thoughts, experiences—joyous and sad with others. He exhibits his self to the world expecting approval or even disapproval and anything except indifference. He expects the posterity to understand and judge him properly even though his contemporaries may fail to appreciate him. Hence, the value or relevance of autobiography to us is in "its capacity to furnish us with models and mirrors that can help us to accept, celebrate, and transform our lives as individuals in the cyclical drama of incarnation and the dialectical drama of historical evolution" 2 (Shapiro 421-422).

**Why Autobiographies?**

Different writers write their autobiographies for different reasons. To William James, the basic function of autobiography is "to cure oneself of guilt and sub-division" (Kazin 79). This is exemplified in the classic pattern of protestant autobiography from *Pilgrim's Progress to John Woolman's Journal.* St. Augustine and Bunyan exult in the triumph of god's unity, Gibbon and Adams resignedly accept the victory of universal decay and Malcolm X is caught in between the forces of religion and history (Howarth 369).

*Resgestae* by Emperor Augustus focuses mainly on the world historical events whereas *Confessions* by St. Augustine dwells on "the inner reflection of a life in which external fact only had an inner meaning" (Weintraub 823). Rousseau, with reference to his *The Confessions* writes, "I have entered upon a performance which is without precedent whose accomplishment will have no imitator. I intend to present my fellow-mortals with a man in the integrity of nature; and this man shall be myself" (3).

***Known and Unknown Indians and Their Autobiographies***

Back home, the autobiographies of our national leaders help us change ourselves into better citizens or at least accept the need for a more democratic and an egalitarian order. They enlighten us on the trials and tribulations of the freedom fighters, and provide a vibrant sense of history unlike the impersonal accounts of professional historians. In the process of reconstruction of history of the nation and of the self, the autobiographies of known and "unknown" Indian(s) reflect the mutual influence of their selves and their specific times.

Gandhi's autobiography, *The Story of My Experiments with Truth,* relates his experiments with truth, his humiliations, his fasts to help him listen to his inner voice and his relentless efforts to attain spiritual perfection. It also shows how it was possible to infuse politics with morality through teaching the lessons of truth and non-violence. Nehru's *An Autobiography*, has been written to enable him to spend his solitude in his jail life through occupying himself with a definite task, to review the past historical events of India with which he was connected, to attain self-clarity (xv) and some peace (208). His work shows how his romantic self has accepted the domination of his political self, how his reason has many times bowed before Gandhian intuition, reveals his preference for democratic socialism and how the boundaries between his individual self and the life of the nation are wiped out. Subhas Chandra Bose's autobiography, *My Struggle*, tells how he has conquered his feelings of inferiority to emerge as a national leader whose private and public selves inextricably mingled as in the case of other national leaders such as Nehru, Rajendra Prasad and Abul Kalam Azad. Azad wrote his autobiography, *India Wins Freedom,* for "the promotion of greater understanding among the different communities as a first step towards greater understanding among peoples of the world" (xiii). M.N. Roy's autobiography reveals his initiation into terrorism, Marxism, his role in the Mexican revolution, his role in the international communist movement, his disillusionment and his propounding of radical humanism and amidst all this, one hardly comes to know much of his personal life. These national leaders portray their public life more vividly than their inner lives.

M.C. Chagla's autobiography, *Roses in December*, relates his liberal education, his career and his principled life. Dom Moraes's *My Father's Son* helps him understand his life's vocation, gives self-clarity and emerges as a literary artifact rather than mere confession in the Augustinian sense or expression of the "whole" truth in the manner of Rousseau. Nirad C. Chaudhuri portrays his environment—familial, social, religious and political—in detail to explain and justify the growth of his individual self under the Empire.

## Can We read Autobiography as History?

Autobiography is a vibrant form and every new work changes the traditional genre to an extent. It is "the most elusive of literary documents" (Olney 3). Reading an autobiography as a closed form might not prove very much beneficial to a reader. The form varies across ages, cultures and according to the specific individuality of the autobiographer. What men of action like Gandhi, Nehru or Malcolm X offer is different from what writers like Bertrand Russel, Mark Twain, R.K. Narayan or Nirad C. Chaudhuri offer in their autobiographies. What Hitler or Mussolini presents is a world apart from things offered by St. Augustine, Rousseau, and Swami Yogananda. What scientists like Darwin and Abdul Kalam relate in their autobiographies is different from issues addressed by writers like Gorky, Sartre or historians such as Gibbon or Collingwood in their autobiographies. Business magnet Iacocca's concerns are completely different from the concerns of P. Sundarayya, an Indian Marxist leader.

The autobiographies of Gandhi, Nehru, Bose and Mandela blur the divisions between history and autobiography, the self and the world or the private and the public realms. The Russian writer Alexander Solzhenitsyn's *Gulag Archipelago* also blurs the distinction between history and fictional element as observed by a critic Matt F. Oza. Like Solzhenitsyn's works, Chaudhuri's autobiographical works too interest us not only as literary artifacts but also as an attempt at vindication of his theory on the British Empire. Chaudhuri writes history but also sustains the reader's interest in his personal life, giving rise to the mixed-genre.

History and autobiography occupy different ends of a spectrum competing with and complementing each other. For a long time autobiography has been seen as a subdivision of biography — which is itself classified as a "variety of history" (Olney 20). At the one end of the spectrum, history appears as good as literature and at the other end, autobiography assumes the shape and significance of a work of history. It is possible to an extent to construct a narrative of independence struggle of India on the basis of autobiographies of the leaders such as Gandhi, Nehru, Bose, Rajendra Prasad, Abul Kalam Azad, Khan Abdul Gafar Khan. Both Nehru and Chaudhuri have succeeded in internalizing the external world through relentless political action or contemplation. The difference between them is that of degree and of personality.

## The Significance of Chaudhuri

The saga of Indian nationalist movement that culminated in partition and consequent repercussions has proved a rich, fertile and inexhaustible source to many Indian English writers. Apart from novelists such as Venkata Ramani, R.K. Narayan, Khushwant Singh, K.A. Abbas, N.S. Phadke, Manohar Malgaonkar, Ahmad Ali, Chaman Nahal, Nayantara Sahgal, Kamala Markandaya and Attia Hosain, historical personages such as Gandhi, Nehru, Rabindranath Tagore, Subhas Chandra Bose, Lakshmi Sahgal, Rajendra Prasad and Abul Kalam Azad have portrayed the national movement. Modern day prominent novelists such as Salman Rushdie, Shashi Tharoor, Amitav Ghosh and Vikram Seth have creatively blended past and present, engaged themselves with the reality that is "India" and interrogated the era of post-Independence India.

Among the galaxy of Indian English prose writers, Nirad C. Chaudhuri occupies a prominent place as a writer who has intertwined his life story with the history of independence movement of the country in an intimate, scholarly, admirable, inimitable and grand style. Chaudhuri has rendered history in the form of autobiographies, a biography of Clive, lengthy essays, tracts and many articles which appeared in various magazines for nearly seven decades. His reputation is international as well as national.

Chaudhuri's theses are too provocative to be left without criticism. They are: the age-old predicament of the Indian civilization remaining an "Indian version of foreign civilizations" such as Aryan, Islamic and European civilizations in succession (Chaudhuri 1951, 188); defeatism in the face of nature (Chaudhuri 1965, 218); "the rise of modern Indian culture as a synonym of the Hindu culture and the gradual decadence of the idea of synthesis of the East and the West into substantial Westernization" (Chaudhuri 1971, 30); "denial of exploitation by the West" (Chaudhuri 1971, 30); and reading of our national movement as a manifestation of hatred (Chaudhuri 1987, 253) and xenophobia (Chaudhuri 1987, 47) of Hindus; the view that ours has been and could only remain Hindu nationalism (Chaudhuri 1987, 24) and the "inevitable decay of Indian nationalism into barbarism" (Chaudhuri 1951, 354).

According to Chaudhuri all his writings are "in one way or the other commentary on [this] very large theme known as 'the impact of Western life and civilization on us in India, and the interaction between the two cultures'" (Chaudhuri 1987, 143).

Under the influence of James Mill, Chaudhuri divides Indian history into three cycles — the Hindu, the Muhammadan and the British; and he sees it as "fundamentally discontinuous" (1951, 480). In each cycle, India has been drawn into the orbit of the then living and most powerful and significant orders (1951, 487-488). Our civilization has been an "Indian version of foreign civilizations" such as Aryan, Islamic and European civilizations in succession. Indian history is "inextricably interwoven with the strands of universal history" (1951, 483). He foresees the inevitable loss of our precious knowledge and culture either through a cataclysmic holocaust or slow, putrid decay (1951, 131). He laments the decline of the British Empire in India as well as of the modern Indian culture created by the westernized Indians in the nineteenth century (1951, 478).

Chaudhuri's greatest sorrow has been the disintegration of a genuine modern Indian culture by the "democratic" or "pop" culture of the West (1987, 146). He observes that Indians in their bid to become a second United States in respect of technology are engaged socially and culturally, in creating a Caribbean Island on a continental scale (1987, 961). In defence of his patriotism he writes that the only loyalty he felt towards his compatriots was in warning them about imminent dangers (1987, xvi; 656).

Although Chaudhuri was an introspective and "unknown" Indian, his autobiographical works can also be read as history for their assertions as well as silences. He has taken up the writing of his autobiography to come out of anonymity and chaos (J. Walsh 98) which he feared, would envelop himself and the country. He wanted to prove to himself and to the world that here was a person of potential significance. His desire for self-projection made him title his work *The Autobiography of an Unknown Indian* (1951) in contrast to *An Autobiography* by a well-known Indian such as Nehru. Both Chaudhuri and India could enter the realm of "proper" history and acquire recognition after 1947.

Chaudhuri refers to *The Autobiography of an Unknown Indian* as "more of a national than personal history" (1951, 474) and "more of an exercise in descriptive ethnology than an autobiography" (1951, 131). He wants to tell "the story of the struggle of a civilization with a hostile environment, in which the destiny of British rule in India became necessarily involved" (1951, ix) and aspires that "the book may be regarded as a contribution to contemporary history" (1951, ix).

The specific form of *The Autobiography of an Unknown Indian* has given Chaudhuri a means to convince others by relating his own experiences and an excuse to conveniently dispense with documentary evidence in support of his historical understanding and conclusions. The turmoil of the self in the setting of chaotic times has given rise to a certain awareness manifested in *The Autobiography of an Unknown Indian.* In spite of the exceptionality or even uniqueness of his personal development, he does not believe that "the value of his narrative as historical testimony is impaired" (1951, x).

In fact Chaudhuri has given sound reasons for making his autobiography a sort of historical narrative. He has concluded that no true history of the Empire would ever be written by historians without personal experience and access to adequate historical sources. Some of the sources have been lost, distorted or suppressed deliberately. The archives of the Government of India at the library of the India Office have been incomplete, burnt down and ridden with confusion on the part of the British officials. The accounts by the newspapers and a few national leaders habituated to write letters or diaries were affected by strict censorship. The proceedings of numerous conferences and formal discussions had pleaded positions but hidden the motives. Moreover the crudities of the style of Indian nationalist myth makers, the uncritical obsession of the British with the withdrawal, the compensatory bias of the shallow intellectual historians who were born to the loyalists of the Empire cannot produce objective history (Chaudhuri. 1987, xvii).

Chaudhuri had also probably chosen the literary form of autobiography since his mind was seeped in English literature and his avid and enormous readings in history provided the stuff of his work. He penned what he strongly believed to be the evolution of Indian history, civilization and freedom struggle. He has mainly depended on his memory based on extensive reading. Many critics have seen him more as a literary figure than a historian since he has mainly relied on his memory but not on evidence. This argument doesn't hold water as memory can guide historical reading and enjoys its own epistemological status. Nehru himself had to depend on memory while writing *An Autobiography* and *Glimpses of World History* from the prison. So, *The Autobiography of an Unknown Indian* can not be expelled from history on the ground that Chaudhuri does not adduce historical evidence to his assertions and he can not be dismissed as a pseudo-historian.

Chaudhuri describes his *Thy Hand, Great Anarch*! as "the first chapter of political history of the very much larger history of the end of European rule over non-European peoples and its cultural complement shown in the decline of modern Indian culture created under the impact of European civilization" (1987, xv). Chaudhuri thus explains the ineluctable decline of India and the rest of the civilized world in Splengerian manner (1987, xxiv-xxvi).

The present writer treats Chaudhuri's autobiographical works more as historical works rather than literary ones. Autobiography is history and even though it is often biased, distorted, inaccurate. Like other forms of history, it edifies us through the self-knowledge and failures of the autobiographer (Forguson 155). An autobiographer's individual perspective may also be representative of a large number of people. The very title *The Autobiography of an Unknown Indian* looks paradoxical because an anonymous person hardly bothers about projecting his own self to the public. But he has titled his autobiography as such because he has not only been projecting his authorial self to win recognition but also expressing artistically the views of like-minded compatriots who may run into millions in India that is vast and populous (1951, x).

For the above reasons Chaudhuri's *The Autobiography of an Unknown Indian* and *Thy Hand, Great Anarch!* prove to be compelling works in these times of conflict between universalism and nationalism in the context of relentless globalization, religious conflicts and the necessity of defining one's identity, his stress on climate rather than on economic factors such as colonialism to explain India's historical backwardness.

Chaudhuri describes the predicament of the nation that has fallen prey to the historical law of imitating a foreign culture that has been more vigorous (1951, 468) and of his own individual self that has doggedly striven to escape the fate of his fellow countrymen (1951, 526).

Individually also, Chaudhuri had longed to westernize himself and advised the Hindu to recover his European soul (1965, 33). His life is a saga of the recovery of his European self that has been frustrated for having been born among "the victims of Circe." He has desperately and passionately fought against Indian space in search of "a historical" or an "imaginary European self" that has become an anachronism even in England. He regrets regarding the decline of even European and American civilizations (1997, 74). This kind of self-conflict forces us to examine the present historical context of nationalism and the importance of Chaudhuri's works.

## Critical Assessment of Chaudhuri

### *As a Litterateur*

M.K. Naik refers to Chaudhuri's "acute sensitivity to the appeal of nature" (162), his "exceptional vividness and immediacy" (161) in revealing a full picture of the growth of his mind and his apparently boundless ego that comes out in "his attempt to give a national dimension to his personal history" (162).

Chaudhuri's creative gifts such as extensively personal and even passionate quality of his doctrine, scholarship, natural audacity, intellectual vivacity and an intense fascination with himself have been highly praised. These creative gifts help to make him "an autobiographer of a rare kind," if not an objective critic of national life (Walsh 1977, 133).

Chaudhuri has been recognized as an "outstanding autobiographer" and as a "superb stylist." The autobiographies of both Nehru and Chaudhuri have been called "modern classics on the intrinsic merits" (Sinha 65).

Chaudhuri's *The Autobiography of an Unknown Indian* was considered to have been written from a purely personal angle (Deva 2). It presents a "cultivated, sensitive, modern Indian personality rarely available for occidentals to meet" (Brown 529).

Chaudhuri's prose shows the influence of Johnson, Burke, Gibbon, Macaulay and Mill (Anjaneyulu 1992, 36). His *Thy Hand, Great Anarch*! exhibits "cerebral quality, stimulating threat, encyclopedic range and allusive style, unconventional approach with exhibitions of pedantry, imitating perversity etc." (Anjaneyulu 36).

The merit of *The Autobiography of an Unknown Indian* lies in its "literary rather than philosophical or sociological aspect" (Mishra 13).

*Chaudhuri as a Historian*

Andre Beteille considers *The Autobiography of an Unknown Indian* as a "serious book which no conscientious student of contemporary Indian history can afford to ignore" (626). He praises Chaudhuri's excellence as an ethnographer in describing a lower middle class home in Calcutta (626) but dismisses him as a sociologist or as a philosopher due to his unbalanced judgments.

Chaudhuri's work "evinces a most conscious and detailed recognition of the fact and consequence of Britain in India" (Walsh 1982, 111). One of the achievements of the autobiography according to Raghavenrdra Rao is to study imperialism as a "cultural problem and it shows how complex, confusing, even ridiculous can be the human drama involved in the Empire-building, Empire-running and Empire-dismantling" (Karnani 34).

In *The Autobiography of an Unknown Indian,* the author objectifies his personal destiny as the destiny of a people, a culture and a nation and is "obsessed by the idea of becoming a full-fledged English man" (Chitre 45).

A.K. Majumdar, a historian, criticizes Chaudhuri's theorization and calls his book an autobiography, thus allowing himself to dispense with evidence and chronological order (29). He points out that Chaudhuri ignores Harappan civilization and Dravidian culture (43).

### *As a Writer of Mixed Genre*

Chaudhuri was a "Niagara of knowledge" (Dikshit 43). He is placed by Srinivasa Iyengar on par with D. P. Mukherjee, Irawati Karve, Kishore Gandhi, M. N. Srinivas who can be called literary artists as well as sociologists (Sinha 33). He writes that Chaudhuri's real aim is to write history, and the autobiographical exercise is merely a means to get the history started (Venugopal 213).

*The Autobiography of an Unknown Indian* has been described as "the most significant, single discursive work to be generated by the love and hate of Indian-British relationships" (Walsh 1982, 115). He notices "the psychological composition or structure which results in a triumph of self-education model of the formative power of language, of its capacity to disturb and re-arrange at the depths of personality" (1982, 122).

*The Autobiography of an Unknown Indian* presents "a landscape in which elements such as social criticism, political history and theory, literary and philosophical reflection are mingled together" (Devi 58-59).

The intellectual hero in *The Autobiography of an Unknown Indian* points out what is fine in the English tradition and builds a bridge of understanding between Britain and India, unafraid of the risk of being dubbed pro-British (Murthy 4-5).

*The Autobiography of an Unknown Indian* draws our attention to "a most authentic Bengali style of English and the work's ambivalence towards British and India" (Gowda Online 13 Nov. 1999). Natwar Singh refers to the innate love of both

Naipaul and Chaudhuri for India in spite of harsh appearance (Dasgupta 106).

While referring to *Thy Hand, Great Anarch!*, David Levy, Veld criticizes the historical element but praises the richness of narration, minute observation and aesthetic sense in the book and sees it useful both as history and literature.

Thus, Chaudhuri has received bouquets and brickbats from his critics who have read him from historical as well as, literary perspectives. He has left an indelible mark on the map of Indian English prose as an impressive autobiographer and as a practitioner of a mixed genre with all its complexities and advantages. His interpretation of Indian freedom struggle has been influenced by his distinctive understanding of nationalism of his times.

## Notes

1. Hobsbawm in his *Age of Extremes: The Short Twentieth Century 1914-1991* writes:

   The pretence that there is a Black, or Hindu, or Russian or female truth incomprehensible and therefore essentially incommunicable to those outside the group could not survive outside institutions whose only function was to encourage such views. Islamic fundamentalists who studied physics did not study Islamic physics; even the most culturally nationalist Frenchmen or Germans learned that operating in the global village of the scientists and technical experts who made the world work required communication in a single language analogous to medieval Latin, which happened to be based on English...(429-430)
2. Shapiro continues that the challenge before autobiography is to "recapture time, shape the shapeless, transform an inner image into a picture-mirror for others, make the flesh into words and words into flesh" (422).

## Works Cited

Ali, Sheik. *History: Its Theory and Method.* Madras: Macmillan, 1978.

Anjaneyulu, D. "Nirad C. Chaudhuri, the Writer Extraordinary." *Journal of Indian Writing in English* 20.1&2 (1992): 25-36. Print.

Anderson, Benedict. *Imagined Communities: Reflections on the Origin and Spread of Nationalism.* London: Verso, 1983.

Azad, Maulana Abul Kalam. *India Wins Freedom: The Complete Version.* New Delhi: Orient Longman, 1988. Print.

Beteille, Andre. "The Autobiography of an Unknown Indian." *Journal of Asian Studies* 28 (1969): 626.

Brown, Norman W. "Concerning Asia." Rev. of *The Autobiography of An Unknown Indian*, by Nirad C. Chaudhuri. *Nation* 15 Dec.(1951): 529.Print.

Bruss, Elizabeth W. *Autobiographical Acts: The Changing Situation of a Literary Genre.* Baltimore and London: Johns Hopkins Press,1976.

Chaudhuri, Nirad C. *The Autobiography of an Unknown Indian.* Bombay: Jaico, 1951.

______ *The Continent of Circe: Being an Essay on the Peoples of India.* Bombay: Jaico, 1965.

______ . *A Passage to England.* New Delhi: Orient Paper Books, 1971.

______ . *Hinduism: A Religion to Live By.* New Delhi: B.I. Publications, 1979.

______ . "View Point." *TLS* 30 Nov. 1979: 63.

______ —. *Thy Hand, Great Anarch! India 1921-1952.* London: Chatto and Windus, 1987.

______ . *Three Horsemen of the New Apocalypse.* New Delhi: OUP, 1997.

Chitre, Dilip."Nirad's Nightmare." *Quest* 62 (1969): 43-52.

Dasgupta, Swapan. *Nirad C. Chaudhuri: The First Hundred Years A Celebration.* New Delhi: Harper Collins, 1997.

Deva, Rajiva. "On Nirad C. Chaudhuri." *Quest* 57(1968): 69-75.

Devi, Lakshmi P. "Adverse Awareness: A Study of Nirad C. Chaudhuri's *The Autobiography of an Unknown Indian.*'" *Journal of Indian Writing in English* 17.2 (1989): 55-59.

Dikshit, Sudhakar S. 1984. "The Brahmin of Oxford." *Illustrated Weekly of India* 26 Feb.1984: 43.

Forguson, Lynd. "Autobiography as History." Rev. of *The Value of the Individual Self and Circumstances in Autobiography*, by Karl Joachim Weintraub. *U of Toronto Quarterly* 49 (1979-80): 139-155.

Gowda, Anniah. 1999. Rev. of *Scholar Extraordinary*, by Nirad C. Chaudhuri Nirad C. Chaudhuri Page. Online.com.13 Nov.

Hobsbawm, E.J. *Age of Extremes: The Short Twentieth Century 1914-1991.* New Delhi: Viking,1995.

Howarth, William C. "Some Principles of Autobiography." *New Literary History* 5 (Winter 1974): 363-381.

Karnani, Chetan. *Nirad C. Chaudhuri.* Boston: Twayne,1980.

Kazin, A. "The Self as History: Reflections on Autobiography." *Telling Lives: The Biographer's Art.* Ed. M. Pichter. Washington: New Republic Books,1979. 74-80.

Kumar, Girija. "The exasperating Nirad Babu." *University News* 3 Feb.1992: 79-83.

Levy-Veld, David. "The Notorious Unknown Indian." Rev. of *Thy Hand, Great Anarch!,* by Nirad C. Chaudhuri 13 Nov.1988: 28-29.

Majumdar, A.K. "Portrait of Indian Intellectual." *Quest* 91(1974): 21-32.

Mishra, Sudhesh. "The Two Chaudhuri's: Historical Witness and Pseudo-Historian." *Journal of Commonwealth Literature* 23.1(1988): 7-15.

Murthy, K.V.S. *Kohinoor in the Crown: Critical Studies in Indian English Literature.* New Delhi: Sterling Publishers Pvt. Ltd, 1987.

Naik, M.K. "The Autobiography of an Unknown Indian: A Note." *World Literature Written in English* 21.1(1982): 60-166.

Nehru, Jawaharlal. *An Autobiography.* New Delhi: Jawaharlal Nehru Memorial Fund / OUP, 1980.

Olney, James. *Autobiography: Essays Theoretical and Critical.* Princeton: Princeton UP, 1980.

Oja, Matt F. "Fictional History and Historical Fiction." *History and Theory* 27.2 (1988): 111-124.

Rao, Raghavendra. "An Epitaph for the British Raj." *Critical Essays on Indian Writing in English.* Ed. M.K. Naik. Dharwar: Karnataka U,1987. 345-358.

Rousseau, Jean Jacques. *The Confessions of Jean Jacques Rousseau.* New Delhi: Rupa Paperbacks, 2000.

Rushdie, Salman. *Midnight's Children.* London: Picador, 1983.

Said, Edward W. *Culture and Imperialism.* London: Chatto and Windus, 1993.

Seabrook, Jeremy. *The Race for Riches: The Human Cost of Wealth.* London: Marshall Pickering, 1988.

Sinha, Tara. *Nirad C. Chaudhuri: A Sociological and Stylystic Study of his Writings during the Period 1951-72.* Patna: Janaki Prakashan, 1981.

Shapiro, Stephen A. "The Dark Continent of Literature: Autobiography." *Comparative Literature Studies* 5.4(1968.): 421-454.

Singh, Natwar. K. "Nirad C. Chaudhuri: The Autumn of Discontent." *Illustrated Weekly of India* 21 Nov. 1982. 18-19.

Venugopal, C. "Growing to Manhood: *The Autobiography of an Unknown Indian.*" Perspectives of Indian Prose in English. Ed. M.K. Naik. New Delhi: Abhiman, 1982, 213-221.

Walsh E. Judith. "Growing up in Britain." *Indian Autobiographies On Childhood and Education under the Raj.* London: Holmes and Meir Publishers, 1983, 96-112.

Walsh, William. "On Nirad Chaudhuri." *Considerations.* Ed. Meenakshi Mukherjee. Bombay: Allied Publishers, 1977. 132-136.

______ " The Meeting of Language and Literature and the Indian Example." *Writers in East-West Encounter: New Cultural Bearings* Ed. Amirthanayagam-Guy. London: Macmillan, 1982. 100-137.

Weintraub, Karl J., "Autobiography and Historical Consciousness." *Critical Inquiry* (June 1975): 821-848.

# 23

# Gender Identity: A Case Study of Durga Khote's *I, Durga Khote*

Krati Sharma

Autobiography is a self-portraiture. It is a medium by which a writer meets with his or her self and introduces it to the readers. Brodski and Schenk indicated, "Autobiography presents as untroubled a reflection of identity as the surface of a mirror can provide. The corresponding assumption has been that autobiography is a transparency through which we perceive the life, unmediated and undistorted"(1). In India this genre of autobiography is used by both the genders to express them selves but there is a difference between their ways of expressing.

Women were few in comparison to male writers as the lives of women were not considered significant enough to write about. As Linda Anderson in *Autobiography* points out, it was not that women did not produce texts, but that they were, as in other genres, deemed to be unimportant, crude or illegitimate, to fail to live up to the necessary test of 'great writing'(86). Women are confined to the 'private realm' and presenting their lives as autobiographies would provide them a way to enter into 'public realm'. Women writers by writing about their lives want to make it very clear that they are not weak, incompetent or aimless. They understand their gender responsibilities of being a woman. It is a challenge to enter the public sphere and talk about themselves and their lives.

Patriarchy has its firm stand in Indian society. It is firmly rooted in Indian society, a woman is either in the control of the father, the husband or the son. Males are the one who are the decision makers. Women's are never given independence of thought and execution of their decision. It's an understanding of the veil, that concept of 'purdha' confines a woman to these 'four walls'. It is within his HOME lies her honour and shame.

It is really difficult for a woman to focus on her life only or be 'self centered'. Their lives are woven round their husband and children in brief their family and they cannot talk only of themselves as male autobiographers have done. Male autobiographers in their work focus on themselves and their career only whereas women autobiographers focus around 'others' and they perceive their lives through others. It is very interesting to trace that women writer of Maharashtra used this genre widely as they are more keen and focused about describing their life because women in India have been traditionally been tellers of tales. They have used myths epics in their local versions, lives of gods and animals. They also narrated the stories related to family histories and memoirs.

The first memoir in Marathi is by Ramabai Ranade (1910) followed by Parvati Bai Atavle's *Majhi Kahani* (1928), Laxmi Bai Tilak's *Smitri Chitre* (1934-36), Kamala Bai Despande's *Baya Karve Bado Puran* (1944), Leela Bai Patwardhan's *Amchee Akara* (1945), Indira Bhagwat *Ya Sadashir* (1948), Satyabhama Bai's *Kalete Diwas* (1964),Yasodha Bai's *Amacha Jeevan Pravas* (1965), Godhwari Parvlakar's *Manush Seva Jev Ho Tum* (1970), Sarojini Sarang Pani (1988) other writers include Durga Khote's *I, Durga Khote*, Leela Chitnus, Usha Kiran, Sunita Deshpande, Radha Bai

Apte and many more. Women in Maharashtra were enlightened about their self projection and they inspire posterity that's why once they started this trend it never seems to have stopped or brought to a standstill at any time.

In the present paper an attempt has been made to glance on the life film actor Durga Khote presented in her autobiography *I, Durga Khote.* Durga Khote (January 14, 1905 September 22, 1991) was an Indian actress, One of the foremost leading ladies of her times, she remained active in both Hindi and Marathi cinema as well as theatre, for over 50 years, starring in around 200 films and numerous theatre productions. The title of her autobiography reveals her search of herself it is beautiful description of convent educated girl married in well to do family which finally met with financial crisis ultimately her decision to be a actress where she performed challenging roles and made a name for herself. In the autobiography of Durga Khote' *'I', Durga Khote,* as the title itself states, the focus is on the 'I', the self of the veteran actress Durga Khote. She belongs to an elite class in Maharashtra. She had her own independent thoughts about her position in the society. She had a convent education. Although she lived in a patriarchal society, because of her status she got freedom to chose her vocation and pursue her interests. Her name is symbolic to the goddess Durga, the goddess of Shakti. Durga Khote used the power and made her own life.

She was born in a traditional Mumbaikar Goud Saraswat Brahmin family (Surname Laud) in present-day Maharashtra. By the age of 26, Durga Khote was a widowed mother with her two young sons, Bakul and Harin. She had to seek work in films in order to support her children. In doing so, she became a pioneer of sorts, as she belonged to a traditional family, and since the film industry at that time was regarded as the preserve of the base and the bawdy. Also, most of the female characters were played by men.

Durga Khote faced with financial problems after marriage, she had to make a living for herself and her two young boys, Bakul and Harin. An educated woman from a cultured, well-respected Laud family, she was definitely one of those who changed the way society viewed a working woman, especially a woman working in the patriarchal world of cinema. Neepa Majumdar in her book *Wanted Cultured Ladies Only!: Female Stardom and Cinema in India, 1930s-1950s* discussed about the entrance of well cultured women in Hindi Film industry in 1930's peculiarly highlighting Durga Khote and Leela Chitnis. Neepa Majumdar in the essay "India has no star" comments, "Her public image was constituted by two frequently repeated details about her: that she played rebellious warrior women, and that she was the first middle class, educated upper caste... woman of good family to dare to become an actress"(80). It was considered disgraceful for women of elite class to become actresses. Ms. Khote faced severe criticism for her appearance in the film consequently.

It wasn't an easy life. The struggle to manage profession and home, the lack of support, the economic hardship, early widowhood, an unsuccessful second marriage to Mohammed Rashid, the loss of her younger son Harin in his prime made her a strong woman.

Durga Khote debuted in a minor role in an obscure 1931 silent film, Farebi Jaal, by the Prabhat Film Company, followed by Maya Machhindra (1932), but was soon promoted to play heroine in the 1932 bi-lingual (Hindi & Marathi) film Ayodhyecha Raja, which was the first-ever Marathi talkie and proved to be a runaway hit, where she essayed the role of Rani Taramati. There was no looking back after that. Indeed, she ventured yet another pioneering trend despite working closely with Prabhat Film Company, she broke away from the "studio system" where an actor has to do contract with studio and they have to work for that studio only in monthly basis. She is one of the first "freelance" actors of that era by working occasionally with the New Theatres, and East India Film Co. (both at Calcutta), and Prakash Pictures. She paved the way for the freelance work in the film industry. In 1937, she produced and directed a film titled Saathi, making her one of the first women to step into this role in Indian cinema. The 40s open for her in a big way, with award winning performances in Charnon Ki Dasi (1941) and Vijay Bhatt's classic, Bharat Milap (1942). For both of the films she bagged Best Actress Award from BFJA Bengal Film Journalists' Association Awards.

Durga Khote married very young and lost her husband at the age of 26. Durga Khote, had an unsuccessful second marriage to Mohammed Rashid which she did in order to support her sons but after a couple of years she came out of that relationship. She led a full life she played many role in her personal life it can be the role of daughter, wife or mother or actress or producer than to a mother in law and grandmother successfully. She justified all of them to a great extent. Durga Khote's *I, Durga Khote* shows the reflection on the consciousness of women writers.

Durga Khote started writing her autobiography without any prior discussion about it to anybody. Durga's son Bakul in *Remembring My Mother* writes:

> "Mother did not discuss the writing of her autobiography with anyone in the family. It was written in three years on her farm '*Retreat*' at Jhirad, her own space, totally, for the first time in her life. Although we never talked about it, I believe she chose the medium of the autobiography to came to terms, with herself, with the swings of fate, the initial joys, the enormous

> tragedies and the overreaching successes in rising above them, and the inviolable turmoil and disappointments of her life. In the process, I believe, she ultimately found her peace (IDK VIII)

These line reveals that Durga found solace in reviewing her life while writing her autobiography. Shanta Gokhle who translated Durga Khote's autobiography in English sees the difference of her style with her contemporaries actors Leela chitins and Hansa Wadkar as they also belong to the film industry Shanta Gokhale in *Translators Note* writes:

What impressed me about *Mee, Durga Khote* was the multi faceted personality of the writer as it came through. One had read other autobiographies by her contemporaries. There was much personal agony there but not too much insight into the profession and certainly no experience of the outside world. Durga Khote, on the other hand, was not just a suffering woman exploited by the world of men – as Leela Chitnis or Hansa Wadkar projected themselves to be in their autobiographies.... Durga had gone out into the world, explored it with zest, and made her own assessment about what she had seen. All these experiences are recorded in her narrative, in a style that is both trenchant and lively (IDK XIV).

Durga Khote played various roles in her life she was not just an actress, but also a business woman, a cultural ambassador and director and producer of plays, films and teleflims. She pens her autobiography in the late 70's as she admits in the preface to the autobiography, she having started writing her autobiography as a means of keeping herself occupied. She had no thought of getting it published. Margo Culley rightly explains for a women autobiography writer, "the real defense against unseemly egotism is the social positioning of the text. Family members and friends have urged her to write her life-story and she earnestly hopes it will be of use to others" (12). Durga Khote accepts that it was her public persona that gave her the publicity, fame, money and self evident right to pen her autobiography.

Durga Khote also questions her own identity. She writes, "Had the financial situation of the Khote family not become shaky than where would I have been? My identity would have been confined to being the daughter –in-law of a rich and powerful family, that's all !" ( IDK 183 ). It was within patriarchy that she got this opportunity to make her own identity. Women writers in India find it very difficult to talk about "I" their own persona or they themselves as an individual. Leena Chandorkar writes Durga has revealed, "her willingness to speak to the public about herself with the bold use of 'I' in the title itself"(125).

Durga got married at a very young age to the only son of Khote family Mr.Vishwanath Khote. Her father-in-law Mr. K.D. Khote was a stockbroker. Her husband was a rich spoil brat he didn't bother about earning money or looking into his father business. Durga was eager to know about their family business. Within two years of her marriage their business was shattered and they lost all their wealth. She returned to her maternal home and was worried about her financial condition. Mr. Khote, was unable to shoulder the family responsibilities. On the contrary, it was the courage of Durga that she decided not to be a burden on her generous father who had given them and his sprawling mansion on Charni Road, Bombay. She began her vocation as a tutor earning a small amount. There are many reasons for accepting that career one could be the careless attitude of her husband Mr. Khote. She writes, "I could not understand how and where to restrict the rudderless life style of Mr.Khote. His bad habit and addictions were growing. He would go to office as and when he wished..... He displayed no concern for the house, the children and the finances" (IDK 80).

She opted this career and decided to move out in the world earn a living for herself and her children. She did not want to be a burden on her father but want to rear her children on her own. Hence she chose her career and independence by default and also because it was a necessity.

Living in the patriarchal society, Durga Khote carried her own identity even as circumstances forced it. When she started her career in films it was her father Mr. Pandurang Laud who decided for her because he didn't want that people should fool his daughter. In one of the incidents he showed his concern when V.Shantaram came to sign Durga for her movie "Ayodhycha Raja" Mr. Laud strictly told Durga Khote "You will remain quiet. You will not speak a word. I will decide everything " (IDK 58). It is from this point we discover that Durga's self-confidence grew with the passage of time. She starts taking her decision. She proved herself a woman of the world, as a professional and as a de-facto head of the family. The references to her father reduced and slowly faded out. Durga, does not mention about his death. Bakul Khote son of Durga Khote in the Introduction of Autobiography states: "The family coffers, which she and her father had filled only in the previous decade, were running dry. In 1930, her profoundly wise, practical and supportive father had launched her on the mission of providing a sound financial future for her family" (IDK IX-X).

After reading her autobiography it is very clear that she is a very disciplined and determined woman. She is painfully systematic in chronicling her life date wise. Each chapter in fact starts with a date, the chapter title "Tour Abroad" starts off, "It was July 1951". This shows her sense of awareness of time. She mentions the date of her film releases, the inclusions of several photographs of her receiving awards, the reaction of others about her success etc.

Durga Khote portrays herself as a woman who never pursued success for its own sake, and showed that the success that she got was not by design but by fortune. She was nominated for the post of President for 43rd Marathi Natya Parishad held in Delhi. She says, "The Presidentship of the MNP has a very prestigious tradition. Political leaders, respected writers, journalists, musicians, actors have graced this post. I did not have that stature but some people have greatness thrust upon them" (IDK 19). Her awareness that did not have the stature shows she could look at herself objectively.

Durga Khote makes strict distinction between her public and private life. She describes her personal and professional experiences in different chapters. Leena Chandorkar writes, "The public and private in a woman's autobiography are problematic because a woman describes herself not only through her public achievement but through her personal relationship as well. This is precisely what makes the autobiographical narratives of publicly successful women difficult. It is her public career that made her famous enough to entitle her to write her autobiography"(138). Durga Khote was well read which is exhibited in the manner of narrating her life. In the views of Shanta Gokhale, "Durga Khote is a good storyteller with a distinct sense of style" (*IDK* XVI).

Durga's husband, Mr. Khote, never bothered to bear the domestic responsibilities nor did he pursue his own job. There was a remarkable quality in him: that he did not stop her when she chose her career. The reason was he had seen the world and being educated in the West, he understood the importance of women's liberation and progress. He visited her when she went for shooting in Kolhapur. He was happy when she bought a car for the family. This shows that he was happy seeing his wife support the family finance as he couldn't do so. It also points out that he enjoyed the financial stability that she provided and he could not. It was a decision of convenience as far as he went. This made the situation comfortable for both.

Durga Khote lost her younger son Hiren suddenly who died due to a heart stroke. She grew upset with the death and tense about the future of Hiren's wife Vijiya and her two sons. Bakul, Durga's elder son, played the authoritative and responsible role like her father. She writes, "Finally, Bakul took the decision Papa had taken thirty seven years ago. He called the DKP [Durga Khote Production] staff over and told them, 'Bai and Vijyabai will come to the office from tomorrow. Put them to work'" (*IDK* 140). These words show although she made her own position in the film fraternity there was also the outward façade of a male head cooperating. She created a place for herself in the society which is still patriarchal. She brought fame and prosperity. She started her own Production house and became a director too. She brought property in Bombay and Jhiraad. It shows, whatever her husband's family had lost, she brought it back single-handedly.

Durga had seen the harshness of male dominancy. She did not want her daughters-in-law to face the same trauma and struggle, and encouraged them to have their own identity. She started Durga Khote Production with the partnership of both her daughters-in-law, Tina and Vijaya. She writes, "Durga Khote Production was born in Goolestan, with Tina, Vijaya and I as partners. The financial investments were entirely mine" (*IDK* 140). Secondly she brought the home in the name of her younger daughter-in-law, Vijaya, when her younger son Hiren suddenly passed away. The motive was to provide her security as she herself had struggle in life. Although she was a strong woman, there were men around her, her father, her husbands, Mr. Khote and Rasheed, and her sons Bakul and Hiren. She worked for their security and convenience. She mentioned Farookh Mehta who was a second father for Hiren's kids. She was impressed by his genuine kindness and his attributes in rearing those kids lovingly.

Durga in her life did those works which were especially meant for men. Under the Durga Khote production House she filmed many documentaries and showed to the society that once given a chance a woman could do anything.

Durga Khote seems to be a strong individual in her autobiography. She faces many obstacles on her own. She started her career as a tutor, then decided to act in films which later paved the way for her to become a producer. She travelled on her own, which was rare then, even now it is not so common. She was the one who invited her would-be daughter-in-law Tina from abroad to stay with her and understand the Indian culture. This shows that she was futuristic and ahead of her times. She is the one who showed the way to other women. Her father rightly complimented her after her first film after *Farebi Jaal* failed. Mr. Laud says in *I, Durga Khote*, "I don't care what the rest of the film is like. But you have shown a way for women to earn a living" (*IDK* 35).

The title of the autobiography *I, Durga Khote* shows distinctively that she wants her readers to know that she is conscious about her 'I' self. She was already a public image, people knew her professionally. Now, she wants to give them a glimpse of her private self. She belonged to Maharashtra where many women writers have documented their life. Women writers state about their life, reflect upon their time and make their so called ordinary lives extraordinary and really worth reading.

Durga Khote was very much concerned about the future of her children, and that was the chief reason for her second marriage to Rashid. She responded when proposed by Rashid. In *I, Durga Khote* she writes about it, "I told Rashid frankly there and then that I was not interested in anything beyond my children's future. I needed help. I needed guidance. If marriage were the price I had to pay for it, I would pay it. I was going into this with eyes wide open. But I would not take on any financial responsibility and I would not give up my work in films. I was offering something like a contract" (*IDK* 97). Rashid accepted all her condition and they married. But with the passage of time differences occured and they separated. She was very much attached to her younger son Harin, whom she lost at a very young age of thirty-six and that made her sad. She gives a detailed description about both her sons, a detailed account of their nature, her joyful moments and emotions with them, their education, their marriages and about their children. All this shows her closeness to her sons Bakul and Harin.

Durga was not an ordinary woman, who followed the social norms or set patterns of society. She travelled on her own, managed financial conditions of her in-laws, herself and her father too. She did not want to control her son in the matter of choice of partners. When Bakul informed her about his decision of marrying a European girl Tina, Durga beautifully explains her logic to him. She said to him in *I,Durga Khote*, "Our lifestyles, the filth, poverty, weather and food here. Will she putup with this happily? Think over all those things first. Don't create unnecessary tensions for yourself. Live in a place where both of you will be happy, whether it is here or in the West. It's your decision" (125). This shows her upright and open mind regarding her son's decision on marriage.

Her autobiography is a chronicle of many pleasures and pains she went through as a woman going out to earn a living for herself and her family. She writes about everything with almost the same degree of passionate attachment or dispassionate distance. Gayatri writes in *Translator's Note*, "We appreciate Khote's portrayal of herself as free willed as well as chained by the opinions of others, capable of acting independently, and yet unable at times to take harsh decisions, putting an end to things that only brought her pain" (IDK XXVI).

Durga Khote uses this genre, beautifully which is very complicated. In her autobiography she contains her beliefs and things, her traditions, her modern approach. She is the one who has seen the world and maintained her financial status. Leena Chandorkar in *Eye Me Myself* states, "Dürga Khote's autobiography reveals the dilemma about placing her sense of self in the mind of a woman who was successful at a time when women celebrities were few and far apart. Durga Khote's splitting of her private and public selves textually as well as literally speaks of her struggles to fit into the mould of a 'good' Indian woman." (20)

She lived her life to the full. She enjoyed her work and got rewards for that too. She took challenges in her life, for example, she went and shot a documentary on the life of labourers working in mines in Orissa. She has given minute details about her granddaughters, their aspirations, her job responsibility and many other important events of her life.

It is a custom in Maharashtra that the name of girl changes after marriage. Durga's name was Bannu before her marriage. She accepted her new name and distinguished herself with her new name. This name given by her in-laws became her identity, and she readily accept it. The success she achieved was then her new identity.

In this paper, the case of Durga Khote is taken up as a woman belonging to a traditional Marathi family she came out from the traditional cycle to find a vocation for herself. She is not seen as a mere shadow of her male counterparts. The male members, whether the father or the husbands or sons, did not hamper the protagonist progress towards establishment of her identity. She has narrated those incidents of her life which were critical for her as a woman but she did not stop herself from facing them and thus created a niche for herself.

## Works Cited

Anderson, Linda. *Autobiography.* NY: Routledge Publications, 2001.

Benstock, Shari. "Authorizing the Autobiographical." *The Private Self: Theory and Practice of Women's Autobiographical Writings.* Ed. Shari Benstock. Chapel Hill: University of North Carolina Press, 1988.

Culley, Margo.ed. *American Women's Autobiography: Fea(s)ts of Memory.* London: The Univ. of Wisconsin Press, 1992.

Chandrokar, Leena. *Eye Me Myself.* New Delhi:New Century Pub,2002.

Freidan, Betty "The Feminist Mystique". New York: N.W. Norton & Company, 2001.

Ghokale,Shanta, Translators Note. By Durga Khote. *I, Durga Khote.* Trans. Shanta Gkhole New Delhi: Oxford University Press, 2006.

Khote, Durga. *I,Durga Khote.* Trans. Shanta Gkhole. New Delhi: Oxford University Press, 2006.

Khote, Bakul. "Remembering My Mother". By Durga Khote. *I, Durga Khote.* Trans. Shanta Gokhale New Delhi: Oxford University Press, 2006: IX-X.

Majumdar, Neepa. 'India has no star'. *Wanted Cultural Ladies Only! Female Stardom and Cinema in India.1930-1950.* New Delhi: Oxford Publications. 2007.

# 24

# Sadhana Amte's *Samidha*— The Beacon of Light for Posterity

Deepali Patil

> Our riches may be taken away by fortune, our reputation by malice, our spirit by calamity, our health by disease, our friends by death; but our actions must follow us beyond grave (Colton in Limaye 36).

Beyond the divisions of gender studies, caste class hierarchies, and feminist approaches lies the pristine beauty of human relationships that is nourished and replenished by complete, selfless devotion and dedication—*Samidha.* Nothing could have been more suitable than this title for the life history of two great lives that in turn shaped many, that embraced hardships, struggle, darkness to enkindle the joys of life for the victimized. Indeed Baba and Sadhanatai Amte's lifelong service to the lepers, tribals and the needy maps out a hard-won victory, not over leprosy which at once invoked ostracism but over the diseased mentality of the society that needs to be cured of deep-seated irrationalities and injustices that at times verge on inhuman perversities and cruelties.

*Samidha*, an autobiography that offers a valuable pen-portrait of Sadhanatai Amte, has to be placed on an entirely different pedestal. Her service for a nobler cause, her immensely commendable share in realizing projects like Anandvan,

Ashokvan, Somnath, Gokul, Uttarayan and equally her unflinching faith in Baba's dreams lend a distinct aura of magnanimity around this woman who belonged to an ordinary family but dared to dream and think larger than life. As an autobiography, this book belongs to a completely different world that is purged of all its differences and carries an unpretentious, simple message of 'love'. It attains glorious divinity as it springs from extraordinary lives like Baba and Tai. It is an autobiography which breaks the cocooned individuality. Although it flows from the heart of Tai, it releases the powerful, all-encompassing current named Baba.

In its peculiar, distinct manner the book unravels the life of Baba, very subtly it exhibits the lives of Tai and Baba revealing their inseparability, two lives merged into one, two sides of the same coin. Surprisingly, in an age when we are consciously speaking about the voices of the marginalized, the women, and the downtrodden, this book cuts through and boldly defies any attempts to be pinned down into any of such divisions and proves to be a pure account, unblemished by ego, self-pride, a complete surrender of everything in favor of humanity. *Samidha* graphically records the acquaintance, brief interlude of wooing and the marital life full of hardships and sacrifice of this unmatched couple. However this 'fairytale romance' has been woven in a greater world, that is not confined to the customary definition of family comprising two plus two, qualified by 'personal' interests. Conversely, 'mutual' is the epithet that rules the extended empire of this duo and endless tribulation for a noble cause formed the vital part of their life.

Baba and Tai chose to swim against the current by leading a life of austerity, turning their backs to luxuries and comforts forever. They voluntarily chose to inhabit this world teeming with deadly snakes, scorpions, monkeys, tigers, bees and bears. All this risk taking and pains-taking was a result of deliberate choice. An inordinate desire to perform an experiment in a world that was gradually losing its sensitivity to issues of vital concern directed Baba to the herculean task. Often selfish motives are found governing the actions but here was a man who along with his wife devised his own "share and care philosophy" that held a long sway in the private and public life of Amtes. Sadhanatai nevertheless refrains from calling it a philosophy, she remarks, "It was the simple art of living based on love" (*Samidha* 55). She particularly mentions that Baba never luxuriated in empty speculations. A principal, if not practicable, was discarded; and practicability was not the only test of validity. It needed to have the sanction of the conscience. This rare, unique experiment began with Shramashram, an experiment in communism, in that people belonging to all castes—such as the mahars, cobblers, scavengers, cane-workers and pardhans—would live together, work according to their own capacity and choice, and pool in their earnings into a community pool.

Baba's experiment was not confined to Shramashram. He inculcated a new discipline into the lives of these people by holding evening prayers, teaching them to read and write, thus making them self-reliant and disciplined. As a man who strongly believed in the dignity of labour, he himself made a practice of hard work, selling out things of daily use at a marginal profit. Even books authored by Vinobaji and Gandhiji were available at Sasta Shitya Mandal. If Baba failed to find any buyers for the books on any day, he would fast.

Sadhanatai too offered her services readily and found many odd jobs consuming her time. Picking lice from the girl's hair, giving them a bath were exercises to instill cleanliness, while making brooms that at more times than one scratched the delicate skin of palms, cooking for many, were activities that brought in the joy of creativity and were invested with serenity and peace of mind. Baba claimed, "I will sweep all the cobwebs of dead customs and conventions, blind beliefs and superstitions with these brooms" (74). Strangely enough what he said in zest, became true in earnest. Just as Tai mastered the art of making brooms, she acquired the skill of milking the cows that initially seemed a painful task, so that along with the titles of 'Annapurna' and 'Yashoda' was conferred another title, 'the milkmaid of Anandwan' (106). Sadhanatai and Baba owned a family where everyone was treated equally and she mentions Baba's revolt at the social discrimination in the midst of R.K. Patil's brother's wedding, the then food minister of Central Provinces. Although the minister was a Gandhian and very progressive thinker, his family was orthodox.

This book abounds in many words of wisdom. Sadhanatai exclaims, "It is common knowledge that your first choice restricts the choices available to you in future. You have the freedom to choose only the first thing. The rest follows automatically. If you make your choice consciously, you will never regret it" (57).

Amtes had to pay a heavy price for their novel experiments in social work. They were treated as outcastes. Yet Amtes never lost their self-respect. When Kamaltai Hospet ordered three cans of ladoos on the naming ceremony of Vikas, or people brought gifts and presents, they were humbly returned. Tai mentions, "this earned us their displeasure" (57) yet it was a rule they had made for themselves that they declined to violate. They desired help but not favor, understanding but not sympathy.

Tai narrates the horrifying episode of Baba's suffering due to snake bite and the resultant agony in which he was made to eat green chilies to curb down the pain and avoid sleep. Fortunately, Mr. Mangalikar's timely help rescued him from the danger.

Their dream of social work steadily took concrete shape in the form of 'Maharogi Sewa Samiti'. The couple had unflinching faith in co-existence and equitable distribution of resources, hence they were automatically drawn to co-operative work. They always identified themselves with the have-nots and faithfully observed the well-known Gandhian principle of simple living. They went bare-foot to all places until chappals were manufactured from discarded tyres in their own institution.

They put their body and soul together without any scruples. In July 1948, Tai was completely bedridden due to typhoid. Baba took charge of all the household chores—cooking, washing, drawing water from the well without leaving any room for distinction between 'masculine' and 'feminine' duties. Sadhanatai aptly notes, had the word 'feminism' been in vogue at that time, Baba would have been derogatorily labelled 'feminist' by the staunch believers of patriarchy.

Tai and Baba found their lives enriched by people like Niranjan Kamble, Dada Patil, Mr. Korgaonkar, Mr. Managlikar, and many more who had a golden heart like them. These people could read the mind of Baba and once convinced about his sincerity and honesty became his devout supporters in no time without even arguing about Baba's occasional fits of anger. Tai would generously cook for any number of visitors at any time and Baba would readily be a partner at housework. Indeed a true romantic couple who chased the dreams for many.

Tai's outlook shows her exemplary faith in this man of action. "Baba is a man of many parts. If I am to mention one quality that has lent charm to this personality, it is his quick perception of other's difficulties and the spontaneous help he extends" (67). Baba even went to the extent of cleaning a mad man smeared in his own excreta. Both had to pay a heavy price for their dedication and sacrifice which was often condemned as "reckless fanaticism" (69). The violation of so-called social norms created a rift between the duo and their family members who criticized Baba's secularism and rebellion against custom as "licentious behavior" (69). Tai had no one to turn to at critical times of need. She suffered from typhoid, feared miscarriage during second pregnancy, received serious head injury that needed four stitches in her ninth month of pregnancy. Such physical pains often intensified the mental agony with none from their family to nurse or console them. Regretfully Tai reveals:

> It was impossible to expect them to have so much understanding and maturity as they were bound by conventions and dead habits. They did not mind spending money on ritualistic worship of their lord, lifeless idols of their favorite gods. They refused to be moved by skeleton-like figures of their fellow beings dying of hunger. The apparition-like faces could not arouse their sympathies. They refused to respond to the dried up tears of the poor who had no energy left even to weep. Any attempt on Baba's part to penetrate their complacency and indifference would have been rendered futile (69-70).

Such speculation demands serious introspection from every responsible human being.

Baba's next venture was to sell the vegetables that they grew, he gave freedom to the customers to pick up the vegetables and pay whatever they liked. This experiment was intended more as a test of human nature than as profit making endeavor. Strikingly, no poor man ever tried to cheat, and contrarily rich people usually paid less than the market rate. Surprisingly Baba never criticized them even when the occasion demanded. His faith in and commitment to constructive work remained unshaken. Likewise, when others censured him, he never felt the need to justify himself. The tranquillity of his mind could not be disturbed by anything. It was the serenity of a sage who lived by his own inner strength. Undoubtedly he was a self-made man and judged himself most strictly of all. Equally strange were his ways of getting the best out of a man, sometimes by asking them odd tasks, sometimes by strange bets, and by testing their mettle. It certainly was his trust in essential goodness of man they inspired him for such experiments. Often such experiments were dismissed as "madness or sheer impudence" (72) by others. Such a voluntary life of exile sometimes was disturbing when it directly affected the children. Prakash and Vikas, both from their childhood were exposed to hostile circumstances and dire poverty. The most blissful period of their life was transformed into a period of denials and refusals. Tai expresses her guilt when she says, "we could not give them even the minimum" or "what we could do for them was less than what the poorest of the poor could have done for their children" (73). They never had 'toor dal' or even biscuits, no woollens to cover themselves in severe winters. They once ate away the 'toor dal' cooked by their neighbor when nobody was around which hurt Tai but she was speechless and could not reprimand them for their obvious temptation. They suffered from nausea and sometimes complained too but their complaints were never entertained.

Baba's confrontation with leprosy was painfully shocking. He saw a human body without any vital signs of life. There were maggots wriggling in the wounds all over a body, indeed a repulsive sight. The ghastly sight sent a wave of fear down Baba's spine. Unable to stand it, he preferred to escape. But a man like him was not an escapist, his rigorous self-assessment and serious afterthought culminated into a history. Overnight brooding initiated a miraculous change within his mind and body and he pledged to serve the lepers, "the most untouchables of the untouchables" (77). A man who had simply no idea about the causes or cure of the disease fearlessly dared to plunge into this unknown odyssey. As Tai aptly remarked, "Passion is the hallmark of our life and work", obsessed with the urge to serve the needy and the diseased, Baba voraciously studied all books available on leprosy. He worked under the guidance from Dr. Wardhekar, the internationally acclaimed specialist in leprosy. Many tried to dissuade him from the hazardous undertaking but Baba's determination never faltered. He risked his own body for the sake of experimenting medication on leprosy.

Despite being a lawyer, Baba completed his scientific study of leprosy in the school of Tropical medicine at Calcutta. During this period Baba himself suffered from tuberculosis, he spat blood, but he placed the lives of lepers above his own ailments. He experienced excruciating pain in the right arm, yet he persisted in writing. Vinobaji discerned his unfailing spirit and wrote, "He who is mentally strong, will never succumb to the disease, but surmount it"(91).

Similar challenges awaited at home too, yet this iron-willed man never yielded to any weakness, nor did he ever contemplate retreat from this untrodden path. Uncompromising, he managed everything as Tai suffered from tuberculosis and its recurrence compelled her to shift to Panhala for recuperation. Nothing deterred Baba from his chosen path; he was like a man possessed.

It was during this brief period of separation that love once again bloomed afresh in the form of letters that bestowed warmth, affection and concern for each-other. Nevertheless, such pure love became the unfailing strength, but not the weakness for both. This phase revealed 'urgent longing and persistent yearning' however it never became an impediment, on the contrary it propelled them to action. For the couple it was never the easygoing proverb of "A sound mind in a sound body", it was always "diseased minds in sound bodies". They were far from being healthy and perennial financial difficulties only aggravated their problems but they faced all the challenges squarely, adhering to the principle of 'never a borrower be'. Their work and life was integrated into one, utterly inseparable.

When Baba started treating lepers under a neem tree in Warora, little did anyone anticipate that the dirty road flanked by thick plantations where no one dared to travel alone would become a solace, haven for many afflicted and forsaken souls. Ventures with the wild—the fox, the bear—became a part of the routine.

> Baba's father, Bapuji's heart sank to see their turmoil and labor. He voiced his anxiety-" It is time for me to enter into vanaprasthashrama, leave for the forest at the evening of my life. But you have made for it with the little ones before I could think of it"( 93). Baba gave a characteristic reply, "Isn't it better to enjoy the romance in youth rather than in old age? (94). This undeniably marked the attitude and the spirit with which Baba looked at life and work, which the couple cheerfully called 'love's labour' (94).

This family was battling against indifferent, callous attitude of the masses, fatal diseases, insensitive, orthodox mindsets, and also uncongenial circumstances. As if the difficulties posed by the human world were less that encounters with the wildlife and the unpredictable, hostile weathers created additional problems. Many a times they had to cross flooded rivers, brave intimidating storms, spend roofless nights in torrents of rain in the midst of sheer darkness and wild animals lurking in the vicinity. Twice Baba survived snake-bites at Anandwan. Prakash was only one and a half years old when a black scorpion bit him. He writhed in agony and pain with no medicine available. Next day a bigger one bit Vikas. In the midst of "great pain, life risked and our helplessness", the lethal sting made Tai ransack the room for the deadly scorpion and to her horror she discovered not one or two but hundreds of them hidden everywhere, in folds of clothes, big containers of foodgrains, scattered everywhere. Once a furious monkey attacked Baba which left him badly wounded. It was in the shadow of this 'natural violence' that they spend their days. Adventures of these diabolic creatures were too many. Once Tai saw three snakes coiled at different corners of the trench latrine, but managed to escape somehow. A majestic tiger became a regular visitor to the camp, hunting down one dog after another. But as nature would have it, it was the 'survival of the fittest'. They stood the tests of time.

Some events truly stand out in the memory. Tai received thirty rupees as prize money for writing in the special column of a magazine called *Stree.* She happily bought a sari for the wife of one of their workers. Such generosity of heart is truly unparalleled and rare to find.

Baba was perfectly at ease with abstract conception of God while Tai had faith in ritualistic and ceremonial worship too. She derived from her complete faith in God when Baba went for a major operation in Mumbai and later to London. She sought to invoke the almighty in her own ways, reading scriptures, performing pujas, observing vratas. Sadhanatai and Baba were certainly a endearing couple. Their romantic life was spiced with brief slight disputes at times. There were occasions at which they fought, yet Tai can boast that she never had to sacrifice her right to hold contrary opinions and Baba was gracious enough to accommodate her dissenting voice.

Moments of success never made their heads swell with pride. The Amtes remained firmly rooted to the ground. Hence the institution flourished in all directions, reaching new horizons, nestling hundreds who were rejected by the world. Leprosy was just the beginning—a tiny trickle. Soon it grew into a spate. Between the trickle and the spate were the years of "struggle, labour, isolation and convergence" (126). After 1957 Baba set up a number of medical centres in different villages. With none of the doctors ready to stay overnight at the leprosy hospital, he shouldered everything alone—cleaning the wounds, picking maggots, dressing and bandaging, cleaning the bedpans that took toll on his own health.

Honesty of purpose is infectious too and when the purpose is pleasure and not profit, it brings peace with it. This *sakshatkara,* a vision of divine humanism invoked the good in many, so that from sensitive writers and poets, eminent politicians, artists and professionals all were drawn to witness these springs of divinity on earth. The expanse of the social work gradually spread to various projects, however it demanded the summoning of all their strengths—both mental as well as physical. Empty dreams can never be fulfilled unless supplemented by concrete skills and the creative frenzy to turn them into reality. Each project tested their patience and endurance, which the Amte family along with their doctor sons proved to have beyond comparison.

Baba started training young volunteers and received overwhelming response from the youth of India as well as keen supporters from all corners of the world. He announced the 'Knit India' programme, which gave simple message that hands are given for construction, not destruction. This message proved to be a directive for all the world which has been infested by the pestilence of violence, slowly corroding all the human values.

> It was awful to see the apathy of the ministers, health officials and their coldness towards issues of vital concern. Acharya Atre, the renowned Marathi satirist writer passed a stinging comment, "Unless the ministers get leprosy they will not come to Anandwan. Baba, you are god on earth and Sadhanatai, a goddess" (135).

Both Baba and Tai could have easily gained political approval as they now had worldwide acclaim for their zealous social service. Yet significantly they refrained from making profits or personal gains on socio-political or economic fronts. Tai particularly draws attention to the fact, "In a country like India, where a majority of the people are ignorant and illiterate, how easy it is to become a leader! Religion, caste, economic inequality, or social injustice-select any one of these attractive issues and begin your cacophony against the establishment! That is all you need to become a leader. Spice up your speech with a bit of rhetoric, and people follow you like sheep. You can become their leader overnight. I wonder how many leaders really take the trouble to study the problem from various perspectives" (154). Baba and Tai never sought anything for themselves.

Anandwan gradually became a home for many destitute and provided them not only a cause for living but offered education and work according to their capacity to make them self-reliant and boost their personal esteem. Muktangan, the open air theatre, was established to give an opportunity to explore their potentials. The next generation of Amtes—Dr. Prakash and his wife Dr. Manda too readily accepted the same path. When Prakash decided to step into the impenetrable jungle of Bhamragad, Baba was ecstatic. Tai very rightfully remarked that, 'living with a man like Baba and all his idiosyncrasies is like carrying a school for twenty-four hours of the day (113).

Public approval was not something the Amtes sought. They never lived in the world of images, hence neither were they lured by fake recognition or fame. Hemalkasa project developed by them was a product of a tryst with the tribals for life. It is beyond imagination to think that they spend seventeen long years of their youth with their little ones in the impenetrable wilderness, in complete isolation without electricity. Their challenges were far too trying, as no food items could be stored in the damp weather, which spoilt everything due to fungus, even tea leaves. Chapatis were a distant dream and vegetables a luxury. They too had to fight deadly epidemics like cerebral malaria and even rampant evil practices like human sacrifice, especially of little children.

Tai would surely have experienced a sense of pride when she declared that none of her children, daughter-in laws or grandchildren ever showed the faintest shade of discontent or discomfort to work in adverse conditions or of pride that they were doing any extra-ordinary work (201). If Manda, has "nestled the whole of Hemalkasa under her wings" (203), Vikas was the architect behind the multidimensional development at Anandwan. He desired the best in everything and for everyone. As is rightly remarked, "the projects that Vikas completed dazzle the eyes of the onlookers, those of Prakash, open their eyes" (247). Tai remarks that "our journey began with nothing" but he is out for 'everything', everything for all. It was a fruitful fulfillment. Tai admits in the prolonged phase of decadence it is difficult to breed honest and sincere workers.

Baba and Tai indeed command reverence for what they were and what they did. They cared for their fellow members, instilled new zest for life by making their lives meaningful, gradually settling these lonely souls into everlasting bonds of family and relationships. They started Uttarayan, a sort of home for the aged, and Gokul, a home for the orphans. The gradually settled workers at Hemalkasa adopted children. Eventually the off-shoots of this firmly rooted dream spread and flowered around. Each one readily contributed for others, developing an ever-lasting bond of love and relationship. Not that the Amtes always encountered enthusiastic well-wishers, they also faced challenges from the self-centered people, 'ready to grab rather than wait'. The unfailing strength of Amtes seems to rest in the perennial source of faith in humanity and the vision to look at the brighter side always. Pain was added to pain and was miraculously transformed into power, collective power born out of mighty pain! (251). The capital invested was pure love. As the ultimate truth, only love survives and is the cause of survival. It is the means as well as the end.

This incomparable life history transcends the ordinary by its intensity and zeal for social service. Significantly never does this autobiography give a feel of being steeped in 'pathos', wallowing in self-pity, nor does it ever harbour complaining tone about the hardships and toil. Such a work would easily capture propagandist approach in quest of recognition and worldwide fame, but it needs to be emphasized that *Samidha* remains completely untouched by any such profit-making calculations. The very fact that Baba single-handedly decided to venture into this world full of deprivation and perilous adventures not only raised him in public esteem but also commanded respect and undaunting support from Tai who unquestioningly followed him. "Unlkie many other autobiographies by women, there is neither the loud protest against male domnation or exploitation, which is common, nor the aggressive self-assertion or justification" (Pawar Shobha, xi).

'Self' and 'Other', identity problems, self-assertion, pre-defined spaces—such truisms that categorize modern world are characteristically absent in this new world that offered genuine love, support and refuge not only to the socially ostracized lepers, but also to the poor and the needy, irrespective of caste, creed or religion. Vinobaji's parting words are a testimony to this history of social service created by the Amtes. The words he uttered were permanently carved in Tai's mind, "there will be another Ramayana here, the Ramayana of social service" (95). This unmatched saga of self-inflicted suffering where 'I', 'my', 'me' the qualifying epithets of the personal world are consciously dissolved under the grand 'we' of a greater family is truly an eye-opener for all those who claim to be or wish to pursue this unattainable goal of servitude. Sadly enough one has to acknowledge that in the rapidly deteriorating world, with a bleak future, such an autobiography is a promising story of endless toil and consequent success. Baba and Tai were the true touchstones who metamorphosed the lives of all those who came into touch with them.

What surrounds us is a morbid picture of world infested with crime, greed, deceit, selfishness, where corruption is gnawing at the human values. Such man-made diseases are threateningly in vogue rather than leprosy or cancer. In such pestilence-stricken world *Samidha* seems to be a divine gift that would help us from drifting apart and tow the lost barks to their destinies of purity, innocence and empathy. The Amtes are the luminous lives that spread radiance in a darkened world. Incessantly working for a great and noble cause, they now have their third generation carrying on the mission of social service. Simply reading this story of complete surrender for a righteous cause would infuse equality, breaking down the shackles of egotistical pride, gender consciousness, and personal space, caste or creed differences. Such a book would certainly enrich the lives of all by teaching us to overcome our weaknesses and securing love, serenity, peace and satisfaction that we always pine for. *Samidha* is a real tribute to godliness in mankind. We have a lot to learn and a long way to go.

## Works Cited

Amte, Sadhana, *Samidha*. Translated. Shobha Pawar. Hyderabad: Orient Longman, 2008. All the later references are from the same text.

Limaye, P.N. ed. *Words of Wisdom*. Pune: Snehvardhan Publishing house, 2004.

Pawar, Shobha. "On Translating Samidha" in *Samidha*. p.xi.

# 25

# The Making of a Woman in Urmila Pawar's *The Weave of My Life: A Dalit Woman's Memoirs*

Shubha Acharya

*The Weave of My Life: A Dalit Woman's Memoirs* is an autobiographical rendition of the author Urmila Pawar but the book combines two extremely important processes in the history of mankind from the Indian context. On the one hand it portrays the struggle of dalit community in its attempt to create an identity of its own and on the other hand it depicts the birth and growth of feminist tendencies in a complex socio-cultural set-up.

In the introduction to the book, Maya Pandit writes, "Autobiography as a genre is said to have begun with the emergence of the sense of individual identity under capitalism". But during the time *The Weave of My Life* was originally published as *AAYDAN* in Marathi. There had been many voices that had already spoken and conveyed the story of their lives. Baby Kamble's autobiography *Jina Amucha* is considered the 'speaking voice' of the Mahar community. There had been others too, like Laxman Mane, Sharankumar Limbaye, Janabai Girhe and many more. Urmila's story can be accepted as a continuation of the voices yet it is significant in experience, in narrative depth and in the making of a 'woman'.

Is *The Weave of My Life* an autobiographical fiction? Does it carry within it the technical features to be considered an autobiography? Are there any digressions from the normal? The questions are best answered with a soulful reading of the book. Urmila Pawar's book can be said to be a full version movie against the trailors that she wrote of her life's stories when she brought out her creative outpourings in bits and parts in various magazines published then. And yes it is a narrative genius because the narration carries the readers on a life journey, giving him/her the juicy details of her experiences, thoughts, views, opinions and reactions. It makes the reader smile, laugh, sad, cry and remark at Urmila's actions and reactions. She allows the reader to open the window to her world and enjoy the journey periodically and grow sentimental at other times. *The Weave of My Life* is an experience to be read, understood, gained and digested.

The novel is an honest monologue of Urmila's life-journey. It combines two strategies of writing techniques, the autobiographical and biographical method of writing. It contains two aspects of a social development, the emergence of the Ambedkerite movement and feminist approach. The novel also portrays two life styles, the urban life spent in Phanasawale, Ratnagirin and Chinchwad in the early half of the book and life in Mumbai in the latter half of the book. But as stated by the famous Marathi writer Shanta Gokhale there is one feature of her persona that runs through the entire account—her ironic view of life and her irrepressible sense of humour.

Urmila states that the moment she realized that she could write about her life, she started penning her thoughts 'weaving' the most precious aspects of her experiences with family, outsiders, and society. Her close relatives aided her bringing out the memories of the past. Urmila's story is a peek into her growth from a notorious child to a famous writer. She finds her voice, her life's goal and creates a place for herself in the process in the world of men and letters. The first sentence of the book, "Women from our village travelled to the market at Ratnagiri to sell things," sets the mind of the reader and the pace of the novel. The word 'travelled' is suggestive of the beginning of the journey. The reader is led on one level through the rocky winding paths of remote places like Phanasawale and the fairly known town of Ratnagiri to the gullies and bylanes of Mumbai, Bhiraunde, Chiplun, with a nostalgic return trip to Ratnagiri and Phanasawale towards the end of the book before finally taking us back to Mumbai. The beginning is a beautiful description of the rural life of the people belonging to the village of Phanasawale. These village folk would walk for miles to the market at Ratnagiri to sell their wares. The women who are the travelers, their topic of conversation, the terrain that they tread and their joys and sorrows are the premise on which the story is built. It seems that the women have been taking this route eternally and Urmila becomes a part of this group sometimes and so does the reader.

The autobiography carries features of a biography in the first chapter of the book. The events and incidents narrated by Urmila about her forefathers are a testimony of the inputs received from relatives and family members. Urmila lost her father when she was in her third standard, so stories about her father's first marriage, his schooling, his marriage to her mother; episodes of her great-great-great grandfather, the man who had founded their settlement at Phanasawale and the Mahar's acquisition of the right to perform various rituals for the villagers are biographical in character. She has written extensively about life in the village from personal experience but amongst the various characters mentioned by her three people stand out as special – her father (Baba), mother (Aaye) and her husband. These three individuals were responsible for the manner in which Urmila shaped her life. She wrote that she hated her father for pressurizing her to study and follow a strict regimen. Her hatred was such that she sometimes prayed that he should not return home. But when he was bed-ridden with severe jaundice, she wanted him to live. She admits that importance of education without gender discrimination was initiated by her father and carried forward by her mother. She has beautifully portrayed the significant role played by Baba in her life and in the life of the villagers. He played a multiple role of a school teacher, priest, family provider (he used to work for a couple of hours every day in the cloth shop of Shri Rangoba Lanjekar) and an advisor. His work kept him away from the house because he would stay close to the place where he worked as a teacher. But he always supported education. His last words to mother on the death bed were "Educate the children". She believes that his insistence that, 'Let the girls go to school. They have to stand on their own feet, be independent. They must also learn to ride bicycles,' captures effectively the ignition to her liberation.

Urmila's account of her Aaye is meticulous. She describes the mother-daughter relationship with pristine clarity. From childhood till she lost her mother, Urmila speaks of her mother as the stoic pillar of strength. In absence of her father, it was her mother who was the controlling force for everyone at home. Urmila's description of her mother as the umbrella of their life becomes pronounced when she writes, "In the past it was my father's hands that worked, now it was hers." She says all her life she hated her mother for being a miser and also for being perpetually busy (Aaye would sit under the vad tree in our courtyard, weaving her bamboo baskets till late at night. That was the last thing our eyes, heavy with sleep, would take in before we went to bed. And when we opened our eyes early in the morning, she would be sitting in the same place (64). Since she was a girl born in a backward caste in a backward region who had lost her father early in life, it was her mother who had to make ends meet. Their meagre condition made life difficult for the children because food was always scarce in their house. But mother worked hard constantly muttering, "God, I have to weave the basket, got to finish that one!" (65). In her childhood Urmila felt that she was deprived of many things because of her mother, but later she realized that it was her mother's methods of making her children understand the true value of 'living with dignity'—'a life of respect'. She did not want them to depend on anybody for anything. It was her training in life that made Urmila strong. The death of her teenaged son brought the mother and daughter together in grief and she understood the reason for her mother's desire to drown herself in weaving aaydans endlessly. Urmila tried the same method and immersed herself in writing.

Urmila has received laurels in her life as a writer and community worker. Her parents were instrumental in laying the foundation for her inclination towards the world of letters. But a partly supportive and loving husband had paved the way for her growth and development as a complete writer. In a conservative and orthodox environment, she dared to fall in love and marry Harischandra. She speaks of life with Harischandra before and after marriage unabashedly. Her teenage escapades with him and sweet experiences immediately after marriage bring a smile on the face of the reader. This is experienced when she writes of her first night with her husband in a crummy lodge with a bagful of live clams, her mother's gift, chattering away under the bed. She has illustrated her husband with utter sincerity which describes their marital life in true light. Like a normal couple they had their moments of happiness, togetherness, isolation and bitterness. After settling in Mumbai, she started working and her work sharpened her writing skills. She wished to complete her graduation and he agreed with much reluctance. She moved ahead and joined a woman's organization but the proactive wife in Urmila confused him. She gained strength from her education and lunged forward to work for social causes, attending sahitya sammelans, writing and publishing.

Urmila wrote that for a man who had since his childhood seen women running a smooth household, Harischandra was perplexed with her behaviour. She gradually understood that her writing, her education, her participation in public programmes and her fame as a writer irritated him. She was equally confused with his contradictory attitude because on the one hand he was proud of her writing but resented her fame as a writer and public figure. However, she states that their relationship withstood all storms. Like all fathers he was angered and objected to their elder daughter Malvika's love marriage to a young man from Uttar Pradesh. Urmila's support to the marriage enraged Harischandra and the marriage drew them apart from relatives and from each other. But destiny and grief brought them together. Mandar's death and Harschandra's illness changed their outlook towards life. She says it pained her to see him suffer and memories of her past life with him surfaced repeatedly overpowering everything else in her life. She remembered him as a student, a lover, a suitor, a husband and a father. The writer in her wrote, "Just as the drying water at the bottom of a pitcher leaves a thin white circle, I could see death creeping closer to the point where life had begun for Harischandra, completing the cycle of life and death." His death left her speechless.

*The Weave of My Life* is not a plain description of a life lived with smiles and tears but is also considered as a milestone in the archives of resources for practising dalit studies as critical and inclusive social science. It depicts Urmila's 'becoming of a modern individual' who emerged from the Phule-Ambedkarite movement and worked ceaselessly to grant individuality to both men and women. She writes:

> "I felt that a woman was also an individual, just as a man was, and was entitled to all the rights of an individual. If man has muscle power, woman has the power to give birth. These are distinctly different capacities and need to be evaluated differently not in the same way. On the other hand, the people of my community often confronted me with, 'Who are those women you are mixing with these days? Take care; they belong to a different caste. Our community does not need their thoughts and values,' while they said this, their way of saying made me feel as if I had joined some criminal gang. I realized that I now had a new vision, a new perspective of looking at women. I had lost my fear. The women's movement had given me great strength to perceive every man and woman as an equal individual. It had taught me to relate to them freely, without any prejudice whatsoever." (248)

Such articulations provide an understanding and investigate the notions of caste, democracy, equality, and freedom. As a memoir, Urmila's book presents the readers with various instances of brahminical subjugation of the dalit groups. It covers nearly three generations of 'inhuman practice' by one section of society on another. Amidst the story of self discovery, she narrates events and incidents of dalit sufferings. The discriminatory treatment in schooling one's child, drawing water from wells, performing religious rituals, celebrating festivals (Holi and Shimga festival) reveal the way of life forced on the 'untouchables' by the 'upper class'.

As a woman born into the Mahar community, Urmila speaks of the manner in which patriarchy 'doubly marginalized' the women folk. Her own experiences present a self-contained world of consensus pitted against a world of uncomfortable co-existence in which the dalits must compromise on their pride and their social standing inorder to survive. She endured the 'distancing' as a child when her mother sent her to deliver baskets to the upper caste houses. The tactics used by their landlady at Ratnagiri to oust them from the rented house and her writer friend Kelaskar's prejudiced behaviour towards her due to his belief that "one has to be born with a high IQ" are examples cited by her of upper class discrimination of the dalits. But the tragic circumstances in which her son died is heart wrenching. A brilliant young boy on the verge of becoming a doctor is driven to kill himself over accusation of reservation to low castes.

Urmila Pawar candidly discusses the conversion of the Mahars into the Ambedkarite fold and the subsequent changes in the cultural patterns with the embracing of Buddhist religion. The changes relieved them from the atrocities of the brahmanical group. It helped them to proceed in the path of self development but a trip back to Phansawale forty years later revealed the utter lack of development in the villages. She conveys a feeling that the change which was supposed to enlighten lives had evaporated into thin air leaving an unchanged atmosphere in the mental makeup of the people although the village was touched by modern infrastructural changes.

In the latter half of the book Urmila emerges as a pillar of female strength making serious efforts to revolutionize thoughts against all odds – the greatest being faced by opposition from her husband. Ashley Tellis, an activist focusing on gay, dalit and women's issues comments that 'In her autobiography *Aydaan*, her deepest love, for her husband, is constantly lashed by his sexism, by his inability to see her as powerful, by his implicit resentment of her growing into the most important dalit feminist writer of her, and many other, generations. She fights him; she fights him to the bitter end. And yet, after his death, she can still offer a stunning portrait of him, swimming in his own particularity, singular and beautiful.

Urmila Pawar's *The Weave of My Life: A Dalit Woman's Memoirs* is a product which, as Shanta Gokhale says, "belongs to the genre of autobiography, which is rarely practiced by Indians as it presents the major issues of class, caste, and gender in the Indian context. Apart from recording a woman's discovery of selfhood and assertion of identity, it also offers a background picture of the Indian (especially Maharashtrian) culture, including interpersonal and intercommunal relations, clashes, and tolerances." Her autobiography brings forth the image of a persona who hopes for the dalit future without politics. She emanates an urge in people to fight caste and prejudice on all fronts, beginning at home and continue it till humanity wins.

## Works Cited

Gokhale, Shanta; Between caste and Gender, *The Hindu, Sunday,* Feb. 01, 2009.

http://www.himalmag.com/component/content/article/125-.html (Well beyond Khairlanji April 2010, By Ashley Tellis).

Pawar, Urmila; *The Weave of My Life: A Dalit Woman's Memoirs*, Stree 2008.

Randhawa, Harbir Singh; *Dalit Literature:Contents, Trends and Concerns,* Sarup Book Publishers Pvt. Ltd. 2010.

## 26

# Coming to Terms with the Self in Andre Agassi's Autobiography *Open*

Kunal Ray

Since the time of Augustine's *Confessions,*[1] autobiographies and biographies are generally perceived as a method of knowing the self. They are like interior monologues which chronicle one's life story beset with problems and setbacks or wallowing in nostalgia and cataloguing a time and era lone gone by. At times, these characters are also reminiscent of Aristotle's tragic hero with one central flaw that causes the mayhem.

The narrative is crafted like a perfect plot that would sustain a reader's interest through the debacles and achievements in a life story which could be exaggerated to elevate the subject and present a near fictional image of the subject of such works to achieve self glorification amongst several other reasons. It could also be a reworking of memory in a fashion that sells. But needless to say, it is always a compelling story.

With the lines gradually blurring between fiction and non-fiction, this question is of particular relevance. Besides, every story is believed to be a confession. Thus, this paper shall seek to explore the confessional traits in the autobiographical work, *Open* by Andre Agassi written in collaboration with journalist J.R. Moehringer[2] and also probe if autobiographies can actually encapsulate the real image of a subject or are they merely representational and selective. The paper will also examine questions on authorship and narrative technique in the context of the book.

The first chapter begins on a dramatic, discordant note:

> I'm seven years old, talking to myself, because I'm scared, and because I'm the only person who listens to me. Under my breath I whisper: Just quit, Andre, just give up. Put down your racket and walk off this court, right now. Go into the house and get something good to eat. Play with Rita, Philly, or Tami. Sit with Mom while she knits or does her jigsaw puzzle. Doesn't that sound nice? Wouldn't that feel like heaven, Andre? To just quit? To never play tennis again? (Agassi 27)

Tennis legend Andre Agassi lays bare his personal history in *Open.* Candidly written, it is an interesting attempt to deconstruct the popular image of the star and humanize the character by chronicling events that speak volumes about his vulnerability and emotional dilemma like any other person. The narrative is peopled with such events that lay emphasis on his real self which would have taken a different shape provided some occurrences and associations could be avoided. What we thought we knew was actually an illusion, a façade created by a person who spent much of his life living for someone else. One also seems to question whether there is any love for the game at all or was it all mere compulsion? Agassi seems in a pressing need to share his story to obtain an outlet to project his real self may be as opposed to the more popular public image. It is an invitation to the deep dark recesses of his mental landscape. He remarkably demystifies his star self to present a more endearing, balanced and relatable humane self. This candid demeanour is an extension of the confessional self of the author which finds literary expression in this book. Susanna Egan talks about a guilty narrator[3] who gets relief through telling his story and Agassi's tale in the overwhelming confessional mode has shades of the same. Confession is also a dialogue and the author adroitly uses this mechanism to establish a communion with his readers and through this entire exercise, he derives considerable satisfaction.

The book rather shockingly opens with Andre's declaration of his hatred for tennis and how the game cost him his childhood. He writes recalling how he loved going to school but was compelled to drop out at the ninth grade to pursue the game with single minded devötion:

> The better I get at tennis, the worse I get at school, which pains me. I like books, but feel overmatched by them. I like my teachers, but don't understand much of what they say. I don't seem to learn or process facts the way other kids do. I have a steel-trap memory, but trouble concentrating. I need things explained twice, three times. Also, I know that my father resents every moment I spend in school; it comes at the cost of court time. Disliking school, therefore, doing poorly in school, feels like loyalty to Pops. (Agassi 34)

Andre had practically no childhood. His contempt for tennis grew manifold when he was denied the liberty that childhood begets. Andre's father, Mike Agassi was a failed boxer whose is an immigrant's story of trials and tribulations in a foreign land. It may also be viewed as an interesting sub-text. Mike was determined to realize his dream of superstardom through his four children and subjected all of them to almost abusive training. The three eldest succumbed to the pressure but Andre Agassi's talent in the sport was evident since an early age. Andre loved football and given an opportunity, would have pursued football as a career but his desires invited his father's wrath and gradually had to be subverted in the face of his monumental inclination to make a tennis star out of his son. Andre Agassi candidly admits his hatred for his father who loomed large like a dictatorial figure throughout his childhood and adolescence. His father was a control freak who only cared for his ambitions. In the seventh grade, Andre was shipped off to the Bollettieri Academy in Florida much against his will. This made him a "rebel" (Agassi 81). He speaks of the Academy as a "glorified prison camp" (74). Again the search for the true self looms large here. The situations compelled that reaction. His tennis flourished at the cost of seeking solace in alcohol and drugs. Nobody objected as long as he won matches. The academy, in Agassi's words, was "Lord of the Flies with forehands" (74).

Agassi also puts on record his hatred and unmatched dislike for his coach, Nick Bollettieri, who is widely, regarded as an innovator whose academy spawned dozens of star athletes. Agassi says Bollettieri was clueless about dealing with children and he suffered every day at the Academy. Aggasi's childhood met an untimely death. He could reconcile himself to his father's cruelty and autocracy much later in life. Almost confronting this dilemma, he writes:

> I stand and feel an overpowering urge to forgive, because I realize that my father can't help himself, that he never could help himself, any more than he could understand himself. My father is what he is, and always will be, and though he can't help himself, though he can't tell the difference between loving me and loving tennis, it's love all the same. (Agassi 202)

The book thus becomes a medium of catharsis for its author. Autobiographies and biographies often convert into mouthpieces but this book is also elliptic in the sense that it relies on implication and suggestion instead of a direct narration. It leaves several things unsaid, inconclusive and open ended thereby involving the readers into the narrative framework. The readers cease to be passive participants and feel invited to partake of the cathartic expression. The universality of the text lies in the emotions chronicled which is a part of the trajectory of any human life. The conversational tone of the narrative also humanizes the central character of the book, Andre Agassi, in this case. This further goes on to prove the prominence of language and linguistic expression in works of autobiographies and biographies. Describing an emotional encounter, with his father, he says:

> He says nothing. Not because he disagrees, or disapproves, but because he's crying. Faintly I hear my father sniffling and wiping away tears, and I know he's proud, just incapable of expressing it. I can't fault the man for not knowing how to say what's in his heart. It's the family curse. (Agassi 165)

Another thought provoking part of this narrative is the discussion on the creation of a public image for a celebrity. Andre Agassi was castigated for an ad campaign saying "Yes. Image Is Everything" (Agassi 131). It was often said that Andre Agassi is a well crafted empty image. But what is of particular relevance here is the amount of scrutiny a public figure invites upon him. No aspect of his life is beyond the public eye. Why was Agassi in search of an image? Was he trying to hide his real, vulnerable self from constant scrutiny? Dramatic tension pervades the landscape of this autobiography and it also transpires between the reader and the narrator. It raises several questions on the composition of a public image and its ingredients and their proportions.

But what is an image? Is an image directly proportional to certain qualities that a public personality has cultivated over the years owing to his achievements in his chosen field of expertise or do we associate an image with aspirations of his followers carefully constructed around his public self by several external factors and agencies? Are our lives awash by multiple images? Are images durable or do the same image transform itself in multiple ways? Are images fleeting or a permanent reserve of time and space? Is Agassi in search of a modernist image? It leads us to probe the greater question whether autobiographies are just an image of the real self of the subject? Can the real self be ever captured in mere words? Is Andre Agassi's real self as it appears in the book a reworking of the interlocutor, J.R. Moehringer? Isn't a large part of the book based on his perceptions of trying to make sense of Andre and episodes from his life? May be he is creating a dichotomy that is non-existent. It could be an image perceived by Moehringer. Is Nick Bollettieri's academy also a well crafted image that green signals the arrival of star athletes? Is an autobiography as dynamic as an image of the real self? This could also be related to the bigger question of authorship. How much of the narrative is to be trusted to unravel the real self of the narrator? It could be seen as a retelling of the same incident keeping the readers in mind as a desired audience. It is at this juncture that autobiographies and biographies take a hagiographic turn. Isn't much of what is desired lost in this process of translation of thought from one person to another? The purpose of literature is to ask important questions and not offer answers on a platter. The narrative quite successfully interweaves these probing questions and makes us re-examine the accepted dynamics of autobiography and biography writing in the process.

In this book, Andre also accepts that during one low period he found solace in crystal myth, supplied by his assistant, "Slim" (Agassi 256) and later lied about it to tennis officials, thus avoiding a three-month suspension. His fans would also be disappointed to know that his hair was also manufactured. He wore a hairpiece all along. But he makes a bold attempt of deconstructing the image people have nursed of him for ages. Winner of eight Grand Slam titles and tens of millions of dollars, with every victory life seemed more vapid for Andre. He immersed himself in alcohol and drugs. Agassi found escape off court surrounded by the surrogate family, he assembled and in most instances paid for, in particular the company of two father figures—his physical trainer, Gil Reyes, and his coach, Brad Gilbert. According to sports writers, these people "fed his ego" (Agassi 141). Was this also an image and a sense of false security and family that nourished Andre and contributed in reconstructing his game, and made possible his extraordinary, late-career resurgence, when, at last finding joy in tennis, he briefly eclipsed his archrival, Pete Sampras. It has been noticed that literary confession may express regret but simply eliminates the burden of sin or guilt. Stephen Spender[4] echoed that confession always comes from an isolated individual seeking wholeness with the human community. Confession, after all, is another form of dialogue. Agassi's sense of isolation and desire to mend bridges is palpable throughout the narrative.

Now coming to the question of remembrances, one is almost compelled to ask how truthful are these? What is the role of memory? Cannot memory be manipulated to accommodate selective representation? Memory could be what we wish to retain and what our present recollection of a past event is. These are constant grappling questions in the realm of autobiography and biography writing. The narration is elliptic and the clues for the questions posed are embedded in the text and may be so are the answers to resolve the queries but the narrative ploy demands the readers to draw their own conclusions without offering any steadfast simplification.

Agassi's marriage to film actor Brooke Shields was a mistake. They were diagonally opposite people and the marriage fell through. Brooke felt Andre had problems of adaptability and refused to partake of new things and experiences in life. One can also examine the role of language in the narrative here which displays the churnings of the mind of the subject and offer an outlet to express the agony and despair of separation from a loved one:

> I tell her she's right, I don't understand. I tell her I don't see how we got here. I tell her how unhappy I've been for so long. I tell her I'm sorry that we've grown distant, that I've grown cold. I tell her about the whirl, the constant whirl, the centrifugal force of this tennis life. I tell her that I haven't known who I am for the longest time, maybe ever. I tell her about the search for a self, the endless monologue in my head, the depression. I tell her everything in my heart, and it all comes out halting, clumsy, inarticulate. It's embarrassing, but necessary, because I don't want to lose her, I've had enough losing, and I know if I'm honest she'll give me a second chance. She says that she's sorry I'm suffering, but she can't solve it. She can't fix me. I need to fix myself. By myself. (Agassi 280)

Soon after divorce in 1999, Andre Agassi courted another tennis star, Steffi Graf, his present wife and mother of his two kids. They both had similar life stories and shared their hatred for the game. Like Agassi, Steffi Graf also had an obsessed parent who guided her to superstardom at the cost of her childhood. There are too may sub-texts in the story and they all merge and contribute to the narrative structure which draws leverage from these incidents. It is perhaps interesting to note here how two stories intersect and there is seamless assimilation with the narrative. The narrative never turns to be droning confession though. It is an instance of combination of elements that contribute to great storytelling. To restore the childhood of several under privileged children and provide them access to good education, Andre Agassi set up Andre Agassi College Preparatory Academy which is a tuition-free public charter school open to students in Kindergarten through twelfth grade in 2001. It was conceived from Agassi's belief that nothing has a greater impact on children's lives than the education they receive. This is not only cathartic but a realization of a dream long cherished:

> Perry and I choose to set the academy in the worst neighborhood of West Las Vegas, where it can serve as a beacon. After months of scouting locations, trying to find a lot that's for sale and affordable and capable of accommodating an evolving campus, we find an eight-acre parcel that meets all our requirements. It's in the center of an urban wasteland, surrounded by pawnshops and homes on the verge of being torn down. It's on the site of the original Las Vegas, the long-forgotten outpost where settlers first arrived, which was later abandoned. I like that our school will be placed on a site that has a history of abandonment. Where better to initiate the kind of change we envision in the lives of children? (Agassi 274-275)

In tandem with the confessional landscape of the book, there is a shift in the narrative towards the fag end with a silent acceptance of Andre's liking for the sport contrary to the beginning of the book. Is this a transformed self of the sportsman speaking who is finally at peace with the world around him? It is interesting to witness his contempt for the game turning into love. How else can you describe that while his contemporaries were retiring, Agassi was training like never before to stay near the top as long as possible? After having played tennis initially for his father and then later because he didn't know what else he could do, over the final years of his career it seems that Agassi was finally playing for himself. Agassi calls the final chapter of the book "The Beginning" (379) and it is clear that he is very excited about life after retirement from professional tennis. Eyes are not trained on him anymore, expectations not riding high, no pre match and post match analysis, no grueling training sessions, no frenzied travelling and far away from the life of a coveted image. He prefers his life of quiet and solitude. Andre Agassi can finally 'play' himself and just be. The narrative restores normalcy in the life and the book thereby taking it to a well-desired conclusive end:

> Rain has been falling off and on all day. Stefanie peers at the sky and says, What do you think? Come on, I say – let's try. I'm willing if you are. Willing. She frowns. She's always willing, but she can't speak for her calf, which has been giving her problems since she retired. Especially lately. She looks down. Darned calf. She has a charity match in Tokyo next week. She's playing to raise money for a kindergarten she's opened in Eritrea, and even though it's only an exhibition she wants to do well. She feels the old pleasure to do well. Also, she can't help but wonder how much game she has left. I wonder the same thing about myself. It's been a year since I walked off the court for the last time at the U.S. Open. It's autumn, 2007. So we've been planning all week to get out there, hit with each other, but now the day has come and it's the one rainy day all year in Vegas. We can't build a fire in the rain. Stefanie looks again at the overcast sky. Then at the clock. Busy day, she says. She has to pick up Jaden at school. We only have this small window. (Agassi 379)

*Open* makes a departure from conventional sports writings. Generally, in such books the emphasis is on discussing details of the game and other technical knowhow takes precedence and the life story becomes a sub-text. Sports biographies and biographers also seem to be feeding an ever expanding industry that consumes any kind of writing with an almost voyeuristic zeal. It appears to be a perfect Capitalist model to churn money. But *Open* is different. I would say it is an anti-sports book which breaks away from conventions in sports writing. It just does not stop at mimicking reality but enhances it and the change begins with the title itself which is an open-ended, inviting proposal to enter the mindscape of a celebrity. The life story and aspirations of a much scarred soul is the anchor of the book and the sports becomes secondary. It could be anybody's story. The subject is the reason for readers to get drawn to the book but they are absorbed into the tale of a life well crafted devoid of hagiographic details. It is the celebration of life and its dimensions which makes the book an experiment in this genre of writing.

## References

1. Usually considered the first modern autobiography.
2. American Pulitzer Prize winning journalist renowned for his memoir *The Tender Bar.*
3. See Egan, Sussana. "The Literary Confession and its Religious Model". *Autobiography: The GreenhavenPress Companion to Literary Movements and Genres.* Ed. Lawrence Kappel. San Diego, CA: Greenhaven Press, Inc, 2001. 40.
4. See Stephen Spender, "Confessions and Autobiography" in *Autobiography: Essays Theoretical and Critical.* Ed. James Olney. Princeton, NJ: Princeton University Press, 1980, pp.120-121.

## Works Cited

Agassi, Andre. *Open: An Autobiography.* USA: Harper Collins, 2009.

Kappel, Lawrence., ed. *Autobiography.* San Diego, CA: Greenhaven Press, Inc, 2001.

Egan, Sussana. Patterns of Experience in Autobiography. Chapell Hill: University of North Carolina Press, 1954:

http://www.studentpulse.com/articles/31/sublime-inauthenticity/how critical is truth in autobiography/scott berghegger.

# 27

# Autobiographies as Negotiations, Religion as Subterfuge: A Study of *Amar Jiban, My Story* and *Amen: The Autobiography of a Nun*

Minu Susan Koshy

> Throughout most of human history, the individual does not oppose himself to all others; he does not feel himself to exist outside of others, and still less against others, but very much with others in an interdependent existence that asserts its rhythms everywhere in the community (As quoted in *Broughton* 2:232).

An autobiography is essentially an attempt on the part of the subject, the "I", to "give an account of itself" (Butler 3). Since the account is inevitably given to an 'other', there is an (un)conscious recognition of the power of the 'other' to confer legitimacy or acceptability upon the subject. As such, there will always be an attempt on the part of the subject, to negotiate with this 'other', so that it (the subject), does not seem to exist outside or against others. However much the "I" may seem to be a dissenting, resisting subject, the fact remains that even the very act of giving an account of oneself, writing an autobiography, is an act of self-justification, an attempt to place oneself in the accepted ethical, moral realm. This attempt becomes more evident in the case of women's autobiographies, as the subjects have to assert their political choices through a medium that is considered as belonging to the 'stronger sex', and at the same time, present themselves as acceptable members of the normative society, which considers the act of writing as something unacceptable in a female. Hence, she has to negotiate with the public sphere if she is to be considered a legitimate "I", which can be placed conveniently in the social order, without disrupting its balance.

As Misch remarks, "the self-assertion of the political will" and "the author's relation to his work and to the public" (Broughton 2:15) find expression in autobiographies. In fact, the author's involvement in the public sphere and the status assigned to him/her are factors that determine the choices he/she makes while giving an account of himself. It is precisely because of the author's relationship to the social sphere and his attempts to come to terms with the norms dictated by the society and its institutions and his assertion through political choices, that autobiographies are essentially negotiations with social norms.

Religion, a highly respected institution of the state, functions successfully as an instrument of imposing norms on the individual, so as to turn him/her into a 'respectable member of the society'. Conformism to religion and its norms can make a person acceptable to the society and failure to do so will invariably make him/her a "dissenting subject", an unwelcome intrusion into the peaceful order of things. ('Unfeminine') females, who write autobiographies and thus encroach upon a sphere meant for men, are in a constant attempt to negotiate with social and religious norms so that, despite their lack of 'femininity', they will not be completely unacceptable in the eyes of the society.

This paper focuses on three autobiographies by women—Rashsundari Debi's *Amar Jiban*, Kamala Das's *My Story* and Sr. Jesme's *Amen: The Autobiography of a Nun*. These three women, through their autobiographies, negotiate with the patriarchal society and try to make themselves 'acceptable subjects' by projecting their adherence to religion and its norms, in their works.

Rashsundari Debi, in *Amar Jiban,* projects her at-that-time revolutionary move of learning to read and write, as a divine gift, which a divine agency compelled her to accept. In *My Story,* we see Kamala Das speaking about the divine love between Radha and Krishna and indirectly striking a parallel between the stories in the Scriptures and her 'illicit' affairs. Similarly, in *Amen,* Sr. Jesme talks within the framework of religion, while opposing the very same religious institutions. The divine agency gains prominence in her autobiography as well.

The three autobiographies under consideration are essentially attempts on the part of the subjects to negotiate with the public sphere, by using religion as a subterfuge for their dissenting ideologies and non-conformist ways of life. Besides religion, there are numerous other ways in which these three women try to negotiate with the norms of the conventional, patriarchal society and make conscious political choices for gaining some degree of acceptance. This paper attempts to look into how *Amar Jiban, My Story* and *Amen* are negotiations of the kind mentioned above, making the authors 'acceptable resisting subjects'.

*Amar Jiban,* the autobiography of Rashsundari Debi, is fundamentally the negotiation undertaken by a 'traditional Indian woman' of the nineteenth century, with the prevalent social norms, so as to present herself as an unimpeachable, conforming housewife, despite her violation of certain guidelines prescribed for women. By learning to read and write, Rashsundari was going against the norms of the conventional society, which considered women's education as the nemesis of the social order—a sign of the Kaliyuga. A woman who was educated was equated to a widow—a cursed 'object' who was bound to bring bad luck to the husband and the family. Rashsundari's attempt at reading was definitely an act of resistance against the dominant ideology of the society. She also speaks of the pathetic plight of the women of those times. She subverts the traditional notion of the woman as the "Annapurna", finding delight in cooking and serving others, the all-bearing "Mother", and the obedient wife. But the remarkable thing is that all this is done in a very subtle way so as not to invite censure. She goes against the norms while at the same time remaining very much within the slot prescribed for her by the society. Through her autobiography, she negotiates with these social norms. This is done primarily by using religion as a stratagem.

In *Amar Jiban*, " we have a triangulated relationship, for apart from the narrating and narrated selves, we have a third entity—the Supreme Lord" (Sarkar 215). From the first section to the last, God is projected as the central character. The Vaishnava sect, to which she belonged, and its rituals and beliefs are highlighted in *Amar Jiban*. In fact, religion is the pivotal point in Rashsundari's autobiography. She seems to center her entire life story around religion and spirituality. Her revolutionary acts are attributed to a divine agency, thereby enabling her to escape the wrath of the society and also to project herself as an acceptable, harmless subject.

*Amar Jiban* starts with an invocation to Goddess Saraswati and the very first section begins with an appeal to the "Lord of the Universe" to bless Rashsundari, who is "an ignorant, mean creature" (139-140). By projecting herself as a humble, meek devotee who begs God for mercy, she devoids herself of any evil that may associate her with the Kaliyuga. Besides, we see Rashsundari Debi talking about Dayamadhav, the family idol, with great admiration and attributing a savior image to Him. She describes her childhood in terms of her relationship with the "Great Lord"(149). Even the few times she talks about her mother, it is mostly with regard to how she initiated Rashsundari into the spiritual world. Here, there is an indirect attempt to project the idea that, for Rashsundari, despite all her 'education', it is God who is important, perhaps more important than even her mother. This is one factor that contributed to this work being considered acceptable. In several places we can see her bending religion to suit her purposes. By eulogizing God, she manages to divert the reader's attention from the 'unacceptable' ideas that she wishes to convey. Thus, she manages to convey her message while at the same time, pleasing the readers with her deep devotion and 'unquestioning belief' in God.

For example, she writes about the burdensome domestic chores she had to do. She had to take over the charge of the household at the age of fourteen, and had to slave over it, going without food for whole days. Yet, being aware of the criticism that she would have to face, she never speaks about this directly. Instead, she chooses to embellish all this with a touch of divinity.

She says: "I would start working at dawn, and I would still be at it until well beyond midnight. I had no rest in between. The Great Lord, however, mercifully made me see it as my own responsibility, so I never resented it" (161), thereby ensuring that her resentment found expression without angering the readers.

Again, she gives a long narrative of how she had to go without food for two whole days, because of her domestic responsibilities. She writes in detail about the happenings that led her to this pathetic condition. But at the end, she adds: "I began to laugh to see the Great Lord try me so. ...Thank the Lord that I was not a sickly creature" (166). Thus, she is the devout woman of the household, who never complains, but accepts her responsibilities and praises God for giving her the strength to carry out her duties.

The reader is convinced that Rashsundari is writing about this, not to express her anguish, but to praise God. The seemingly innocent act of praising god is a major way in which Rashsundari negotiates with the social order so that she is not targeted for her 'outrageous' act of complaining about something which is 'the lot of good women'. She makes sure that nothing that she says can be interpreted as 'against God or religion'. Even while talking about her bitter experiences, which God, as *Adhikari*, inflicted upon her, she ascertains that she adds something more to make the readers feel as if she is praising Him. This is seen mostly when she describes her marriage (when she was separated from her natal family) and the loss of her sons.

> *Adhikari*, this is a most curious theatre. You have shown yourself in so many different roles, costumes. At first, you assumed the roles of my parents, brothers, sisters, relatives, near and dear ones. You brought them to me and then you took me away from them. Who can tell what you are going to do; who knows when the curtains will come down, which play is going to come to an end. No one else can know any of this. *Adhikari*, you took away all my dear ones, after you had brought them to me. I was filled with pain. But you soothed it away. (209-210)

Again:

> *Adhikari*, who can describe your many qualities? ...you snatch away my son from my breast, from my arms. I do not know where you had brought him from, I do not know where you take him away. When you take him away from my arms, I wish

> you had taken away my life as well...What unnatural pain lashes out at such times!...Only those who have gone through that pain know what it is like. And you know, as well... (210-211)

Rashsundari's status as a woman from an affluent, orthodox family, and her desire to read and write and come out with an autobiography, were at odds with each other. Embracing one openly would have meant sacrificing the other. Rashsundari used religion as a tool to balance the two spheres. This becomes most evident when she writes about how she learnt to read and write. Since she knew that education was prohibited to her and that learning to read and write would invite social ostracization,she used religion as a ploy to fulfill her wish.

In *Amar Jiban*, she says repeatedly (but in different ways), that she learnt to read and write only because God wished her to do so. She says that she prayed to God to teach her to read, and then had a dream in which she was reading the *Chaitanya Bhagabat*. She depicts this as a divine gift, and also a signal from God. Again, her prayers to lead her to the book find fulfillment when her husband leaves the book somewhere within her reach. Depicting these as signs from God, she convinces the readers and the society that her education is God's gift, something that God *made* her accept...hence justifying herself. Again, she is in a constant attempt to prove to the reader( and thus, to the society) that her desire to learn came out of her intense yearning to read *Chaitanya Bhagabat* and that she was interested only in religious texts. "Little by little, a desire took shape in my mind and I came to be possessed by a single wish: I will learn to read, and I will *read a sacred text*" (italics mine) (168). Again, "...the Great Lord did grant me my wish. I was dying to read, and I read enough to satisfy myself. I gradually finished all the books that the house possessed – *Chaitanya Bhagabat*, *Chaitanya Charitamrita*,

*...Gobinda Lilamrita, Bidagdha Madhab, Premabhakti Chandrika, Balmiki Puran...*"(186).

Rashsundari Debi talks about the sufferings women had to undergo during those times, in a society that was rigidly patriarchal. But again, to escape being labeled an 'unacceptable' subject, she portrays all these as the will of the divine agency, who cannot be questioned. She talks about her marriage (which was very evidently an oppressive institution for her, even though she doesn't say that openly): "The bird was thrust behind the cage, the fish fell into the net. However, that was His will, one cannot question it" (154). "Whenever she refers to the social order, Rashsundari describes it as God's design. God is, therefore made the author of the patriarchal discipline, responsible for her sufferings" (Sarkar 229). But she ensures that her resentment is masked as eulogy for God.

Rashsundari Debi subverts religion in another substantial way as part of negotiating with the social order, to justify her political choices. This is found in the way she uses the Vaishnavite eulogisation of the illicit love between Radha and Krishna. To reach a higher level of spirituality, to become one with God, Radha has to transgress the boundaries imposed upon her by her *sansar*. Similarly, to fulfil God's desire ( by learning to read and write), Rashsundari has to transgress the norms prescribed for her by the patriarchal society. Thus, her transgression is justifiable in the eyes of the society. Again, she considers Krishna as a father figure, thereby appealing to the Vaishnavite sensibilities of her society (although in a way that subverts the traditional view of Krishna as 'lover' or 'son'). She talks profusely about God and her deep devotion to him. She describes all her actions as powered by a divine agent, so that nobody can fault her for her 'unfeminine' deeds. This way of glorifying religion and God as a ploy to shift focus from her so-called improper attitude is the major technique that Rashsundari Debi uses in *Amar Jiban* to place herself in a 'legitimate space' in the social order.

A similar way of negotiating with social norms using religion as a subterfuge can be seen in Kamala Das's *My Story*. *My Story*, written at a time when Das was on the verge of death was quick to be condemned as the story of an 'immoral' woman, who was bent on misguiding the 'innocent, gullible, good' women leading 'normal' lives, unmarred by infidelity and 'illicit relationships'. Das's outspoken and open way of talking about her extramarital affairs invited strong criticism from the conservative society of Kerala, especially from the Nair community to which she belonged. She was branded as a nymphomaniac, a foil to the traditional Nair woman. It was perhaps because of this ostracization that she was forced to "drop contradictory hints, first confessing it was nothing but the truth and then declaring it was just a wish-fulfilling fantasy, an alter-life she had created for herself" (Das vii).

But even within the autobiography of a subject who resists so strongly as to invite censure, we see elements of negotiation and compromise, whereby she, in a way, appeals to the society to deem her 'acceptable'. Like Rashsundari Debi, Kamala Das also uses religion in a significant way to support or justify her revolutionary actions. In her case, the *parakiya* love of Krishna and Radha, becomes the pivot on which she locates her love life.

Das often uses this 'illicit' relationship, which nobody finds objectionable, to justify her extra-marital affairs. She seems to say that her romances were not the 'lowly' actions of a nymphomaniac, but a search for true love...a love that can only be found in Krishna. She says: "The only heroine whose sex life seemed comparatively untumultous was Radha who waited on the banks of Jamuna for her blue-skinned lover. But she was another's wife and so an adulterous"(Das 24). Yet, religion finds no fault with this love. So, since Das's affairs are no different, they need not be seen as licentious. To add to this, she makes a direct comparison between one of her lovers "the handsome dark one"(171) and Krishna: "'You are my Krishna', I whispered kissing his eyes shut. ...I carried him with me inside my eye lids, the dark god of girlhood dreams...The sea was our only witness. How many times I turned to it and whispered, 'Oh, sea, I am at last in love. I have found my Krishna...'" (174-5). Here, the comparison she strikes between the sea and Kalindi (the river at Vrindavan, which was the sole witness to Radha and Krishna) is remarkable.

Also, she says: "Yes, it is true that I loved him. ...At the first touch of his body, all my past infatuations were obliterated" (178). The terminology used is essentially an attempt to demarcate the boundaries in her relationships with men and also to legitimize them. While all her other extramarital relationships are subsumed under the term "infatuations", that with the man who resembled Krishna is "love". As this love obliterates the infatuations, the latter do not exist anymore. What exists is her love for this man, who is Krishna for her. Since Radha's affair with Krishna doesn't come under attack, at least in mainstream religion, there is no reason why Das's affair should be considered 'immoral'. Also, she tries to give the idea that it was as a result of her search for God that she ended up in 'licentiousness', thereby justifying herself in front of the society and assuming the role of a traditional Hindu woman seeking refuge in God.

> Like alms looking for a begging bowl was my love which only sought for it a receptacle. At the hour of worship even a stone becomes an idol. I was perhaps seeking a familiar face that blossomed like a blue lotus in the waters of my dreams. It was to get closer to that bodiless one that I approached other forms and lost my way. I might have gone astray, but not once did I forget my destination... (112)

Das uses religion as a logical way of legitimizing her 'transgressions'. She attempts to make herself fit into the traditional notion of a 'good woman'. For this, she uses another method as well—she talks about her love for Krishna too as legitimate because 'good Hindu women' like her great-grandmother's sister Ammalu, also wrote love poems addressed to Him. "Most of the poems were about KRISHNA. To Him she had been faithful. My chastity is my only gift to you, oh Krishna, she wrote in her last poem" (17). Das writes about her boundless love for Krishna:

> Through the smoke of the incense I saw the beauteous smile of my Krishna. 'Always, always, I shall love you', I told him, not speaking aloud but willing him to hear me, 'only you will be my husband, only your horoscope will match with mine...'(87).

In *My Story*, we can also see Das turning to religion for refuge quite often. She writes a lot about the precepts of Hinduism, like God as the ultimate truth and only relation, life as being nothing but a stage-show, death as a merging with the divine being, etc. She writes:

> ...I turned to Krishna. I felt that the show had ended and the auditorium was empty. Then He came, not wearing a crown, not wearing make-up, but making a quiet entry. 'What is the role you are going to play'? I asked Him. '...I am not playing any role, I am myself', He said. ...He had come to claim me,

> ultimately. Thereafter He dwelt in my dreams. Often I sat cross-legged before a lamp reciting mantras in His praise. (179)

Again:

> In actuality....Who am I? ...We are burdened with perishable bodies which strike up bonds which are also unreal and perishable. The only relationship that is permanent is the one which we form with God. ...I shall pass through all the pathways of this world, condemning none, understanding all and then become part of Him. Then for me there shall be no return journey... (181)

These are statements that indicate her attachment and belief in God. But there is more to it. They are statements with which Das claims to be a part of the normative society. Religion and her devotion are subtly turned into tools for negotiating with the public sphere. They become one of the ways in which Das attempts to gain the image of a 'feminine', traditional Nair woman, as opposed to that of an 'immoral' woman. She, in a way, subverts religion in various ways to absolve herself of her 'crimes'.

In *Amen:The Autobiography of a Nun*, Sr. Jesme also uses religion as a stratagem for her non-conformist way of life. She uses religious ideas and ideals to justify her actions, especially the revolutionary one of leaving the convent, which made her unacceptable even to her own family. Her autobiography itself is an attempt on her part to defend her decision and thus gain acceptance in the social order.

A remarkable thing about *Amen* is that the autobiographer talks only within the framework of religion. She says that "it is only a revelation of a part of my [Sr.Jesme's] life. It neither starts at the very beginning nor comes up till the present—the curtain falls when I leave the convent" (Author's note, xii). That is to mean she talks only about that part of her life when she was defined entirely by religion. Her life after leaving the convent is completely hidden away, so as not to invite social ostracization. Thus the very frame of the autobiography is a negotiation with the norms of the society and the religious community to which she belongs.

Sr. Jesme, while talking about her life before joining the convent, talks about the utmost importance accorded to religion in her family, despite hers being a not-so-traditional Catholic one. And also about her religious disposition. "Despite enjoying many such simple pleasures, even then there is a spiritual and mystical pull within me towards Jesus.... From childhood, Jesus has been beside me" (Jesme 10-11). She attempts to bring to the forefront the religious calling that she had from her childhood. She writes several times about her experiences with Jesus with passion:

> "I turn to my beloved Jesus for an intimate talk. Almost in a trance, I spend an hour in his presence.... The Holy Mass seems to be a divine banquet where Jesus, my Spouse receives me as His bride....Spiritually, I am raised to the Heavens and I realize that I can only be His. No more marriage for me. No more worldliness. He is my only refuge, my rock, my fortress, my way, my truth, my salvation, my joy—my everything" (13-14).

During her novitiate she feels the "'midriff astrain'—a physical experience of the Lord possessing the body" (39-40). Such experiences of closeness with the Lord are mentioned in *Amen*, basically as a way of convincing the reader that she genuinely had a religious calling and she is not 'Satan in disguise' as the society depicted her to be, after she left the convent.

Sr. Jesme's progressive attitude invited severe criticism from the religious authorities. Her way of education through films and art( which was unacceptable to the Church and its Heads) was one factor that made her a controversial "cine-nun"(122). She considered cinema as a way to reach God. "Films remain for me an important activity and a medium of communicating His message...If we are to look beyond the letters of the laws laid down for our Congregation, and for the Church in general, we need such new mediums"(109). Such statements are clear negotiations with the social and religious norms that Jesme undertakes so that the choices she made do not turn her into an anti-religious nun. Besides, by highlighting her novel ideas, she manages to convince the progressive section of the society of the logic behind her choices. This is evident when she criticizes the propagation of age-old ideals of blind obedience to norms which do not have any relevance in the present age.

The crucial moment in Sr. Jesme's story is her leaving the convent. This one action of hers made her detestable not only to the community, but also to her own family. Here, like Rashsundari Debi, she projects a divine agency as the force which made her take that particular choice. What she says about this is notable:

> I spend three whole days in the chapel where the Blessed Sacrament ...is visible through the glass door....I silently gaze at Him, with only one request: 'Speak to me directly. Now I will believe only Your words'. Nothing happens for three days, but in the evening of the third day, He opens His eyes, parts His lips and speaks. "Why do you say you had been in the convent for twenty-six years? Count and see how many years have passed after you left home for CMC." I count and am puzzled at the number thirty-three. These are the number of years that Jesus spent on earth.

> "Jesme, your life in the CMC is over. So far, you have been undergoing only 'desert experiences'. Now you are going through the 'death experience' at the same age as I did. You are dying for the CMC. Don't blame anybody. I'm doing it through them".
>
> "Jesus, what am I to do?"
>
> "Before the thirty-fourth year, you will leave CMC. You will have a new life from then on".
>
> "Jesus, where? When? How?"
>
> "Jesme, you are to lead the lay-religious...there are many who need your help". (157-58)

Her decision is thus not against God's will, but rather a submission to it. Throughout her autobiography, Sr.Jesme tries to project the image of her being the compliant devotee carrying out God's will. Even her decision to publish her autobiography in English (so as to obtain a wider readership base) is prompted by God.

> Once during Mass I asked Jesus, 'When will Amen be published in English?' When I came home, I got phone calls from *Times Now* and *Aaj Kal* as they wanted to interview me....Later, there were interviews from Hong Kong and London via video-conferencing and live interviews from different channels. Could Jesus have heard my prayer so swiftly? On the heels of this coverage, English publishers approached me, one after another, and I was obliged to seek legal counsel. After negotiations, I selected Penguin Books India. (Author's note, viii)

Negotiation through religion takes place in another significant way as well. In several places, she strikes comparisons between herself and Biblical characters who were wronged, particularly Jesus Christ. In the extract given above, she strikes a direct parallel between her and Jesus. Again, before going to Delhi, when the

Vice-Principal, who had plotted against Jesme says "Bless me Jesme", she considers it as a plea not to curse the former. "For, the guilt feeling, similar to that of Judas's, might have prompted her to utter those words" (161). After leaving the convent, she meets her mother and she writes about this meeting: "Returning from there, we go to Amma's,...Like Jesus and Mother Mary meeting in the Fourth Station of the Way of the Cross, we look at each other" (169). Writing this way, she manages to portray herself as a wronged character like Jesus, misunderstood by the society. There is also an unexpressed hope that her 'divinity' would be proved one day, just as in the case of Jesus.

Sr. Jesme, also makes double-speeches, so as to convey her dissenting ideologies in a way that would appear to whitewash the religious institutions, while at the same time registering her protest against them. An excellent example is the way in which she talks about the utter poverty in which the nuns were forced to live, while all the money was being squandered by the higher authorities. She writes about the meager allowance given to the nuns and the misery they had to undergo. But, at the end, she adds: "Still, the poverty endured by the poor is indeed graver than what we experience in the convents. The professed sisters get all their necessities from the convent. We are blessed to be free of any worries in the world. As safe as in 'Noah's Ark', we live more secure than the richest Ambani or Bill Gates" (77). Immediately after this, she speaks about how she used to weep for lack of money to buy even the basic necessities. She speaks about how her superiors used to torture her. But she often manages to convince the reader of their helplessness as well, as most often their decisions against her were due to orders from higher authorities.

Sr.Jesme talks very much within the frame of Christianity, despite her opposition to its institutions. And she ensures that the society gets to know about this. In *Amen*, she writes in several places about her loyalty to Christianity and to the Church. She says: "I ...can very well declare that I left the CMC holding the hands of my Spouse Jesus and Mother Mary" (xiii), "I am for the Church—my Amen is to Jesus, to the Bible and to the Church. I can proudly affirm, as St Teresa of Avila, that I, too, am the valiant daughter of the Church" (178). Also, she highlights the fact that many of the people associated with the Church are in support of her. She quotes what Sr Alphy said: "We live the ascetic life inside the Four Walls, you live it outside; that's the only difference I see now...There are many in the convent who love you and would like to meet you; but none has the courage to do so" (171).

She writes about similar sentiments being expressed by Christians, even Catholics, and also by priests including the Archbishop Rt.Rev.Andrews Thazhath who said "that as far as he is concerned, I [Sr.Jesme] have only quit the Congregation of Mother of Carmel but am still the loyal daughter of the Church"(178). These are again attempts on the part of the subject to convince a social order that ostracizes her that she is after all still acceptable to the Church, and a question as to why then should the normative society consider her as somebody to be kept at a distance. Thus, in *Amen*, religion becomes the instrument with which Sr.Jesme negotiates with social norms as well as the attitudes of the social order, in order to become an acceptable woman once again.

Besides religion, Rashsundari Debi, Kamala Das and Sr. Jesme resort to various other means to negotiate with the social order, so as to find a legitimate space for themselves. This can be seen when Rashsundari portrays an image of herself as a 'damsel in distress', a fearful, timid woman who always requires help from a male figure (often symbolized by Dayamadhav). Her exaggeration of her sense of propriety shown when she narrates how reluctant she was to be seen by her husband's horse, her extreme ignorance about marriage, all are conscious efforts on her part to pacify the traditional society of the nineteenth century. She successfully manages to present herself as a 'good woman', even though she did something that was prohibited for her by the patriarchal society. She was very much conscious of the injustice meted out to women and while condemning it, she makes sure that she attributes it all to divine will. Immediately after describing her tiring work in the household, she thanks god for her good health, and adds that if it had not been so, if she had been sickly, "What would have happened to my children?"(166), thereby becoming the 'traditional Indian woman with her eternal, self-sacrificing concern for her children' and thus pleasing the traditional readership.

Again, she, knowing full well how her husband too was responsible for her suffering, writes: "The man who was my master was a good person. But it is most difficult to abandon the custom of the land. That is why I suffered so" (172), making sure that she gives the image of being loyal to her *karta.* Her way of "telling all the truth but telling it slant" (as quoted in Harish 7) helped her negotiate in a successful way with the norms of the society, thereby making her revolutionary actions justifiable. Kamala Das attempts to do this mainly by declaring that it was her search for love that made her seek refuge in extramarital affairs. She puts the blame on the patriarchal society which found nothing wrong with her husband carrying on sexual relationships with several women, as a result of which she "made up her mind to be unfaithful to him, at least physically" (90). By adding "at least physically", she is again trying to conform to the stereotypical 'good woman whose heart always belongs to her husband' (even though it is very clear that she never shared any emotional intimacy with her husband but was close to several of her lovers). At the same time she negotiates with the male-dominated society by regressing occasionally to the role of the Nair woman, with a phobia of sex, saying: "I hate to show myself naked to anyone..." (67), terming sex as a brutal "attack" (84) etc. She tries to appeal to the people of her home state by hinting at her love for the Nalapat House and its surroundings. An attempt to pacify her community is on when she writes about her return, at least for a short while, to 'the Nair woman's way of life', wearing the traditional dress, lots of jewellery and a line of sandal paste on the forehead. When she says "People like us, who believe in the essential dignity of human beings..." what she intends to do is to identify herself with a certain group of people, thereby declaring to the society that she is not a complete misfit.

The same is the case when she states that "*Like the majority of city-dwelling women* (italics mine) I too tried adultery once..." (177).Thus, what she seems to say is what she did is not a transgression, but something that many other people do, but the only difference is that they hide it, while she talks openly about it. Similar is the case when she says that notoriety is not uncommon for writers, as the non-writers can never reach the heights attained by writers and hence will not be able to understand them.

Even when she writes seemingly arrogant statements like "City fathers, friends and moralists, if I were a sinner, do not forgive me" (178) and "If my parents had ...pointed out the wrong path and the right, I would still have led the life I led"(204), she is, in a way, declaring that she has no regrets or rather, she doesn't find herself guilty, thereby denying the society the right to brand her as a sinner. The ultimate proof that she is in a constant attempt to negotiate with the social norms is her frequent change of stance about the 'truthfulness' of her autobiography. It was perhaps to find a legitimate space for herself in the scheme of things and to thwart ostracization that she declared that her work was fictional. *Amen* is not any different.

The very fact that Sr. Jesme uses fictitious names for the persons and institutions she talks about shows the process of negotiation going on. Also, in several places, she highlights her 'noble deeds', like helping poor students, being considerate even to her enemies, consideration for the *cheduthies* in the convent etc, so as to paint the picture of herself as a 'good sister'. Stressing on the Vow of Obedience, she justifies herself for her compliance with injustice, especially in the case of the administration of the colleges where she worked.

Jesme equates her story with that of Sr. Abhaya and Sr. Anupama Mary, thereby legitimizing her account of her pitiful life as a nun. She uses the autobiography as a means of proclaiming that she was falsely implicated in the misdeeds of the Church and its authorities. She also writes about how she was targeted and harassed by her Superiors. And how ultimately all these led to her leaving the convent. She too, like Rashsundari and Kamala Das, is in an attempt to place herself in a legitimate space in the social order, negotiating with its norms.

Thus, in the three autobiographies under consideration, we see a constant process of negotiation with the social norms( which reflects the political choices that the subject makes) going on. But it remains a fact that the degree of this negotiation is not the same in the three works, each belonging to a different century altogether. *Amar Jiban*, published in the nineteenth century, is a book of double-speak.

There is not a single place where Rashsundari registers her protest directly, or if she does, she manages to add a compromising statement immediately afterwards, so as to please the patriarchal society of her times. Every single element of resistance to the accepted norms is enfolded in a sweet coating of words indicating conformism.

In the case of *My Story*, which came out in the twentieth century, there is a delicate balance between negotiation and resistance. While on the surface level, she registers her opposition to social norms in a direct way, there is an undercurrent of negotiation with these very same norms going on, as elaborated upon before.

But in *Amen*, there is a radical shift. Although there is a process of negotiation and compromise going on, there is over and above it, an assertion of the rights of the individual. Sr. Jesme does not hesitate to retort against her brother or her superiors when they try to contain and suppress her. And for this, she gives little or no justification. Her wearing a churidar after leaving the convent and not a saree (which is the 'prescribed' dress for a middle-aged woman in Kerala) itself is a symbol of how she asserts her individuality and choices without waiting for the society to choose for her. She doesn't hesitate to condemn the Church for its misdeeds. Nor does she hide the fact that she did not receive any financial support from the religious authorities despite what the Canonical Law says. And in her work, unlike in the case of Rashsundari Debi and Kamala Das, there is very little of double-speak. Negotiation with the accepted norms occurs in a way that does not compromise of the basic identity of the subject.

The reason for this decreasing level of negotiation in women's autobiography may be attributed in part to the changing times. With the increasing participation of women in the public sphere and their emancipation, especially in the economic arena, there is more of freedom, space for self-expression and a little less fear of ostracization. The status of the subjects too matters. It was Rashsundari's status as an upper class housewife dependent upon her husband that made her resort to an extreme way of negotiation.

Kamala Das, again an upper class woman, but one who had financial independence (at least to an extent, since she owned property and also earned money through her writing), was in a position where she had to place herself in a legitimate space by negotiating with norms, at times radically, at times minimally.

And in the case of Sr. Jesme, a financially independent woman, precisely because of her already marginalized status (since in a way, as a nun, she was isolated from the mainstream society), could give an account of her which is not completely a negotiation with the social order.

As different from a man's autobiography (where negotiations do occur, but in a way that does not lead to the individual compromising himself in a radical way), what we see in a woman's autobiography is essentially radical negotiations with the social norms... attempts to become acceptable subjects. *Amar Jiban*, *My Story* and *Amen:The Autobiography of a Nun* are proof of how women give accounts of themselves in such a way that their actions do not lead them to complete isolation from the society and community. There is always an ongoing process of negotiation with the normative society and its prescriptions in women's autobiographies in different ways and varying degrees that reflect the sometimes non-conformist political choices of the women, so that the female "I" is not rendered "unfeminine/ unacceptable".

## Works Cited

Broughton, Trev Lynn, ed. *Autobiography.* 1st ed. 4 vols. New York:Routledge, 2007. Print.

Butler, Judith. *Giving an Account of Oneself.* New York: Fordham University Press, 2005. Print.

Das, Kamala. *My Story.* Noida: Harper Collins Publishers India, 2009. Print.

Harish, Ranjana. *Indian Women's Autobiographies.* New Delhi: Arnold Publishers, 1993. Print.

Jesme, Sister. *Amen: The Autobiography of a Nun.* New Delhi: Penguin Books India, 2009. Print.

Sangari, Kumkum, Chakravarthi Uma, ed. *From Myths to Markets: Essays on Gender.* New Delhi: Manohar Publishers, 1999. Print.

Sarkar, Tanika. *Words to Win:The Making of Amar Jiban: A Modern Autobiography.* Kolkata:Zubaan Books, 1999. Print.

28

# A Critical Analysis of Robert Lowell's *Life Studies*: Confessional Poetry as Psycho-Analytical Autobiography

**Jyoti Sharma**

Diaries, letters, reminiscences, autobiographies and confessions may be grouped together as literature of personal revelation. In each instance a large part of the interest resides in the conscious or unconscious portrayal of the artist's life. We may say that confessions are the most personal or subjective of all literary forms. Poetry, as a form of literature, is best suited for the expression of the poet's innermost feelings and sentiments. Allen Ginsberg explained his interpretation of Confessional Poetry with the following quote from his poem "Howl":

> [To] stand before you speechless and intelligent and shaking with shame,
>
> Rejected yet confessing out the soul to conform to the rhythm of thought in his Naked and endless head...

The Confessional Poets exposes the subliminal pain buried deep in their disturbed psyche with such touching sincerity, that the reader is unwillingly drawn towards their world and even found themselves identifying with their unusual state of mind. They have a personal charisma which is quite unique and which is reflected in their poetry. Indebted to both Romantic poets and French Symbolists for their introspective ponderings on the darker realms, the movement dramatized everyday human angst with unsparing technical mastery. Robert Lowell scrutinized his marital discord and emotional breakdowns. Anne Sexton explored her abortions and depression; Sylvia Plath charted her suicidal tendencies. Confessional poetry's tone of guilt-ridden despair was not limited to the page. The movement lost many of its practitioners to suicide, including poets Sylvia Plath and Anne Sexton.

Robert Lowell is one of the most influential poets of the 1950s and 60s. His pioneering work, *Life Studies*, was the catalyst that stimulated the sudden blooming of a new literary movement which was termed "The Confessional Poetry". M.L. Rosenthal first applied the term *confession* to Robert Lowell's work. One definition of what makes a poem 'confessional' was offered by Irving Howe, who argued that a "confessional poem would seem to be one in which the writer speaks to the reader, telling him, without the mediating presence of imagined event or persona, something about his life."[1] The new 'confessional' poems removed the mask that poets had been hiding behind and provided an insight into the private lives of the poets. The label 'confessional poetry' in many critics' views over-simplified and undervalued the nature of the poetry of Lowell, Sexton, Plath and other confessional poets. The confessional poetry is indeed poetic autobiography, where the poet writes about his life without compromising on the art of writing poetry. Some critics undervalue the art of confessional poets, simply because they draw the subjects of their poetry from their own life.

We should not reduce confessional poetry to psychological case studies, thereby missing the rich complexity of their poetry itself. These poets tried to remove the veil from their souls and tried to capture the real life within the deep recesses of their hearts. Their voice is the representative voice of their particular age – a manic age of alienation. Seneca records Aristotle saying, "No great genius was without a mixture of insanity". The confessional poet's are certainly psychologically disturbed people who are also great poets. These geniuses who write "with a mixture of insanity" definitely force the reader to look at the world through the confessional poet's eyes. The poet's descriptions can make our hearts pound slightly faster while making us uneasily smile. Their poetry is definitely a reflection of the manic modern times.

Milton tried to justify the ways of God to men and William Wordsworth propounded his philosophy of Nature through his poetry. Every age finds an expression through its representative poets. The confessional poets represent the modern age of alienation and instability. Despite being extremely private their poetry reflects the larger discords of the emotional landscape of the western conscience. By expressing their deep turmoil of contemporary soul, their poetry gains universal appeal.

Lowell's poems are directly connected with the events of his life. As Walt Whitman has famously said, "Lowell was simmering, simmering, simmering; *Life Studies* brought him to a boil."

The significance of *Life Studies* in literature, as Vereen Bell's statement tells us, is great.

> It gave celebrity and respectability to a mode of writing in America that would soon be known as "confessional". As a model and as a symbolic breakthrough, this volume became a land mark in the history of American poetry's evolution. It made new possibilities of meaning accessible to poetic understanding and had a strong influence upon two different generations of younger poets, particularly upon poets who had been Lowell's friends or students as well—Anne Sexton, Sylvia Plath, Adrienne Rich, Allen Williamson, Frank Bidart. The

> poems of Life studies were mainly about Lowell's own family and their poignantly thwarted expectations.[2]

The book *Life Studies* is divided into four sections. The second and fourth sections are directly confessional and autobiographical. The second section of *Life Studies* is subtitled "91 Revere Street". It is superb prose autobiographical piece. The fourth section subtitled 'Life Studies" contains intensely confessional poems. These two sections form the bulk of the book and both sections are woven together and complement each other. The prose autobiography, "*91 Revere Street*" is the preamble to the autobiographical poems of the sub-section "Life Studies." Both sections studied together present a superb psychoanalytical autobiography of Robert Lowell.

### 91 Revere Street

The most confessional and autobiographical section of the book *Life Studies* is the prose piece entitled "91 Revere Street". It first came out in 1956 in *Partisan Review*. It is superbly written prose autobiography; which provides the background for all the poems in the book, especially for the highly confessional poems of the last section. Just like his confessional poems, the prose autobiography too is not a simple narration of the events of his life. The psychological and emotional development of the child Lowell is expressed by the use of realistic images, detailed descriptions of the house and furniture, short pieces of conversation, deep exploration of the relationships of his parents, grand parents and other ancestors.

"I lean heavily to the rational," Lowell said in the "Afterthought" to the first *Notebook* "but am devoted to surrealism." This is very true of "91 Revere Street". The title itself gives a factual detail – the address of the house, where Lowell spent his childhood, the most impressionable part of his life. The writer is the adult Robert Lowell, who discloses his childhood memories seen through the eyes of the child Lowell. The vision is thus intermingled – the adult vision narrates the feelings and emotions of the child, while analysing the situations that influenced the child Lowell. The adult Lowell transforms every childhood episode into a psychological experience. In the *Life Studies* poems as well as in the prose autobiography Lowell:

> Wasn't a child at all –
> Unseen and all seeing, I was Agrippina
> in the Golden House of Nero...
> ('My Last Afternoon with Uncle Devereux Winslow')

"The unseen and all seeing" child characteristically records all the family disgraces, failures, neurosis and quarrels. The failure of this family is the symbol of the degradation of a culture.

The prose autobiography begins with the account of his Uncle Mordecia Myers who was "my Grandmother Lowell's grandfather". Initially, the detailed description of Mordecai Myers seems a bit disproportioned. But soon the reader realizes that Lowell is preparing the background for his father's character sketch. Lowell says in "91 Revere Street":

> Bailey Mason Myers! Easy going, Empire State Patricians, these relatives of my grandmother Lowell seemed to have given my father his character. ("91 Revere Street", 12)

In this section, Lowell also presents an account of his own character and that of his family members in a humiliating manner. The embarrassments, the degradations, the humiliations are vividly described. In this context, Lowell's somewhat disproportionate emphasis on Major Myers's portrait makes him a symbol of humiliation of his family.

"The account of him is platitudinous, wordy and fond, but he has no Christian name and is entitled merely Major M. Myers in my cousin Cassie Mason Myers Julian—James's privately printed biographical sketches..." His portrait has undertones of confessed embarrassments. His "full lipped smile was good humouredly pompous and embarrassed." "He was a dark man, a German Jew... a man like George-III's pomaded, disreputable son Prinny", the Prince Regent, or he was one of those "Moorish-looking dons painted by his contemporary Goya..." This is how Major Myers has been described. Lowell admits that he spent a "tame" and "honourable" life and after his death "he was remembered soberly as a New York State Gentleman". Lowell's mother admired him as the one properly dressed and dieted ancestor in the lot we had inherited from my father's Cousin Cassie. The paradox in Major Myer's character is brought out in the following lines.

> Poor sheep dog in wolf's clothing! In the anarchy of my adolescent war on my parents, I tried to make him a true wolf the wandering Jew! Homo Lupus homin! (12)

Mordecai Myers's description is immediately followed by the description of Lowell's childhood; his mother's property disputes and finally the family getting quarterly payments from the Mason Myers Julia-James Trust, and eventually Lowell's father's resignation from the Navy on the gamble to doubling his income in business. This autobiography is particularly about the two yeas Lowell spent with his parents at "91 Revere Street" Lowell says:

> 91 Revere Street was the setting for those arthritic spiritual pains that troubled us for the two years my mother spent in trying to argue my father into rejoining Navy. (19)

The vivid explorations of his parents' attitudes, relationships, opinions, mannerisms and speech habits are a means to express their psyche, and its effect on Lowell's own personality. As a small boy, Lowell was "quite without hero worship" for his father, whose actuality seemed so inferior to the photographs he once mailed from the "Golden Gate". Most of "91 revere Street" tries to express and explain his father's growing sense of inferiority:

> My father had been born two months after his own father's death. At each stage of his life, he was to be forlornly fatherless...By the time he graduated from Annapolis he had a high sense of abstract form, which he beclouded with his humour. He had reached, perhaps, his final mental possibilities. He was deep – not with profundity, but with the dumb depth of one, who trusted in statistics and was dubious of personal experience. In his forties, father's soul went underground: as a civilian, he kept his high sense of form, his humour, his accuracy, but this accuracy was henceforth unimportant, recreational, horse de combat. His debunking grew myopic; his shyness grew evasive; he argued with a fumbling languor. In the twenty two years father lived after he resigned from the Navy, he never again deserted Boston, and never became Bostonian. He survived to drift from job to job, to be displaced, to be grimly and literally that old cliché, a fish out of water." (17-18)

The first three lines of the passage bring out Lowell's buried sympathy and understanding for his father, whose childhood experience and upbringing are held responsible for his meek nature. The Freudian myth has become internalised. Lowell is involved in an entangled, in the father-son dynamic, yearning for closeness and understanding and realising the need for balance. Lowell's father has been brought up by two women – "a mild widowed mother and an intense widowed grandmother". Lowell's sympathy for his "forlornly fatherless father" turns into sharp and excessive criticism, when he says that his father reached his final mental possibility by the time he graduated. Lowell goes to he extent to say that in his forties his "father's soul went underground." In the major part of "91 revere Street" Lowell seems bitterly critical of his father, perhaps, because his father's meekness had an adverse effect on his own personality. And Lowell could never forgive his father for this. Lowell is quite critical of his own schooling. Lowell describes the school as "entirely a woman's world" where being a boy meant "to be small, denied and weak". Just like his school, Lowell's home too, is dominated by women, his snobbish, ambitious and persuasive mother. Lowell's childhood is a mute witness to his parent's constant arguments and discords. Later in Lowell's poems about his own marriage his arguments and discords with his wives remind us of his patents' married life. It seems that he has inherited the maladjustments of his married life from his parents.

In his famous poem "Man and Wife" Lowell says:

> Now twelve years later, you turn your back
> Sleepless, you hold
> Your pillow to your hollows like a child;
> Your old fashioned tirade-
> Loving, rapid, merciless_
> Breaks like the Atlantic Ocean on my head.

These lines remind us of an account of his parents' violent arguments:

> All day I used to look forward to the nights when my bedroom walls would once again vibrate, when I would awake with raptures to the rhythm of my parents arguing, arguing one other to exhaustion. (19)

Lowell also says:

> I writhed with disappointment on the nights, when my mother and father only lowed harmoniously like cows, as they criticized Helen Bailey and Admiral De Stahl. (19)

The child Lowell is so much accustomed to the discords that they have become part of his existence. Lowell grows up, and continues to relish marital discords, now in his own marriage. He describes his wife's "old fashioned tirade" as "loving, rapid and merciless".

Most critics have highlighted Lowell's discrediting of his father, but few have emphasised his negative feelings for his mother. Lowell's portrait of his mother is of a woman, who is not only dominating, but also manipulating, mean, snobbish and scheming. She hated her husband's naval life:

> Mother had violently set her heart on the resignation. She was hysterical even in her calm, but like a patient and for bearing strategist, she tried to pretend her neutrality. One night she said with murderous coolness, 'Bobby and I are leaving for Papa's." This was an ultimatum to force father to sign a deed placing the Revere Street house in Mother's name. (19)

The mother is extremely class conscious:

> She did not have the self–assurance for wide human experience; she needed to feel liked, admired, surrounded by the approved and familiar. Her haughtiness and chilliness came from apprehension. She would start talking like a grand dame, and then stand back rigid and faltering, as if she feared being crushed by her own massively intimidating offensive. (32)

Lowell's mother is too much attached to her father. She admires his flattering bossiness, and in contrast, finds her husband "savouries, un-masterful, merely considerate". The child's view of his relationship with his parents is summed up in a single line:

> I bored my parents, they bored me. (19)

The child's vision of his parents is bleak, while the only ray of hope was his "white haired Grandfather Winslow". Lowell says:

> ... he was all I ever wanted to be: the bad boy, the problem child, the commodore of his household. (28)

Another man who Lowell admires was Commander Billy, who "even when breathed the power that would make him a vice-admiral and hero in World War II" (45). Unable to idolize his father, Lowell is constantly in search of father surrogates and idolizes powerful men like Grandfather Winslow and Commander Billy.

"91 Revere Street" is the confessions of an isolated and lonely child, growing up amidst the doubts and detachments of his old parents and other grown ups. The manner of "91 Revere Street" comes close to the mode of psychoanalysis. Lowell said to A. Alvarez in an interview that he recognized psychoanalysis as a dominant mode for the American interpretation of reality. "And it strikes me; this may be true of my peculiar history: brought up as a protestant, then a catholic convert. When that goes and we look at it another way, Freud seems the only religious teacher."[3]

George McFadden pointes out in an article that Lowell's use of Freud in *Life Studies* often goes unnoticed because Freudian myths "have been so widely internalized by now that we take them for granted."[4] J.F. Crick points out that Lowell's autobiographical piece "is a disturbing, bizarre comedy of a house and its inheritance: a house which is both microcosm of a certain strata of the Boston upper-class world and with its class and racial stresses, the story of United States."[5] The central home of the work is failure – of a family, a city and a culture. Internalized oppressions speak with a certain voice and it definitely had an enormous effect on him. His *Life Studies* is a story of the self realization of the unconscious. Everything in his unconscious seeks outward manifestation and his personality longs to evolve out of its unconscious states and makes an effort to experience itself as a whole.

## Autobiographical Poetry of the Sub-section "Life Studies"

The first eight poems of the subsection 'Life Studies" are associated with his grand parents, parents, aunts and uncles. The first poem of this section is "My Last Afternoon with Uncle Devereux Winslow". The poem, an elegy on the death of Lowell's uncle Winslow, is the longest and the most suggestive poem about his uncle. The elegy begins with an outcry by young Robert at the age of five:

> I won't go with you. I want to stay with grandpa!

It is a very natural and commonplace outcry by five year olds, but Lowell's poetic brilliance has compressed a lot of suggestive meaning in this single line. On the stylistic level, it makes the poem's diction conversational and natural from the very beginning. On the thematic level, this one line suggests that, Robert, the child is more attached to his grandfather than to his parents. These sentiments are gradually developed in this poem and other poems of this section. The opening speech also suggests the child's rebellious nature. The elegy is an epitome of the other themes taken up in the "Life Studies" section.

The description of Aunt Sarah's life shows psycho-neurotic tendencies in the family. Later in this section Lowell writes about his own mental illness. An almost hysterically nostalgic pain at the loss of the past is epitomised in the lament for a young uncle that concludes the poem. In the poem, the characters of his grandfather, his great aunt Sarah, and his uncle Devereux are portrayed through various aesthetic analogies. His grandfather's personality becomes vividly alive in the following lines:

> Like my grandfather, the décor
> Was manly, comfortable,
> Overbearing disproportioned.

Aunt Sarah's "soundless" music on her "dummy piano" is an expression of her life. The life of Aunt Sarah, like the soundless music, fails to touch anyone. Her life, like her music is aimless, static, lonely and futile. Uncle Devereux stands as if posed for "The engagement photograph". He is wearing the war uniform for a volunteer Canadian officer. The uncle's character is portrayed in terms of the various posters on the wall. The reader is totally unprepared for the lines:

> My uncle was dying at twenty nine.

Hugh Staples says that the line is shocking in its suddenness as E.M. Forster's "Gerald died that afternoon." Initially one is shocked to read about the young uncle's impending death, but later on we realise that from the beginning the poem was about death – the death like life of the Winslow family. In the eyes of the child Lowell, his uncle is a hero, representing super-human strength and splendour.

> His blue coat and white trousers
> Grew sharper and straighter.
> His coat was a blue jay's tail,
> His trousers were solid cream from the top of the
> bottle.
> He was animated, hierarchical,
> Like a ginger snap man in a cloths press.
> ('My Last Afternoon with Uncle Devereux')

It is a splendid image, but there is death like stillness in the description. Its perfection makes it seem lifeless:

"In Memory of Arthur Winslow" and "My Last Afternoon With Uncle Devereux" are both divided into four sections, but the development of these elegies is entirely different. In the first elegy, there is a progression from sickness to burial scene to lamentation for the dead man and to a prayer for his salvation. In first part of this poem, there is a word picture of Lowell's grandfather's summer home, as the fascinated child Lowell saw it. The central character of this part is Arthur Winslow "no longer the ruthless, godless capitalist of the earlier elegy, but a kindly if misguided man who has tried to place his individual stamp on his environment."[6]

The second part is the little boy's image of himself. This small stanza is full of particular factual details:

> I was five and a half
> My formal peal grey shorts
> Had been worn for three minutes.

It is only in the final part that the little boy's hero, Uncle Devereux appears and the poet refers to his impending death. There is no reference to his uncle's salvation. The motif of consolation, which was considered essential in any classical elegy, is totally missing here. Lowell does not talk directly about the loss his uncle's death would make on the family as Milton does. But Lowell's poem is no less elegiac. His Aunt and Uncle's last honeymoon is sentimental and pathetic, especially so, since they are leaving three baby daughters behind.

The next poem of this section, "Dunbarton" (the title refers to the sight of the family graveyard), takes up the theme of the boy's special relationship with his grandfather. Lowell says:

He was my father. I was his son.

The child's attachment to his grandfather seems out of proportion in the following lines:

In the mornings I cuddled like a paramour
In my Grandfather's bed,
While he scouted about the chattering greenwood
stove.

In 'Grandparents' their relationship is tender and sentimental:

Grandpa! Have me, hold me, cherish me!
Tears smut my fingers...

The next six poems of this section deal with the poet's parents, particularly their deaths. The admiration and affection Lowell expresses for his grandparents is nowhere seen in the poems about his parents. The first poem 'Commander Lowell 1887-1950' gives us a living portrait of Lowell's father – a pathetic figure, a misfit in the crowd and a failure in his career and marriage. Lowell mercilessly exposes the weaknesses of his father. In the end of the poem, his father's failures are contrasted with his earlier achievement which was followed by little that justified his early promise:

Smiling on all,
Father was once successful enough to be lost
In the mob of ruling class Bostonians.
...And once
Nineteen, the youngest ensign in his class
He was "the old man" of a gunboat on the Yangtze.
(Commander Lowell '1897-1950')

Philips Hobsbaum comments on these lines of the poem;

> That final touch consolidates the sea imagery that is glimpsed in hints throughout the poem. The naval officer that showed up badly among the weekend sea dogs, the bold singer whose anchor weighed him down in an inappropriate occupation, the owner of a vainglorious house whose only seaman like attribute was a drawing room ceiling coloured sea blue – all these aspects of the protagonist are subsumed in the last three lines which show the commander's moment of glory when for once in his life he was the most responsible person around. The source of compassion here is the sense of time. There is pathos as well as irony in the juxtaposition of age and youth: the boy of nineteen, the youngest ensign in his class is the old man of the gunboat. There is pathos even in the customary term for a commander. We are not told what plague or battle reduced the compliment of the crew to this pass. What we know is that the point so quietly made at the end of the poem contrasts heroically with the blunders and vanities narrated in the verses. The conflict between potential and achievement is nonetheless keen because we arrive at the end to find a picture of a man who reached his peak too early – like Othello who beat the Turk at Aleppo – and who's life, therefore, slid down hill all the way."[7]

The poem is saved from becoming a narration of mere naked factual details of his father's humiliations by Lowell's artistic fusion of pathetic facts with a wry humour and a touching irony:

> He wasn't at all "serious",
> When he showed up on the golf course,...
> They wrote him off as "naval"
> Poor father, his training was engineering!

The poetry acts out the sad but jaunty concept of a man going down with all flags flying. Sylvia Plath's 'Daddy', John Berryman's 'Dream Song, 384' and Anne Sexton's 'All My Pretty Ones' are all confessions about the poet's fathers. None of these poems, however, can boast of the kind of compassion, wit and humour exhibited in Lowell's poem about his father. In the end of

'Commander Lowell' the protagonist emerges as a pathetic character, a victim of circumstances.

In 'Terminal Days at Beverly Farm', the next poem in this section, we see Commander Lowell at Beverly Farms after his second stroke. This poem continues the chronicle of his father's pathetic retirement, last illness and death:

> Father's death was abrupt and unprotesting.
> His vision was still twenty-twenty.
> After a morning of anxious repetitive smiling,
> His last words to Mother were:
> "I feel awful."
>
> ('Terminal Days at Beverly Farm')

Commander Lowell is a man who drifts with time and takes life as it comes. He is "unprotesting" in life and also in death.

In 'Father's Bedroom' and 'For Sale' we linger over the neat details of the room in which the father died. 'For Sale', a fourteen-line poem, is much more suggestive than it seems at the first reading. The cottage in which Lowell's parents lived and his father spent his last days, is on sale. The description of the empty cottage is analogous to the deep void in the mother's heart. Though Lowell's parents were nowhere shown as a very loving couple, yet the intimacy born out of living together for decades is present in all the poems. The cottage is now "empty, open, intimate", "waiting for the mover/on the heels of the undertaker" The end of the poem shifts to the sentiments of the mother, who has always been dissatisfied with her husband, but after his death, suddenly realizes that life without him is aimless:

> Ready, afraid
> of living alone till eighty,
> Mother mooned in a window,

as if she had stayed on a train
one stop past her destination.

The next poems 'Sailing Home from Rapallo' and 'During Fever' are devoted to the mother. 'Sailing Home from Rapallo' is about Lowell's mother's death and burial. The first stanza is rare, direct expression of the poet's emotions for his dead mother:

Your nurse could only speak Italian,
But after twenty minutes I could imagine your final week,
And tears ran down my cheeks...

The next stanza is about Lowell's journey from Italy to Dunbarton with his mother's body. The class consciousness, even at the time of death, is movingly ironic. Lowell writes:

Mother travelled first class in the hold.

Lowell's elegies do not have the basic motif of a true conventional elegy. Except for the first three lines, the reference to grief at death of his mother is totally absent. There are many psychological confessions implicit in the poem, the most important being his parents' absurd class consciousness, and the ultimate degeneration of the family.

'During Fever' is the concluding poem concerning his parents' life. Lowell's daughter is in fever, but it is only the first stanza that tells us about his daughter's fever. The next stanza is about Lowell's life with his parents, when he was a child. The third stanza describes mother's master bedroom and the "nuptial bed" which was "as big as a bathroom" the last stanza is about "those settled years of World War One", when "the un-emancipated woman/ still had her Freudian papa` and maids!"

The last six poems of *Life Studies* focus on the poet's adult life – about his confinement in mental hospital, about his five month imprisonment as a conscientious objector, about his married life, and about himself as a person.

'Walking in the Blue' is a poem about one morning spent at McLean's, the mental hospital. The poem is in the first person. 'Waking in the Blue' and other poem about mental illness started a new mode of writing about the dramatized confessions of psychiatric illness. This poem has not a single iota of self pity or sentimental tears, which are very common in other confessional poems of lesser poets.

T.S. Eliot has said that "the emotion of art is impersonal." In 'Life Studies' poems, Lowell has expressed his personal life in a typically impersonal manner. He writes about his own mental illness and confinement in the mental hospital as if he is writing about someone else. He is an observer as well as a participant in the events. He is not only recording the data or using a camera to record the events, the way John Berryman does in 'The Hell Poem'.

'The Hell Poem' is not about the poet's experience, but about the recorded facts in a mental asylum. No particular mention of the hospital is given, nor are the inmates living individuals. Lowell gives particular details of the mental hospital, the inmates are individuals not types, and he himself is one of them. He is not merely an onlooker, but a part of the crowd. Sylvia Plath admired the mental hospital poems of Lowell. She once commented: "Robert Lowell's poems about his experiences in a mental hospital, for example, interest me very much."[8]

Lowell does not generalize, but gives particular details, making the poem much more realistic. The night attendant props up his head in 'The Meaning of Meaning'. Stanley is now in the sixties. He was once a "Harvard All American full back," he wears a "crimson golf-cap". The poem is full of such particular and precise details. Marjorie G. Perloff says that Lowell's most pervasive images that of hospital and prison merge in this poem. The inmates of the asylum feel a sense of confinement that is repeatedly emphasised: "his 'agonized blue window' admits no fresh air from the world beyond the sanatorium; his razor is 'locked'. Indeed time itself seems to be poisoned here." In between the limits of clay, the hours constitute a meaningless vacuum, and there is no escape for the patients under the surveillance of the "crew haircuts/ and slightly too little nonsensical twinkle" of the Roman Catholic attendants. The hospital prison world, moreover, is perilously close to the graveyard. As soon as the day breaks, the poet is overwhelmed by a sense of inner emptiness and the fear of death:[9]

> Absence! My heart grows tense
> as though a harpoon were sparring for the kill.

Time factor is very important in the poem. The poem begins with "Azure day" and describes the poet's morning in the mental hospital. The poem is about one particular morning, but the past and future intrude in the poem. The past of Stanley and Bobbie gives these characters beyond the mental hospital. Lowell sees his own bleak future in the lives of other inmates. Written in free verse, the poem gives the effect of casual conversation and understatement. The use of rhyme, assonance, repetition and alliteration is extremely deft, giving Lowell's free verse a tone of calculated ease. Marjorie G. Perloff says, "Te danger of the Lowell made...is that the poem too easily becomes self indulgent confession on the one hand or random description of objects on the other. The special strength of a poem like 'Waking in the Blue' is that Lowell manages to mediate between self and world, personal response and external reality, consistently endowing the particular detail with typicality and universality."[10]

The next poem of this section, 'Home After Three Months Away' brings the poet home again after three months' confinement. Lowell's return is not merely to his home, but to reality itself, after the treatment of his mental illness at McLeans mental hospital. Hugh. B. Staples remarks: "One would expect a note of jubilation, a sense of release, but in contrast to the analogous case of W.E. Henley's 'Discharged' we have a mood of contemplative meditation not rhapsody."[11] The poet is home after three months at the mental hospital. On his retune he finds many changes, but the little daughter's affection for her father is the same. His daughters little pranks convince the poet that he still has a lot to live for:

> Our noses rub,
> each of us pats a stingy lock of hair—
> they tell me nothing's gone.
> ('Home After Three Months Away')

Hugh B. Staples says, "Lowell's art is of the variety that conceals art."[12] In this poem, the poet, writing in conversational free verse, describes commonplace incidents of domestic life. Compared with other poems, the poet is here in tender, loving and humorous mood. The details of home life have been chosen with great care so as to give us a picture of a normal healthy household. The end rhymes are much more numerous than they are in other poems. After his mental treatment and regain of mental health, he has accepted the order of things in society and come to terms to reality. The order that has returned into his life is reflected in the order and systematic rhymes and rhythms of the poem.

On the whole, in 'Home After Three Months Away' the poet tries to reassess his own life and his relation with his family. He longs for and makes efforts to bring some order in his life. In the early part of the poem, the poet is concerned only about the past and the present. Towards the end of the poem, the thoughts of future intrude. The tulips are now turned to weeds:

> They cannot meet
> Another year's snowballing enervation.
> In the last two lines Lowell abruptly returns to his own state of mind:
> I keep no rank nor station
> Cured, I am frizzled, stale and small.

The two intensely personal declarations are entitled 'Man and Wife' and 'To Speak of the Woe that is in Marriage'. Marjorie G. Perloff remarks on 'Man and Wife' that it is "a highly condensed presentation of a complex personal drama; the movement from a tranquilized present in which life itself is feared and denied, to the memory of a romanticised bohemian past, and back to the present with its open eyed realization that marriage is torture but also salvation.[13]

The poem, a colloquy addressed to his wife, begins with the image of husband and wife reclining on "Mother's bed". The morning rays of the sun bring back memories of the previous night which was not a very pleasant one. Devoid of love and passion it was a sleepless night made bearable by tranquilizers. The rising sun does not bring hope for the couple; it dyes them in "war-paint". In the beginning of the poem the images (like war-paint, ignites the morning, murderous fine-days etc) present a picture of a couple, whose marriage is full of unpleasantness, ugliness and hatred. But the very next lines change the mood of the poem. "All night I've held your hand" makes it a ruefully tender love poem. The poet addresses his wife as

> Oh my petite,
> The clearest of all God's creatures.

He recalls a very different night of their first meeting, when he was very young and a novice:

> Hand on glass
> And heart in mouth

He was trying to out drink the Rahvs and fainted at the feet of his future wife. He also remembers the "shrill invective" of his wife, which has not changed even after twelve years of marriage. The last stanza again brings us back to the present. The forlorn, lonely and dissatisfied wife hugs a pillow:

> Your old fashioned tirade-
> Loving, rapid, merciless-
> Breaks like the Atlantic Ocean on my head.

'Man and Wife' dramatises the strains and stresses of the poet's twelve year old marriage to Elizabeth Hardwick. Hugh B. Staples has called it the only love poem in *Life Studies* while Philips Hobsbaum describes it rather as a record of marital humiliation. We may judge the poem as a confession of the humiliating moments on Lowell's married life, but at the same time, Lowell's love for his wife is also expressed. With a few deft strokes, Lowell has painted a picture of the complexities of love; not only its tenderness, warmth and compassion, but also its humiliation, indignity and shame. Lowell's achievement is in reaching such heights of sincerity in his poetry.

The second marriage poem in *Life Studies* is a monologue by the wife. The poem is a frank accusation of the wife for the unjust and humiliating behaviour of her husband;

> Oh the monotonous meanness of his lust...
> It's the injustice...he is so unjust –
> Whisky blind, swaggering home at five.

alcoholism – are un-poetic.They argue that these themes should be dealt in biographies or psychiatric case studies. These critics fail to see the vast scope of poetry. What is the scope of poetry? We may ask. Lynn Alterbernd and Leslie L. Lewis describe the nature of poetry:

> ... poetry is closely related to mankind's deepest concerns. It not only records the comments on events but also helps to define our response to them...poetry can accommodate itself to new ways of living, because it is also an expression of the unchanging and universal essence of human experience.[17]

Robert Lowell's *Life Studies* is certainly one of the best poetic psychological autobiographies of the modern times.

## References


1. Irving Howe, "The Plath Celebration: A Partial Dissent" in *Sylvia Plath: The Woman and Her Work* ed. Edward Butscher, London: Peter Owen, 1979, p.233.
2. Vereen Bell, "Robert Lowell", in *Voices and Visions: The Poet in America.* Ed. By Helen Vendler. p. 429.
3. A. Alvarez. "A Talk with Robert Lowell", *Encounter*, Feb. 1975. p.45.
4. George McFadden, "Life Studies: Robert Lowell's Comic Breakthrough", *PMLA 90*, Jan. 1975. p.97.
5. Quoted by V. Ramakrishnan in *Crisis and Confessions Studies in the Poetry of Theodore Roethke, Robert Lowell and Sylvia Plath.* p.110.
6. Marjorie G. Perloff, *The Poetic Art of Robert Lowell.* p.146.
7. Philips Hobsbaum, *A Reader's Guide to Robert Lowell.* p. 82.
8. From an interview and reading of poems made by Sylvia lath for the British Council.
9. Marjorie G. Perloff, *The Poetic Art of Robert Lowell.* p.168.
10. Ibid., p. 175.
11. Hugh B. Staples, "Beyond Charles River to the Acheron: An Introduction to the Poetry of Robert Lowell", in *Poets in Progress*, ed. by Hungerford Edward. p.35.
12. Ibid., p.35.

13. Marjorie G. Perloff, *op.cit.*, p.93.
14. Ibid., p.1.
15. Robert Lowell, "On Skunk Hour" in *Robert Lowell, A Collection of Critical Essays, Twentieth Century Views* ed. by Thomas Parkinson. p. 131.
16. Ibid., p. 132.
17. Lynn Altenbernd and Leslie L.: *A Handbook for the Study of Poetry*. p. 1.

29

# Experience of Discrimination and Dalit Identity as Reflected in the Dalit Autobiography of Omprakash Valmiki's *Joothan*

Grishma Manikrao Khobragade

Dalits in India have to face common discrimination and cruel treatment from upper caste. It is to be noted that the caste system and a social identity based on caste are prevalent only in India. Indian society is full of caste discrimination, a fact which many studies point out. In spite of several anti-caste discrimination laws and provisions, violation of these norms is a regular feature. Even the UN has been making efforts to combat discriminatory practices still faced by dalits of India.

It is estimated that India has even failed to uphold existing laws against caste discriminations and violations of human rights. Further, Dalits are also seen segregated in all walks of life and forced to live in deplorable conditions and there are many cases wherein they are abused on all counts by the people of upper castes. Violence against dalits is manifested in all kinds of inhuman atrocities, rapes and murders. Hence, caste discrimination is also considered as the root cause of violence against dalits and it acts as hidden apartheid in India.

'Untouchability' is a term closely linked with discrimination. It can be traced from ancient time in Indian society operating as a social institution. Untouchablilty also has its own socio-economic reasons behind it – causes which divide the society into different fragments having different social status. In the present time, the practice of untouchability is pervasive both in the rural and urban areas and this has affected all aspects of daily life. Dalits often reside in separate locations such as slums, with separate wells or water tanks in many villages in India. They are frequently not allowed to take out processions on public roads which pass through the settlements of higher caste. They are denied entry to temples, are made to find menial work under the most humiliating conditions and are abused by the upper classes. Although India has prohibited caste discrimination in its Constitution, in practice this is not seen enforced. The continuation of the practice of untouchability is thus contrary to constitutional provision of abolition of untouchablilty (Article 17) and different criminal laws are enacted to eradicate such a social evil. Discriminating a person on the basis of his caste is, on record, prohibited. Along with this law, the government allows positive discrimination of the depressed classes of India, to empower them.

Dalit literature is often used to encourage their culture and to proclaim their, self-respect, identity and rights. As atrocities against the dalits continue in the society, dalit literature continues to be protest literature. With reference to this protest ideology, Anil Chauhan rightly comments:

> The ideologies of the protest movement among backward classes are characterized by relative deprivation in the religious, economic, political, civic and educational areas of social life. These are pivoted around conflict and opposition at different structural levels. Ideologies of the backward classes' movements are double edged, expressing the feeling of dissatisfaction, dissent and protest with the existing situation and working out a positive programme for removing the malady. The former

> typifies protest and conflict and the latter, social transformation and change.[1]

Dalit writers, therefore, not only bring out the problems that dalits faced under rigid Brahminical social structure, but also make efforts to eradicate the superstitions and disparity in their community. Though all dalit writers have not touched upon the issue of caste discrimination and hegemony very effectively, still the impact of dalit literature amongst dalits as well as on other community is noteworthy. Through the literature a new social consciousness is infused among the dalit community and this impact or sensitivity may manifest itself in political action in future. Dalit literature in itself is none less than a movement in the Indian cultural history, in which dalits play a significant role in cultural revival and social restoration.

This paper endeavours to identify how dalits have used autobiography as a means of assertion against caste prejudice by looking at the famous dalit autobiography of Hindi, *Joothan* (1997) by Omprakash Valmiki. This paper exposes the miserable story of dalit experience on the basis of caste discrimination in modern India. According to the theoretical studies of Margo Perkins and Barbara Harlow, dalit autobiography has been used as a means of political assertion by dalit writers. For Margo Perkins and Harlow, the autobiographical narrative is perceived as the real location of the power struggle, where the voices of dalit contest the institutionalized narrative of the dominant group. Harlow writes:

> If resistance poetry challenged the dominant and hegemonic discourse of an occupying or colonizing power by attacking the symbolic foundations of that power and erecting symbolic structures of its own—resistance narratives go further still in analyzing the relations of power which sustain the system of domination and exploitation.[2]

The significant contribution of dalit autobiography exposes the persistence of caste-based discrimination and the power structures and belief systems that support the practice of untouchability.This is certainly true of Omprakash Valmiki has concerned in various forms of social activism. He shows his major form of activism through his writing. Autobiography is a form of allegation and resistance in its own right.

*Joothan* begins in the village during the autobiographers' respective childhoods, and both narratives follow the protagonist's gradual move to the cityseen at first as a space of modernity, and thus new freedom from untouchability. This is initially reflected in the protagonist's experience of pain. In the village, where caste identity is known and acknowledged, pain is experienced bluntly, as forced exclusion or even as physical violence. When the experience of humiliation and discrimination ends inthe revelation of the writer'suntouchable identity. A sense of progress through education and to the city is not interpreted as a fundamental move away from the community, despite the sense of alienation expressed in the story. Instead, it is understood by the autobiographer as a process realization of one's communal 'dalit' identity, which then incites him to fight to regain the rights and self-respect for him and his community. Life events are not related to experiences of caste discrimination or to education and the development of the protagonist's political consciousness, events such as marriage or the death of parents, are swiftly passed over with a few paragraphs, rhough the idea of progress from the rural to the urban bursts apart towards the end of the story.

The strength of dalit autobiography is its use of the author's life-experiences of suffering as a means of political allegation. By writing about his own experiences as a dalit, Omprakash Valmiki reveals an objective in his autobiography. He says:

> Being born is not in the control of a person. If it were in one's control, then why would I have been born in a Bhangi household? Those who call themselves the standard-bearers of this country's great cultural heritage, did they decide which homes they would be born into? Albeit they turn to scriptures to justify their position, the scriptures that establish feudal values instead of promoting equality and freedom. (133-34)

The objective of dalit autobiography is to expose the reality behind the institutional narrative that caste no longer functions as a significant force in democratic India. In fact, untouchability was abolished by the Constitution of India and there is no longer caste-based discrimination in government jobs, public schools, transportation, etc. Valmiki does by constantly narrating his experiences of pain as segregation due to the continued practice of untouchability. He writes:

> I was kept out of extracurricular activities. On such occasions I stood on the margins like a spectator. During the annual functions of the school, when rehearsals were on for the play, I too wished for a role. But I always had to stand outside the door. The so-called descendents of the gods cannot understand the anguish of standing outside the door. (16)

He narrates various examples of his life story. Valmiki relates how he was patiently kept out of the chemistry lab "on some pretext or the other", and despite protesting to the teacher of the school, nothing was done to enforce the equality of every student in spite of of caste to use the lab. He writes:

> Not only did I do poorly in the lab tests in the board exam, I also got low marks in the oral, even though I had answered the examiner's questions quite correctly. (65)

As a dalit student his own experiences are universal. Suffering and pain experienced as degradation, as segregation, or as actual physical violence, all serve the narrative, that is to depict the existing experience of untouchability. For dalit readers, pain is a uniting phenomenon.

There are numerous subjects within the autobiography, all bound by his identity as a 'dalit' *Joothan* gives a more complex picture of subjectivity where the central character and the dalit community are connected in a complex web of meaning. In *Joothan,* the protagonist Valmiki is an individual, and yet his individuality is often subdued by those who see him only as a faceless member of his community.

The central character constantly faces a clash between the negative identities imposed on his from the outside. The protagonist's own subjective independence is also bound up in a close relationship with his caste community. He faces personal prejudice and is also deeply sensitive to the pain of other oppressed dalits. Valmiki's personal success in education is interpreted as a success for the entire dalit community. As his father repeats throughout the narrative, it is Valmiki's personal responsibility to improve his caste through his individual achievements. The paradox is that his own development as an individualoptions that are open to him and barriers that come in his wayis largely affected by the growth of the dalit movement as a whole. Omprakash Valmiki was born and brought up in the Bhangi caste in UP. His autobiography often polishes over inter-*jati* conflict between the Chamar and Bhangi Dalit communities.

In dalit autobiography, the individual uses his narrative to raise his voice against caste oppression. All individuals hold multiple identities of their community. We find one example in the autobiography—that dalit women, are almost absent in *Joothan.* Though the writer associates himself with other friends and his community, he keep silence regarding his wife, Chanda who only appears for short moments in the story. The structure of prejudice in dalit autobiography thus reflects the writer's desire to reestablishing links with the dalit community. Though born in rural dalit area, the autobiographer, through learning and professional success, has left his community and entered the urban middle class. There is not only a sense of physical separation but also divisions due to education and financial status. Through the process of narrating their life-story with a focus on their dalit identity, dalit writers are able to come together into a powerful group which can then assert itself against the main obstacles. They still face the continued practice of untouchability.

The story of autobiography focuses on events that highlight the pain of experiencing caste discrimination, and exposes its persistent practice in modern India. Thus, the autobiographer values events that strengthen the fact of untouchability. Most of the narrative time focuses on these events. When in response to the insults of an upper caste Tyagi, Valmiki'smother forcefully refuses to accept the *joothan*. As Valmiki describes:

> That night the Mother Goddess Durga entered my mother's eyes...My mother had confronted him like a lioness. 103).

Valmiki has attempted to negotiate the challenge of securing narrative authority by emphasizing the experience of discrimination and dalit identity as two necessary criteria for writing. He negotiates the issue of authority to represent the dalit community by presenting his autobiography not as a result of his desire for personal identification, but as a response to the requests from the dalit community for representation. After Valmiki's short autobiographical essay was published in a journal, he comments:

> . . . responses came even from far-flung rural areas. The Dalit readers had seen their own pain in those pages of mine. They all desire that I write about my experiences in more detail. (17)

While class-based issues certainly come up in the autobiography where pain is experienced as hunger, the story is clearly driving forward and given meaning by issues of caste. The accepting of *joothan*, leftover scraps of food, is interpreted by the author in the context of his caste rather than class identity. Thus, the dalit autobiography is not simply the narration of a dalit's life-story, it is used by the dalit writers as a means of political assertion.

Thus, *Joothan* serves as a rebellious space within the literary community in which the writer can speak out against untouchability that caste no longer functions as a social force in democratic India. Thus, the autobiography also serves as a means for dalit writers to reclaim narrative authority over the construction of the dalit self, while dominant Indian society has identified dalits as inferior. The dalit autobiographer 're-writers' selfhood, so to speak, in his description of his life and the life of his community.

Valmiki's autobiography serves as a list of all those dalits, the author believes, have contributed to the movement. He describes the activities of Marathi dalit writers, of various editors who published dalit articles in their magazines, and of dalit social activists. *Joothan* constitutes a socio-cultural record of the dalit community. It also details events in the political history of the dalit movement. *Joothan* includes descriptions of the Gawai Brother's incident in Poona 1978 and the protest activities of the Dalit Panthers in response to the affirmation movement for the renaming of Marathwada University after Dr. Ambedkar, the anti-reservation protests in Gujarat, and the 1984 incident.

His story is to expose the caste discrimination in present times. It attacks the basis of caste discrimination in various ways but focuses on the realistic experiences of discrimination. The autobiography serves the additional function of re-affirming and strengthening the link between the individual dalit writer and his community. An increasing understanding and awareness of the contribution of dalit autobiography must also take into account the cultural and historical processes under which he arose in the Hindi region including the social location of the dalit writer himself. Dalit autobiography is considered a form of political assertion for a number of reasons.

Valmiki depicts the painful experiences of his life-story. *Joothan*[3] is called a narrative of pain and it also carries historical truth. It tries to bring out the socio-cultural accounts of dalit life in public. The social and political disparity, socially and culturally constructed caste awareness in the society, forms the source of dalit literature. These writing encourage other marginalized writers and also readers to relate to feelings, conditions and the authenticity of the dalit writer.

## Works Cited

1. Anil Chauhan, *Dalit Politics and Identity* Reviewed in Social *Scientist,*Vol.31.No.5/6 (May-June.2003.) pp.93-96. *Documenting Dissent: Contesting Fables, Contested Memories and Dalit Political Discourse,* Shimla: Badri Narayan, IIAS, 2001, p.165
2. Harlow, Barbara. *Resistance Literature.* Methuen and Co.: London. 1987. 85.
3. Omprakash Valmiki, *Joothan—An Untouchable's Story,* translated by Arun prabha Mukhherjee.Columbia University Press, June 2008.

## 30

# Partial Confessions in Bill Clinton's *My Life* and Michael Jackson's *Moonwalk*

V. Rajesh & J. Jaya Parveen

### Introduction

Isabella Rossellini is an Italian actress, filmmaker, author, philanthropist and model. During the book-signing ceremony of her autobiography *Some of Me*, she says, "Some of the people thought I was a channeller or a clairvoyant and that amused me incredibly" (Lauerman1997). Not wanting to disappoint her readers, she announces at the beginning of her book: "The reader should not expect confessions, revelations, not even the truth. I lie. I always did." As the title implies, her autobiography *Some of Me* reveals only a little about her, not all (Lauerman 1997).

This is true about every autobiographer. Whenever one writes an autobiography, people think that they have become saints, channellers, clairvoyants, or true souls to reveal all the truth about their lives. They forget that they are still human beings with their own virtues and vices. Not only Isabella Rossellini's autobiography, but anybody's autobiography can reveal only a little, not all. Autobiographers try to understand themselves and their lives by writing for others. They might have forgotten a few events, their perception and understanding of a few events may vary from others, memory may magnify or diminish the effects of a few events, etc. Some may conceal, distort, or recreate truth for the sake of saving their reputations. Some may confess fully while others make partial confessions.

*My Life* is Bill Clinton's autobiography published by the Knopf Publishing Group in 2004. In the book, he has narrated his childhood memories, love, family, political experiences, etc. He has described many people who influenced him in his private and public lives. *Moonwalk* is Michael Jackson's autobiography published in 1988. The title is derived from Michael Jackson's signature dance move by name 'Moonwalk'. The dance move presents the illusion that the dancer is stepping forward while actually moving backward. It can be a metaphor to the lives of great personalities who seem to move forward in name, fame, money, etc. while actually moving backward in health, mental peace, family, love, etc. Bill Clinton and Michael Jackson have made confessions in their autobiographies which are not complete but only partial.

## Partial Confession in Bill Clinton's *My Life*

Bill Clinton was the 42nd President of the United States. He held office from 1993 to 2001. He was accused of perjury, abuse of power, and obstruction of justice. These cases failed while his real downfall started with Paula Jones lawsuit and Lewinsky scandal. Independent Counsel Ken Starr dealt with Clinton's land deals in the name 'Whitewater'. After that, he conducted investigations on the termination of White House travel agents, misuse of FBI files, sexual harassment, etc. The Lewinsky scandal brought a worldwide discontent on Clinton's role as the US President. Though Clinton has a stained reputation, he received an advance of US$12 million for his book *My Life*. More than 2,250,000 copies are sold around the world.

*My Life* has 957 pages which is quite long for a non-fiction. This is criticised by Jon Stewart: "I have to confess, I did not finish the entire book; I'm on page twelve thousand" (Stewart 2004). George Bush makes fun of it by saying that the book has ten thousand pages (Bush, n.d). Clinton's former advisor, Dick Morris, refutes the data and details in Clinton's autobiography. He has published a book called *Because He Could* criticising Clinton for presenting factual inaccuracies in *My Life*. *Because He Could* is a frank and perceptive deconstruction of the story Clinton tells in his autobiography. (Paperbackswap.com, n.d)

Men can never befriend truth completely. They can try hard to match their perceptions with reality, but never bring the exact reality in speaking or writing. "No doubt it was scrubbed up and buffed by other hands and fact-checked to within an inch of its life, but it's still the testament of the defiant, half-smiling figure on the cover: the man from Hope, Arkansas, originally known as William Jefferson Blythe III" (McCrum 2004). McCrum also says that Clinton has planned to write a good book, but betrays his ambitions in a self-indulgent, over-therapised ramble.

Bill Clinton claims that most of his qualities are attributed to his parents and grandparents. He has the reputation of doing anything fast. He loves big challenges and adventures. He acknowledges that his father's early death is the reason for that. "The knowledge that I too could die young drove me both to try to drain the most out of every moment of life and to get on with the next big challenge. Even when I wasn't sure where I was going, I was always in a hurry." (*My Life* 9)

Clinton attributes to his grandfather James Eldridge Cassidy for his compassion for the blacks. He calls him the first male influence on his life. He is an incredibly kind and generous man. Clinton adored him throughout his life. He treats both the whites and blacks equally. "It was rare to find an uneducated rural southerner without a racist bone in his body. That's exactly what my grandfather was" (*My Life* 12). Clinton's grandfather whipped his mother for calling a black woman 'nigger'. As a shopkeeper, he gave a lot of food items to the black people on credit. That is why Clinton has always believed in 'food tickets'.

Roger is Clinton's stepfather whom his mother Virginia Kelley married in 1950. Virginia liked Roger because he was jovial, affectionate to her son, and generous. But he was a drunkard with self-doubt, binge drinking, and adolescent partying. One day he fired a gun at his mother after a fierce fight. Critics say that Clinton owed to his stepfather's terrifying violence for his unruly behaviour in the public life. (McCrum2004)

Clinton was reflective even in his young age. In the Junior English Honors class, Clinton had to write an autobiographical essay. In that he confessed that he had contradictory thoughts. "I am a living paradox—deeply religious, yet not as convinced of my exact beliefs as I ought to be; wanting responsibility yet shirking it; loving the truth but often times giving way to falsity. I detest selfishness, but see it in the mirror every day." (*My Life* 48)

Some of his friends, family members, and colleagues never learned the ways of life. He struggled to be different from them, but surrendered to evil and resembled them often. He wanted to get rid of his ego. But many a time, he failed. He says, "What a boring little word—I! I, me, my, mine . . . the only things that enable worthwhile uses of these words are the universal good qualities which we are not too often able to place with them

—faith, trust, love, responsibility, regret, knowledge." (*My Life* 48)

According to Clinton (2004), most of the problems arise in life because of leading 'parallel lives'—an external life that takes its natural course and an internal life where the secrets are hidden. "When I was a child, my outside life was filled with friends and fun, learning and doing. My internal life was full of uncertainty, anger, and a dread of ever-looming violence" (*My Life* 106). Clinton may be apolegetic, but critics think that he tries to find reasons for his setbacks. They say that he is cooking the 'parallel lives' theory in defence of his behaviour in the White House. (McCrum 2004)

Gennifer Flowers, Elizabeth Ward Gracen, Sally Perdue and Dolly Kyle Browning have made complaints that Clinton had sexual relationships with them. Kathleen Willey declares that Clinton had attacked her sexually before four years. Juanita Broaddrick announces that Clinton had raped her before twenty years. The cases of Paula Jones and Kathleen Willey portray Mr. Clinton as an official who misused his power and exploited his female subordinates. In *My Life*, Clinton has confessed only his extramarital relationships with Gennifer Flowers and Monica Lewinsky.

Clinton is a controversial figure. His book is too personal and revealing. So it invites a lot of open comments and criticisms. According to Kakutani (2004), the book which has more than 950 pages is sloppy, self-indulgent, and eye-crossingly dull. Readers can hear the voice of a man prattling away, not for the reader, but for himself and the history. He has devolved into a hodgepodge of jottings: part policy primer, part 12-step confessional, part stump speech, and part presidential archive in his autobiography *My Life*. (Kakutani 2004)

## Partial Confession in Michael Jackson's *Moonwalk*

*Moonwalk* is Michael Jackson's autobiography. He had written the book with the help of Shaye Areheart, and Jacqueline Kennedy Onassis edited the book. In it, he talks about his parents, Jackson 5, show business friends, plastic surgery, girlfriends, popworld superstardom, etc. He describes his journey as a young boy with gifted musical talents, a global pop superstar, and a sad figure haunted by lawsuits, paparazzi, and failed plastic surgeries.

Jackson calls James Brown, Sammy Davis, Fred Astaire and Gene Kelly 'the real showmen'. According to him, the artistic and social distinctions like high art vs. low art, sophistication vs. vulgarity mean nothing. He remains the King of Pop forever for this fans. According to Tucker (1988), Michael Jackson was a supremely gifted and beloved artist who was held captive by his upbringing, by his fame, by his power, and by himself. According to Tucker (1988), his autobiography contains drab show-biz cliches and aimless anecdotes. "Had it been written by anyone else, *Moonwalk* could be dismissed as an assiduously unrevealing, frequently tedious document.... A book like this is just another commercial for the self, a plug for his latest product—his new album *Bad*." (Tucker 1988)

The father-son relationship was never smooth in Jackson's life. His father Joseph Jackson was a mystery to him, and his father knew it. "One of the few things I regret most is never being able to have a real closeness with him" (*Moonwalk* 5). He felt indebted to his father for safeguarding his fortunes. He yearned to understand and love his father completely which remained a distant dream. "To this day I'm so thankful he didn't try to take all our money for himself the way so many parents of child stars have... But I still don't know him, and that's sad for a son who hungers to understand his own father. He's still a mystery man to me and he may always be one." (*Moonwalk* 6)

Jackson acknowledges that his father groomed him and his brothers for talent contests. He spent a lot of money and ime working for them. He calls him a great trainer. "Talent is something that God gives to a performer, but our father taught us how to cultivate it" (*Moonwalk,* 10). At the same time, Jackson suffered a lot in his father's hands. He underwent long hour practice for the stage shows. His father beat him and his brothers if they didn't do well during practice. "If you messed up, you got hit, sometimes with a belt, sometimes with a switch. My father was real strict with us—real strict." (*Moonwalk* 11)

Jackson is very defensive, making his father angrier. "I would fight back and my father would kill me, just tear me up" (*Moonwalk* 11). His mother was very supportive and protected him from abuses as far as possible. After dance performances, his brothers hugged and kissed him backstage. He felt very happy and so wonderful for all of them. But he regrets that his father never participated in the felicitations. "I loved it! I mean, we hug all the time. My whole family embraces a lot, except for my father. He's the only one who doesn't." (*Moonwalk* 86)

Jackson says that his first love was Diana Ross (an American singer) who mothered and made him feel right at home during music tours. His first real date was with Tatum O'Neal who was a child actress when he was a teenager. After that, he was romantically serious for a while with Brooke Shields. There were many women in his life whose names he doesn't want to reveal in his autobiography. "There have been a lot of wonderful women in my life, women whose names wouldn't mean anything to the readers of this book, and it would be unfair to discuss them because they are not celebrities and are unaccustomed to having their names in print" (*Moonwalk* 70). He concludes by saying that he values his privacy and respect theirs as well.

He felt insecure and self-conscious as an adolescent. Even pimples disturbed him a lot. "I know that a case of acne can have a devastating effect on a person. The effect on me was so bad that it messed up my whole personality" (*Moonwalk* 39). He thinks that wearing one glove contributed to his unique style. "I felt that one glove was cool. Wearing two gloves seemed so ordinary, but a single glove was different and was definitely a look" (*Moonwalk* 88). He wore white socks, and it became a fashion. After *Thriller*, wearing the pants high around the ankles become a fashion. He admits that he loved to start new trends though they looked absurd for some people.

Jackson is accused of lightening his skin tone to look fair. In *Moonwalk*, he says that he altered his nose twice and added a cleft to his chin. He says that he had never altered his cheeks or eyes. He had never thinned the lips or done dermabrasion or skin peel. He felt bad when the press accused him of surgically altering his appearance. He says, "I don't care what anyone else says—it's my face and I know." (*Moonwalk* 92)

Journalists often say, "What happened to truth? Did it go out of style?" Jackson declares that he was really hurt by those words. He says, "Journalists seem willing to say anything to sell a paper. They say I've had my eyes widened, that I want to look more white. More white? What kind of statement is that? I didn't invent plastic surgery" (*Moonwalk* 100). He regrets that many people have had plastic surgery, and journalists are not criticising them. He says that most of what they print are a fabrication. In his autobiography, he does not reveal that he suffered from vitiligo, a skin disease.

When talking about his privacy, he accepts that he was obsessed with it. He says that people staring at anybody is understandable, but not easy always. He exclaims that he liked wearing the surgical mask given by his dentist after pulling a teeth to avoid germs. He adds that he wore sunglasses to avoid looking everybody in the eye and concealled a bit of himself. He says, "There's so little privacy in my life that concealing a little bit of me is a way to give myself a break from all that. It may be considered strange, I know, but I like my privacy." (*Moonwalk* 107)

Michael Jackson was accused of owning a private chimp at home. It's name was Bubbles. It slept in a crib in Jackson's bedroom, used his toilet, ate candies, and accompanied him wherever he went. He mentions about it in his autobiography. He says, "I'm crazy about monkeys, especially chimps. My chimp Bubbles is a constant delight. I really enjoy taking him with me on trips or excursions. He's a wonderful distraction and a great pet" (*Moonwalk* 110). This treasured pet was a source of joy to the singer, but drew a lot of mockery from the media.

Jackson was considered bizarre and eccentric, obsessed with recapturing his childhood. He always loved children. He says, "They energise me—just being around them. They look at everything with such fresh eyes, such open minds. The only demand they make is to be treated fairly—and to be loved. I think that's what we all want." He wanted to be an inspiration for the children. He wanted them to like his music. According to him, children were the toughest audience. "Their approval means more to me than anyone else's. It's always the kids who know which song is going to be a hit." (*Moonwalk* 108)

Jackson visited children's hospitals and helped the needy. He felt very sorry for them, and says, "It's so sad for children to have to get sick. More than anyone else, kids don't deserve that. They often can't even understand what's wrong with them. It makes my heart twist. When I'm with them, I just want to hug them and make it all better for them" (*Moonwalk,* 109). He adds that when he faced problems with his skin and adolescent growth spurts, kids never let him down. Only they understood that he was the same person inside though he was no longer little Michael outside. "I've never forgotten that. Kids are great. If I were living for no other reason than to help and please kids, that would be enough for me. They're amazing people. Amazing" (*Moonwalk* 109). His love and affection for young boys were seen as a harmless eccentricity until the 1993 sexual allegation case against him by a 13-year-old boy, Jordan Chandler.

Jackson was exposed to bad things even in his childhood. Along with his brothers, he watched a girl taking off her clothes and panties, and throwing them to the audience. The men picked them up, sniffed them, and yelled. They looked into the ladies' bathroom through a hole in the wall from a musician's dressing room. He watched a stripper who threw away all the dresses at the end of the dance and revealed that he was not a woman, but a man. "My brothers and I would be watching all this, taking it in, and my father wouldn't mind." (*Moonwalk* 15)

Though Jackson seems to confess everything about his childhood, he has concealed quite a lot of information which is presented in his biography *The Magic, the Madness, the Whole Story* by his lifelong friend Randy Taraborrelli. Jackson's father instructed young Jackson to crawl under the tables and look at the panties of women as a part of their performance. Jackson's brothers were interested in groupies and prostitutes. They took advantages of female fans too (Taraborrelli2009). Jackson seems to have had no interest in them. According to Taraborrelli (2009), young Jackson was conflicted between his religiously strict mother and his promiscuous father, and he got sexual perversions due to his very early exposures to sex. He has not revealed these things in his autobiography.

There is a rumour that Jackson slept in an oxygen chamber to help him stay young. He tried to buy the bones of Joseph Merrick called the "Elephant Man" by giving $500,000 to the London Hospital Medical College $500,000 (Edwards 1987). There is no reference to these events in his autobiography.

## Conclusion

McCrum relates all the confessions and self-justifications of Clinton to his future campaigns and political intentions. He says, "There are many fascinating moments in Bill Clinton's story, but after *My Life*'s 957-page campaign he remains a tragic figure". According to him, Bill Clinton's autobiography is the manifesto for his third and most important campaign: his continuing appeal for history's mandate. "It is often said that if he were to run for office tomorrow he would win by a landslide. *My Life* lends some weight (nearly 4lbs) to that argument. This is a campaigning document. Alas, a book tour is a poor substitute for the campaign trail." (McCrum 2004)

Several complaints of sexual misconduct and harrassment are charged against Clinton throughout his career. McCrum says that peole who are aware of the Whitewater and Lewinsky scandals know how candid Clinton is. Yet *My Life* is utterly self-serving. "For every line of contrition, there are two of self-justification. For every attempt at atonement, there is yet another display of self-aggrandisement." *My Life* is described as the mirror of Clinton's presidency – a heterogeneous mixture of self-indulgence, lack of discipline, extra-length speeches, statistics, lies, partial confessions, etc. (McCrum 2004)

In *Moonwalk*, Jackson has confessed a few things about his own personality, father, girl friends, career, etc. But the confession is only partial as he does not mention anything about the much-expected Elephant Man and hyperbaric oxygen chamber, and reveals less-convincing reasons for owning a pet monkey, having crippled nose, wearing one glove, sunglasses, and mask, etc.

For concealing or interpreting truth in his own way, Jackson says, "What one wishes is to be touched by truth and to be able to interpret that truth so that one may use what one is feeling and experiencing, be it despair or joy, in a way that will add meaning to one's life and will hopefully touch others as well. This is art in its highest form. Those moments of enlightenment are what I continue to live for" (*Moonwalk* 112). This is further justified by the statement of Tucker (1988) in *The New York Times*: "Just because he signed a contract with a publisher for an autobiography doesn't mean he felt the need to reveal anything about himself."

## Works Cited

Abimboye, Demola. "The Man, His Weird Ways". Published on 5.7.09. Retrieved on 22.03.12 from <http://www.newswatchngr.com/index.php?option=com_content&task=view&id=1080&Itemid=1>.

"Because He Could". *Paperbackswap.com.* n.d. Retrieved on 20.3.12 from <http://www.paperbackswap.com/Because-He-Could/book/0060784156/>.

Bush, George. (n.d) "President and the Press". *Radio and TV Correspondents Dinner.* n.d. Retrieved on 21.03.12 from <http://www.youtube.com/watch?v=aGSZaN5IKVA>.

Clinton, Bill. (2004) *My Life.* US: Knopf Publishing Group.

Edwards, David. "Michael Jackson Bids for the Elephant Man" *CBC Radio Interview.* Broadcasted on 17.6.87. Retrieved on 25.3.12 from <http://archives.cbc.ca/arts_entertainment/music/clips/16930/>.

Jackson, Michael. (1988) *Moonwalk.* US: Random House.

Kakutani, Michiko. (2004) "Books of The Times; A Pastiche of a Presidency, Imitating a Life, in 957 Pages". *The New York Times.* Published on 20.06.04. Retrieved on 22.03.12 from <http://www.nytimes.com/2004/06/20/us/books-of-the-times-a-pastiche-of-a-presidency-imitating-a-life-in-957-pages.html?pagewanted=all&src=pm>.

Lauerman, Connie. (1997) "Partial Confession: Isabella Rossellini's New Autobiography Tells Some But Not All." *Chicago Tribune.* Retrieved on 20.03.12 from <http://lubbockonline.com/news/070397/partial.htm>.

McCrum, Robert. (2004) "Still Pressing the Flesh". *The Observor.* Published on 27.06.04. Retrieved on 21.03.12 from <http://www.guardian.co.uk/books/2004/jun/27/biography.politicalbooks1>.

Mcdowell, Edwin. (1988) "Michael Jakcson Writes His Story." *The New York Times.* Published on 18.4.88. Retrieved on 20.03.12 from <http://www.nytimes.com/1988/04/18/books/michael-jakcson-writes-his-story.html>

"Music's Misunderstood Superstar". *BBC News.* Published on 13.6.05. Retrieved on 21.3.12 from <http://news.bbc.co.uk/2/hi/entertainment/4584367.stm>.

Stewart, Jon (2004) "Bill Clinton Pt.2" *The Daily Show with Jon Stewart.* Published on 09.08.04. Retrieved on 22.03.12 from <http://www.thedailyshow.com/watch/mon-august-9-2004/bill-clinton-pt—2>.

Taraborrelli, Randy (2009). *The Magic, the Madness, the Whole Story.* US: Grand Central Publishing.

Tucker, Ken. "Summer Reading; Firing Your Father Isn't Easy". Published on 05.06.88. Retrieved on 22.3.12 from <http://www.nytimes.com/1988/06/05/books/summer-reading-firing-your-father-isn-t-easy.html?src=pm>.

# 31

# Biography and Other Cognate Forms of Narrative Prose

**Dhara K. Chotai**

> For there is a virtue in truth. It has an almost mystic power. Like radium, it seems able to give off for ever and ever grains of energy, atoms of light. It stimulates the mind, which is endowed with a curious susceptibility in this direction as no fiction, however artful or highly coloured, can stimulate it. (AB 33-34)

> [novel enables] the most thorough knowledge of human nature, the happiest delineation of its varieties, the liveliest effusions of wit and humour to be conveyed to the world in the best chosen language. (*ATN* 16)

Biography and novel, the two different forms of narrative prose, stand on an equal pedestal for encompassing human nature. Both narrativise the events of human life but both have different objectives, perspectives and vistas for their enterprise. The present paper aims at analyzing the difference between the form of biography and other forms of narrative prose like the novel, story and history. It is an attempt to understand different aspects of biography with reference to these forms; it simply endeavours at knowing the one with reference to the other.

## Defining the Differences between Biography and Other Forms of Narrative

The word 'biography' is derived from the Greek roots *bios*, i.e. life, and *graphein*, i.e. to write. It is often translated as 'Life Writing'. John Dryden first used the term in 1683 to describe the literary work of Plutarch as "the history of particular men's lives" (*FMGL* 330). Subsequently, numerous attempts have been made to define the genre. Harold Nicolson quotes approvingly the *Oxford Dictionary's* definition of biography in his *The Development of English Biography* as "The history of the lives of individual men as a branch of literature" (*DEB* 7). Likewise, in *The Nature of Biography*, John A. Garraty defines biography as "the history of a human life" or "the record of a life" (*TAB* 14). He explains, "It is thus a branch of history, each life a small segment in a vast mosaic..." (*TAB* 14). But biography is not a branch of history; for history is not a mosaic of lives, that is, a vast accumulation of biographical sketches, but a generalized narrative concerning events, movements and institutions. Thus, the phrase "history of a life" as used by Nicolson and Garraty is rather misleading according to Paul Murray Kendall. He further says that the alternate definition offered by Mr. Garraty, "the record of a life" is not much more satisfactory. For the term 'record' implies documentation, severely factual account, an objective marshalling of evidences, and not biography which hopes to recapture the sense of life being lived.

Biography is likewise often defined as the story of a man's life. But 'story' is as unsatisfactory in its way as the term 'record' is. As 'record' implies sheer fact, 'story' implies fiction. Story, with its fictionalised element, leads us away from actuality.

Thus, biography is neither the history nor the record nor the story of a man's life. Considering that biography represents imagination limited by truth, facts raised to the power of revelation, Paul Murray Kendall defines biography as "the simulation, in words, of a man's life, from all that is known about that man" (*TAB* 15). Thus, numerous attempts have been made to define the term biography, and in the process it is discriminated from history, story and record as they are established concepts in themselves which carry the shadows of their nature and elements which are not exactly found in the form of biography.

## Distinction of Purpose in Biography and Novel

As stated earlier, biography deals with truth; it aims at truthful transmission of personality, which symbolizes lofty thoughts and deeds to raise and grace the human dignity in every civilization. It avails for the fellowmen direction when he is torn between the two aspects of human nature, which is very well explained in the following quotation by Andre Moruis:

> Plato conceived of the human soul as perpetually drawn by two horses, one white and the other black, one dragging him up towards the highest, the other dragging him down to the lowest in his nature. For several centuries humanity was forced to forget the existence of the black charger. Perhaps our own age denies the existence of the white horse a little too lightly, but a good biographer, in my view, is one who can see both white and black and can show how a man who has this difficult pair do drive and succeed as well as fail. (*AB* 31)

Nevertheless, a novel also deals with human nature; it also sets examples like biography but unlike biography it cannot enliven the human mind with living experience because it does not deal with truth. So when a reader reads a biography he relates the events and deeds of the subject of biography with real life, and is constantly reminded of something which really existed at some point of time in human history. So he thinks at the back of his mind 'this is how it was' and in the process visualizes an individual moving on the pages of biography. This aspect of biography convinces the reader more with the marvels of its character and the consequences of human actions. However, fiction has its own charm and power to influence human mind because human frame of perception is electrified zone where constantly new equations of understanding takes place with every experience. But one thing is sure—while reading fiction the reader is conscious of its imaginative aspect which makes him think 'this has never happened', and the very sense of connectivity with the element of truth of events and character is disconnected.

So a reader is not inspired by the truthfulness of the actions and deeds as he is in biography. Of course, novel also arouses powerful feelings; every work of art, in so far as it arouses the emotions and thereby the desire to act, touches upon morality. But biography comes much more closely to it, because the credibility of the narrative and the reader's conviction of the real existence of the people in the narrative make its influence immensely stronger.

## Subject in Biography and Novel

In a novel, the author invents a story, characters and their actions where as a biographer does not invent, rather, he discovers the life—a story, a character and his actions. His discovery is based on microscopic study and rigorous research which he carries out to unearth material about the life of his subject. As Andre Mouris writes, it is:

> The truth which biography demands, is truth in its hardest most obdurate form; it is truth as truth is to be found in the British Museum; it is truth out of which all vapor of falsehood has been pressed by the weight of research. (*AB* 33)

As a result this activity he comes across materials like letters, and diary of a man; his own works, which bear a mark of his personality; works of those who have written about him; conversations and correspondences written about him by their witnesses; the memoirs of his contemporaries, etc. which help him to comprehend different aspects of his subject's personality. In contrast to this, fiction is pure imaginative writing, here the author invents the story line, characters and setting which in turn is based on his life experience. But he is free to choose from his life experience particular shade of reality of his choice, which befits his imaginary story line and characters. A novelist can foresee his characters and the events of his work of art, whereas, a biographer cannot foresee his character and the events of his life, rather it is very difficult for him even to understand his subject after amassing available material, because a human being is like an enigma and therefore it is impossible to foresee his actions, ideas and emotions. Andre Mouris writes how and what does a modern biographer think aobut his sub:

> Here is a man. I possess a certain number of documents, a certain amount of evidence about him. I am going to attempt to draw a true portrait. What will this portrait be? I have no idea. I don't want to know before I have actually drawn it. I am prepared to accept whatever a prolonged contemplation of my subject may reveal to me, and to correct it in proportion to such new facts as I discover. (*AB* 12)

Thus, in biography the life of a subject is a drama of infinite complexity of which we know not, of which we never shall know, the end. On the other hand, a character in novel, as said earlier, is built up of what the author has put into it; it is the creation of a human intellect and, as such, is accessible to a human intellect. Andre Moruis explains that a character may be complex in novel also, but even then it is "an ordered complexity" (*AB* 39) and we can grasp it. Moreover, the characters in the novel have one more advantage over the characters in biography. The characters of a biography are not as well adapted as those of a novel to relieve a reader of the necessity of acting and judging, since they have actually existed. And therefore, sometimes the characters of a biography stir the moral impulses of readers at the expense of aesthetic emotions.

History deals with the fragments of the vast roll of events and a vast number of persons are part of those events, whereas a biography deals with the cosmos of one individual, whose life is sharply defined by two definite events: birth and death. It feels the canvas with one figure, and other characters, however great in themselves, must always be subsidiary to the central hero. The events of the period revolve round him like in Ptolemaic system stars revolve round the sun. Biography in relation to history is very well explained Andre Mouris in the following lines. He asserts:

> The biographer must not try to play the historian too long. Their objectives are different. Biography is the story of the evolution of a human soul; history should be for him what it is for the portrait-painter, the background against which he sets his model. (*AB* 98)

## Pattern of Composition in Biography and Novel

The 'Pattern' of the novel, the quality of arrangement makes it an intelligible work of art. At first sight, here, a biographer seems to be in trouble, because his is not that easy job to find a pattern of his work as a novelist can do. Except for the rare cases, when he is writing a history of a man whose life has already been constructed by himself (in terms of his diary, letter, autobiography, historical narrative, etc.) he is, as asserted by Andre Mouris:

> ...obliged to take over a shapeless mass, made up of unequal fragments prolonged in every direction by isolated groups of events which lead nowhere. There are deserts in every life, and the desert must be depicted if we are to give a fair and complete idea of a country. (*AB* 174)

These deserts are long periods of empty monotony; but sometimes such periods throw up the colour of the livelier periods into greater relief. For a biographer it is very difficult to unearth such periods in his subject's life as they remain silent without any evidence; they are reflected neither on the pages of subject's writing nor on the minds of the people around him, who, usually happened to take note of his actions and their interconnections in different sections of his life.

In this regard, a novelist is fortunate to envisage a life which is perfectly grouped round a single passion. Thus, the biographer has greater difficulty than the novelist in composition. However, a biographer has one compensation, as elucidated Andre Mouris:

> ...to be compelled to take over the form of a work readymade is almost always a source of power to the artist. It is painful. It makes his task more difficult; but at the same time it is from this struggle between the mind and the matter that resists it that a master piece is born... some of the most felicitous word-pictures have been the result of the limitations imposed by the formal rigidity of classical verse. (*AB* 174-175)

The biographer's task is to resist the resistance of a material to carve a statue of the mind of his subject, which even after process remains uncarved, it is the sense of completion in the mind of reader while reading the last word of a work that an image of the mind emerges, and it lives a lasting impression by virtue of its invisibility. The problem with some of the novels is that their construction is too free. Being at liberty to fashion his characters as he likes or wants, novelist sometimes lose the design or pattern of construction. This excess of construction springs from an excess of freedom.

After the study of history of the novel, Andre Mouris is of the opinion that the best novelists often impose restraints upon themselves and proceed to search for situations and documents in real life just as a biographer would do. A series of events thus borrowed from actual life and then transmuted by the novelist's art will always ring truer than entirely imaginary events. For example, Meredith borrowed many of his characters from real life; Tolstoy utilized the history of his own family in his *War and Peace.* But the novelist has the freedom and space to cut out with the surgeon's knife the growth of parasitic events to accord with his plans and his passions; whereas the biographer is doomed to live with his malady. He has to cover the whole story of life without ignoring or disturbing any fact or idea or information and impart a truthful shape to marble of his subject's identity.

## Timeframe for a Biographer and a Novelist

A biographer while writing a biography or while thinking about his subject goes to the past; he thinks in terms of 'was', 'would have been', 'might', 'might have been', 'could', 'could have been', 'has', 'had' and 'had been'. He can never talk in terms of 'is' and 'will' about his subject's life. Unlike a biographer, a novelist is free to employ 'is', 'was', 'will', 'can', 'could', 'would', 'may', 'might', etc. In short, a biographer is working on the past in the present and a novelist is working on the past, the present and the future at all times. Further, when a biographer starts his line of action, he sees through the beginning, middle and end of his narrative, whereas, a novelist does not know entire narrative before he really ends it (in a sense that a biographer does). A reader of a biography may know about the changes of fortune in advance, but still he would like to observe and go through a slow march of events and experience an aesthetic elevation. In the words of Andre Moruis:

> ... when we read a life with the events and the end of which we are already familiar, it seems to be walking in a stretch of country which we know already, and to be reviving and completing our recollections of it. The peace of mind with which we accomplish this familiar walk is favourable to the proper aesthetic attitude. (41)

## Timeframe for Biography and History

Paul Murray Kendall writes in his *The Art of Biography* that "Both history and biography explore the remains of yesterday and, as arts, interpret those remains" (*TAB* 4). But they differ in their core concerns: the historian frames a cosmos of happenings, in which men are included only as event producers or event sufferers; and the biographer explores the cosmos of a single being. Further, history deals with generalizations about a time, about a group of people in time and about an institution while biographer deals with particulars of one man's life. Additionally, modern biography is primarily concerned with individuality and with truth. This very test for individuality differentiates it from history because history deals with general events, it deals with the general fortunes of the community and the exploits, thoughts, and purposes of the individual who had so marked a share in them.

## Point of View: Biographer and Novelist

Andre Mouris suggests three points of views. They are:

1. To see everything through the hero's eyes.
2. To see everything through the eyes of each one of the characters in turn.
3. Or to take the point of view of a creator.

And he advises that in biography only the first one is preferred. A biographer views the events, circumstances and people around his subject from subject's point of view, whereas a novelist represents this configuration from his point of view. He narrates and reflects what is there in his mind about the subject/character and his life, so here the writer of fiction comes in the centre, whereas in biography since a biographer is suppose to see through the events and circumstances from the subject's point of view, a subject of biography becomes the centre. Further, the subject in the centre is viewed by biographer from all possible points of periphery to comprehend all the facets of his personality. This can be well explained through the following diagram:

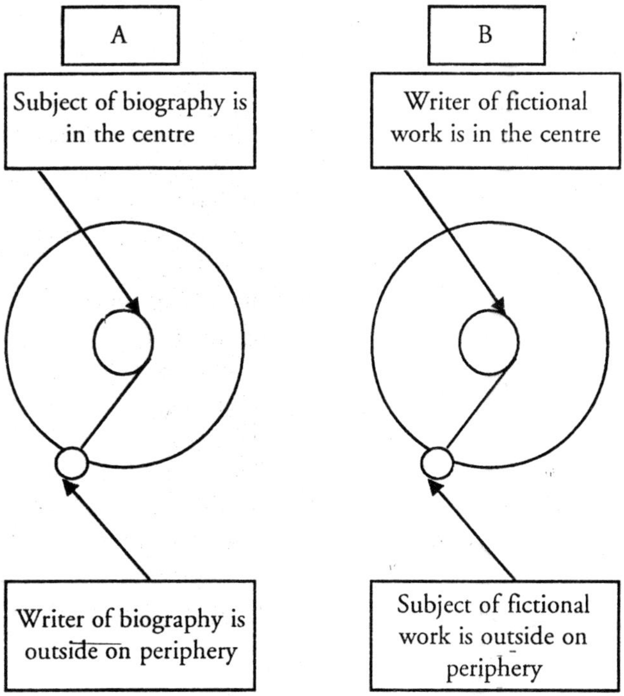


**Figure A** **Figure B**

As Figure A shows, in biography the subject, i.e. 'human being', is in the centre and is observed by an author, another human being, from the periphery with a view to see him and analyze him from all possible angles/perspectives. In figure B the situation is different. Here the fiction writer is in the centre because he creates a work of art from his individual perception about objects being viewed by him from a chosen angle in his work. So here observer is in the centre, whereas in biography the observer is outside the centre to view the centre from different perspectives.

To conclude it can be said that a human being when he writes he constructs, when he is written he is constructed by others, in terms of identity, it is a passage for a biographer to understand his subject from how he was known to how he was. In fiction it is a voyage for an author to an unknown terra firma of his own self, which ironically, in turn is based on his known configuration of his own self. He writes himself on the pages of his work under the garb of different characters playing different roles of human nature as understood by him. Both biography and novel articulate the hidden common note of human nature but both adopt different objectives, perspectives and manner to represent the vivid and infinite complexity of a human event. Even though, both as a work of art attempt to arouse in their readers a quintessential element that resides in every human soul to understand and approve their noblest aspirations. It is here, on the receiving end that the creator of a biographer and other forms of narrative prose convene a meeting to act over the frame of human perceptions leading towards actions.

## Works Cited

Kendall, Paul Murray. *The Art of Biography*. London: George Allen & Unwin LTD., 1965.

Liddel, Robert. *A Treatise on Novel.* London: Jonathan Cape Paperback, 1965.

Mourois, Andre. *Aspects of Biography.* Tran. S C Roberts. London: Cambridge, 1929.

Muir, Edwin. The Structure of the Novel. Bombay: Allied Publishers, 1966. Nicolson, Harold. *The Development of English Biography.* London: The Hogarth Press, 1959.

32

# Knowing the Unknown: A Study of Autobiographies of Indian Women with a Difference

Charusheela H. Patil

## Introduction

In a country like India, the traditions and customs are not only followed but lived up to. The status of women in India is largely determined by the gender and not by inherent qualities or by their social and economic status. In olden days, they were bonded with various them relationships which did not allow to realize the identity. As a result they could not express themselves candidly. In spite of these social barriers, they have managed to carve a niche for themselves in a male-dominated society in India. One of the major instruments that they used to assert their identity was express in words, i.e., trough writing.

Women's literature in India has evolved to show common experiences, a sense of sisterhood and a range of female experiences that question the patriarchy. From this phenomenon emerged a genre called autobiography, "writing about the self ". No doubt there were other genres of self-expression, but women can express through it with ease and mastery. Considering this very aspect of self-expression through autobiography, I have selected to study such autobiographies which deal with not only the rebellious actions of those who have overthrown the customs and traditions of society but those who have shown extraordinary talent by adopting social services and Indian Administrative Services. The stories of selected autobiographies are with a difference. *India Calling* (1934) by Corneilla Sorabjee, *Look Before and After* (1956) by Shoilabala Das, *My Reminiscence* by Renuka Roy, *I Dare* Kiran Bedi.

These women's autobiographies exhibit that they have shown extraordinary concern for the society than to their personal experiences and advancements. Gender-based discrimination was never a matter of concern for these women. Autobiography is an inward journey of the author's life from childhood. The genre of autobiography became more and more popular in the twentieth century as education became everybody's concern. Its another major feature is authenticity and truthfulness.

India has a history of the emergence of women's writing that began with the advent of Buddhism. It was the freedom offered by religion, the way of life it offered to women, and the principle of equality that it propagated which allowed women to pen down their thoughts for the first time. Around eighteenth century, however, with the social and political upheavals, such as loss of kingdoms, arrival of the East India Company, women's writing again became an issue of women's status. They were looked down upon as a rebellious act. The trend of educating women began again in the late nineteenth century with the rise of the Reformist Movements in India. This led to a new stage in the development of women's literature in India. The earliest women writing the reformist period was Savitribai Phule, who along with her husband championed the cause of women's education. Her writing carries the mark of an activist and a scholar. This tradition of writing for social reform was continued by other woman,

Pandita Ramabai of the same generation. Women's writing in the twentieth century moved towards feminism combined with actual political reforms in the women's status. Some of the women took writing as a tool for expressing their personal life and experiences. Hamsa Wadkar, a stage and television actor, narrates the experiences of being neglected and a wretched life. The legacy of penning down the memorable experiences was shouldered by other contemporary women as well. As a result the genre of autobiography gained much attention from the people.

Indian autobiography in English has a comparatively short history. Indian English writers started to write autobiographies in English in the early decades of the twentieth century. Among them were social reformers like Raja Rammohun Roy, who wrote a short account of his life, politicians like Jawaharlal Neheru, Mahatma Gandhi, Sarojini Naidu, etc. These autiobiographies obiviosly represent their political and social activities and their experiences. M.K. Naik and Shyamala Narayan in *Indian Literature 1980-2000: A Critical Survey* (2001) have revived the various autobiographies published in India. All these writers come from different states of India. They have different domestic, economic as well as social background. Their autobiographies portray the variety of Indian life and at the same time they narrate exciting stories of how they became what they finally turned out to be. They are also sensitive, conscious and observant witnesses to their own times; therefore, to read their life stories is to acquaint oneself with a whole bygone era.

Autobiography is a way to organize the story of life and it reflects on the past in order to better understand the present. It is usually a story that one tells about oneself. It is a form of introspection. When an author writes about his past, it is not free from emotions. People are interested in the actual lives of others and want to know about the others' past, and feelings and desires. Onley says, "The explanation for the special appeal of autobiography is a fascination with the self and its profound, its endless mysteries which leads to develop the culture of confession".

This paper aims at surveying the autobiographies of Indian women writers who have actually not been a part of literary traditions but their contribution to literature has made a strong mark in the flourish of the genre of autobiography. Through this paper, an attempt is made to draw attention to such autobiographies on the basis of intensity and authenticity with which the authors want their experiences to be understood by the people. An exhibition of extraordinary talent by the selected Indian women who have shown the courage in breaking away from the customs of society has a crucial role in redefining the status of Indian women. A detailed study of these will reveal that these women are associated with Indian administrative or political services. To begin with let us take Corneilla Sorabjee.

*India Calling* (1935) by Corneilla Sorabjee is an autobiography of India's first woman lawyer, who struggled against the suppression of women. She belonged to a Parsi-Christain family. She was inspired to choose her job by observing the plight of women who visited her mother. Her book depicts the gender discrimination encountered by her not only in India but also in England where she went to study on a Government of India scholarship. She emerged victorious from her ordeals and succeeded in becoming a lawyer. Her autobiography deals with her concern for improving the sad conditions of the women in Indian society.

Shoilabala Das, a brave lady from Orissa, in her autobiography *Look Before and After* (1956), Shoialabalal Das was determined to achieve success that made her a "born fighter", "a blunt woman". She received high education, often in boy's colleges, which contributed a lot towards moulding her personality. She was an adopted child of Madhusudan Das, who was an important political leader of Orissa. He sent her to Cambridge to take a teachers' training course, on her return she helped him in the affairs of the Orissa state. Her bold attitude and forthright manner got her an honorary post of a magistrate in Orissa. She later became a member of the State's Public Service Commission and held many public posts later in life.

*My Reminiscences* (1982), an autobiography of Renuka Roy, described how the frank atmosphere of family helped her in developing her identity. In the conservative Indian society, Renuka as a girl child was welcomed with pomp and ceremony. Renuka's marriage with Satyajit Ray is a turning point for Renuka. She was a follower of Gandhji and Satyajit Ray. She was a freedom fighter and fought especially for the women's rights and laws related to divorce. She enjoyed various dignified posts in the government during 1952-1957: She served as a minister for relief and rehabilitation. From 1957 to 67, she remained an elected member of parliament. From 1958 to 1960, she remained an active member and Head of the Planning Commission of Social Welfare and Welfare of Backward Class. Her autobiographies are more a piece of social documentation than memories of self-contentment.

Throughout much of her career, Kiran Bedi got more service and productivity out of the staff that were assigned to her. From changing the traffic situation in Goa with a mere 25 cops to getting the respect of the outsider-unfriendly state of Mizoram as Police Commissioner, her ability to marshal her resources shines through. What's amazing is that it often took just this one person, and maybe a few others, to cause massive changes in the police systems and operations. *I Dare*, Kiran Bedi's autobiography, reveals the various aspects of her dynamic personality, especially about her leadership.

Leaders basically act as catalysts for positive change. While today leadership in literature is mostly about CEO's, the magnitude of social change that Kiran Bedi has started is much more impressive than that. One of her famous postings was as Inspector-General of Tihar Jail in Delhi. Before she arrived, it was known to be a hell-hole. Drugs, physical abuse, corruption, disease, prisoner deaths were common. The book tells the story of the innovative methods—mostly rehabilitation and correctional efforts that managed to change a place like Tihar in such a short span of time. Another aspect of undaunted leadership is that Kiran Bedi often found huge opposition from politicians but in spite of that she proved herself a lady with extraordinary courage.

This study will remain incomplete if it does not discuss the iron lady of India, Mrs Indira Gandhi though she has not written her autobiography.

Indira Gandhi was hugely influenced by life and works of Mahatma Gandhi. She was very close to her father. The bond between them further strengthened during the time Nehru spent in prison. He exchanged letters with his daughter that made her aware of the current political condition of the country. The letters also helped her in developing a perspective and vision about her country. She actively participated in the Quit India Movement in 1942 for which she was imprisoned. She was the third Prime Minister of independent India. She also became the first woman Prime Minister of the country. She was a lady with a strong will power and tremendous self-belief. She ruled India for 16 years, and her tenure at the top ensured India never lacked in courage and developmental policies. She showed her true mettle during the Indo-Pak war in 1971. She was truly an Iron Lady. She was assassinated on October 31, 1984.

The above discussed women have paved the way for generations of women, given courage and confidence to the next generations. As a result today we can see women accomplishing the unconquered areas like Military, Navy and Air Force, etc.

## Works Cited

Iyengar, K.R. Srinivasan. *Indian Writing in English*. New Delhi: Sterling Publishers, 1993.

Naik, M. K. & Narayan Shymala, *Indian Literature 1980-2000: A Critical Survey* (2001).

Onley, James. *Metaphors of Self: The Meaning of Autobiography*. Princeton University Press, 1972.

Roy, Pascal. *Design and Truth in Autobiography*, Harvard University Press,1960.

Sodhi, Meena. *Indiian Writing in English: An Autobiographical Mode*, Creative Books, 1999.

*The Art of Autobiography in 19th& 20th Century England*, Yale University Press, 1984.

## 33

# "In 'Black' and 'White': William Styron's *The Confessions of Nat Turner*— Historical Truths or Distorted Facts?"

**Payel Dutta Chowdhury**

The development of African American writings may be traced back to the slave narratives. The Middle Passage and the experience of slavery are the period of dissolution of the black identity and any sense of homogeneous culture integral to the idea of community. Whatever is written about the experiences of the Middle Passage essentially represents the trauma of shame, pain, suffering, and the struggle for survival. In the absence of sustained fictional narrative, traces of the sense of community feelings or the strong desire to achieve that amidst sufferings in varied forms, is reflected mainly in some of the autobiographical narratives and songs.

For the African Americans, cultural representation in the early stage was mainly oral, and it was only in the eighteenth century that some form of written literature developed. The slave narratives, the earliest form of written expression, may be regarded as a reaction against the forced silence imposed on these people during the time of the Middle Passage. This enforced silence continued during the days of slavery in plantations. Faced with this deliberate design to enforce cultural amnesia and a consequent displacement and dislocation of the sense of community, the slaves on the plantation put up a strong resistance by bringing together memory and experience to narrate and keep alive a unique history which may be viewed as an assertion of the subaltern voice. The oral tradition was the foundation on which the subalterns based their strong sense of protest in the process of reconstituting the sense of community and consequently the achievement of political power.

*The Interesting Narrative of the Life of OlaudahEquiano, or GustavusVassa, the African, Written by Himself* (1789), widely regarded as the prototype of the slave narrative, claims that blacks could represent themselves effectively through the written form. Equiano's narrative stresses on how he was "first torn away from all the tender connexions that were", as he says, "naturally dear to my heart..." (Gates 140). Separated cruelly from his near and dear ones, he relates aggravated distress in the form of the auction where "without scruple, are relations and friends separated, most of them never to see each other again" (Gates 161).

The importance of autobiographical elements is also underlined by Harriet Jacobs in *Incidents in the Life of a Slave Girl* (1861), where she states, "It has been painful to me, in many ways, to recall the dreary years I passed in bondage..." (Gates 245). Jacobs'narrative, like many other slave narratives, brings to light the different harassments that she had undergone as a slave. With the abolition of slavery in 1865, the slave narratives changed their perspective. The Abolitionist Movement enabled social activists and writers like Sojourner Truth in *The Narrative of Sojourner Truth* (1878) and Elizabeth Keckley in *Behind the Scenes, or Thirty Years a Slave, and Four Years in the White House* (1868) to dare death to tell frankly of a life offering rape, pain and desolation.

The projection of the manifold atrocities of slavery, futile attempts of many runaways, and slave revolts became the central themes of not only black writers, but in due time many whites who took it upon themselves to tell these stories from the point of view of the blacks. In this context, the Pulitzer Prize winner *The Confessions of Nat Turner* (1967) by William Styron, which received many critical accolades as well as backlashes, may be reviewed and re-read in order to justify the book as the real "confessions" of Nat Turner – an authentic biography or merely a fictional narrative of a slave rebel by a white writer. Styron's book is based on a (supposed-to-be-true) account of Turner's confessions published by a lawyer, Thomas Ruffin Gray, in 1831 titled *The Confessions of Nat Turner: The Leader of the Late Insurrection in Southampton, Virginia.* Styron's interest in slavery had its roots in the stories he heard from his grandmother, who had owned slaves, and his desire to re-tell the story of Nat Turner was ingrained in him during his childhood days while reading about Turner's revolt in his school textbooks. Styron's book was published during the zenith of the Black Power Movement and the Black Civil Rights Movement, a critical time when African American writers and activists favoured black separatism over integration. Nat Turner's revolt, upon which Styron based his book, is probably the most widely known slave uprising which made the probability of abolition seem impossible in Virginia.

Turner, a black American slave, who led the Southampton insurrection, has for a very long time been the focus of many cultural and historical debates. He was the dominant figure among a trio of insurrectionists who led major uprisings – starting with Gabriel Prosser in 1800, then Denmark Vesey in 1822, and ultimately Turner in 1831. These uprisings, which resulted from powerful urges to be free, were in most of the cases uprooted even before they could cause major damages to the whites. Turner's revolt was one of those very few ones which was a great success in creating havoc and deaths of nearly fifty-five white Virginians. Just prior to his revolt, the Virginia state legislature had argued extensively about the issues of slavery. It seemed greatly probable that abolition at last would turn out to be a reality as strong anti-slavery sentiments were being expressed in the western states of Virginia. Turner's bloody revolt made all dreams of abolition an impossibility, and in fact, life became all the more dreary for the Virginian slaves. The rebellion, no doubt, created panic in the minds of the slave owners and resulted in much white bloodshed, but it also led to the deaths of many blacks as well as the capture and execution of the chief protagonist. The worst part of the rebellion was that many Negroes did not support their counterparts and as Turner confesses all that he could do was feel enraged "...above all at those Negroes who refused us or fled us or who had become the enemy – those spiritless and spineless wretches who had turned against us" (Styron 398). Turner's "confessions" to Gray before he was executed revealed, however, his complete lack of remorseas he says, "I fear I would have to plead not guilty to everything, because I don't feel guilty. And try as I might I simply can't feel – as you put it, sir – a pang of remorse" (Styron 393), and the tragedy for him was nothing but a desirable outcome.

William Styron's *The Confessions of Nat Turner* is not just a mere account of the 1831 revolt, but also a detailed description of Turner's life – his childhood, education, religious views and beliefs, bonding with other slaves, opinions on his white masters, etc.—as well as projections of the dreadful life of the slaves as revealed through many incidents. Born to a black woman owned by a plantation owner named Turner, Nat's early life was devoid of the usual miseries faced by the children of the plantation slaves. Unlike other "nigger" children, he did not know the meaning of hunger as he confessed "to be the child of the cook is to be, as my mother constantly points out, the 'luckiest little nigger' live"... (Styron 139). However, passing his early days in almost next to doing nothing, his life takes a definite turning once he is caught reading a book that he had stolen from the Turner library.

As the proportion of blacks increased in the 1700s, white anxiety about possible uprisings grew and more systematic controls over slaves became commonplace. Various legislative measures were passed to prohibit slaves from learning to read or write. In such a situation, the discovery of a black child with a stolen book was supposed to lead to grim consequences. But surprisingly Turner's master uses the young boy to test his long-held belief that slaves can be educated and, if allowed, can lead a respectable life.

Nat grows to be the pet of the white family, is taught by the family members and shows great promise as he masters his subjects with ease. Styron, however, does not present a one-sided perspective of benevolent white masters; if his book abounds in accounts of good people like Samuel Turner, Miss Nell, Miss Sarah and many more, the cruel and racist Benjamin Turner and Nathaniel Francis also exist there. Even though the brother of Samuel Turner.

Benjamin has very contrary views to slaves being educated. In a conversation with another like-minded person, Dr. Ballard, he says, "I'll swear to you that if you show me a little darky whom you've taught to read the complete works of Julius Caesar forward and backward in the original Latin tongue, I will show you a darky who is *still* an animal with the brain of a human child that will never get wise nor learn honesty nor acquire any human ethics though that darky live to a ripe old age. A darky, gentlemen, is basically as unteachable as a chicken, and that is the simple fact of the matter" (Styron 164-165). Nevertheless, Turner's life goes pretty smooth in the plantation and as a result of his education, he displayed strong religious feelings and became a preacher among the other slaves. Styron's depiction of Turner's early life is amidst many revelations and discoveries of being born a black and slave, but a fortunate one for being able to receive education and much kindness from his masters.

The 'confessions' of Turner reveal many disturbing events which occurred in his later life. Even though he receives assurances from his benevolent owner that he would be set free one day, that event never takes place in his life. Circumstances changed, however, and the owner sold Nat. Subsequent and more cruel owners failed to keep the long-ago promise of his freedom and for the first time in life, Nat learnt what it was to be a real slave. This betrayal added to his fury and frustration towards all white people and resulted in his resolution to wipe out the whites. Styron's book vividly presents the wretched condition of the slaves through many incidents narrated by the protagonist which sharpened his desire to create mass havoc.

A noticeable fact in Turner's decision to revolt is his choice of equality over freedom. Instead of considering freedom, probably by the umpteen numbers of chances that he had in fleeing to the North, he decides rather on revenge killings – even of those white people who had been kind to him. In this context it is important to understand the real condition of the free blacks at that point of time. Even though the free blacks enjoyed relative autonomy as compared to the slaves, but they also faced several restrictions which kept them at a lower social and economic status to the whites. They were not allowed to vote, serve on juries, use the same public facilities as the whites and above all, were not given employment in most of the cases, which resulted in several free blacks dying hungry.

Turner, in his confessions, presents the misery of such people in the depiction of a poor free black family that he encounters – where he finds the small child dead in the arms of the mother – which makes him ponder at "the dark rumor passed among the slaves that a number of the free Negroes in the country were starving." (Styron 287) Several other issues which brought out the sufferings of the slaves are raised in Turner's "confessions", issues like the separation of the black family and the continuous attempt of negating any possibility of the formation of a black community.

Turner records an inhuman "entertainment" of the whites to force two Negroes to fight against each other which makes him realize that "...of the indignation and wrongs that a Negro might endure – blistering toil and deprivation, slights and slurs and insults, beatings, chains, exile from beloved kin – none seemed more loathsome, at that minute, than this: that he be pitted in brutal combat against his own kind for the obscene amusement of human beings of any description – but especially those so mean and reptilian in spirit, so worthless, so likewise despised in the scheme of things and saved from the final morass only by the hairline advantage of a lighter skin" (Styron 306). Styron's depiction of such incidents in his book makes readers understand the reason behind the fury of Turner and his decision to take revenge. Turner's "confessions" provide ample ground for readers to have an insight into the workings of the mind of a slave who uses his education and religion as tools to defend his rebellion and the mass killings.

It is imperative to get a real glimpse of Styron's depiction of Turner's mind and his views on the condition of the black slaves, the question of their liberty and his pride in being a black in order tounderstand his remorselessness at the tragedy. The false promise of freedom and the atrocities of the various slave masters after he left the Turner plantation acted as the major factors leading towards his rebellious attitude. It became his "divine mission to kill all the white people in Southampton..." (Styron 258), even though he realized it all the while that the massacre that he desired will not bring about real liberty for the blacks. Nevertheless, the fire of revenge against the whites took concrete shape in his mind due the hopeless condition of the blacks that he encountered every day and which made him realize "with an intensity I had never known before that, chattel or unchained, slave or free, people whose skins were black would never find true liberty...." (Styron 298) However, Turner was not one to let things take its own course and sit back doing nothing. He chose with great deliberation four black men who had suffered in their own ways as slaves or free men and now joined hands with Turner in his great mission of revenge. Turner takes regular Bible classes for them and other slaves, all the while making them realize the divine purpose of their mission. He makes elaborate plans of the rebellion, stage by stage, of "slay(ing) all. No hostages, no impediments, nothing to encumber. All.The only possible way." (Styron 330) but at the same time is determined on avoiding the exploitation of white women – "Must sternly prevent violation of females. We shall not do to their women what they have done to ours." (Styron 330) Styron provides his readers a detailed understanding of Turner's psyche in the way he held his head high and urged all blacks to do the same. He proves to be a great leader as he instils in the slaves the sense of pride in being black: "Black folk ain't never goin' to be no great nation until they studies to love they own black skin an' the beauty of that skin an' the beauty of them black hands that toils so hard and black feet that trods so weary on God's earth....Pride, pride, everlasting pride, pride will make you free!" (Styron 311) However, it is this same leader who is actually not able to kill his victims when the time comes. Styron's detailed description of Nat's inability to strike his white victims and his success in killing only one of them provides us with a problem as well as a deeper understanding of the actual mental makeup of this black rebel.

William Styron's book brings to light several incidents in the life of Nat Turner, an educated religious slave-turned rebel – incidents which make the readers understand the true implication of being black and probable reasons behind many black uprisings like Turner's. As contemporary readers, when we look at Styron's book, the time gap (which occurs as a result of the actual confession which was given in 1831 and Styron's book published in 1967) acts as a boon for us to review Turner's life, his revolt and more importantly Styron's depiction of the rebel in a more critical manner, without being affected by several praises and backlashes that the book received post-publication.

The book received strong dissent and hostility from many black writers who denounced it as a fabrication and alleged Styron of having distortedthe black history.

Critics have questioned the authenticity of Styron's depiction of Turner's confessions and one particular author who probe deep into the matter discloses on her reading the actual trial manuscript that she "noticed that Thomas Gray was not Turner's attorney" and that "Turner pleaded innocent" during the trial and further records her finding "no mention in the transcript of a confession or of Gray" (Foster).

Several other critics have noted Styron's tampering with historical facts as he himself recorded that he gave a more human and pious nature to Turner in his book rather than the "dangerous religious lunatic....a psychopathic monster" he found in Gray's text. (Row)

Styron is also found guilty of concocting the relationship between Turner and Margaret Whitehead, the only white whom he actually kills. In the absence of historical records pertaining to this relationship, he takes the liberty of imagining and portraying a sexually charged relationship between the rebel and the victim. Many black writers and critics expressed their vehement dislike of Styron's narrow projection of the experiences of the black people who, they felt, did not have the capability to look into the mind of a black for the simple reason for being a white.

Finally, with the publication of *William Styron's Nat Turner: Ten BlackWriters Respond* (1968), a direct attack on Styron's book was made for distorting historical facts about a black slave rebel. A collection of essays by black writers, critics, magazine editors, psychiatrists, librarians, academicians, the ten writers vociferously claimed that "Styron's novel utterly fails the simple test of honesty" and that "in terms of getting into the slave's psyche and his idiom, it is a monumental failure" (Row)

Nevertheless, Styron's book won the Pulitzer Prize and several accolades including some even from black writers and critics like Cornel West, Henry Louis Gates and James Baldwin. Gates encouraged the making of a film based on Styron's book and Baldwin observed that a white writer had "begun to write the common history – ours" (Row). Styron, however, took the criticisms in a light manner and dismissed *Ten Black Writers* as "intellectual squalor" (Row).

As contemporary readers, we are no doubt presented with the difficulty of offering any solution to the dilemma of fact v/s fiction as any opinion may be regarded as biased and lacking first-hand knowledge. We may, however, safely say that Styron's book still holds good as it provides an insight into the mind of a slave rebel, bringing out the various atrocities that the blacks were subjected to, even though we are aware of certain liberties that the author has taken in depicting some situations and relationships. Certain distorted facts about Turner's life do not demean the authenticity of the portrayal of the miserable condition of slavery, particularly in the absence of undocumented historical facts.

Styron's best-seller, in fact, laid bare the true perspective of black sufferings and the history of many slave revolts and established itself as a book that "challenged black Americans, historians, and social critics, for it raised questions on Turner, black history, and the 'true' character ('Sambo' or 'rebel') of the slave in the South" (Mellard). Over the years, several conflicting views have been expressed on Turner's revolt and his "confessions" and the authenticity of Styron's book; however, it remains alive in the readers' mind as a testimonial of the way in which slavery corrupted and diminished the very essence of being human.

## Works Cited

Foster, Sharon Ewell. "The Truth about Nat Turner".http://www.theroot.com/views/truth-about-nat-turner. (Posted on 23rd August, 2011).

Gates, Henry Louis, Jr. and Nellie Y Mc Kay, eds. *The Norton Anthology of African American Literature* (1st edition). New York: W.W. Norton & Company Inc., 1995.

Mellard, James M. "Documenting the American South: Nat Turner, 1800? – 1831".http://docsouth.unc.edu/neh/turner/bio.html.

Row, Jess. "Styron's Choice".Sunday Book Review in New York Times.http://www.nytimes.com/2008/09/07/books/review/Row-t.html?_r=1. (Published on 5th September, 2008).

Styron, William. *The Confessions of Nat Turner*. New York: Random House, 1970. (First published in 1967).

34

# What They Told Us About Their Lives— Autobiography, Biography and Memoirs: Literary Perspectives

R. K. Bhushan

> If a cartographer presented us with a map of the world that did not include the continent of Africa or that was mistaken about its configuration and major features, we would certainly protest. But literary cartographers have long been precisely mapping the continents of fiction, drama, and poetry, all the while pretending that autobiography was not there or simply coloring it a toneless black. Aristotle makes no mention of autobiography: therefore it does not exist. However, from St. Augustine to Sartre, autobiography is a form of literary art, as an examination of some of its characteristic rhetorical resources and themes will show. The value of the autobiographical tradition, its relevance to our lives, lies in its capacity to furnish us with models and mirrors that can help us to accept, celebrate and transform our lives as individuals and as participants." *(The Dark Continent of Literature: Autobiography)*
>
> —Stephen A. Shapiro

Autobiographies, biographies and memoirs, reminiscences, diaries and travel accounts have always fascinated the reading public everywhere for a variety of reasons since the times ancient. These have been found to be highly motivational and inspirational; these have also brought about a transition or a turning point in the lives of the readers. Many from the reading public of this literature have confessed how readings of life stories or recollections and reminiscences influenced the daily course of events in their own lives, shaped up their mind, enlightened their outlook and carved smoother paths to higher destinations which helped them not only achieve great happiness in personal life but also they cheered and brightened the environment for others to realize their life for better purposes. Easily understandable reason is that those who write their autobiographies, or those whose life stories are attempted by others, or those who record their reminiscences, or those who write their daily diaries, or record some events, or influences from their life in their diaries are the people who were either born with unique identity, or they created such an identity by dint of their zeal for life lived in industry and diligence, superb determination, unfailing faith in their silent resolve and strong will, unmindful of the setbacks or rebuffs. This was done to create happiness for themselves and leave behind milestones guiding on the paths to the fresh and beautiful regions of life and love. Even the diaries and travel accounts have been an integral part of this genre by and large. The record of observations and impressions of these writers of diaries and travels have held the interested readers throughout in wonder and stimulated their taste for life.

These great souls denied to themselves what ordinary souls crave for and fight for to express their rowdy shadows; instead they used their natural gifts for the lasting benefit of posterity. The garden of life is ever adored with the ever-refreshing fragrances of these brilliant and glowing flowers. This genre of literature in all languages is marked by truthfulness, honesty, straightforwardness and integrity otherwise it loses the sheen and shine of literature. We know the welcome such Literature packed with lies and falsehood receives! That is the reason that the autobiographical and biographical literature remains an ever-fresh and rapidly growing area for writers, readers, practitioners and scholars and a fertile area for further research. *So what they told us and what they tell us about the life they lived, the life they observed, the life they felt and the life they wanted others to know and accomplish with faults and failures, wisdom and success in bruises and breezes have much to reveal, understand and possess and experience what we rarely know the bliss of living. They make honest claims to tell the truth, the whole truth and nothing but the truth. However, the justification of these claims is decided by the well-informed and enlightened readers. These writers can't risk twisting or distorting the truth respecting the demand of the art of life and have to be and are required to be conscientious to a degree.* (The italics have been used to particularly emphasize the significance of these thoughts and views about this almost neglected genre of literature.)

Some of these writers have gained greater richness in living and they have written two/three/four or even five autobiographies, though different biographers have attempted the biography of the same person from their own angle unfolding the unknown. Even then, we may rue that this significant, factual and honest form of literature has been ignored without any sensible reasoning. Stephen A. Shapiro has very pertinently observed to assert and establish the relevance and importance of autobiography as an indispensable form and part of literature. He says:

> Autobiography has been unjustifiably ignored by contemporary literary critics who tend to assume that it is not a form of "imaginative" literature. But autobiographers do not simply copy themselves down; all forms of story-telling are creations that depend upon the conventions of art. Great autobiographies are frequently organized thematically and utilize all the rhetorical resources of fiction and drama. As symbolic forms that unfold the patterns of entire lives, autobiographies have enormous educational value as models.

Abraham wrote three autobiographies (1858-60). Simone de Beauvoir, one of the most important cultural historian of the twentieth century, and also the most thoughtful critic of society was known for her thunderous voice and forceful writings for feministic studies, especially socio-psychological conflicts and clashes in the lives of women. She is also famous for her non-monogamous relations, and wrote her autobiography in four volumes: (1)Memoirs of a Dutiful Daughter (1959); (2) Prime of Life (1963); (3) Force of Circumstance (1965); (4) All Said and Done (1974).

She was a philosopher-woman and a woman-philosopher who lived with greater than immense capacity for potential challenges. Her close association and intimate relations with Sartre roused her to the irresistible force of existential issues, and she emerged as the guiding force of the Existential Movement.

Siegfried Sassoon wrote his autobiographical memoirs: (1) Memoirs of a Fox-Hunting Man (1928); (2) Memoirs of an Infantry Officer (1930).

Taslima Nasrin, the famous author of *Lajja* from Bangladesh and very well known for her bold and unrestrained utterances and writings on the freedom, rights and dignity of living a meaningful life, has written five autobiographies: (1) My Girlhood (1999); (2) Crusty Wind (2002); (3) Speak up or Split into Two (2003); (4) Those Dark Days (2004) (5) *I am not Fine but You Stay Well, My Beloved Country* (2006).

We expect more from the pen of this remarkably handsome woman gifted with envious intellectual subtlety and sharpness and the courage of complete conviction, in the years to come.

Even the 31-year old British woman, Katy Price, has written four autobiographies and has declared to write one autobiography every year.

And the beauty, and also wonder, is that such lives hold great interest and favour with the biographers who work their own information and reflection and affection in truth-telling while writing about the lives of such writers. So some biographers attempt one life.

## Memoirs and Autobiographies

There is no autobiography that is not a memoir in certain respects and no memoir can be written without autobiographical contexts. Pascal says that the memoir writer's intention is not self-examination. Memoirs are not a pure autobiography. The diary, journal, memoir, reminiscences, travel accounts and letters are all manifestation of the writer's self. However, their perspectives are different. An autobiography tells the story of a person's involvement and participation in the process of his growth and becoming an identity in life in the world. It may involve the role and influence of a person or persons, book or books, the general environment, the situations and events in one's own or social life on the development of the narrator's personality.

Memoirs are generally written by those people who have played a distinguished role in some particular, significant course in history or focus their chief attention on some event of great public importance in which their own role was that of the guiding or the driving force. Thus a very thin line divides the memoir from autobiography. The difference is only of focusing. Memoirs are generally on the outer world and people and events in the life of the writer whereas autobiography is more on the inner world of the writer. In memoirs, there is emphasis on personalities and events and even situations that influenced or impacted the course of the writer's life or even brought about a dramatic turn in his or her life. Coles's *Dictionary of Literary Terms* defines memoir as "a form of autobiography. Memoirs, however, typically emphasize events and personalities other than the writer's." We have Daniel Defoe's *The Memoirs of a Cavalier* (1720). Also we have Siegfried Sassoon's autobiographical memoirs: *Memoires of a Fox-Hunting Man* (1928), *Memoires of an Infantry Officer* (1930), and Thackeray's *Memoirs of Barry Lyndon* (1844).

## Biography

Generally a biography means an account of a person's life written by someone else. The biographer relies on his personal information, historical evidence such as letters, reminiscences, diaries of a person about whom truth-telling is the sole purpose. *Handbook of Literary Terms* by X.J. Kennedy defines biography as "a branch of historical scholarship. It yields a written account of a person's life. To establish and interpret the facts of an author's life, a biographer uses all the available evidence-not just personal documents such as letters and diaries, but also the stories and poems for the light they shed on the personal record." To be precise, a biography is a sequential record of factual details written after thorough scrutiny of relevant available information and record. However, today biography and autobiography have been defined in far-extended boundaries and as such have assumed wider significance of meaning. It is no longer the literary record of the personal lives of the saints or the stories related to the rise and fall of princes as it was presumed in the post-classical Europe. We see how biographies began to appear after that-from the sixteenth century till the present. Edwin Arnold wrote poetical biographies of Mahatma Buddha and Jesus Christ—*Light of Asia* and *Light of the World* respectively. It would be more appropriate to say that biography is a rich tribute to autobiography. Some other famous biographies are *Life of Dr. Johnson* by Boswell; *Lives of Poets* by Dr. Johnson; *Eminent*

*Victorians* and *Queen Victoria* by Lytton Strachey; *Napoleon* by Ludwick; *Adolf Hitler* by James Bunting. There are biographies of Tagore, Aurobindo, Paulo Coelho.

We can safely classify and categorize this genre as follows:

1. Memoirs by Women.
2. Memoirs by Men.
3. Pulitzer Winners: Biographies and Autobiographies.
4. Celebrity Biography.
5. World War II Memoirs.
6. The Best Spiritual Autobiographies.
7. Best Diaries and Autobiographies.
8. Artist Biographies.
9. Jail Diaries or Prison diaries.
10. The Biographies of Great Statesmen.
11. The Biographies of Great Philosophers.
12. The Biographies of Great Scientists.
13. The Biographies of Great Poets.
14. The Biographies of Great Novelists.
15. The Biographies of Nobel Laureates.
16. 100 Great Men.
17. 100 Great Women.
18. Dictionary of Greek and Roman Biography by Smith.
19. Great People of Faith and Wisdom, published by Reader's Digest.
20. Makers of Modern India Series.

It is interesting to note that in each of the most of the classified titles, dozens and, even hundreds, of books have been written. This is the information of a very limited mind on the subject; how much more there will be, I can't say and with the personal limitations now, I can't dare go further. However, it can be concluded that people throughout everywhere have felt the urge to share their life experiences with others and also others' life experiences still with others. This area in literature has ever continued to grow and widen with remarkable fertility and serious interest of the scholarship. There has been an equally wider growth in the meaning and application of this genre.

Today biography may be understood as an exact presentation of the life history, not life story, of an individual. Hence the biographer has to be conscious, scrupulous and conscientious in his brave venture to write about the facts of the life in an analytical and interpretative manner. Such an attempt alone creates a unified impression of the inner and outer life of the subject with the influences and imprints.

Roger Fowler in his *A Dictionary of Modern Critical Terms* has dealt with the subject with greater clarity and in very reasonable detail. The elucidation of the topic is not only informative but interesting also. He explains the accepted meaning of the biography and goes on to discuss the same century-wise with major writers and works. Then he elaborates the meaning, its application, its usage and practice in the twentieth century in the context of fictional and documentary techniques, personal history, first-person narrative and /or tape recorded novels, and also focusses on the truth-telling claims of the biographer based on the available evidence, the range of his personal knowledge in the light of the licence of his society to publish it. Roger Fowler says: "it ignores the central issue of what kind of reality language can sustain." He acquaints us with defining identity, creating identity and even unique identity while explaining truth, fiction, whole truth, varnished truth and plain truth in view of the traditional and changed and changing application of the meaning of this genre of popular literature. He adds "For many new writers-for example in the emerging African countries (Achebe, Ngugi, Soyinka) and in Negro American circles (Baldwin, John Williams, Jean Tooner)—*autobiographical art is not a device for summing up the accumulated wisdom of a lifetime but a means of defining identity*" (italics mine).It reduces to meaninglessness the distinction between novel and autobiography. In this respect, we can trace the unity between Ralph Ellison's *Invisible Man* (1965) and J.P. Clark's autobiography: *America, Their America* (1964) notwithstanding their different genres.

My interest and fascination for autobiographies and biographies have remained unflagging in spirit and zeal since my college days. I remember the prescribed prose book, *Paths of Greatness,* in our B.A. Class. This book was an anthology of the extracts of the biographies of great philosophers, scientists, religious teachers like Plato, Galileo, Sir J.C. Bose, Jesus Christ, Saint Ravi Das etc. Our great teacher put his best, as ever he did in teaching poetry, prose and the history of literature, in provoking our profound and lasting interest in the lives of the immortals of mankind. Thereafter, there was no looking back. Then I used my summer vacation in reading *Living Biographies of Great Philosophers, Living Biographies of Great Scientists, Living Biographies of Great Poets,* all by Hana Lee Thomas and Dana Lee Thomas. These authors have written the biographies of great novelists and statesmen also. I felt the magic of their simple, spontaneous and lyrical prose style in their story-telling and, even after more than four decades, I remember a lot about the highly captivating and dramatic openings and endings about their lives.

These readings were of immensely motivational and inspirational use to my students in my teaching. Today also I make liberal use of all this in my lectures whether on general topics or literary talks.

Justice G. D. Khosla's portrayal of the deeply heart-rending and poignantly moving life story of the last Mughal Emperor of India interspersed with the translation of a large number of his Urdu verses in *The Last Mughal* also enhanced my interest. The poetical and fictional biographies of Prince Siddhartha, Mahatma, Buddha too left their indelible mark, further tendering my emotions and thoughts with delicacy and pain. Thomas De Quincey's *Confessions of an Opium Eater,* Shelley's *Ariel, Lives of Poets* by the Great Doctor, *The Dictator of His Age*, Dr. Johnson, Boswell's *Life of Dr. Johnson* continued to strengthen my interest in the study of autobiographies and biographies.

Mahatma Gandhi's *My Experiments with Truth* shaped and sharpened very early my concept of truth and morality at the personal, social and professional level and never dared to reshape that. How orthodoxical it seems today! But I remained and remain stuck up. Pt. Jawaharlal Nehru's *Autobiography* and *Prison Diary* inspired intellectual interest. Nehru's prose is simple and remarkable for its brilliance loaded with his deep intellectual and subtle understanding and insight into men and matters, people and politics, with motives laid bare and bathed with equally subtle philosophy, humour, wit, satire and pathos and inimitable sense of patriotism. Even personal reflections are many fathoms deep and touch the enviable level of objectivity in subjectivity and carry the reader to the refreshing and glowing zeniths of the Alps, the Himalayas, the antiquity of the places and prisons enriching his domains of knowledge and curiosity.

Puran Singh's *Paths of Life* introduces us into new areas of poetic prose coloured in rich tenderness, and we participate in his childhood enchantments amidst the virgin beauties of nature leaving us tenderer than the tender. These soul-bearings from his early childhood to the later years of his life running into almost 110 pages reveal the freshness of eternal emotion and sentiment bathed deep in humanity. So are Dostoevsky's *Notes From a Dead House!* Even *Adolf Hitler* by James Bunting roused my interest and I had a better understanding of this monstrous ruler than what I learnt from his *Mein Kempf.* Nirad Chaudhuri's *The Autobiography of an Unknown Indian* also made a fascinating study which inspired me to read sparkling Khushwant Singh's *India* and *New India.*

The reader's interest in the perspectives of autobiographical and biographical literature is influenced and determined by his own leanings to know more about the persons who lived and struggled through the labyrinths of life of reader's own interest. Such an attitude shapes up his own prospective and prescriptive for a better and brighter look ahead. Today when the individual life is under severe constraints of social, professional and personal kind and becomes confined in his her own shell in spite of wider social networking areas and platforms provided by fast-track technology, there emerges an urge to share one's lived experiences in black and white and in letter and spirit. Perhaps this is the reason that this genre has received fresh stimulus and impetus. So we have a large number of autobiographies and biographies seeing the light of the day everyday everywhere. The choice of the reader has also become astonishingly wide. The earnest reader feels interested in the life-stories of people from different walks of life. This isalso decided by the natural and acquired instinct of his/her personality. One might have started with the autobiography/biography of a missionary or a philosopher or a statesman but, at a later stage, one's interest might have directed one to the study of poets, scientists, business magnates, generals, singers, dancers, sportsmen etc. the unchallengeable fact is that the reader has an aromatic and appetizing diet on his big menu.

For this purpose, I would like to present the following list which, I am sure, will inspire and motivate the general and particular reader:

1. Nelson Mandela: *Long Walk to Freedom* (1995)
2. Bill Clinton: *My Life* (2004)
3. Vinod Mehta: *Lucknow Boy: A Memoir* (Penguin India)
4. Robert Graves: *Goodbye To All That* (Penguin, U.K. 2009)
5. A. N. Wilson: *Dante in Love*
6. Claire Tomalin: *Thomas Hardy: The Time-Torn Man* (Penguin U.K.)
7. Jude Morgan: *The Secret Life of William Shakespeare*
8. Alexander Harris: *Virginia Woolf*
9. Matthew Hollis: *Now All Roads Lead to France: The Last Years of Edward Thomas*
10. Sarah Freeman: *Bronte in Love*
11. Claire Tomalin: *Charles Dickens: A Life*
12. Earnest Hemingway:*A Moveable Feast: The Restored Edition*
13. Vladimir Nabokov: *Speak, Memory* (1966)
14. A.P.J. Kalam: *Wings of Fire*
15. Pilloo Mody: *Zulfi, Mera Yaar*
16. M.C, Chagla: *Roses in December*
17. Walter Isaacson: *Steve Jobs: The Exclusive Biography.*

The list can be multiplied into pages but the purpose of provoking the reader's interest in fascinating variety and diversity is amply served with this. To add to our flavour, we have hundreds of biographies of men and women who changed the world; certainly, these inspirational people will change the world of the reader too! Why not take a fruitful chance with no risk/s but all dividends?

I may be excused for not remembering the publishers and the years of publication of many of these autobiographies and biographies though they were a relief and a solace in the decades of tumultuous life. Still some significant sources are mentioned as under.

## Works Cited

Birren, James E., Ph.D and Reyes, Anita C. MS: *Bibliography of Autobiography, Memoir and Reminiscence Literature,* Ethel Percy Andrus Gerontology Centre, University of Southern California, Los Angeles, California, July 2008.

Coles: *Dictionary of Literary Terms,* Rama Brothers, New Delhi, 1996.

Fowler, Roger (Ed.): *A Dictionary of Modern Critical Terms* Routledge, London, 2003.

Iyengar, K. R. Srinivas: *Sri Aurobindo: A Biography and A History, Sri Aurobindo International Centre of Education, Pondicherry,* Aug.1985.

Kennedy, X. J, Gioia, Dana, Bauerlein, Mark: *Handbook of Literary Terms-Literature, Language, Theory,* Pearson Education, India, 2007.

Maxwell, A. James (Ed.): *Great People of Faith and Wisdom-How Their Lives Changed Our Lives, Reader's Digest Services,* 1984.

biographyonline.net;

www.google: Autobiographical and Biographical Literature.

# 35

# Dr. Sharankumar Limbale, a Dominant Literary Voice Striving for Liberty, Justice and Humanity for Dalits: A Literary Interview of Writer of Renowned Autobiography *The Outcaste*

Arvind M. Nawale

Sharankumar Limbale (b. 1956), a well-known dalit activist, writer, editor, critic and author of 40 books is one among the most renowned dalit voices in India. Most of his writings are in Marati and translated into English and other languages. At present, he is working as a Professor Regional Director (Pune Division) of the Yashwantrao Chavan Maharashtra Open University, Nashik. He is a good academician as well as a writer and he occupied so many positions till date. He is an illustrious writer and his writings mostly rest on the dalit struggle and identity. He is known for his poetry, short stories and particularly for his master-piece, autobiography *Akkarmashi* (2004). His autobiography is written in Marati language and translated into Hindi, Tamil, Kannada, Punjabi, Gujarathi, Malayalam languages. Anyhow, it caught the attention of the world especially after translated into English as *The Outcaste* by Santhosh Bhoomkar. He got many awards and won the wider acclaim from the public for his literary talents. His critical work *Towards an Aesthetics of Dalit Studies* (2004) is considered as a most resource book on dalit criticism. He is a member of many academic and cultural organizations and many scholars did and engaged in active research on his writings. He won prestigious 14 awards for his literary and social contribution. His other books include Udrek (poetry collection), *Bahujan, Zund, Hindu, Upalya,(novels) Dalit Brahman,(short stories) Dalit Sahityache Saundarya Shastra (criticism)* and so on.

AN: *Thank you for agreeing to this interview. Please tell us a little about yourself. Who is the true Sharankumar Limbale? Dr. Sharankumar Limbale, a Professor or Sharankumar Limbale, a dalit autobiography writer. Which Limbale do you love most?*

SL: Sharankumar Limbale as an author. I love my writing because of its commitment to the movement and masses. I am writing for social change. It is my responsibility being an author and born as dalit. I am tightly fastened with expectons of downtroddens. I can't survive witout masses. I am not human being but a living weapon. I am a war. My writig is a battlefield. It is my noble duty to write for dalits.

AN: *Who/what made you want to write?*

SL: Thoughts of Dr. Ambedkar and dalit movement inspired me to write. Atrocities against dalit made me to react. My writing is reaction against brutal and unhuman caste system. Equality, freedom, justice, democracy are streams of my blood. I never tolerate injustice against common man irrespective of his caste. I want to see a beautiful nation without exploitation, corruption and atrocities. From thousands of years dalits are neglected. Now we are aware of our rights and power. Dalit literature is a manifesto of our movement. My life is part and parcel of dalit movement. Movement is MY LIFE.

*AN:* *You are one of the major voices in dalit literature. How did Dr. Ambedkar's writing and thoughts influence the writer in you? Can you say about your journey as a dalit writer? Apart from Dr. Ambedkar, who else has made an impact on your writing?*

*SL:* I am writing from my schooldays but it was an immitaion of high caste authors. It was not true feelings. I came in contact with dalit movement in my youth and I am changed totally. This change is new birth for me. It made me to march towards masses. But it is true the writing of Marathi progressive writers influenced me in my college days to think.

*AN:* *What books have most influenced your life most?*

*SL:* *An Annihilation of Caste* by Dr. B.R. Ambedkar, *Golpeetha* by Namdev Dhasal and *Baluta* by Daya Pawar. These books are searchlights in my life.

*AN:* *As a child, what did you want to be when you grew up?*

*SL:* I wanted to be an author. It was my lovable dream. But dalit movement made me dalit writer. Now I can't write imaginative, false and entertainment literature.

*AN:* *Will you please tell us something about your childhood memories? What was your parentage and bringing up all about? Has this background flowered the writer in you?*

*SL:* I have written my autobiography *The Outcaste: Akkarmashi.* It is published by Oxford University Press. Please see it. I have written everything in it. It is not an autobiography of a person but a social document of dalits.

It is helpful to understand me as well as the dalit community and its struggle.

AN: *What inspired you to write your much acclaimed autobiography, The Outcaste?*

SL: My different and defamed life story. Daya Pawar wrote his autobiography named *Baluta* and then Laxman Mane wrote his autobiography *Upara*. These two books are well received and debated. There was a need to come forward and to continue this literary form. This was the beginning, I feel, to place me on the public front because my life has social meaning. It is the example of dalit community and how they are harassed. I have written this book for a social cause.

AN: *How did you come up with the title, The Outcaste?*

SL: I, translator Santosh Bhoomkar and editor Mini Krishanan of this book decided the title. It matched the original *Akkarmashi*.

AN: *How did your family help in your writing?*

SL: No.... no. they are uneducated. I took help from my friends. I had discussed with them when I was writing. This was a beginning period. No one knows how to write and what to write in a dalit autobiography. Daya Pawar was the pathfinder. We followed him.

AN: *How did your family members react on your confessional mode of writing? Was there no disliking on your confessional mode? For example—You described in your The Outcaste in a very frank language how you were an outcaste, your childhood where you and your fellow dalits were beset with grinding poverty and hunger as well as rank inequity by high-caste Indians. You describe bigoted incidents in your public school where you and other dalit children were expected to accept leftover food from the high caste children. You also were not allowed to draw water from public wells. You had to wait for high caste people to draw the water for you and pour it into your hands or cups. You exposed how dalit women have been either beguiled or forced into sexual encounters with high caste men. The high caste men, who think touching a dalit might "pollute" them, never think themselves to be 'polluted.' while raping a dalit woman. What were the reactions of your family and relatives after the publication of the book?*

*SL:* At the first time of publication, I had been attacked by every one of my family and community. When my autobiography received and well debated I became a hero, then the resistance became normal.

*AN:* *Is any distressing/ embarrassing experience you faced after the publication of The Outcaste?*

*SL:* Before publishing the book only my villagers knew that I was an outcaste boy. Even today sometime I face ill-treatment, especially in marriage engagement of my children, but not in movement and social life.

*AN:* *Are experiences depicted in your writing based on someone else you know, or events in your own life?*

*SL:* Movement is person for me, friend for me, society for me, life for me and mother for me. I have depicted only the movement.

*AN:* *Name a few others outside of family members that you feel supported you.*

*SL:* My friends. Suryanarayan Ransubhe, Nishikant Thakar, Laxman Gaikwad, N.M. Shinde, Hrishekesh Ayachit and others.

*AN:* *Are you feeling optimistic about the possibilities of creating a social change through your literary work? Do you think it's important for writers to be socially active?*

*SL:* Yes.

*AN:* *What is your biggest struggle with your writing?*

*SL:* Time is the biggest struggle.

*AN:* *What are some of the unexpected and notable responses to your writings?*

*SL:* The great writer Amrita Pritam, Kamaleshwar, Rajendra Yadav, Ramnika Gupta, Alok Mukherjee, Arun Mukherjee, Hon. Sushil Kumar Shinde, Ajit Kour are the persons who admired me always.

*AN:* *You got many awards and won a wider acclaim from the public for your literary talents. That's really great! How have your life and/or your relationship with writing changed since such awards?*

*SL:* No ...no. Awards are only recognitions. Awards can help to reach the public at large but can't change the writing process. I am not writing for any awards. I am writing for a social cause.

*AN:* *With the growing translation of works by dalit writers from various regional languages into English, dalit literature is on the edge to attain a national and an international attendance as well as to masquerade as a major defiance to the traditional concepts of what forms literature and how we read it. What do you think about it?*

SL: We have to understand the caste system of India, and then we can understand dalit literature in the true sense. But it is impossible for every reader to do so. Literature is a mirror of society. One can understand through dalit literature the social structure of Indian society which is based on discrimination and inequality. No one can read dalit literature for entertainment. It is a literature of social cause and for social change. Readers can know the social reality about Indian dalits through dalit literature. One can take inspiration to struggle against injustice in one's life. Dalit literature is a noble message to live and let live as human beings.

AN: *What do you think of the future of dalit literature?*

SL: Whenever there is caste system and inequality in society dalit literature will be there to defend human values.

AN: *What do you think the future holds for a dalit writer?*

SL: We should think to rebuild a beautiful and progressive India. We should work together to minimize the age-old gap between dalits and non-dalits. We should prepare to be ready for new changes because of globalization. We should talk on national problems. We should talk on population, unemployment etc., command man. We should talk on brotherhood and sisterhood.

AN: *What aesthetic considerations should be taken into account in interpreting dalit writing?*

SL: I have explained in detail in my book *Towards An esthetics of Dalit Literature* published by Orient Longman.

AN: *Is it appropriate to apply to dalit literature, the criteria used in assessing the work of non-dalit writers generally, and high-caste Hindu writers in particular?*

*SL:* Why not? How can we compel literary critics to follow our parameters? One can use one's criteria to assess dalit literature. It is another way to understand the dalit literature. It will help us to know the other side of our literature and we should welcome our critics. This is the healthy way. We should welcome and appreciate our critics. It is the need to assess the dalit literature on the basis of art, but no one dares to do it.

*AN:* *Your novel, Hindu translated from the Marathi into English, mirrors the present-day conflicts in India and intensely demonstrates the negations within most individuals, their negotiations, densities and the plight of women who suffer gender discrimination regardless of their caste. Please tell us, where did the seed for this novel come from and how did you develop it?*

*SL:* I have written a trilogy. *Hindu* is the second novel in this trilogy. I want a good translator to translate this trilogy.

*AN:* *What kind of criticism do you prefer to have about your writing?*

*SL:* Very welcoming, encouraging and supportive.

*AN:* *What are you working on now? What can we expect soon?*

*SL:* I am writing a book in Marathi. Only Marathi readers can read it soon.

*AN:* Thanks. Let your pen run and keep on running for issues around you. All the best for your future literary ventures.

# Index